Hawaii, the Legend that Sells

HAWAII, the Legend that Sells

BRYAN H. FARRELL

The University Press of Hawaii
Honolulu

The University Press of Hawaii acknowledges
the assistance of the Andrew W. Mellon Foundation
in the publication of this book.

Library of Congress Cataloging in Publication Data

Farrell, Bryan H.
  Hawaii, the legend that sells.

  Bibliography: p.
  Includes index.
  1. Tourist trade—Hawaii. I. Title.
G155.U6F28   381'.4591969044   81–16177
ISBN 0–8248–0766–9   AACR2

Contents

Figures

Tables

Acknowledgments

THIS study is the result of the efforts of several institutions and literally hundreds of people who gave me firsthand information. The views expressed are my responsibility alone. Transient contacts met on the beach, at a conference, or at a public hearing provided useful ideas without formally identifying themselves. Funds and services, for which I am most grateful, were provided by Canada Council, the Long Foundation, the University of Victoria, and the University of California at Santa Cruz. I am grateful to Chuck Y. Gee, Dean of the School of Travel Industry Management, University of Hawaii, who provided services and made it possible for me to consult with faculty members and again with industry and community leaders during the final revision phase of the manuscript.

I received considerable assistance from the work of researchers DiAnne Reid Ross and Lisa Baird Evans who were simultaneously collecting materials for the tourism project of the Center for South Pacific Studies. Other assistance was kindly provided in Hawaii by Anna Lee Farrell, by numerous county officers, and by the staff of the publications department of the Department of Planning and Economic Development in Honolulu. Valuable help was given by research student Gail Suzuki who, working in Honolulu interviewed thirty-five informants in government, industry, and community groups while closely examining the Hawaii State Plan, the State Tourism Plan, and the processes involved in visitor industry planning. These persons are acknowledged by her elsewhere.

Special thanks for their particular contributions are offered to the following persons, all of whom gave valuable time or offered worthwhile suggestions: Sophie Ann Aoki, Susan Arakawa, Art

Asher, Tom Ashley, Bruce Benson, Wendell Brookes, Effie Cameron, Jeff Chang, David Ching, Willard Tim Chow, Dexter Choy, J. F. Conrad, Nora Cooper, Elmer Cravalho, G. L. Lip Crothers, Ray Dash, Jack Davis, Cathryn Dearden, Richard Denning, A. DeRegos, Ernest Donehower, Keith Duke, Dewey Eberley, Kenneth Emory, Pardee Erdman, Tom Fearon, Arthur Fernandez, Paul Ferreira, Ben Finney, Bernice Flood, Angela Franco, Joe Franco, Gordon Gibson, Stanley Gima, Guido Giocommetti, Ed Greaney, Charles Gregory, Lorraine Green, Tom Green, the late Thomas Hamilton, Charlie Hamura, Chris Hart, Paul Higa, Wesley Hillendahl, Tony Hodges, Ted Hori, Ralph Hukushima, John Hyer, Garner Ivey, Elizabeth Johnson, Donald Johnson, Frank Kaanamo, Carl Kaiama, Joe Kealoha, Marion Kelly, Noel Kent, Jean King, Tony Kinores, Ken Kirchmeyer, John Knox, Ron Kondo, Dave Kong, Nona Kong, Karl Korte, Adam Krivatsy, Gay Larned, Aaron Levine, Juanita Liu, Joseph Long, Rod Lowe, Philip Lowenthal, Paul Mancini, Len Mason, Dick Mayer, William Merrill, Jack Millar, Timothy Mitchell, Howard Nakamura, Eleanor Nordyke, Gwen Ohashi, Robert Ohata, Pamela Takiora Ingram Pryor, Stan Raymond, Thomas Rohr, Peter Sanborn, Willis Sanburn, Robert Schmitt, David Shearer, Elizabeth Shearer, Anthony Silva, Richard Silva, Les Skillings, Frank Skrivanek, Leiomalama Solomon, Allan Sommarstrom, J. M. Souki, John Souza, Earl Stoner, Hannibal Tavares, Haunani-Kay Trask, Cynthia Texeira, Lynn Thompson, Ivan Tilgenkamp, the late George Tompkin, the late Louis Van Der Linden, Alexa Keaunui Vaught, Ronald Vaught, John Ventura, Ned Wiederholt, Peter Wilson, Tamara Wong, Kenneth Wood, Teichi Yamada, Joseph Young, and JoAnn Yukimura.

Chapters of the initial drafts were read and commented upon by Toshio Ishikawa, Colin Cameron, John Kelsh, and Peter Krippl. They, of course, have no responsibility for the views expressed. Dean Edward Barnet, first dean of the School of Travel Industry Management, University of Hawaii, read the unrevised manuscript in its entirety and provided excellent extensive critical comment.

Grateful acknowledgment is made to the *Annal of Tourism Research* and to the *Western Geographic Series* for permission to use published materials that appear in modified form in chapters 10 and 11 and the maps in the first three chapters.

Maps were drawn by John Bryant and Ian Norrie, cartographers at the University of Victoria, and portions were updated by Paddy Farrell at Santa Cruz. Special thanks are offered to Iris Wiley, and to the staff of The University Press of Hawaii. Typing of the first drafts was done by Dianne Norris. Final typing, constant revising, and painstaking editing were the work of Gretchen Miller at the Pacific Research Unit, Santa Cruz.

Throughout what came to be a prolonged and extensive exercise, I was aided considerably by Billye Farrell, whose wide reading, extensive knowledge of Hawaii, and observation of human behavior provided perceptive insights on many fundamental questions which might otherwise have been overlooked.

To everyone I owe an immense debt of gratitude, especially to the last two persons who, unlike others, suffered the stresses of constant revision: as the situation in Hawaii seemed to change markedly every few months to the extent that even the author began to believe that although rewarding, writing about tourism in Hawaii could become a never-ending, permanent, full-time job.

Introduction

TAKE a group of breathtakingly beautiful volcanic islands set in the blue Pacific as close to paradise as you wish; join them politically to a highly populated advanced nation where people have more money and time to play with than any place on earth; introduce jet air travel cheap enough to beckon a factory worker or a typist; provide affordable, attractive accommodations, staff them with beautiful, warm, and hospitable people; and the results are staggering. This is not fantasy. This is the story of Hawaii, the Pacific's most developed tourist area.

Hawaii has just completed three decades of accelerated tourism. The 1950s, starting from a mere 46,600 visitors in the first year of the decade, averaged an impressive 22 percent increase annually for the remaining years. The 1960s were boom years, spectacular because during the last five years of the decade the annual visitor increase alone averaged almost 200,000 a year—an average yearly increase for the decade of 19 percent. The third decade was not quite so startling but still remarkable. In the 1970s, rates were erratic but nevertheless, in spite of a recession year in 1975, averaged close to 11 percent with annual increments closer to 300,000. In 1967 the state received its one-millionth visitor for a single year. In 1972, the two millionth arrived. In 1976 the three millionth made his appearance, and the year 1979 saw close to the state's four millionth visitor. The end of the decade also signaled a steep downturn in visitor arrivals, a downturn associated with a national recession. Visitor expenditures in the three decades went from $24.2 million to over $2.5 billion and the number of hotel rooms from fewer than 3,000 to almost 53,000 in 1979.

You might well question these spectacular results and ask

whether they did not have startling effects on Hawaii. The answer would have to be that they indeed did—the effects both good and bad. This book concerns itself with these impacts and the interrelatedness of the manifold forces brought to bear on man and nature in Hawaii through tourism. This holistic view of tourism sees it either as a matrix of numerous overlapping and intersecting systems reminiscent of a series of circles within a complicated Venn diagram or as a steel ring puzzle in its tangled complexity. What I propose to do here is to look at each ring separately, then in association with all others in the puzzle.

A Context of Forces and Values

There are some who speak of the fragility of tourism. If this means that the industry must be finely tuned to produce the highest quality tourist experience, be economically healthy, do the least possible damage to land and society, and retain the respect of visitors and the people, then I will agree. But from another viewpoint one might look at Hawaii's tourist industry until the end of the 1970s as having been particularly resilient. During the last twenty years, it has felt the impact of the Vietnam war and adjusted and readjusted to the appearance and disappearance of the lucrative military R&R (rest and recuperation) trade. It has seen an increased awareness among citizen groups wanting to impose controls or change directions in the interests of the environment, local ethnic groups, or the maintenance of good quality surf. In the wake of growing environmental awareness came a host of environmental regulations and procedures. Such changes were certainly linked with, if not central to, a newly emerging counterculture. And just as Hawaii drew migrants and tourists, it also attracted a new transient countercultural population which came with a distinct life-style that was a novel and at times uncomfortable element of Hawaii life.

The period also saw Japan develop as a major industrial power and a valuable source of tourists who perceived vacations differently, needed to be approached differently by the industry, and spent generously. Japanese investment funds poured into Hawaii and, as the state's first major incursion of foreign capital into the visitor industry, were met with mixed local reactions. The early 1970s saw the first major gasoline shortage, which for too few was an ominous warning of things to come, but for those with millions of dollars tied up in the industry, the effect was chilling. Later in the decade new sport (tennis) and entertainment (disco) emphases appeared. Destination areas on neighbor islands, where space was plentiful and life quite different from Oahu, created multiple golf courses, thereby competing with and diminishing the initial hold of Waikiki.

If the 1960s were years of expansion characterized by the struggle for civil rights, increased consideration of minorities, the growth of megalopolis, doomsayers, and activism related to the "we want it now" syndrome, the 1970s turned inward. People now thought of jobs and economic survival where previously they had talked knowingly about an approaching era when physical survival would be critical. The first oil crisis of 1973 and the 1974–1975 mainland recession added more reason. People grew more concerned with their destiny, their consciousness, themselves. The environment, falling in importance, took a less elevated place. The women's movement advanced noticeably. Women drove buses, repaired telephones, became chief executive officers, real estate brokers, and businesspersons of distinction. On other political and economic fronts, the country became absorbed with trying to beat inflation, bolster the value of the dollar overseas, develop relations with China, and solve problems in the Middle East.

The OPEC countries continued to raise the price of oil to crippling proportions while mainland citizenry felt duped by what they saw as national and international manipulation. High oil prices had a resounding impact on Japan's economy and produced a steadying influence on the rate of increase of Japanese visitors to Hawaii.

Without a doubt, the 1980s will see as many changes, concerned probably with efforts to decrease domestic inflation and to control and turn around the economic recession that finally arrived. Other concerns will be with a testing of values, the changing international status of the United States, international monetary crises, and the availability and cost of energy. All will have implications for Hawaii, some possibly resounding. Recession and inflation have already taken a toll. By the last quarter of 1979 and into 1980 the number of visitors to Hawaii had sagged ominously.

I have already mentioned megalopolis, the end product of what William Irwin Thompson calls the "Los Angelization of America" and Alvin Toffler might call the end product of "brute force technology." This monumental urban occupation of space, its ugliness, smog, crime, and other social problems has been a factor in underlining the attractions of Hawaii; massive escape from these conditions by those who can afford it has been a major contribution to the tourism success story of Hawaii. The growing revulsion to metropolitan crowding, urban vulgarity, and pollution is unlikely to abate. The open space, beauty, and tranquility of Hawaii, along with the excitement, will continue to provide incentives for visits and increased migration from unpalatable regions of congestion and stress if economic conditions and energy availability allow it.

Tourists, Travelers, and Leisure

This study is concerned mostly with the interaction of tourists with people and land. For present purposes I see tourists as people who want to get away from it all. They are in Hawaii not in the course of earning a living but primarily for pleasurable leisure which can be relaxing, physically invigorating, educational, instructive, or just plain experiential.

Valene Smith in the introduction to *Hosts and Guests* says: "A tourist is a temporarily leisured person who voluntarily visits a place away from home for the purpose of experiencing a change."[1] Nelson Graburn in the same work views tourism as a special form of play which involves travel, relaxation from tensions, and the opportunity of becoming a nonentity.[2] Dean MacCannell, who has done as much as any writer to analyze the tourist and his behavior, describes the tourist as a sightseer, mainly middle class, "deployed throughout the world in search of experience."[3]

The traveler, on the other hand, has a goal in mind, arriving in Hawaii to complete a business deal, to confer with members of the state administration, or to repair specialized equipment at a Honolulu hospital. The traveler role is also a useful guise for the intellectual snob who cannot conceive of himself as a leisured tourist. He purports to travel always for a worthy enlightening reason and would not be caught dead with a camera. Despite the excuses and the guises, he too, like all of us at some time or other, is still a tourist seeking a special experience. Nor is this activity less worthy than any of the others that occupy our leisure, our nonwork moments.

The industry fequently uses the word "visitor" for tourists. Anti-tourism factions deride this device. "They're still tourists," they say as if the outsider carries with him some pernicious affliction. "Tourist" is a perfectly reputable word but I see nothing wrong with "visitor" and if from time to time "tourist" develops unfortunate connotations and the use of "visitor" removes these then why not use it? In offical state language, "visitor" is used and is so commonplace it raises few eyebrows.

But "visitor" does have other uses and could be considered in some circumstances a shade different from "tourist." Is the person who rents a house on the Big Island for three months just a tourist? Is the condominium owner who spends several months of each year on Kauai a semipermanent seasonal resident? I could accept visitor in both situations. Difficulty arises as to where to draw a line, if this is necessary, between resident and visitor. When a relative visits from the mainland, he or she is neither "traveler" nor "tourist" but a "guest." Some have raised another distinction: guests are invited but visitors just arrive.

In the following discussion I largely ignore the distinctions I have discussed concerning tourist, traveler, and visitor. I know that the most marked impacts which raise concern are made servicing tourists. As well, the tourist industry in all its ramifications draws working travelers to Hawaii by the thousands, and the social and intellectual impact, because of the opportunity for closer relations with local people frequently denied tourists, may be considerable. But tourist, traveler, visitor, guest, semiseasonal resident, or, as we will consider later, the tourism-oriented inmigrant, all contribute to the overall tourism-related impact on both people and land.

The Approach

Because no one writer can be intimately aware of every activity at every place, it is my intention to pay more attention to some impacts of tourism least covered in documents concerning Hawaii, to consider generally the contemporary Hawaii scene, and to draw case studies from land development on the island of Maui, which has emerged during the seventies as a premier island destination area of Hawaii. In a number of ways, Maui is representative of Hawaii as a whole. It does not have the high degree of urbanism or the military installations of Oahu, yet the type of leisure land development completed, planned, and under construction is representative of similar activity on all major islands. Four large projects and two coastal strips were studied. Each occupies hundreds of acres and each will ultimately support populations of many thousands of persons. Each project provides employment for a large number of workers during construction and in basic and nonbasic service industries afterwards.

The work for this book was carried out in a series of studies during the course of a decade—the seventies. Earlier observations were made in 1948, 1951, 1961, and 1965, and in every year from 1969 to 1981 for a total period of twenty-seven months. During this time well over one hundred persons were interviewed. For Maui, I initially postulated "that because nearly thirty years will have elapsed between the planning of the first major project (Kaanapali) and the emergence of the last (Makena), and because attitudes during this time have changed radically, the planning process and its implementation will inevitably mirror changing social values." It was considered that development would reflect changing goals and values through such outward manifestations as greater public participation in planning, lower densities, the preservation of scenic views, greater access by the public to amenities around which developments were built, and a much greater concern for environmental quality. It was also postulated that large-scale planned-unit development served the welfare of the community better than small-scale subdivisional development. This book attempts to show the extent to which these hypotheses are valid.

Although conclusions concerning Maui are applied where appropriate to the state, other themes are addressed directly to Hawaii as a whole. Some of these are as follows: that continuing agriculture is essential to a healthy tourist industry; that a concept of balance (see chapter 14) should be an integral part of planning; that the public, the government, and the "operators" are together coequal components of the tourist industry; that successful tourism can be expected in the future only if the public is deeply involved in every facet of planning and discussion; that baseline research, continuous monitoring, and the setting of limits must be done now; and that what has evolved as the Hawaii tourist industry is an expression of the interaction of an introduced economic activity, limited resources, a unique environment, conflicting values, and numerous cultures.

Although Maui is put under the microscope, the island is used just for illustrative purposes. Fieldwork was conducted on every island and case studies and examples were drawn from all major development areas. Several assumptions have been made. First, that tourism is an obvious way for Hawaii, a relatively small state with limited resources, to earn what amounts to export income from the sale of services and amenities. Second, that tourism will continue into the distant future—it is not going to stop. Third, that tourism does not exist in a vacuum and, to understand its full meaning, it is necessary to go back into history and then to proceed toward the present in a context of social, political, economic, and environmental change.

Two major notions guiding this study then are the interrelatedness of systems (remember the steel rings) and appropriate context. Whenever case studies are developed more fully, they are cited to illustrate a social, economic, or environmental element or problem which otherwise might have been missed. These include using investment as a psychological strategy, environmental law to maintain privacy and territory, the provision of shoreline walks and beach access as a response to changing community views, the deeding of land for community recreation as a political reality, the maintenance of a precise balance between agriculture and tourism, public hearings as an expression of social disparities, and the interaction of interest groups as an educational, social, and psychological exercise.

This is not meant to be the type of traditional exposition of tourism seen elsewhere and applied to Hawaii. Many economic questions are dealt with effectively elsewhere by others. Greater attention is given here to the various impacts and human interactions as experienced or learned about in the course of research for this work. The outcome is an approach to tourism through the medium of land and people. This is perhaps the only way to illustrate tourism's manifold ramifications and to show without any doubt the value of not separating the activity from any of the main elements upon which it is based and in which it operates.

CHAPTER 1

Setting the Stage: Background to Present Development

LONG before the original Polynesians sailed to Hawaii in magnificent double-hulled canoes, before the arrival of significant organic life, millions of years into the past, Hawaii was the scene of spectacular activity.

The Pacific Basin is made up of several gigantic, rather mobile paving stones roughly resembling movable pieces of broken shell which slide on the surface of a boiled egg. The real world paving stones, called plates by geologists, have been migrating about the face of the earth for many millions of years. The Pacific plate, a particularly large one, moves laterally on the earth's crust, drawn dynamically toward the interior of the earth. It has, for eons of time, been moving and continues to move somewhat erratically, across the Pacific Basin on a path roughly southeast to northwest. But this is only part of it. In the north central Pacific, in the vicinity of the island of Hawaii, is a "hot spot" operating like a giant welding torch from within the earth. As the Pacific plate passes over it, as it has for twenty-five million years, it cuts through the crust to form volcanoes, allowing gases, steam, ash, and lava to extrude on the ocean floor 18,000 feet below the ocean surface.[1] Basaltic domes, formed of layer upon layer—like onion skin—of volcanic materials, appear. At the time of the first human visitors to Hawaii the domes had appeared as a chain of volcanic islands, some rising to almost 14,000 feet above sea level. And to give substance to the theory, the chain of major Hawaiian islands does in fact today trend 350 miles in the direction noted. As we would expect, Kauai in the north is the oldest island, followed by Oahu, Molokai, Lanai, Maui, and finally, with numerous examples of active volcanism, the Big Island of Hawaii. And as if the plate were performing on cue, new volcanoes have been discovered along the

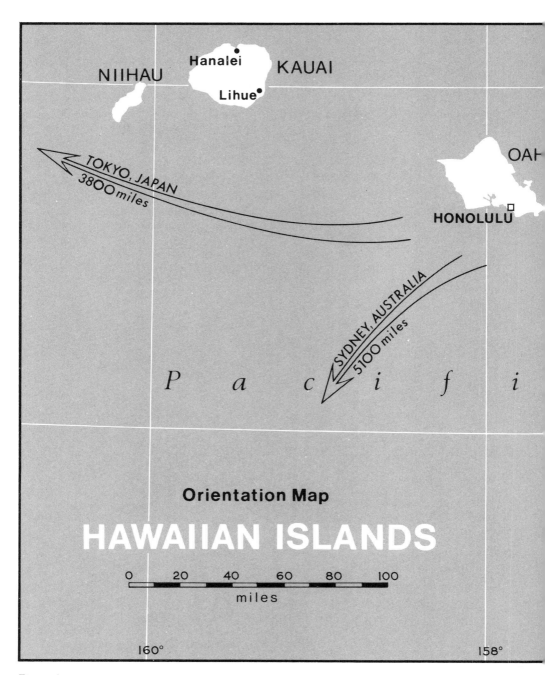

Figure 1.

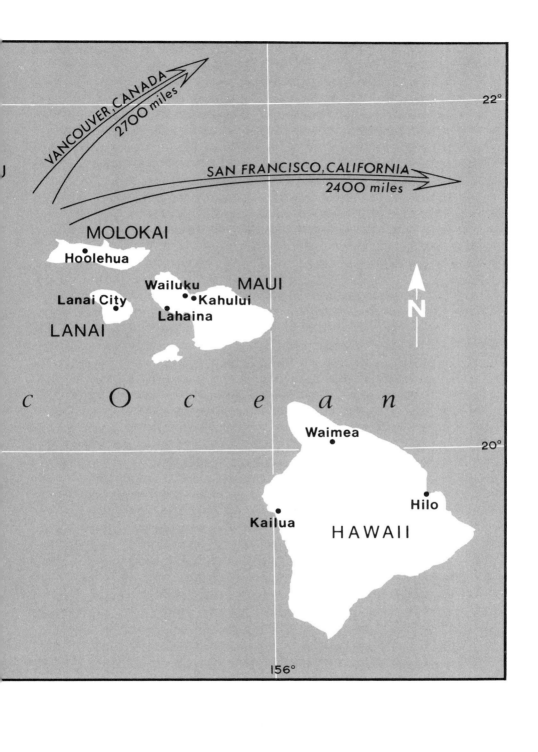

trend line to the southeast. These ultimately will become the new-est of the Hawaiian series. The process continues indefinitely.

In older areas where the direct effects of volcanism seem no lon-ger a threat, on the more sheltered coasts away from the constant battering of storm waves, or in protected bays away from the damaging effects of fresh water, coral reefs have been building over long periods of time in warm, shallow, well-aerated water. Healthy reefs developed quickly in pace with the action of destruc-tive ocean waves on their seaward margins. Millions of years of the disintegration of coral by storms took a natural toll of the reef but nevertheless provided a resource of inestimable value to the Hawaiian Islands: long, dazzlingly beautiful coral sand beaches.

Today the Hawaiian group of islands stands majestic and spec-tacular. Jagged skylines and dramatic coasts, especially on the windward sides of islands, present an impressive view. In older areas millions of years of erosion have subdued more ragged forms. In all areas erosional forces have had to compete with vol-canic building and, in some places, recent lava flows have over-whelmed and obliterated thousands of years of down-cutting by rivers. Together the islands, large and small—over 130 in total but eight of major importance—cover 6,450 square miles.

The group, although often referred to as subtropical, lies within the tropics between 19° and 22° N latitude. Because it is north of the equator and more toward the eastern Pacific, the group falls within an area dominated by the great regular tropical easterlies found on the southern margins of subtropical high pressure circu-lations; these are commonly referred to and with good reason ro-manticized as trade winds. Temperatures are mild tropical. Mean temperatures at Honolulu for the coolest and warmest months are 71° and 78° F. Extremes vary from 57° to 88° F. In all areas as the heat of the day approaches, trade winds take over as a natural air conditioner making conditions pleasant, if at times windy. Like all trade wind areas where Pacific high islands are involved, the changes in climate are startling from wet sides to dry sides, a situation expected where winds for a very high percentage of time blow from the same quarter. Windward areas are wet, wetter with increasing altitude. During storms a myriad of streams cascade down the steep rocky slopes. Waterfalls abound and as the plunge-pools at their feet cut backwards, great hunks of jointed, fractured basaltic rock drop downward to disintegrate and be transported toward the sea.

In the high interiors, rainfall totals may be anywhere from 200 to 500 inches a year. The erosive power of large volumes of water causes the heads of adjacent valleys to migrate together eventually to form spectacular knife-edge barriers between nearby river systems. Water falling on the outcropping of certain porous rock types is taken downward rather than running off the surface and contributes to the overwhelmingly important underground water supplies of Hawaii, the main source of water for residential use.

On the wet sides of islands, where at sea level rainfall may range from forty to fifty inches annually, broadleaf trees and shrubs form true rainforest. This is certainly true in exposed valleys 500 feet and higher in altitude. Remoteness from other Pacific areas resulted in the original rather meager number of species. Over the past century and a half, these have been augmented by numerous introductions of flowering species from South America, India, China, Southeast Asia, and elsewhere in the Pacific. The beautiful plumeria (frangipani), gardenia, and pikake now so closely identified with the islands are all introductions as are the night-blooming cereus, shower trees, jacarandas, oleanders, and bougainvilleas.

After hundreds of years of early indigenous Hawaiian settlements a harmony of people with their environment may have developed together with a degree of stability. About this we can only guess, but with a limited technology and only survival and ceremonial needs the land was treated gently. Early Europeans brought cattle, goats, sheep, and all types of introduced crops and plants; during this ecologically disturbing process "accompanied by a never-ending stream of new exotic plants . . . whole vegetation types were destroyed."[2] Yet in the wake of this destruction, which could have been but was not minimized, there arose pineapple and sugar cane fields, cattle ranching, and diversified agriculture, all of which are now closely related to and essential to the maintenance of a healthy tourism and a balanced economy.

At the beginning of the tourist boom of the 1960s, Raymond Fosberg wrote the following:

> Now almost all the vegetation types that are commonly seen by visitors excepting . . . those around Kilauea Volcano are largely . . . non-Hawaiian plants. And most of the people who live [in Hawaii] do not even know this. The cane, the pineapple, the guava, the papaya, the showy trees that line the streets, the weeds that invade

the gardens . . . and the coconuts are all newcomers brought by
man from elsewhere. Even the ornamental hibiscus which sym-
bolizes Hawaii . . . is a creation of man. Almost no Hawaiian plants
have been brought into cultivation.

Man came and found a strange and wonderful flora and fauna . . .
He has not yet succeeded in completely destroying them, but he has
made more progress in that direction than in almost any other . . .
One might hope that the people of Hawaii would realize what they
are losing and demand that at least bits of it be saved. Their de-
scendants might even . . . appreciate the chance to see and enjoy
some of the wonders of old Hawaii.[3]

Twenty years later I feel the chances of something worthwhile
being saved, though not great, are much better than in 1961 when
the statement was made.

What Fosberg says is perfectly true. The new introduced flowering plants are a resource of inestimable value to both local people and tourists. Nurturing the original flora and fauna can
produce results of equal local and tourist interest and should be
given high priority. With wise leadership and thoughtful approaches, Hawaii can maintain a healthy balance between new
and old vegetation covers in each area, conserving the environment in such a way that people and nature can exist side by side.

On the drier sides of islands where rainfall may be from five to
thirty inches a year, the contrast from the wet may be startling.
The vegetation covers the ground sparsely. It may range from a
more open savanna-type forest with indigenous grasses to dry-land
xerophytic communities often on newer volcanic material and
dominated by kiawe, wiliwili, prickly pear cactus, and other such
species. With water, the "desert" blooms. It is on the drier, rainshadow sides where clearer skies, sunshine, more predictable
weather, and white coral beaches abound that the tourist goes and
new resort areas have sprung up. All coastal areas have a tourist
potential but it is in the leeward, protected areas where tourism
has achieved its highest development.

Hawaiians and the Land[4]

The original Polynesian occupiers of Hawaii made their first land-
falls in Hawaii from the Marquesas and Tahiti starting about A.D.
650.[5] When they arrived they found high islands of great beauty

covered in a vegetation undisturbed by human or animal habitation. They brought with them tropical crops that had been stored within their canoes and continued the practice of subsistence farming they had learned in the islands of eastern Polynesia. Here in Hawaii, living remotely from other Pacific groups, they developed a unique way of life and a socioeconomic organization related to past heritage but intimately connected to the new environment into which they had settled. Land tenure reflected the changes taking place.

There may have been three, four, or more systems of land organization operating at different times in Hawaii. Dole suggests at least one system prior to European contact.[6] Another came with development of the Hawaiian kingdom and another with the redistribution of land in the Great Mahele of 1848.[7] Certainly, in the last three systems, although radical changes took place moving from one to the next, the control of land has always been in the hands of very few people and land control and politics have been intimately related in one way or another. Meller and Horwitz stress that as in the past, and for some time to come in Hawaii, "the control of land will remain a central theme in the State's social and political evolution."[8]

When the first Europeans arrived, land was organized in quasi-feudal cells, a system which has some parallels with the situation today. Each island was ruled by an individual of extremely high rank. Beneath him were powerful high chiefs, *ali'i-nui*, who controlled major blocks of land. The biggest identified pieces were triangular *ahupua'a*, their apexes toward the interior and broader bases often along the coast. *Ili*, lesser divisions within the *ahupua'a*, were managed by minor chiefs. Further toward the base of the pyramid, within each *ili*, were the gardens of the *maka'ainana*, untitled men, peasants, who through service and food production supported themselves, their families, and the chiefs at various ranks.[9] The *maka'ainana* were in fact tenants-at-will. Rights to land could be abrogated at any time by chiefs who always had the controlling hand. But within this tough authoritarian rule, families usually occupied the same land for generations.

Well before contact it seems the common man may have had more extensive rights to land than he had in the nineteenth century. Probably as the result of continual warfare and the dependence on a strong leader for survival, most rights to land had become identified with chiefs, especially a strong man who subdued opposition and threats to the security of the land by aggressive leaders from other areas.[10] Kamehameha, paramount chief of the large island of Hawaii, with warriors and European weapons overcame the forces of all major islands. In this manner he made himself absolute ruler of the group. He made a marked break with former tradition by making sure that his own family became hereditary rulers of the future, something quite unknown previously. Reallocation of territories on the death of an island ruler was abandoned in favor of the control of land remaining with those already in control. On Kamehameha's own death, the new procedures worked in the favor of the royal family who retained control with the assistance of their chiefly supporters. It was at this point that the principal of hereditary "ownership" of land was initiated.[11] Such a change in political and land organization was a crucial element in contributing to today's land situation. I see it as evidence that because land tenure was obviously not a sacrosanct matter to persons of great distinction and authority, other marked changes under similar circumstances could have as easily taken place in the past.

During the early decades of the nineteenth century, a close rapport developed between the politically minded haole (Caucasian) and New England missionaries (and their lineage), both of whom frequently served as advisors to the royal family and later as ministers in the cabinet of the Hawaiian government. The outsider saw with enthusiasm the potential of Hawaiian land and with some unremitting persuasion and initiative what might be done with it by an astute entrepreneur. Its ownership—despite its undefined title and not understood system of rights—was made all the more desirable when it was realized that already for some its use was said to have been obtained by gifts of little value, perhaps a little money or as reciprocity for services performed for the royal family. As the influence of the non-Hawaiian community grew so did pressure for the wholesale acquisition of land.

In 1835 as the result of missionary insistence, the government approved the lease of a tract of land at Koloa, Kauai, to a group of "respectable businessmen," Ladd & Co., one of whom had been trained at Yale Divinity School.[12] For a few years after that time, they planted sugar cane and ran a mill with modest success but after some scandalous adventures, the group went bankrupt in 1844. (More later concerning the Koloa-Poipu Beach resort, essentially the same area first pioneered in the western manner by Ladd & Co. almost a century and a half ago.)

The Polynesian rulers had for several decades developed a better realization of the land's role in these changing times both as a future resource of importance for Hawaiian people and as a means of assuring for the rulers an affluent style of living. The sales and resales of land, the auctioning of property, and the use of land in payment of debts by foreigners were considered highly undesirable. In view of these trends, it was now felt necessary for Hawaiian leaders to reassert control over a resource which was showing increasing signs of becoming uncontrollable. In 1842 Kamehameha I, in an effort to restrain what he considered to be objectionable activity, proclaimed that land would be available only for lease after consent had been obtained from both the premier and the king. The apparent firmness seemed doomed to failure because as Kelly put it: "Pressures for changes were powerful and the developing commercial community was looking for new ways to invest its increasingly large profits."[13] Outright purchase rather than leasing was what the expatriate community was after and it became inevitable that all possible pressure would be exerted on the government to bring this about.

Persons other than Ladd & Co., with missionary help, got large-tract long-term leases. The missionaries for their part felt that the leases would stimulate rural activity and employment and would be a healthy antidote to objectionable urban drift to Honolulu and other centers affecting Hawaiians at the time. Three groups—the government, the New England missionaries, and the haole community—all had their own agendas. The land situation was rapidly changing.

Haoles and the Land

Outsiders were getting extensive control over large parcels of territory. They pursued their goal of attaining full title to land with relentless determination. There were merchants with money to invest, the early sugar plantations were proving successful, and the pressure on government to make more land available was increasing markedly. Haole demands finally resulted in legislative action.

In December 1845, a five-man land commission, the Board of Commissioners to Quiet Land Titles, was appointed by Kamehameha III to investigate land claims and conflicts and to confirm or deny the validity of claims. The commissioners really had another mission in mind, a completely new system of land organization and rights. The board developed "principles" for evaluating the situation. These criteria resulted ultimately in recommendations to take great areas away from the king and redistribute them to new rightholders who would be granted title and the right to their ultimate disposal. In effect, a new tenure was created involving the king, the chiefs, and the government. Most importantly, the door was left open for outsiders to enter a system which was more to their liking and in which they could exert the control they had determinedly worked for. The recommendations, after lengthy discussions between various parties, became law in 1848.

This became known as the *Great Mahele*, the greatest revolution the land of Hawaii had ever known. It divided and reallocated the king's land three ways: crown land (less than 1 million acres) remained the king's personal, privately owned land; government land (more than 1.5 million acres) was to be used for the future support of the legislature; and *konohiki* land (1.5 million acres), which had been under the de facto control of the chiefs, was now by law their own. Two years later, as something of an afterthought, the bulk of the Hawaiian people were awarded their ancestral subsistence garden plots, *kuleana*, amounting to only 30,000 acres.[14]

By 1850 aliens possessed virtually all they had been pressing for especially the right to purchase land in fee simple. The common people owned less than 1 percent of the land; most of the remainder, for a short period at least, was technically in the hands of the king, government, and 245 chiefs.[15]

The rapid exploitation of both the Hawaiian people and their lands was not just a matter of Caucasian rapacity; indeed it was aided and abetted by the ruling families and influential chiefs,[16] although it must be argued that they had little knowledge, at the time, of the effects of their actions.

With hindsight, it seems that the events to follow would be inevitable. Great tracts of land were bought from the government and individual chiefs or their heirs. Even the rank-and-file Hawaiians were quickly persuaded to dispose of their small acreage. By 1936 only 6 percent of the original awards made to commoners were in Hawaiian hands.[17] With land easily available, plantation companies proliferated and recruiters for the sugar estates combed the world for cheap tractable labor. This they found in China, Japan, Portugal, the Philippines, and in other places (see chapter 9). Hundreds of thousands of Asian laborers arrived during the nineteenth and early twentieth centuries. Although substantial numbers of them returned to their homelands, many more remained either because they thought their futures lay with Hawaii or because plantation work did not provide the expected monetary rewards necessary for a triumphant return home. The basis of today's cosmopolitan Hawaiian population was laid at this time.

After arrangements had been made for easy entry of Hawaii sugar into the United States by the Reciprocity Treaty of 1876, sugar production flourished. The first effect of the treaty "was to cause a boom in sugar which turned the heads of some of [the] shrewdest men and nearly caused a financial crash"—so wrote Professor W. P. Alexander twenty years later.[18] A discriminatory tariff levied by the United States in 1890 provided an unwelcome impediment to development, but fortunately this was removed four years later. One result of the growth of the sugar industry was that several influential companies (the sugar factors or agencies) were organized to provide special purchasing, marketing, accounting, and other services for a growing number of plantations. In time, virtually all the industry was brought under the influence of the factors. After a series of purchases and the absorption of smaller and faltering estates, most of the agricultural land of the island group came under the control of but a few major corporate entities. This process continued well into the middle of the present century and was still continuing as recently as the 1950s.

Out of the sugar factors who controlled 96 percent of Hawaii-grown sugar, by the 1920s several had arisen to dominate the industry. For a long time these, for the most part, directed the Hawaii economy: H. Hackfeld and Company, a German firm later bought by American Factors (Amfac); Theo H. Davies and Co.; Alexander & Baldwin; C. Brewer and Co.; and Castle & Cooke. In the 1930s every one of these companies had at least one missionary descendant among its directors. Alexander & Baldwin had six![19] Several of the agencies are major commercial conglomerates today, all retain agricultural land as well as their other commercial interests, and three of them—Amfac, Alexander & Baldwin, and C. Brewer—are heavily involved in the visitor industry. Castle & Cooke may ultimately develop Lanai for the same purpose.

Between annexation by the United States in 1898 and World War II, land in Hawaii was used primarily for agricultural purposes, although new public uses were becoming increasingly important. Sugar acreage grew from 127,000 acres at the beginning of the century to almost a quarter of a million acres in the mid-1930s. The same period saw the decline of diversified farming and the rise of pineapples as the second major plantation crop. By the third decade of the century, 79,000 acres of pineapples had been established.

To compete with countries where costs were much lower than in Hawaii, it was quickly learned that local agriculture would have to depend on highly efficient well-managed plantations, a substantial use of technology, and the imaginative use of research. This last activity took place under the direction of the Hawaiian Sugar Planters' Association and the Pineapple Research Institute.[20] All this achieved remarkable success despite economic setbacks and legislative bombshells like the Jones-Costigan Sugar Control Act of 1934 which reduced the quota of Hawaii sugar allowed to enter the mainland market.

During the first four decades of this century, attitudes changed and so did the use of the land. Agriculture was still important but new uses for defense, education, transportation, and recreation grew in significance. The Forest Reserve Act of 1903 authorized the designation of vast amounts of public and private lands as forest reserves to prevent soil erosion, improve water yield, and in part to prevent wanton burning of forest margins by ranchers wanting to increase areas of pasture.[21] It was also designed to repair the accumulated damage of poor land management, the devastation by grazing animals liberated and protected in the late eighteenth and nineteenth centuries, and especially to ensure ample water supplies for lowland sugar producers. During the forty-year period, hundreds of thousands of acres were set aside under gubernatorial orders for forest reserves and national parks, while smaller but still significant areas were allotted to military use, airports, education, and other public uses.[22]

The use of land for leisure developed slowly. By the 1840s, with a population of 8,000, Honolulu had five hotels and six boarding houses. For the next three decades the small but growing town catered to a significant number of transient guests—whalers, seamen, and traders. The first Hawaiian Hotel was established in 1855. The second, which later became known as the Royal Hawaiian, opened its magnificent doors in 1872. Here was a hotel occupying some four acres, "a credit to the City," and reported by the *Hawaiian Gazette* as "that flower of the islands . . . a monumental edifice . . . comparable with anything to be found on the mainland."[23]

The next hotel of impressive proportions which actually catered to tourists, as opposed to travelers, was the imposing Haleiwa Hotel opened in 1899 at Waialua at the head of the Oahu Railway and Land Company's line on the north shore of Oahu. The trip to Haleiwa became so popular, the railway journey so memorable, and the on-site facilities so good that without exaggeration Haleiwa during the early years of the century represented Oahu's first "off-Honolulu" resort destination area. Haleiwa was situated at the end of the railway just as Waikiki, later, was to be found at the end of the trans-Pacific steamer route.[24]

Closer to Honolulu several places offered accommodations —the Seaside Annex, formerly the beach annex of the Royal Hawaiian; the Moana Hotel (1901) at Waikiki; the Alexander Young (1903) downtown; and several smaller hotels in Honolulu.

At the end of World War I there were three major hotels in the downtown area—the Alexander Young, the Pleasanton, and the Royal Hawaiian. At Waikiki, a mile or two out of town toward Diamond Head, there was the Moana, the Seaside, the Halekulani, the Waikiki Inn, and the Outrigger Canoe Club (founded in 1908). During the 1920s, when the number of tourists was around 13,000 annually, a new Seaside Hotel was built, the Matson Navigation Company opened the present Royal Hawaiian (1927), and in the following year the Niumalu was added. These together with numerous small hotels, guest houses, and cottages had, by World War II, entirely changed the complexion of Waikiki as it was in its earlier days, described by Judd as "a swamp exploited [first by Hawaiians for taro and later] by Chinese farmers who raised ducks and bananas."[25]

One or two shipping lines ran cruises to Hawaii and the visitor orientation was shared disproportionately between Honolulu and Waikiki where a concentration of hotels was developing. The fledgling tourist industry was symbolized by a few staid and elegant hotels, the exploits of Duke Kahanamoku, and a number of South Seas movies with their mellifluous musical scores. Despite the manner in which certain kamaaina residents decried the tourist industry, it reflected, in comparison with today's frenetic ambience, well-to-do formality in an atmosphere of quiet charm.

World War II, defense spending on Oahu in the postwar years, economic boom conditions on the mainland, and eventually statehood in 1959 catapulted Hawaii from the insular, isolated, novel category into the mainstream of American life. Thousands of mainland military servicemen had their first taste of the tropical Pacific in Hawaii during World War II and the Korean War— impressions which continue to thrive in their minds. Nor did movements of military personnel cease after the wars. Military spending continued to pour millions in federal funds into the island economy, especially during the Vietnam war. Finally, to meet the demands of a stepped-up economy, fast, cheaper, more frequent commercial jet airline services commenced in 1959.

Hawaii Approaches the 1970s

Little in Hawaii may be satisfactorily understood unless it is appreciated in an appropriate context of history and change. After statehood, political power rested firmly with the Democratic party. Prior to this time and up to 1954, the state had been in the hands of the landed aristocracy—sugar, pineapple, and related interests. Thomas Hitch called these "the sugar-pineapple-land-capital 'haves' "—represented by the Republican party. The Democrats, he saw, represented "the small business-wage earner-laboring 'have nots'."[26]

The situation was not as simple as this may make it appear. Although there was a marked shift in political power, this did not also represent an economic shift. Although economic changes since the transfer of political power and statehood have been significant, economic power remains where it formerly did even as the base of power has been extended considerably. Political transition had two phases: the first, 1900–1954, from an absolute feudal monarchy to an economic ruling class, and the second, 1954 to the present, to a government having a much wider constituency, including labor representation.

These changes have resulted in highly centralized government, just as it was in the nineteenth century, tempered by pioneer, progressive legislation in the areas of land use, taxes, and labor. The same forward thinking has provided an ideal climate for spectacular economic development over the past two decades. Until World War II, Hawaii was strictly an agricultural state with 42 percent of the civilian labor force working in sugar and pineapple. When tourism came to the islands in the mid-1950s, it heralded a period of unprecedented prosperity. Even the worst economic year in this post-1955 period, including a mainland recession in the mid-1970s, was not as bad as that experienced in the post-war decade of stagnation, 1945–1955. Agriculture then showed no promise, unemployment reached 10 percent, and, from 1948 to 1954, some 80,000 more persons left Hawaii than arrived. This was offset by an excess of births over deaths which ultimately produced a net decline in total population of around 10,000.[27]

The pre-1954 history must be viewed as a springboard to later happenings. It prepared the stage for tourism's resounding success and continued acceptance during the following decades. Events preceding 1954 and the burgeoning tourist industry contributed to weakening the traditional hold of the landed oligarchy on the economy. Resiliently, some of its members soon were making plans to infiltrate the visitor industry. Tourism was not merely a novel infusion into the economy: it helped break the community's deeply ingrained plantation dependency. By bringing people to Hawaii, tourism was both a symbol and a manifestation of economic turnaround. The industry broke a general feeling of remoteness by psychologically bringing the community closer to the American mainstream. In retrospect, some argue that it was then that Hawaii bought the host of problems it has now to contend with. Few, however, would argue that a dramatic economic change was not needed.

In time the visitor industry did much to improve the employment picture; in addition it counterbalanced an increasingly bleak future for agriculture. For many people it provided local economic opportunities which kept family members in the district and drastically reduced the need to migrate to the mainland for work. At the time of statehood, the alternatives to tourism seemed depressingly inadequate to sustain on their own the enthusiasm of local leaders. Nothing else seemed able to demonstrate the political and economic integrity of the land.

The Hawaii Economy Today

Agriculture, economically strong or weak, has always been fundamental to Hawaii's economy and way of life. In comparison with that of other Pacific groups, Hawaii's economy appears stable and mature. As an island group, it is highly anomalous in that it derives its relative sophistication and economic importance from its strategic location as a Pacific extension of the United States.

Unlike other places intent on breaking colonial connections, statehood reinforced its pre-1959 linkages. Hawaii's metropolitan associations make a startling difference. Its basic agricultural economy has long since been eclipsed by a mainland contribution—
federal spending—and, since the mid-1960s, by tourism.

As Pacific islands with a typically restricted range of resources,
Hawaii has depended substantially on its exports for overseas income. These include federal expenditures in Hawaii, tourism receipts, and agricultural income. In 1980 federal outlays in the
state were over $3.3 billion, approximately 10 percent ahead of
visitor industry receipts. The greatest single item of federal expenditures, $1.9 billion, was for nondefense purposes; the remainder,
a noticeably lower amount, was for defense (see table 1). Most of
the nondefense spending represented health, retirement, and dis-
ability   insurance   disbursements   through   the   Department   of
Health, Education, and Welfare. Other substantial sums went to
the Department of Transportation, the Civil Service Commission,
the Department of Labor, the Department of Commerce, and the
Veterans Administration. The importance of federal spending cannot be stressed enough here, as the common belief by many mainlanders is that the state is supported almost entirely by tourism.

The 1980 visitor expenditures of $3.0 billion came from the ar-
rival of almost four million tourists. The year's rate of increase
was the second consecutive yearly increase below the average for
the decade, and the first in over thirty years in which an absolute
decrease in visitor arrivals was recorded. Although an impending
downturn signaled in 1979 had arrived, tourist expenditures still
increased by almost 15 percent, just keeping pace with inflation.

TABLE 1. *Hawaii Income (in millions of dollars)*

	1940	1950	1960	1970	1979	1980
Commodities						
Sugar	60	124	127	189	346	595
Pineapple	46	102	119	139	223	229
Federal Expenditures						
Defense	40	147	373	639	1,310	1,399
Other		56	113	439	1,663	1,908
Goods and services						
Tourist and other visitors	12	24	131	595	2,600	3,000

SOURCES: For 1950 and 1960 statistics, *Annual Economic Review*, 1970 and 1971, Bank of Hawaii,
Honolulu; for 1970, State of Hawaii, *Data Book* 1978 (Honolulu: Department of Planning and Economic
Development, 1978); for 1980, *Economics Division*, Bank of Hawaii.

The third category of income, agriculture, is smaller in comparison, about $1 billion in which sugar came first with $595 million, followed by pineapple with $229 million. Livestock raising, dairying, and other aspects of diversified agriculture follow with an accumulated total of about $172 million, noticeably less than that for pineapple. For the past two decades employment has reflected the two major indigenous economic activities. From 1959, employment in agriculture dropped from 19,800 to just over 15,000 in 1980. During the same period. the increase in hotel employment rose from 4,500 to almost 25,000.

Because agriculture has such a close relationship to tourism chapter 7 has been devoted to it. Suffice it to say here that only fresh pineapple and some areas of diversified agriculture show limited promise for the future. Although sugar resulted in a spectacular income in 1980 it dropped in 1981, and its immediate past history has been one of woeful instability. As intended by state and county policy, diversified agriculture together with aquaculture is being promoted wherever possible. Big things are hoped for in these areas but what product will succeed well beyond the others is yet to be seen: flowers, indoor plants, papaya, macadamia nuts, vegetables, or shrimp. The sugar-pineapple mainstay appeared threatened at every turn and during the past decade was weak and erratic; increasing costs and low receipts took their toll. Now both are stronger, but for neither is the future guaranteed. As sugar strengthened in 1979–1980 and pineapple growers saw bright days ahead, I wondered whether anything more than a hopeful wait-and-see stance was warranted. One must always remember that statistics indicate very little about the underlying story.

Tourism, whose receipts grew 400 percent during the decade 1968–1978, is so potent a force and yet in many ways so vulnerable no one group within the community can afford to become complacent and be lulled by its past success. It is no surprise then that diversified agriculture which will spread the economic base, help keep people in the rural area, and secure the land from the inroads of less desirable uses should be vigorously encouraged despite its mixed bag of minor successes and the paucity of information available on markets and their potential. No one has, of course, given up on sugar especially in the immediate period when demand exceeds supply, or on pineapple and livestock, all struggling but still more important than diversified crop agriculture.

Since 1968 Hawaii chronically has had an adverse balance of

payments with the mainland and foreign countries. This has varied somewhat erratically from $16 million to $513 million annually with an average around $250 million. A major component of the state's expenditures in 1978 of $6.3 billion was $1.8 billion for industrial commodities including machinery, equipment, lumber, and chemicals; $1.2 billion for fuel; and $371 million for imported foods and beverages. About $1.4 billion were payments to agencies of the federal government which, happily for Hawaii, spends or disburses more than twice this amount in the state.

The least stable of the above items is fuel whose costs rose by two-thirds between 1977 and 1978. It could easily double during the next few years, diminishing much which is gained·from tourism or agriculture. The state administration is fully aware of the problem and has set as one of its priorities the development of self-sufficiency in energy, putting to use as many indigenous sources as possible. The high cost of fuels is a two-edged sword for Hawaii. It directly diminishes state income and indirectly, through higher airfares, reduces the number of visitors.

In a state well equipped for agriculture, large purchases of food from the mainland need considerable reevaluation. Much of this is related to the tourist industry. This, in terms of the industry's multiplier effect, is identified as leakage, a process that weakens the economic impact of the industry. Another major reason for food importation is the strong cultural ties many people still have with the diet of the place of family origin. When I walk through markets in Honolulu, Hilo, Lihue, and Kahului, I see merchandise straight from the Orient. But more importantly, three-quarters of the stock is indistinguishable from that found in mainland food markets. Mainland merchandising is a most pervasive force and mainland eating patterns die hard. If consumers so choose, it is entirely possible to substitute, to a much greater extent than at present, papaya, pineapple, and local juice for imported breakfast items and local beef and salad vegetables for flown-in corn-fed beef, head lettuce, and imported tomatoes.

Just as fuel prices and Hawaii's vulnerability have caused a marked reevaluation of local resources, so too might spiraling inflation of consumer prices cause a similar reassessment of the manner in which local resources might be better used. The astronomical levels to which mainland beef prices are projected to rise could greatly benefit the livestock industry. By using local resources more effectively, the economic impact of tourism is increased while the state dependence on this particular source of income is lessened. Local gains would more than offset losses.

The percentage share of Hawaii's overseas earnings is interesting. For the past decade and a half, income from federal sources has been reasonably stable varying from 40 to 50 percent of the total. Agricultural commodities' share of exports has steadily fallen from about 26 percent to less than 10 percent while the sale of goods and services which can largely be attributable to the tourism industry has more than doubled from about 18 to 41 percent.[28] Of the payments that are made, commodity imports have remained about the same for the past fifteen years at around 50 to 54 percent.

The real benefit of tourism to the economy is a complicated matter which must take into consideration not only the industry's receipts but also outlays for food imports, fuel, and building materials together with expenditures of the state and the counties for providing an infrastructure for its support: police, fire, park maintenance, airports, and highways, to mention only a few. If the industry grows at a rate beyond a certain threshhold it more than provides for employment needs locally and jobs must be filled by in-migrants attracted by opportunities in Hawaii. In these circumstances, the financial burden and social repsonsibilities of state and local government are much greater than they would otherwise have been. Now they must provide extra for education, health, recreation, and other services for newcomers, most of whom have been attracted by the state's industrial growth. Here another element enters the scene. Not only are cars, food, fuel, building materials, and machinery imported to support the industry but labor as well.

In 1970 a consulting firm, Mathematica, completed a cost-benefit analysis to determine the benefit of tourism to state and local governments. The conclusion of this survey was as follows: "Visitors to Hawaii easily pay back their costs to the State government taking into account the direct and indirect revenues they provide and the direct and indirect public costs incurred on their behalf."[29]

For various reasons the analysis expected the ratio of benefits to costs to decline in the future. In the late 1970s, patterned on the Mathematica report, the State of Hawaii concluded its own analysis in preparation for the state tourism plan. It confirmed Mathematica's initial findings and found that the ratios had indeed declined as forecast. The reason for this is not specifically known, the state study being more comprehensive than the Mathematica survey and not strictly comparable. The new study reported that "Hawaii's State and county governments receive more revenues from visitors than they spend on the visitors' behalf." Thus, the lower ratio might be attributable to two things: one, it might represent a decline in the benefits of tourism, or, two, "the net benefits of tourism growth to Hawaii's State and county governments had been exaggerated"[30]—that is, overestimated in the first place by Mathematica. The original report's forecast that the net benefits of tourism to state and counties were inversely proportional to the number of recent in-migrants in the labor force was confirmed, and in addition the state found "that the net benefits of Tourism growth to Hawaii's State government are much greater than benefits to its county governments."[31]

The state of course returns a proportion of its gains to the counties in the form of school support and numerous other state projects. The benefits to both state and counties become obvious in a chapter to follow.

CHAPTER 2

Contemporary Leisure Development

THE present population of Hawaii—civilian, armed forces and their dependents, and daily visitors—amounts to over one million. In 1980, the resident population alone reached 965,000 persons. By far the greatest number, 762,000, lived on Oahu, and most of these were concentrated in the capital city of Honolulu. The rest were spread over the remaining islands. Populations for the larger islands were 92,200 on Hawaii (the Big Island), 63,000 on Maui, and approximately 39,000 on Kauai. Oahu, as expected, is the most densely settled with over 1,400 persons per square mile. The other islands, in comparison, have great open areas and are relatively sparsely settled: 25 people per square mile on Hawaii, 83 on Kauai, and 106 on Maui. Of the total, 125,000 were military personnel or dependents.

The most critical problem in Hawaii is population growth, which not only creates stress on island resources but also aggravates most other problems. Hawaii's population has already achieved a low birth rate of only two children per family. The average age of the population is young, and death rates are low. If we disregard net migration, it is estimated that with closely balanced birth and death rates, the population would stabilize by the middle of the twenty-first century at a figure 40 percent higher than in 1970.[1]

The problem however is in-migration. In 1960 the resident population of Hawaii was 642,000; in 1970, 775,000; and in 1980 close to 965,000. By the last decade of the century, certainly by the turn of the century, the resident population may reach 1.3 million. Between 1970 and 1980 it increased by an average rate of 2.3 percent per annum. Between 1970 and 1980, while the natural increase for the state was 93,800, net migration excluding military was 100,900.[2] In-migration for the period was considerable. Some migrants from other states eventually return to the mainland along with some long-term residents. Alien migrants are, in comparison, much less mobile and the numbers arriving are particularly high. In 1975 it was estimated that Hawaii received 10.4 aliens per 1,000 resident population in contrast to the United States average of 1.8. What is known for certain is that from 1969 to 1979 aliens in the state increased 20,000, or 40 percent. This entry of both citizens and aliens is of central concern to the administration and to state and county planners. An intercensal growth rate of 33 percent compared with the nation's growth rate of 9 percent is a matter of great concern.

I have already pointed out the relationship between tourism and population, and this vital relationship will come up again and again. An obvious figure of some importance is the total number of tourist arrivals in the state. It allows people to "oo" and "ah" and say "how long until the next million?" but outside its practical use for airlines, some planning, and its symbolic uses, its utility is limited. What is useful is the average daily tourist census, or the full-time population equivalent (FPE) of millions of visitors each year. In 1980 this averaged close to 100,000 daily. For 1990, a tentative figure is 150,000; for 2000, 182,000. In the light of present conditions these estimates may need revision. We do know that tourism adds to the state the equivalent of the populations of the counties of Maui and Kauai. Over and above the resident population, Hawaii resources must contribute substantially to the sustenance of the FPE. The ratio of tourists (FPE) to residents is almost 1:10. Given present rates of growth, it could be that within three decades there would be the equivalent of one tourist FPE to every resident family in Hawaii or a daily population well in excess of today's total population of all neighbor islands.

Tourism Boom—Predisposing Causes, Influential Forces

During World War II, the Korean War, and the Vietnam War, hundreds of thousands of military personnel either trained in Hawaii or arrived in Honolulu en route to their final destination. To these people, the myth of the South Seas, passed on from father to son, became something of a reality and many planned to return with their families. In more than three decades since World War

II, North Americans (and later Japanese) have become more affluent, their disposable income greater. The result is that mobility, at least on the North American mainland, is of second nature. With increased affluence came vacations of a month or six weeks rather than two weeks and, for growing numbers, vacations twice a year. To stimulate movement to Hawaii, promotion has been essential. The intensity of advertising has increased and its potential as far as new markets and new angles are concerned never seems to diminish. Where once there were minimal connections, eight major airlines now carry visitors from the United States and Canada.

In the 1960s the economy fare from the mainland to Honolulu was $110. By 1970, the $85 thrift fare (now only a memory) had appeared along with the box lunch, and package tours brought the secretary and the pensioner where once Honolulu had been the preserve of the dowager and the financier. By the end of the 1960s the greatest volume of trade was provided by prearranged group travel which kept a large number of hotels and construction companies in business. By the mid-1970s the economy fares were very much higher but at $126 still better value than a decade earlier. By the end of the decade, as we shall see later, stiff airline competition again started to benefit the consumer, at least temporarily (see table 2). Then, by early 1981, the standard fare was over $250, and having a drastic effect on visitor arrivals.

In the late 1960s, R&R servicemen and families made up a significant portion of visitors. This ended, but the momentum continued. A 1971 survey showed that 35 percent of visitors was returnees who had enjoyed the islands at least once before. Since then the percentage has increased five points. Another development of the 1970s was a substantial increase in the number of Japanese tourists who discovered Hawaii after the Japanese government liberalized the use of foreign exchange outside the country. Japan's

TABLE 2. *California-Hawaii Travel Time and Cost*

Travel Time Index (1935 = 100)		Cost of Travel Index in Constant Dollars for Lowest Regular Fares (1935 = 100)	
1935 by ship	100	1935 by ship	100
1940 by B-314	16	1940 by B-314	353
1958 by DC-7C	8	1958 by DC-7C	108
		1970 by B-707	76
1975 by B-747	5	1975 by B-747	43

SOURCE: Thomas H. Hamilton, "Tourism in Hawaii" written for The Encyclopedia of Hawaii, 1976, manuscript in Hawaii State Archives.

economy was booming, air fares were cheap, and frequent service connected Tokyo to Honolulu. As a result of revaluation of the yen, the Japanese tourists found that as the seventies proceeded they could buy considerably more than they could in 1971. Understandably Hawaii became economically very attractive. Later, as the result of economic reversals in Japan, this trend slowed. The devaluation of the dollar encouraged more mainlanders, rather than spend a summer in Europe, to travel to Hawaii where they would find in 1974 the most reasonably priced hotel rooms of any major tourist area in the United States. This combination of economic patriotism and good value was relatively short-lived. Hotel tariffs later increased markedly.

A final major consideration in boosting the visitor industry has been the rapid growth of convention facilities in Waikiki and on every major island. As the decade progressed, so increased the number of convention visitors. Convention attendance in 1978 was reported as 53 percent greater than the previous year. Part of this was the result of two conventions alone bringing 42,000 persons to Hawaii, almost as great as the total of all visitors in 1950. Nor did the 1973–1974 energy crisis have the expected negative impact on tourism. Although movement in Hawaii was restricted, the curtailment of travel on the mainland resulted in extra visitors leaving for Hawaii in preference to risking unpredictable conditions at home.

As effects of the first energy crisis approached normality in 1975, recession slowed conditions on the mainland and arrivals in Hawaii. This was followed by a rapid recovery of Hawaii's economy, but on the mainland inflation and high foreign payments for imported petroleum resulted in a rapid weakening of the dollar. As we approached the eighties, conditions started to look as though they were repeating the early seventies but with greater magnitude. The energy crisis returned and mobility was restricted on the mainland. Cheap fares again made travel to Hawaii attractive, and the weakened dollar made travel to Hawaii by foreigners advantageous and travel abroad costly to Americans.[3] Each way, Hawaii was to benefit until a protracted United Airlines strike, the grounding of DC-10s, winter storms in Hawaii, and milder weather on the mainland reduced the tourist flow and consumed the gains. Then by the first quarter of 1980 as the result of higher air fares, higher room rates, and the impacts of inflation and recession, visitor totals had dropped almost 6 percent. This rate of downturn did not continue and the year ended with a decline of less than 1 percent. The year 1981 was predicted as a "no growth" year for the economy. Airlines were applying for further fare increases and the immediate future looked far from bright.

The Tourism Regions

For most of this century and certainly since the mid-1950s, the main island of Oahu, the major city Honolulu, and that highly publicized visitor enclave Waikiki have dominated the tourism scene. Despite the fact that incredible growth has taken place on the outer or neighbor islands, especially Maui, there is still a long way to go for neighbor island resort regions to achieve anything like the intensity, concentration, and excitement of Waikiki. Except for about an eighth of the total visitors who go first to Maui or arrive directly by overseas aircraft on the Big Island and remain on neighbor islands, virtually everybody spends time at Waikiki.

The *State Tourism Study* designates, outside of Waikiki, fifteen tourism resort regions whose designated names I will use in this study. It must be pointed out that these are planning designations and within each there may be several well-known places with their own local names (fig. 2).

On Oahu there are two partially developed areas and two more proposed. The two operating regions are Kahuku in the north and Makaha on the dry west coast. The other two are the Ewa (West) Beach region south of Makaha and Queen's Beach region east of Diamond Head. The four regions are discussed in greater detail later in this chapter as are the regions of Hawaii and Kauai.

On the Big Island well-developed areas can be found in the major urban center, Hilo, and at North Kona on the dry rainshadow coast. On the same coast are two newer emerging regions: in the north the famed South Kohala region, site of the Mauna Kea Beach Hotel, and an extension of the Kona Coast at South Kona.

Kauai has four designated areas extending along the Windward coast from the Princeville region in the north, which contains Hanalei as a subcenter, to the Lawai-Poipu region in the south. This latter area is best known now by the center of activity at Poipu Beach. North of Poipu is the Nawiliwili region and further north still is Wailua-Kapaa. The Wailua-Kapaa region is by far the most developed and well known while the others are in the developmental stages.

Maui County is divided into three resort areas. The west coast

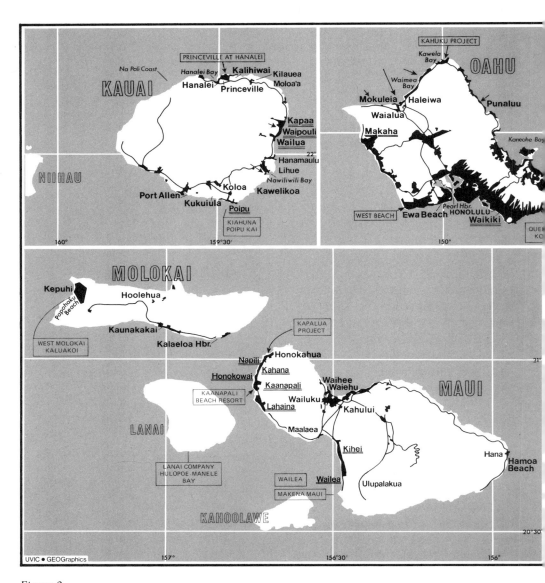

Figure 2.

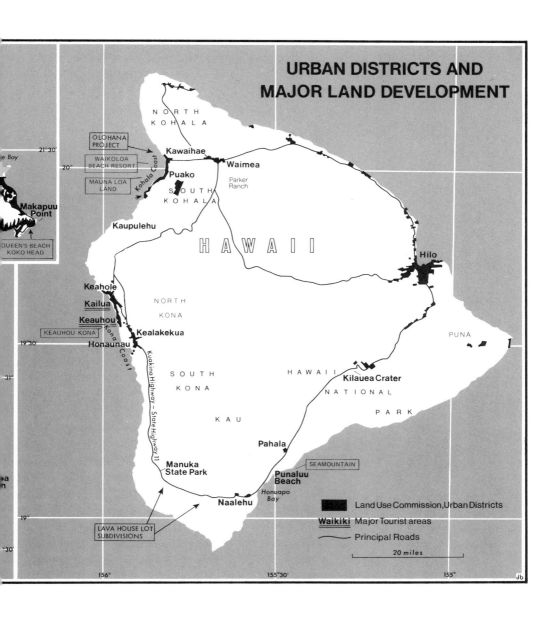

URBAN DISTRICTS AND
MAJOR LAND DEVELOPMENT

e Bay

21°30'

20°

Makapuu
Point

QUEEN'S BEACH
KOKO HEAD

21°

19°30'

19°

30'

OLOHANA
PROJECT

WAIKOLOA
BEACH RESORT

MAUNA LOA
LAND

NORTH
KOHALA

Kawaihae

Waimea

Puako

Parker
Ranch

SOUTH
KOHALA

Kaupulehu

HAWAII

Keahole

Kailua

NORTH
KONA

Keauhou

KEAUHOU KONA

Kealakekua

Honaunau

Kona Coast

Kuakina Highway – State Highway 11

SOUTH
KONA

HAWAII

Hilo

PUNA

Kilauea Crater

NATIONAL

PARK

KAU

Pahala

Manuka
State Park

SEAMOUNTAIN

Punaluu
Beach

Honuapo
Bay

Naalehu

LAVA HOUSE LOT
SUBDIVISIONS

Kohala Coast

■ Land Use Commission, Urban Districts

Waikiki Major Tourist areas

~ Principal Roads

20 miles

156°

155°30'

155°

Jb

of Maui has two of these: first, the Kapalua-Lahaina region, which includes, from north to south, Kapalua, Kahana, Honokowai, Kaanapali, and Lahaina; and, second, the Maalaea-Makena region, which encompasses Maalaea, Kihei, Kamaole, Keawakapu, Wailea, and Makena. Both regions have undergone considerable development but, in terms of what is planned, much is yet to come. The third region in Maui county is the recently opened Kaluakoi area of West Molokai.

The Resources on Which Tourism Is Based

For centuries Hawaiian land provided all needed resources. Later, through commercial agriculture, the land continued to provide the bulk of Hawaii's monetary income. Most recently, the land has been transformed into a conceptual resource—economically the most valuable.[4] Collectively, this may be viewed as an ambient resource, that special combination of elements such as a warm, sensuous, and nondebilitating climate; exciting coastal and mountain scenery; warm, clear ocean water; uncluttered open spaces of cropland, forest, and park; and one of the most interesting cosmopolitan populations in the world.[5] These are the amenities of Hawaii which contribute to what M. Clawson calls a resource-based recreation area.[6] In the Mediterranean, the increasing use made of the ambient resource is called by A. S. Svendsen the sunshine revolution,[7] something equally appropriate to Hawaii.

Relatively few people understand that tourism, when approached with sensitivity and taste, can be a resource-creating activity. It can also have a negative aspect and consequently becomes a "resource" for a very minor part of the community—an anti-resource, to coin a term. The human creation of a huge tourism concentration such as Waikiki, despite its mixed effects, is nevertheless a resource which deserves nurturing and improvement. Some excellent examples of resource creation are taking place at Kapalua, Wailea, and South Kohala, but they cannot retain their positive aspects if they or areas about them deteriorate appreciably.

As a recreation area Hawaii has many advantages: it is far enough from the visitors' home areas to impart feelings of physical separation; it possesses a romantic South Pacific mystique associated with the early history and literature of the area; and above all it has an abundance of sunshine. Its brightness startles. The vivid colors of sea, vegetation, flowers, sky, and clothing are difficult for many temperate latitude visitors to believe. The climate is warm, seldom too hot, and cooling trade winds make life extremely pleasant. Volcanoes and torrential mountain streams have etched startling mountain landscapes. Dramatic black basaltic coastlines are dotted with postcard-perfect golden yellow sand beaches.

State and federal lands constitute 48 percent of the total area. A large amount of this is either park or open grazing land. These together with forest reserves and over two million acres in agriculture provide great open spaces largely free of human habitation—a refreshing alternative to growing urban settlement.

The people of Hawaii are physically attractive. Their ethnic heterogeneity does much to forge a distinct social group which, although culturally diverse, has enough in common in manners and local custom to evoke an authentic local Hawaii life-style (see chapter 9). If visitors find Oahu, which still has its charms, too crowded, then they are bound to find in the neighbor islands a rare tranquility. The quality of such tranquility is difficult to define. It has to do with the preserves of open space, ruralness, warmth, and hospitality. This has come to be known as the aloha spirit of Hawaii, something which the visitor industry has capitalized upon.

The particular things that appeal to tourists are many indeed. One can only generalize here what these might be: the physical beauty of the land, the diversity of cultural, historical, and archeological resources, the sense of calm and quiet. While there is not a European urban richness, the sensitive and seeing traveler is as well rewarded in Hawaii as in any other place in the world.

Anatomy of the Industry

To understand the tourist industry, one must have an appreciation of raw statistical data.[8] Too many numbers, however, tend to detract from the themes I wish to explore here. As a compromise, I have compressed into this section a series of statistics only as necessary preparation for what follows.

For three decades, until 1979, the visitor industry grew at a healthy pace. The 0.5 percent decline in visitor arrivals for 1980 was even worse than the low 1.4 percent growth estimated by the Bank of Hawaii. The best forecasts are now expecting after a current period of decline a flattening off, followed by low to modest growth at a rate much lower than the recent 9 percent average of the past decade. With a present visitor count near four million annually, a 5 percent increase—the rate suggested by the State Tourism Plan—would bring an additional 200,000 visitors, close to the figure for total visitors at the end of the boom in the 1960s when the rate of increase was around 16 percent. At this point, a 10 percent increase, historically rather ordinary for Hawaii, would bring 400,000 more visitors, an increase which would have been considered colossal by fair-minded observers of the early seventies. Past increases must be placed in world perspective; in relation to increases in Spain, other Mediterranean countries, and the Caribbean, that of Hawaii is not out of line.

About a quarter of the total number of visitors come from Asia or Oceania. The remainder, classified "westbound," arrive via the North American continent, mostly from the United States. At the end of the seventies, of the total visitors arriving, almost three-quarters were from other states, one-seventh from Japan, and one-thirteenth from Canada.

At one time, before World War II, most visitors arrived by ship preparatory to a long and elegant stay in Hawaii. Now surface travel is insignificant except for the recently inaugurated seven-day Hawaiian Islands cruises originating from Honolulu. The tourism revolution has been as much a transport revolution as anything else. By 1965 those arriving by ship had dropped to 7 percent and by 1977 to 0.3 percent. It is now true to say, cruises excepted, that everybody travels by air.

Of the westbound visitors, most come from major United States urban areas where more direct air travel is readily available and where many travel agents are actively engaged. Big cities providing more than 50,000 tourists each a year are Los Angeles (around 200,000), San Francisco (130,000), Chicago (110,000), New York (around 100,000), Seattle, Anaheim, and San Jose. Nine of the top twenty cities are on the Pacific coast which understandably provides a third of Hawaii's visitors. In the west, air fares to Hawaii are cheaper than from elsewhere, and living on the Pacific ocean gives residents a greater community of interest with Hawaii. California provides a quarter of the visitors and after this only the states of Washington, Illinois, and New York, each with approximately a 5 percent share, are worthy of notice. Regionally the Pacific coast leads, followed by the Midwest (one-fifth) and then the

Atlantic Coast–New England (one-fifth). With recession conditions, California and Alaska have held fairly steady while visitors from the farm and industrial states farther east have dropped off markedly.

About 280 flights a week leave the North American continent for Hawaii. Eight airlines are involved. Of the total number of flights to Hawaii all but a few, which terminate in Hilo, are destined for Honolulu. United Airlines handles more than half the traffic followed by Western and Northwest which share almost equally about a quarter of the remainder. An aspect of Hawaii's vulnerability was demonstrated during April and May 1979 when United Airlines was on strike. Its impact was staggering. Repercussions were felt in the visitor industry, the food markets, and in numerous industries which depend on air transport for essential parts and raw materials. Some areas reported a 30 percent visitor decline. About half as many flights arrive from Asia and the South Pacific as arrive from North America.

Once in Hawaii there is a complex schedule of regular flights to the major islands. There are three major interisland carriers, Hawaiian Air, its chief competition, Aloha Airlines, and a newcomer, the much smaller Mid Pacific Air. Between them more than 50 flights depart Honolulu daily. Small commuter airlines account for a small amount of air traffic. Commuter airlines come and go. Interisland airlines too are extremely sensitive to the changing fortunes of tourism. Both major carriers depend on tourism for over half of their traffic. In January 1980, as the result of a tourism slump in what is normally the busy season, Hawaiian's traffic was down almost 12 percent, necessitating employee layoffs.

In late 1978 the Airline Deregulation Act came into force. Within the United States it allowed companies to lay claim to previously unused commercial airline routes, engendering fierce competition in the airline business.[9] Changes occurred but what will finally happen in Hawaii is yet to be seen. As a noncontiguous state in terms of the act, Hawaii may not feel the direct effects of the legislation until after 1981. Possible effects may include drastic discounts and innovative marketing devices to keep the big planes full and competing with each other. Early waves hit Hawaii several years ago. Continental Airlines announced in November 1978 that it would introduce the first direct nonstop route Hawaii-Denver-Kansas City. This was followed immediately by a similar announcement by United. Hawaiian, Braniff, and Continental then received approval for a new Portland, Oregon-Honolulu route with all but Hawaiian offering an initial $99 round-trip promotional fare.

Each month in 1978 saw an increase in visitors arriving in Hawaii. During the year many more visitors from eastern and midwestern cities arrived as the result of United Airlines' cut-rate fares which "touched off a stampede by other airlines to lower their fares [and put] the cost of a Hawaii vacation within the reach of thousands of people who never before could afford such a trip."[10] As a result of price cutting, the charter flight business just about disappeared.

Hardly had the first effects of deregulation appeared when counter forces began to appear in 1979. Not only did oil companies start to allocate supplies of aircraft fuel but also the price shot up. Continental Airlines discontinued its direct flights to Hilo and standard fares moved inexorably upward. Fare increases related to inflation and the price of fuel are likely to characterize the industry in the future.

The longer a visitor stays in Hawaii, hotel capacity will be used more economically and visitors will spend more apart from lodgings. An increase in the length of stay also eases stress on the environment, both physically and humanly. The average length of stay, 10.7 days in the late seventies (nearer to 10 days in 1980), is over 7 days shorter than it was in 1960 and the declining trend has been marked over a period of twenty years. Besides inflation and recession conditions, there are several explanations for this state of affairs. More people have been taking vacations more than once a year, a wider cross section of United States society including wage earners with shorter vacations have been traveling, and more people have been arriving on group inclusive tours (GITs) which cater to persons of moderate incomes with shorter vacations.

During the decade 1967–1977, westbound individual status tourists (FIT: free independent traveler) declined from just under three-quarters to just over half of all tourists, while after their 1971 inauguration GITs increased to almost a half. The group tour accounted for much of the constructional activity at Waikiki and has been the backbone of Waikiki's success. With a drastic decline in charter flights and discount fares, a reversal is taking place. Although counties are talking about high quality tourism which encourages FITs, these people are now coming in greater numbers without specific encouragement. This might be associated as well with a greater number of returnees and a greater degree of sophistication on the part of tourists who feel they can now handle Hawaii on their own. To help the FIT, United Airlines offers a full service called ITCH (Instant Tour Confirmation in Hawaii). This computerized service can arrange reservations with more than half Hawaii's hotel room inventory. Very soon this may be raised to 80 percent.

About three-quarters of all tourists to Hawaii go to the neighbor islands as well as to Oahu. In 1977, 28 percent of visitors stayed on Oahu exclusively while 12 percent went only to a neighbor island without visiting Oahu.

By October 1980, Hawaii had close to 56,000 hotel (hotel-apartment-condominium) units—34,200 on Oahu, 10,500 on Maui, 6,300 on the Big Island, and 4,700 on Kauai (see table 3).

For 1980, a bad year following an active period of new construction, occupancies for Waikiki hotels averaged 72 percent and for the neighbor islands 63 percent. Kauai with a less vigorous building program than Maui averaged 69 percent followed by Maui's 66 percent and 53 percent for the Big Island. This represented a decrease of 10 percent in Waikiki and 14 percent on the neighbor islands over 1978, an "average" year. In all areas the highest occupancy rate can be expected from Christmas to about April. The nearest Hawaii has to an off season is the relatively short period between the end of the summer, school vacation in September and the Christmas buildup.

Difficulty in arranging accommodations because of excessive demand can become a deterrent; in business terms continuous high demand suggests a need to expand available accommodations. Under such circumstances this could mean a high occupancy rate in the 90–100 percent range at all times. If this were met by building new hotels, the occupancy rate might be expected to

TABLE 3. *Room Inventory: Hotel-Condominium-Apartment*

	1955	1960	1965	1970	1975	1980
Oahu	2,628	5,716	11,083	21,217	25,699	34,173
Hawaii	451	581	1,387	3,486	5,486	6,299
Kauai	152	237	860	2,609	3,314	4,707
Maui	222	291	1,456	2,720	6,192	10,521
TOTAL	3,453	6,825	14,786	30,032	40,691	55,700

SOURCE: Hawaii Visitors Bureau.

drop at least temporarily. Consequently, lower occupancy rates do not always indicate depressed economic conditions, especially over the short run.

A Tourist Profile

I have already said something about the character of visitors to Hawaii, when they visit, where, and for how long. Almost 40 percent of them are back for a second, third, or more trip to Hawaii— a solid statement of support for the industry and how it is run. Most of those arriving will be staying in hotels or apartment-hotels and only a little short of 90 percent states unabashedly that they are in Hawaii for pleasure as a major purpose.

More women than men visit the state and the average age of all visitors is forty-three. One out of every two who visit is a college graduate and after the visit, 90 percent feels that Hawaii has produced an experience well above average.

The big spenders in Hawaii are Japanese ($213 per day); low spenders are Canadian (about $65). The average spent by a mainland tourist, westbound, is $77 per day and of this three-fifths is allocated to lodging, food, and beverage. More is spent on Oahu, where the opportunities especially in Waikiki are greater than on neighbor islands. Independent visitors (FITs) spend less than GITs, but as a tenth of all FITs stay with relatives or friends, their expenditure for food and lodging is consequently lowered considerably. It would be justifiable to assume that the remaining 90 percent of FITs spend more than tour group members. Tour group visitors are usually in Hawaii for the first time and thus spend more on entertainment, sightseeing, interisland travel, and gifts than other types of tourists.[11] With a marked increase in the number of FITs traveling now to Hawaii the expenditure profile can be expected to change as well.

Waikiki and Oahu

The impact of man on the Hawaiian environment has been the greatest on Oahu, and nowhere has it been more fascinating and brutal than on the 360 acres which constitutes Waikiki. In the 1940s, before the real impact of air travel, Waikiki's beautiful golden beach provided the stage for several low, elegant, and charming hotels, green lawns, and well-cared-for parks (fig. 2).

Beyond the stores and restaurants lining Kalakaua Avenue, the main thoroughfare, was a scattering of one- and two-story private wooden houses and apartments extending in diminishing concentrations back to the Ala Wai Canal. Tourism's development was dramatic. It grew from an enthusiastic roar by the 1950s to a resounding crescendo in the 1960s when concrete monoliths were constructed in every available space. Still, from a room count of 10,700 in 1967, the number grew to 25,000 in a little more than a decade. The rate of increase was unbelievably fast until 1971 when growth flattened out after most prime areas, zoned appropriately, had been taken up.[12] By this time two new regulations were enforced; apparently foreknowledge of these encouraged the earlier frantic activity.

Land values and taxes rose so high that spindly highrises grew from handkerchief-size lots, and older hotels were dismantled to

Waikiki. Towering highrise hotels overlook golden coral sand beaches and the Pacific Ocean. The cluster of buildings is the core of Hawaii's visitor industry. (Hawaii Visitiors Bureau photo)

allow for new structures. This process may last indefinitely. Many historic coconut palms were lost in a forest of concrete piles reaching the sky in a jagged fretwork of architectural confusion. Automobile exhaust collected in great quantities in traffic-clogged, man-made canyons. From daylight to dusk the cooing of Hawaiian doves was not to be heard amid the clamor of jackhammers and pneumatic drills reverberating against cliffs of concrete. At nightfall when the noise of construction temporarily ceased, the intermittent wailing of police sirens punctuated the relative quiet of night. The end of this seemingly ceaseless activity is now in sight. Although 28,000 hotel units (as opposed to apartment units) may be approved by the early 1980s, anything approaching the 31,000 room limit is unlikely for some time.

No writer speaks about Waikiki in a complimentary manner. Outsiders and insiders alike point to Waikiki as a design disaster, a mistake to be avoided at all costs. Yet of its approximately 4 million visitors annually the great majority appear fascinated by their experience, and the generally higher occupancy rates suggest that far from being repelled, tourists come back in great numbers.

What happened was the responsibility of all concerned. The developers were no more to blame than those allowing the situation to happen. With hindsight and new values the situation may be viewed in a dozen different ways. Waikiki's initial momentum reflected times which have already changed significantly. The pattern laid, the momentum continued and Waikiki now consolidates. The lessons were painfully learned. Jets fly overhead, the swinging booms of gigantic cranes, although fewer in number, have for almost thirty years been a permanent feature of the landscape. During the same period hard hats have been as commonplace as aloha shirts. Symbols commonly associated with transience became virtually permanent. There is, after all, the old joke about the Dillingham crane being the state bird. One changing situation overtook another in the pursuit of the tourist, and the dust of construction did not settle for three decades, if it can be said to have settled yet.

Despite the fact that an end to growth is believed to be not too far off, 1978 and 1979 were bumper years for construction in Waikiki—they contributed close to 60 percent of new construction. Moving at a juggernaut pace over the past decades, Waikiki has become a matter of growing concern to the state, the city, the community at large, and the industry.

Attempting to Solve a Problem

For over seventy years people have been surveying Waikiki, planning for its future, legislating for its improvement, and writing about it. The "physical resources" volume of the *State Tourism Study* lists twenty-eight efforts to do something about Waikiki over a period of seventy years. The first was in 1906, the last in 1976. Certainly this won't be the last survey to be attempted, just the last listed.[13]

The first survey was the plan of Mr. L. E. Pinkham, president of the Board of Health, who aimed to drain and reclaim the Waikiki area (chapter 8). Even before this happened he proposed seeking "a desirable optimum population," placing utilities underground, building a storm water system, and establishing building setbacks on all streets. One can only wish for visionaries of the caliber and prescience of Mr. Pinkham today. In 1906, he wrote: "With the Pacific coast increasing in population, wealth, and enterprise almost miraculously and the Orient awakening, the Pacific Ocean will become a pond and Honolulu a point of call to a degree now incomprehensible."[14]

Numerous studies took place before 1963, but it was in that year that a citizens' advisory committee was set up by the mayor to assess the situation and make recommendations. It did so in 1966 with little result. Three years later Mayor Frank Fasi appointed a planning advisory committee. This committee, evaluating the 1966 report, prepared the *Action Plan for Waikiki*, published in 1970. The major problems identified fell into two categories: inadequate facilities and services (streets, transport, recreation, beaches, and social services) and undesirable environmental characteristics (crowding, lack of open space, and poor aesthetics).[15]

The problems, the committee said, arose from inappropriate zoning, inadequate planning, political inaction, and error. The committee reaffirmed a building ceiling of 26,000 hotel rooms proposed a year earlier by a Hawaii Visitors Bureau Waikiki task force. To this was added 11,500 apartment units. The 1970 report noted that "Waikiki still has the opportunity to prevent the seeds of deterioration from flowering and flourishing into destructive blight. However, this opportunity will not last forever."[16]

As a consequence of the recommendations, a state act of 1971 voted $9 million for far-reaching road, drainage, and sewer improvements, which people expected would be effected by 1975.[17] By 1977, as the result of a number of delays including strained relations between the state and the county, less than $5 million had been allotted. Large numbers of essential projects still needed funding. These included widening Waikiki beach, dredging Ala Wai Canal, improving canal and Ala Wai boat harbor water quality, acquiring mini-park land, improving traffic circulation, widening roads, and extending sidewalks. Almost three years later in 1980 the state was accused of not making its contribution. It would, it said, if the county met its obligations. A new county administration is now in office and for the new mayor Waikiki is a top priority.

Apart from advertising and other types of promotion, Waikiki *is* the concrete symbol of Hawaii tourism. It is the springboard for further experiences in Hawaii. Yet its overall management runs counter to primary rules followed by any first-class resort area —the creation of an unassailable image of environmental, design, and architectural excellence with a human infrastructure to match. Without a doubt the present unplanned chaos has primitive charm capable of stimulating the type of excitement found on Kalakaua Avenue. There will be few, however, who will challenge my assumption that when ultimate ceilings are reached and occupancy is high, with increasing age and little attention to improvements, the special *je ne sais quoi* of Waikiki will be badly tarnished. It will no longer be the attraction it was in the 1960s and the 1970s, especially in comparison with the quality offered by neighbor islands. But as it will remain Hawaii's major tourism symbol, Waikiki souring will have a marked effect on the state.

In 1976, at last, the Honolulu City Council stepped in and took decisive action after existing regulation and legislation had failed: Waikiki was designated a Special Design District (SDD). Despite the oft-quoted ceiling of 26,000 which in 1969 was lauded as "the industry policing itself," in the face of a permissive local government, this and similar recommendations proved to be nothing more than talk and good intentions. The ceiling of 26,000 was a long way off, and good intentions were affordable. In 1979, the 26,000 ceiling was passed. Before the SDD took effect the contemporaneous zoning permitted 68,000 rooms in Waikiki. The present SDD limits hotel rooms to 31,000 and an average daily population of about 65,000 persons, a figure fast approaching.[18] No limit is set for apartments or apartment rooms, but the new regulations require lower densities for all rooms, hotel and apartment, by decreasing the floor area ratio (that is, ratio of floor space to land space).

While it is hoped that the SDD will control Waikiki growth, the SDD adds another level of potential regulation while allowing only condominium development. Existing legislation, including the coastal zone management program (chapter 5), already contains much that could help relieve the crowding along Waikiki's littoral. Although the SDD is thought to provide desirable regulation for Waikiki, the Department of General Planning's own figures indicate that 37,000 units may still be available in a pinch.[19] This is roughly equivalent to the early 1980 level of Waikiki units plus the total rooms available on Maui.

The example of Waikiki is a telling one. Its worst characteristics—and visitor patronage attests to its best—are the result of apathy, abhorrence of regulation and its implementation, special-interest pressure, lip service instead of action, and a laissez-faire attitude that no matter what somehow all will be well. In Hawaii, with many things worth protecting, including Waikiki and the tourist industry as a whole, those days and attitudes should be things of the past.

In studies carried out by the City and County of Honolulu's Department of General Planning, special attention has been given to Kakaako, a small, old district, two miles northwest of Waikiki, mountainside *(mauka)* of Ala Moana Park.

The Ward Estate, a major Kakaako landowner, suggests that, as part of the already planned redevelopment, "some tourist-oriented development . . . in the vicinity of Kewalo Basin" would be appropriate.[20] A 1979 staff report of the Department of General Planning recommended some hotel development, perhaps no more than 1,000 rooms and certainly not a major destination resort.[21] The site would be ideal for business travelers and conventioneers, the impact would be no greater than many other types of possible development, and it would provide jobs in the Honolulu area where they are needed.

The early development of Kakaako would have at least a minor physical and possibly a much larger psychological effect. In the view of Oahu neighborhood boards, especially those representing residents of central Honolulu, the slowing of Waikiki's growth is an important problem; for more than half of them, "a very important problem."[22]

Off-Waikiki Development

Away from Waikiki on Oahu, two areas have been developed at Makaha and Kahuku. Two others are in the planning stage. The furthest advanced is at Makaha region on the dry side of the island adjacent to famous surfing beaches. Here Capital Investment Co. Ltd., largely catering to the rich, started a project involving hotels, condominiums, residences, and recreation areas. The success the developer expected, however, was never realized, thus casting a cloud over future development that is other than residential. The Makaha resort area is on the valley floor. Residential areas flank the central core and occupy the valley mouth. Already about 2,400 units have been built, only 8 percent hotel and the rest condominium and apartment. The most recent proposals suggest 400 additional hotel and 1,000 apartment units by 1990. So far a number of buildings have become second home projects. Most flank the shoreline and some the golf course, a green oasis in the dry brown landscape. Overall, as *Tourism in Hawaii* puts it, the development is "in a country-club atmosphere," set in almost 1,400 acres.[23]

Besides surfing, for which the area has an international reputation, there are numerous sandy beaches and fine diving and fishing sites. This abundance of resources makes the sunny Waianae coastline, with its series of good beach parks, a major recreation area for Oahu residents. A new state park is being planned in the area to preserve some of the last remaining wild shore areas on Oahu. This too will become a major resource.

On the northernmost portion of the island is the Kahuku region near Kahuku and Kawela, forty miles north of Honolulu. Here approximately 900 acres, part of the 15,000-acre estate of the late James Campbell, have been set aside for resort development. Although not as dry as Makaha, rainfall is low, less than 40 inches, a contributory factor to a successful Hawaiian resort.

There are five waterfront sites between Kahuku Point and Kawela Bay. One major hotel, with close to 500 rooms and a golf course, has already been built on a spectacular point overlooking the sea. The Kuilima Hyatt Hotel and about 400 condominium units are the forerunners of what the Prudential Insurance Company has planned as a major destination area with several more hotels, another golf course, commercial space, and 1,900 condominium units. Developers see something in the vicinity of 7,000 total units, 6,000 of which were allowable under the General Plan design for Windward Oahu. A new study of May 1979 by the Department of General Planning which incorporates views of neighborhood boards recommends a limit after 2,700 new hotel rooms have been built.[24] Scenic attractions abound in the area and the Polynesian Cultural Center at Laie is in easy reach of the proposed destination area.

Good surfing areas exist from Sunset Beach to Kahuku, and the state tourism study stresses that in no way should these be interfered with during development. The area, which already supports considerable local recreation, is less remote than Makaha Valley. A study by Mak and Ah Mai indicates that by the year 2000, a population increase of 17,000 to 23,000 could be expected, raising the district population to possibly 40,000 if the resort area is developed as Prudential plans.[25] This prediction provided the basis for protests by district resident groups and generated studies such as "The Future of Resort Development on Oahu," cited above, to ascertain community attitudes. The present situation is that the county will approve expansion in the area only with the consent of local residents. If resistance is too strong the Kuilima Resort Community as planned may never eventuate. As the area is the focus of Oahu's diversified agriculture, the community's determination to preserve one of the island's last bastions of rural living could scuttle a most ambitious development scheme. Like a number of others in Hawaii the situation is very delicate.

Despite objections, the first phase of hotel development came, as it did in several other places in Hawaii, at a time when sugar growing was a declining activity. In a confused state of reorganization, the sugar mill at Kahuku was closed. The hotel and associated activity offered employment for 600 persons and the old mill became a speciality shopping center. The growth of the area has been slow, the development at the present stage is unobtrusive, and the surroundings are tasteful—all requisites of a successful high quality destination area.

The present Hawaii Kai residential development near Koko Head is already part of greater Honolulu. The Queen's Beach project is a proposal of the Hawaii Kai Development Co. Ltd. which has plans for creating a resort-recreational-residential area near Queen's Beach extending roughly between Makapuu Point and Koko Head park. About 3,000 hotel and 445 residential units have been mentioned as a possibility. The entire area has been an urban district for some time and a request was made for 100 acres to be zoned by the City and County of Honolulu for resort, apartment, and commercial purposes. No concrete proposal has yet been made to the city, which sees the possibility of only 800 hotel rooms being built between 1985 and 1990.

The advantage of the project is that it will give visitors an urban alternative to Waikiki very close to interesting tourist attractions: Hanauma Beach Park, Sea Life Park, and Makapuu Beach Park. There are two private golf courses close by; however, the area suffers in a way similar to Kahuku. Coastal recreation amenities are already heavily used on the edge of urban Honolulu. Heavier use will be counterproductive. Like attractive areas elsewhere in Honolulu, the area has well-established population concentrations and the additional 3,000 in population projected would be about the limit which could be readily absorbed. An associated problem would be employee-generated traffic from other parts of Honolulu. For the present county administration Queen's Beach and West Beach (see following) do not have a high priority for development; with the consent of local residents Kuilima and Makaha do.

In the Ewa region, West Beach Resorts ultimately hopes to develop a first phase of approximately 660 acres along the western portion of the Ewa plain at Honouliuli. All together at this stage 10,200 units are proposed, all but 3,000 condominium and apartment units for hotel use. A golf course, a 700-slip small craft marina, a tennis facility, and two shopping centers are part of the proposal. The adjacent shoreline has recreational potential and the project is in easy reach of the Waianae coast beach park system to the north. Two theme parks have been given county approval, and both, the Caneland and the Kahe Point parks, will be virtually adjacent to the project when it is started. What is described is the resort portion of a major development which will include an alternative to the Honolulu harbor: Barbers Point deep-draft harbor, 12,000 acres of urban development, thirteen residential villages, and a marina.[26] If the numbers requested were approved, it would become one of the largest developments in Hawaii. At present no more than 3,600 units, 2,400 hotel, are seen as a possibility by 1990. Honolulu's draft development plans would allow a maximum of 3,100 hotel units only.

Development will certainly not have full local approval. People on the Waianae coast have shown considerable hostility to tourism. The neighborhood boards report that almost 70 percent of the Waianae population feels development will bring an undesirable population increase, which is estimated by the city's consultants to be around 30,000 persons.[27] It is argued by some local residents, however, that if the rewards of tourism are more accessible to local residents, antagonism and a current hostile climate to tourists may well diminish.

In the past decade several other projects have been discussed, with preliminary design work completed. So far, however, outside Honolulu only Makaha and Kahuku are in operation. West Beach and Queen's Beach seem the most likely to start in the future.

Neighbor Islands

In 1961, 55 percent of tourists visited the neighbor islands. By the end of the seventies they were receiving almost 80 percent of the state's visitors. In 1980 almost 22,000 out of 56,000 "hotel" units were located outside Oahu. Today Waikiki no longer has the dominance it once had.

There are many obvious reasons for this. Many of Hawaii's visitors come from California where ocean-front facilities are frequently overcrowded. The congestion and activity of Waikiki are therefore to be avoided. Neighbor islands give greater visitor satisfaction than Waikiki in this way. More people visiting Waikiki now have the means to travel to the neighbor islands as well. People visiting Hawaii for the second, third, or fourth times have seen Waikiki and are now moving to other parts of the state. Neighbor islands have outstanding recreational facilities including many first class golf courses and, in comparison with Waikiki, new and uncrowded accommodations. This all adds up to a much greater appeal of the neighbor islands than was formerly the case—a fact amply demonstrated during 1971 when, although visitors to the state increased by only 4.1 percent, visitors to Maui increased by 19 percent, to the Big Island 12 percent, and to Kauai 11 percent. Helping to account for this shift were the activities of the Hawaii Visitors Bureau, the national magazine pictorial spreads by some neighbor island resort areas and county visitor associations, joint promotional ventures with nationally known manufacturers, and advertising in Waikiki trade papers. Discussion of the above trends assumes the present recession a temporary setback with its own characteristics. During a period of soft economy some visitors are deciding they can afford to travel to Waikiki but no farther.

This is reflected in lower than normal occupancy rates on neighbor islands.

Hawaii: The Big Island

At the beginning of the 1970s Hawaii County's performance in the visitor industry was vigorous, showing statistically more promise than any other neighbor island. Consistently more people visited the state with the intention of going to the Big Island than to Maui. To meet this demand, more construction took place in Hawaii County than elsewhere away from Waikiki.

During the decade the momentum slowed and concern for the county's growth rate developed. The situation was distorted by shifting visitor distribution patterns mainly as the result of Maui's spectacular success. At the beginning of the decade Hawaii and Maui counties were running neck and neck, but by the end of the decade Hawaii provided less than a third of neighbor island rooms to Maui's half. Hawaii's approximately 6,000 rooms represented 12 percent of those available in the state.

Loyal observers interpreting these statistics say, with justification, that Hawaii presents completely different tourist fare from other counties and should not be compared with Waikiki or Maui. It does not have Maui's long stretches of usable beaches but it does have widespread and interesting coral areas, deep historical interest, broad open spaces, fascinating biota, unsurpassed geological formations, and active volcanoes.

Hilo and North Kona Regions

Interisland airlines most frequently use two airports: Hilo, the main center of the region, and Keahole, six miles north of Kailua, in the North Kona region. Keahole serves the dry western Kona coastal area, and Hilo, the wet eastern coast. In addition Hilo, as a minor international port of entry, receives mainland flights. Both places have been long established, and tourism development consequently has taken place. The Hilo region, with Hilo as the old established port, has always provided for travelers. A more recent attempt to combine its more utilitarian functions as county seat with a resort area has met with limited success. Places of historical and cultural interest abound, a fascinating drive brings Akaka Falls into range, a longer drive brings one to Volcanoes National Park, and within the city itself the Wailuku River State Park is a restful and pleasant diversion. Consistently, though, occupancy of its approximately 2,600 accommodation units has been low. Fourteen hotels dominate the inventory, and no plans are in evidence for further development in the area.

Of all places on the Big Island, the North Kona region, more usually known as Kailua-Kona, has undergone a transformation over the past twenty years. This portion of the Kona coast, with almost 60 percent of Hawaii County's public accommodations, is already the most extensively developed resort area on the island with shopping, entertainment, cultural, and historic functions. Major hotels dominate the room inventory: apartments and condominiums provide about 15 percent. Until recently this included the venerable Kona Inn, a link with Hawaii tourism's past. Unfortunately, the inn no longer exists as such; rather it now houses professional and business offices, indicating the drastic change that has come to the area. Development now includes almost 3,000 rooms in fifteen hotels and almost as many condominiums. The area core extends from Kailua to Keauhou along a narrow apron of low level land. At present, 10,000 hotel and 9,000 apartment units are still allowable.

Slightly farther inland, noticeably higher in elevation, and just south of Kailua, the permanent settlements of North and South Kona parallel the coast along the Kuakini Highway. These two mauka-settled regions help provide labor for the coastal resort areas which bring people and wealth to the area. Both *makai* (oceanside) and mauka regions are functionally distinct. One serves a hinterland of grazing, truck farming, orchard growing, and coffee cultivating, and provides light industry, construction, government, and commerce. The other is oriented toward pleasure, relaxation, sportfishing, and the appreciation of the historic significance of old Hawaii. The district has been developed rapidly into a major tourist destination area and can be compared with Wailua-Kapaa on Kauai or with the Lahaina-Kaanapali area earlier in the 1970s. Development was helped considerably by the opening of Keahole airport in 1970 and the constant use made of it by the two major interisland carriers since.

A major component of the core area, six miles south of Kailua, is the Keauhou-Kona resort project of the Kamehameha Development Corporation, a subsidiary of Kamehameha Schools and the Bernice Pauahi Bishop Estate. The development, one of the major planned developments of the state, once referred to as a "community of leisure," is in an early phase developing 525 acres of the 2,000 acres available. By 1977 it was operating three hotels with over 1,300 rooms and close to 150 apartments. The long-term plan of the development is to provide 3,000 hotel rooms, 2,000 apartment units, and 1,000 single-family homes.

The project, which already has a club house, golf course, and fifteen tennis courts, estimates employment will increase from the present level of 1,000 to 2,500.[28] This would not be all. The district population could be increased by many thousands more.

There are a number of other projects in the North Kona area, some of which have advanced only in a minor way or have fallen into a state of limbo. Since publication in 1972 of the pioneer work *Tourism in Hawaii: Hawaii Tourism Impact Plan*, only a few of the proposed grander resort plans have come to fruition. With every year, financing large-scale development projects becomes more difficult and, if conditions depart from near perfect, hotel interests are often reluctant to contribute.

South Kohala

Thirty or forty miles north of Kailua-Kona is the South Kohala region, where ambitious and spectacular resorts and facilities may be expected to develop. Present unbuilt capacity is in the vicinity of 20,000 units. Already the area is famous for the plush 310-room Mauna Kea Beach Hotel developed by environmentalist-developer Laurance Rockefeller and sold in 1978 to United Airlines for $51.5 million. At present, other than the one hotel, about 100 condominium units, and recreational facilities, there is little to be seen of the 7,200 hotel units and 5,400 condominiums and apartments planned for at least three major projects. Several others await approval to proceed.

The Mauna Kea Beach Hotel was initially a part of Laurance Rockefeller's larger Olohana Corporation project which plans for an investment of $230 million on 4,000 coastal acres from Kawaihae Bay south past the Mauna Kea Beach Hotel at Kauhaoa Bay to Hapuna beach. The full project includes several hotels (1,100 rooms) near sandy beaches overlooking the water, 2,500 single-family dwellings, and 4,000 condominium units. The project will bring people to enjoy magnificent surroundings, to live in eight residential neighborhoods, and to play on two golf courses. Then the present population of about 400 persons will swell ultimately to 8,000.

The other well-known area is Transcontinental Development Corporation's 31,000-acre residential and resort development at Waikoloa just south of the Olohana Corporation's property and until 1979 operated by Boise Cascade. The development started in 1969 on former ranching land. Seven years later with resort zoning for 500 acres, it had a golf course, club house, village store, post office, equestrian center, and 140 residents at Waikoloa Village, 900 feet above sea level on the slopes of Mauna Kea. Here at the village homes are being constructed and housing lots sold.

Six hotel sites were planned by Boise Cascade to use over 500 acres of prime waterfront land. Together they will have no more than 3,000 rooms. In addition to the hotels, there will be up to 11,000 multi- and single-family residential units. The village is to be surrounded permanently by 10,000 acres of open space for hiking, riding, and other recreational activities. Over 8,000 other acres may eventually be sold as 20-acre farmlets.

Despite its locational advantages on the relatively new Queen Kaahumanu Highway from Kailua to Kawaihae, its outlook onto beautiful Anaehoomalu Bay, access to fine beaches, and a sunny dry climate, development at Waikoloa has been slow. Building on its small coastal frontage at Waikoloa Beach Resort—as opposed to Waikoloa Village which is inland—has been held up by litigation and problems with utilities. After many years of work on the property and a long period of negotiation, the company still did not have its first anchor hotel, an essential in Hawaii resort development.

One hotel, the Royal Waikoloan, was to be built by the First Hawaiian Development Corporation and managed by Sheraton, the second by E. W. Westgate and Associates and managed by Westin. Both ran into snags concerning financing. Water supply and the provision of infrastructure on the property contributed as well to the failure to establish a hotel. With the purchase of the Mauna Kea Beach Hotel by United Airlines, its subsidiary Westin then had a hotel interest in the area.

By 1976, 970 house lots and 38 condominium units were completed. Then in 1978 the project was up for sale after well over $40 million had been invested. Additionally, 31,000 acres had been initially rezoned, the biggest area to be designated urban in Hawaii County. "We should never have given them that much zoning," said former Council Chairman Robert Yamada. "It should be given on a piecemeal basis. This is the way to keep check on a developer. Unless you set a time limit, [he] will find any reason to delay if he thinks it necessary.''[29]

The development was hardly an overnight success. In 1979, a decade after first development, ownership changed, and it looked as though the project had started to move. The first hotel was started at Anaehoomalu Bay where sufficient land exists for a golf course, five other hotels, and twelve condominium apartment sites.

Ranching has been a traditional activity in the district since 1803. With the sale of land for development by the Parker Ranch this changed. The ranch, one of the most famous of the United States, breeds Hereford cattle and its headquarters at Waimea lends distinction and interest to an area just beginning its experience with visitors.

There are three other projects close by between Waikoloa and Olohana's Kawaihae project, which have long been undergoing initial planning. Mauna Lani Resort Inc., owned by the Tokyu and Mitsubishi Corporation, has, at Puako, 4,000 acres of which 800 acres were rezoned in 1976 to allow first phase development. Some 3,000 hotel rooms and 3,300 residential units are envisaged. The development plan designates four to six beachfront hotels, a central historic preserve, a driving range, a racquet club, and residential areas along each fairway of an eighteen-hole golf course. By the early 1980s, a 350-room hotel and 75-unit condominium block will be completed. A golf course is already constructed. It is the intention of the developers that the resort should provide a locale for the international business community to gather for seminars and for high-level business and cultural discussions.

Immediately east and mauka of the planned Mauna Lani resort, Signal Hawaii, Inc., hoped to develop a substantial block of land for resort residential uses. From its original area it sold 3,000 acres to Thomas Nakahara of Hilo and to Puako Heights Investors. The land was zoned agricultural and one plan was to develop mini-ranch lots no smaller than five acres.

All resorts in the region have been held back by lack of water. New sources have now been found after exploratory drilling by state and county, and by the early 1980s transmission lines should be supplying coastal resort areas.

The Big Island started the seventies with vigor. Later in the decade it lagged behind until hopes were rekindled and it seemed to be sailing a totally new course.

Kauai: The Garden Isle

At the end of the 1970s, Kauai had over 4,100 rental units, of which less than three-quarters was hotel with a respectable occupancy rate. It had one-fifth of neighbor island room capacity, and forecasters predicted that if Kauai County and the community let up on their hard-nosed attitude to growth, Kauai could be another Maui. The fact that Kauai has developed different attitudes is a topic I discuss in chapter 12.

To many visitors the island of Kauai, the Garden Isle, is the most picturesque and tropically lush of all Hawaii's islands. Parts of the Na Pali coast are as isolated as any wilderness in the state. "This is an island," Scott Stone says, "where tourists are genuinely liked instead of merely being tolerated as on Oahu."[30] This was in 1969. A decade later I would say this was conditionally true if the tourist in turn showed respect to the residents. Because the resort areas of Kauai are on the windward side of the island, tourist eyes are constantly turned toward luxuriant fern grottos, verdant rainforests, and prolific waterfalls. As the oldest major island in the group, its surface has long been etched by streams fed by some of the heaviest rainfall in the world. Its high jagged skyline, frequently wreathed in clouds, provides a fascinating backdrop to coastal activity. And Waimea Canyon is a grand sight indeed.

Lihue, the main town, is pure country, giving a hint of what is to be found elsewhere, whether at Haena or Koloa. Of all the Hawaiian islands, I find Kauai most reminiscent of the South Pacific —Tahiti in its bold outward form, Fiji in its lush agricultural ambience. One does not have to drive far to find interesting rural settlements, acres of waving sugar cane, small ports, papaya growing, and on the way to Princeville at Kilauea, experimental aquaculture. Sophistication does not thrive on Kauai—rural tranquility does.

Half the completed development on Kauai has been in the Wailua-Kapaa area. The remainder is divided between Poipu, Nawiliwili, and Hanalei-Princeville. Six small motels are found at Lihue, the county seat.

Wailua-Kapaa

The Wailua-Kapaa region, already substantially developed, extends from Hanamaulu north of Lihue through Wailua and Waipouli to Kapaa. The allowable capacity is around 5,800 units. The dozen hotels and apartments account for just over 2,500 units. In the Wailua-Kapaa district, considerable coastal development has already taken place. Nui Pia Farms Ltd. has 190 acres, most of which are "urban"; of these, 108 acres of waterfront property are currently being developed for resort, residential, and commercial uses. Development has taken place on both sides of the coastal highway. Already within this Wailua-Kapaa corridor, there are five hotels on oceanfront land and several others within about 200 yards of the beach. About 2,500 further units are planned or proposed; approvals for many, however, must be negotiated with the planning commission and the Kauai community. This would indeed follow the usual pattern on Kauai over the past several years. Most recently after what has been another Kauai cause celèbre, the green light has been given Pacific Standard Life Insurance Co. by a narrow margin in a split council to develop twenty-five of sixty-five acres of the old Nukolii Dairy farm at Hanamaulu south of Wailua. The first phase calls for a 350-unit hotel and 150 condominium units. The ultimate goal is 1,500 units.

In November 1980 a public referendum resulted in a 2 to 1 vote to downzone the site and stop the construction to which a wide public representation objected. Construction nevertheless continued, and in February 1981 Kauai Judge Kei Hirano ruled that despite the referendum construction could continue. The case will be appealed. The entire subject of Nukolii will no doubt make legal and social history. It has close parallels to Makena, which will be mentioned later. Never before to my knowledge has a community spoken so cohesively and firmly against a particular tourist development. There have been other cases on Kauai and in Lahaina, Maui, but never with such a high potential for conflict.

Princeville-Hanalei

The Princeville region is one of the most attractive parts of Kauai. Centered on Hanalei Bay, it is easily accessible to impressive scenic coastland both to the east and to the west of the bay. Hanalei, an attractive village, is the site of early settlement, taro gardens in the lower Hanalei valley, and historic buildings—all in an atmosphere of isolation away from Oahu's crowds. This is a remoteness to be savored still. Oldtimers would say it has gone already. Within a decade few will disagree. Already within the area are eleven apartment and condominium buildings representing less than 600 rooms. Club Mediterranée-Hanalei Plantation (formerly a resort, now a condominium) overlooks the bay and at Princeville, a few miles on the Lihue side of Hanalei, the former Hanalei Beach and Racquet Club provides accommodations as do a number of condominiums. Development so far seems small scale in relation to great adjacent landscape areas yet only dotted with buildings. But this is not the intention of the operators of the Princeville resort project who have plans for the most extensive, spectacular, and potentially elegant Kauai development now underway. "Princeville at Hanalei," planned as a recreational and resort community, occupies 10,000 acres of the former Princeville Ranch. The resort is being developed by the Princeville Corporation, 90 percent owned by the Denver-based Consolidated Oil & Gas Company. Its size, in relation to present development which has yet to blossom, is staggering and already it is able to boast a first-class Robert Trent Jones twenty-seven hole golf course (Princeville Makai), nineteen tennis courts, and seven miles of coastline from which beaches are accessible.

This is conceived as a grand development: an entire new resort town, several hotels providing 1,000 rooms, and about 2,700 residential units, a considerably scaled-down version of earlier published plans. Already probably $60–$70 million have been invested in the development which includes half a dozen condominium complexes, club houses, the Princeville Village Center, and an airstrip.

In comparison to some large developments Princeville got off to a very slow start. Two major subunits foundered financially and the Racquet Club, now standing in lieu of a hotel, had a similar fate. Now after a decade, the first hotel, a 300-room low-rise structure is being developed by the Marriot Corporation—not without community objections.

Princeville has had a long haul. Unlike some developers, the Princeville Corporation did not have land it already owned. When development first started other areas closer to the beaten track competed with it successfully. Other resort regions in the state were more popular for the purchase of condominiums and lots. They were also in drier areas but brochures try to capitalize on this fact by saying, "Rain is usually a late night, early morning gift to Princeville." Observers have felt the scale of the enterprise was to its disadvantage. At one stage, buyers had felt that there was so much offered there was no need to hurry to make a purchase.

A frequent strategy in resort development is to establish a major hotel as an anchor to create a special image from the start. This has been done recently with success elsewhere. This was not the case at Princeville, and the development suffered. Timing seemed wrong then. Now it is probably right. Some competing areas are becoming cluttered, occupancy on the island has been high, and although occupancy is still low at Princeville, its time is probably coming. Buildings are all low profile; forty feet is the maximum. With its great emphasis on lots and, perhaps in the future, ranchettes, it could be difficult to exert the long-term control some high-quality resort developments aim for. In the meantime residents have all the space in the world in the most unurban urban enclave on Kauai, which really does look just as the glossy brochures portray it.

Nawiliwili and Poipu Beach (Lawai-Poipu)

The Nawiliwili-Lihue region deserves mention for two reasons. First, it is small and geographically separate, and its nearly 800 units provide for most of those who are strictly business travelers to Kauai. Second, in a commanding position on Nawiliwili Bay is the Kauai Surf Hotel with 600 rooms, far more than any other hotel on the island. The convention center which it houses brings the hotel 25 percent of its guests.[31] While some will recommend a Kalalau Valley trip or a hike up the slopes of Mount Waialeale, the world's wettest mountain, cognoscente I have met would never miss the bar at the Kauai Surf for local color.

Common references for the State Tourism Plan's designation of Lawai-Poipu, located on the southeast tip of Kauai, are Poipu, Poipu Beach, or Koloa-Poipu. This is an interesting area with some good beaches including the best bodysurfing beach on the island. The focus of the area is a coastal strip extending from Spouting Horn in the west to Makahuena Point and mauka to Koloa. The area has at present about a dozen establishments—several small hotels and smaller condominium buildings—bringing the total to about 1,130 units, which makes it considerably larger now than the Princeville-Hanalei area. Its potential in terms of what is already built or proposed, 3,800 units, falls a little short of the northern region. In other respects it is quite unlike Princeville. Its location tends to confine it, and its hotels are cramped together on its better beach area. In comparison with the one large planned unit development of the north, it lacks recreational facilities and sufficient accommodations for its mostly independent travelers.

The latter deficiency will be remedied soon when the waterfront Island Holiday's Waiohai Hotel of 47 units is replaced by a newer version with 460 rooms. With the Moana Corporation's Kiahuna development between Poipu and Koloa, the region will add a golf course and greater accommodation capacity. "And then," says Don Timbie, manager of the area's Japanese-owned Sheraton Kauai, "that will make us a real destination area."[32] "The real problem," says Bill Johnson of the Kauai Surf at Nawiliwili, "is in the future if Kauai does not provide the roads and support facilities for the large number of visitors that will be coming." Without the facilities, he feels Kauai might start losing visitors to other islands.

Condominiums

I frequently refer to condominiums throughout this work as an element second in importance to hotels. Yet in some resort areas, they are overwhelmingly important; indeed, some resort areas, in existence a number of years with condominiums, have still to establish their first hotel.

The importance of condominiums is masked by the fact that they play both an indefinite and changing role in the overall tourist industry. At any time it is not known how many units in a resort complex are available for a rental pool, how many are rented individually by owners, and how many are never rented. No figures give a true indication. Because of a diverse and uncertain contribution, including at times what has been considered unfair and illegal competition with hotels, the more organized parts of the tourist industry tend to overlook condominiums in their promotional efforts. What can be stressed is that statistics quoted paint a truer picture for hotels than for condominiums.

Newer, little known condominiums may have actual occupancy rates of 15–20 percent in "off months." But each complex has its own story. In some, only a small proportion of owners may wish to rent so that at certain times of the year the building might seem virtually deserted. This is often the case with high-value units. In some moderate-value units, owners are anxious to have as high a return as possible. Whether rental occupancy as opposed to actual occupancy is high could depend on the activity of the management and the owners' association. In some resort areas, condominium rentals are well organized. The owners who so desire may list units with the Hawaii Visitors Bureau, and there is a growing number of resort region agencies oriented toward listing and renting condominiums.

Management and ownership arrangements vary greatly. In some cases owners agree with management that occupancy of units will be only for a certain definitely scheduled period. In this way the complex can be run largely as an apartment-hotel with a guaranteed number of units always available for rent. Over the last few years some developers have been selling units on a time-sharing basis. If periods are for a month, a 100-unit block could theoretically have 1,200 owners and 100 percent occupancy virtually all the time. Unlike hotels, condominiums pose serious social and community questions. As yet few groups or counties have faced up to the real long-term effect where condominiums dominate tourist accommodations or where condominium conversions and, to an extent, time-sharing in areas peripheral to tourism cause greater demands on the availability of local housing.

Large or Small Scale?

Maui case studies, which will be described later, enlarge upon several characteristics already becoming evident.

Waikiki, Poipu Beach, Wailua-Kapaa, Hilo, and Kailua-Kona are all examples of what I call small-scale development. This appellation includes even Waikiki which, although massive, represents numbers of single individual or corporate operators running hotels and condominiums often on minimally sized lots. Frequently there are significant areas of buildings cheek by jowl all presenting a mishmash of unplanned heterogeneity. Each individual development is planned, indeed some may be as elegant as one would find anywhere, but no complex is planned in relation to its neighbors and, overall, the entire district usually lacks manageable coherence. Such regions make for high building and human densities, unaesthetic design, and limited recreational facilities. On the positive side, such resort areas frequently offer an abundance of retail stores, ample restaurants and entertainment, and a crowd-generated excitement seldom matched in large-scale developments.

The large-scale development occupies an extensive area as a single unit. In the small-scale category, thirty acres is large. Large-scale developments range from several hundred to several thousand acres and more. Planning is characterized by a grand all-encompassing design—coherence and theme in landscaping, circulation, and the placement of buildings. Most projects are presented to local governments as planned unit developments; counties may maintain control while the developer, after paying his dues (outlined later), gets the flexibility and planning he wants. Once underway, it is possible for the developer to keep control of every aspect of development from the design, the standard of restaurants, and the night-lighting system to the materials used for drapes and details as minute as the placement, color, and size of trash cans.

There are advantages and disadvantages in both types of development. Uniformly high quality can be maintained in large-scale projects which are likely to respond better to community views and to local government direction. Except for location and associated physical amenities there is a degree of sameness which may stifle character. The tendency is toward clinical quality and uniformity and few show any degree of imagination or creativity. One may be differentiated from the other in terms of management; or the presence of a superior rather than just a good hotel; by condominiums worth $450,000 rather than $250,000; by the presence of a museum, art center, or botanical garden; or by an Arnold Palmer versus a Robert Trent Jones golf course. Generally, visitors and condominium residents are white, upper middle class, and enjoy golf, tennis, and other leisure pastimes.

Small-scale developments may have the characteristics of dynamism and excitement. In a mature region the elegant and the seedy stand side by side as do the traditional and the new, the substantial and the plastic. In Waikiki the monstrous Sheraton-Waikiki towers over the old Royal Hawaiian and one at once empathizes with the old lady as claustrophobically she is surrounded by menacing concrete giants. In small-scale development, no matter how big, local people circulate as a matter of course because it's all part of *their* town. This does not happen to the same extent in large planned unit developments. If nothing else, small scale has character—or had it. How else would there be (or could there have been) a Queen's Surf, or a Kona Inn, a Halekulani, a Hana Maui, a Pioneer Inn, or even a Blue Max? But then again who knows what large old buildings will be revered in half a century: the Mauna Kea Beach Hotel in South Kohala, if it is not already? the Sheraton Maui at Kaanapali? By then large-scale operations may have developed something of lasting value, something historic that emerges as the result of interaction between environment and creative human beings. Many of the new developments reflect the creativity of an innovative planner or a thoughtful architect—admirable amid the myriad of unplanned small-scale muddles.

CHAPTER 3

Maui: The Valley Isle Comes to Life

ECONOMIC analysts looking at Hawaii in the post-World War II years would have seen Maui as a typical neighbor island county in the throes of economic lethargy. The impact of tourism and the military, so important to Oahu, had for the most part passed Maui by. In many ways this was fortunate. When development eventually did come, important lessons had been learned from Oahu.

While Waikiki strained under the burgeoning growth of visitor numbers, relatively few persons visited the neighbor islands. In 1956, 90 percent of total visitor days in Hawaii were spent on Oahu and 1 percent on Maui. By the mid-1960s, the tourist lag, the greater degree of inaccessibility compared with Oahu, and the lack of development on Maui all were beginning to change. Furthermore, there had been time, in theory at least, for planners and developers to take stock of the situation and prepare more rationally than would otherwise have been the case for Maui's future. Signs of development were welcome. In the early 1960s, the island's population was lower than it had been forty years previously. For many, Maui offered little. Greater agricultural technology reduced the need for plantation laborers, and young adults left the island in great numbers for better opportunities elsewhere.[1]

Visitors to Hawaii stayed for a number of days on Oahu and visited other islands for a short, added experience. Of these visits, many were only during the daylight hours. Figures for overnight visitors are telling (table 4). By 1963, Maui, the Valley Isle, received more than a quarter of all visitor days and a much greater proportion of total visitors, but many of them still just stayed overnight—others, as in the past, just passed through during the day.

Visitor units, especially if occupancy rates are high, are another indicator of potential tourist volume and change. When planning for Kaanapali resort began in the early 1950s, the island had only 176 rooms; by the mid-1960s, the number was 1,200; by the mid-1970s, it was over 6,000.

Previous examples have shown that Maui development per se is not unique nor are its projects as potentially large as some on other islands. What is unique is its ebullience, its comparative rate of growth, its popularity, and its image of efficient county management and economic well-being. It does include the longest established of the neighbor islands' planned unit developments, Kaanapali; one of the most ambitious in terms of financial involvement, Wailea; and one, Kapalua, which has consciously set its quality sights so high that the rich from around the world are clamoring to be associated with it.

That which applies to tourism on Oahu is appropriate in large measure to Maui as well. But there are other elements that help to account for the county's spectacular growth during the 1970s. Of primary importance is a fifty-mile stretch of western shoreline from Lipoa Point to La Perouse Bay or, in resort terms, from Kapalua to Makena. The coastal scenery and beaches are some of the finest in Hawaii—they are breathtaking. Offshore, just a short distance away, three other islands—Kahoolawe, Lanai, and Molokai —enhance an already exciting seascape. Two islands are always in view and in some areas even three may be seen at one time. Beach parks have been developed by the state and county so that local people and visitors alike can take full advantage of this lovely area (figs. 1 and 3).

The southern part of the narrow coastal lowland lies in the rain shadow of the majestic 10,000-foot volcanic dome of Haleakala while the north, not quite so well protected, is flanked by the 5,000 to 6,000-foot peaks of the West Maui mountains. As a consequence, the coastal lands receive maximum sunshine and, except in winter, low rainfall—the ideal formula for tourist use. Precipitation ranges from a meager six to ten inches in the south at Kihei and Wailea (fig. 4), to a moderate 30 to 40 inches at Kapalua —dry in comparison with the 300 to 400-inch totals among the West Maui mountains.

Maui, like the island of Hawaii, has exploited its spectacular volcanic terrain. A forty-mile journey to the summit of Haleakala provides a truly awesome view of the ever-changing brick-red crater landscape, a distant glimpse of the major peaks of Mauna

TABLE 4. *Neighbor Island Overnight Visitors and Visitor Expenditures*

	Neighbor Islands	Maui Co.	Hawaii Co.	Kauai Co.	State Visitor Expenditure ($ Million)	Neighbor Island Visitor Expenditure ($ Million)	Maui Co. Visitor Expenditure ($ Million)	Hawaii Co. Visitor Expenditure ($ Million)	Kauai Co. Visitor Expenditure ($ Million)
1967	443,175	304,437	286,590	275,461	380	89.6	31.5	31.5	26.6
1970	637,518	447,985	445,401	410,075	595	153.0	54.5	53.4	45.1
1975	1,310,459	931,863	769,779	632,821	1,360	332.4	143.9	107.1	81.4
1979	1,972,737	1,419,773	860,940	825,366	2,620	672.3	340.9	172.2	159.2

SOURCE: Hawaii Visitors Bureau Research Department.

TABLE 5. *Maui Profile*

Year	Population	Ethnic Background	Percent 1970[b]	1975[c]	Place of Birth[c]	Percent	Land Use	Area (acres)
1960[a]	35,717	Hawaiian and part-Hawaiian	28	23	Maui	49	Sugar[d]	47,500
		Japanese	25	25	Oahu	10	Pineapples[d]	32,400
		Filipino	23	15	Hawaii	2	Vegetables[d]	1,200
1970[a]	38,700	Portuguese	10	4	Molokai	5	Grazing Lands[e]	171,400
		Caucasian	9	21	Lanai	2	Forest[e]	20,000
		Chinese	2	1	Kauai	1	Forest Reserve[e]	155,900
		Puerto Rican	2	0	Elsewhere in U.S.	18	National Park[e]	17,700
1980[a]	63,100	Other	1	11	Other countries	13	Urban[e]	6,000
							Other	13,800
							TOTAL	465,900 or 728 sq. mi.

SOURCES:
[a] Department of Planning and Economic Development.
[b] *Maui Community Profile*, State Planning Systems—Community Action Program Honolulu, 1970, p. 42.
[c] *1975 Census Update Survey* (Honolulu: Maui Economic Opportunity Inc., 1976).
[d] State of Hawaii, *Data Book* 1978.
[e] Proceedings, Land Classification Service, Land Study Bureau, University of Hawaii, 1969.

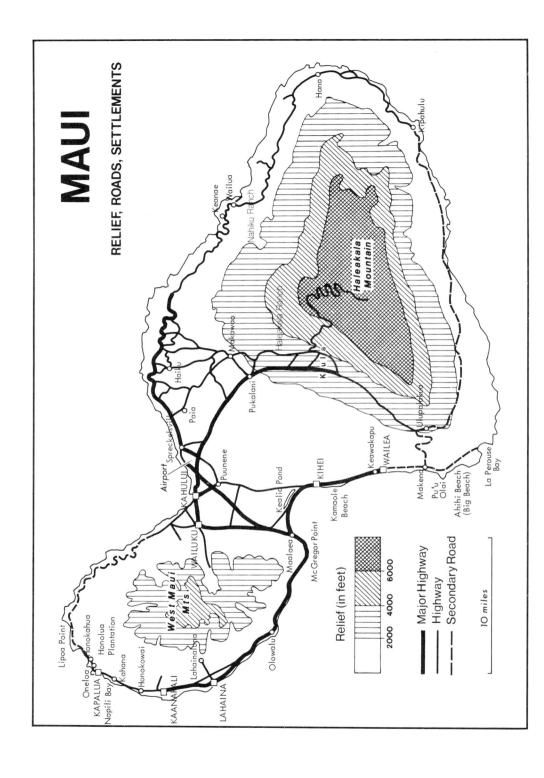

MAUI

RELIEF, ROADS, SETTLEMENTS

Hana

Kipahulu

Wailua

Keanae

Nahiku Ranch

Haleakala Ranch

Haleakala Mountain

Makawao

Haiku

Kula

Paia

Pukalani

Spreckelsville

Airport

Puunene

Keawakapu

KAHULUI

Kealia Pond

KIHEI

WAILEA

Ulupalakua

Makena

Pu'u Olai

La Perouse Bay

Kamaole Beach

Ahihi Beach (Big Beach)

WAILUKU

Maalaea

McGregor Point

West Maui Mts

Olowalu

Lipoa Point

Honokahua

Honolua Plantation

Oneloa

KAPALUA

Napili Bay

Kahana

Honokowai

KAANAPALI

Lahainaluna

LAHAINA

Relief (in feet)

2000 4000 6000

Major Highway

Highway

Secondary Road

10 miles

Kea and Mauna Loa on Hawaii, a commanding picture of the West Maui mountains, and an aerial view of the sugar-rich central valley thousands of feet below.

Outside Haleakala, which is popular and well-advertised, the potential of the mountains is barely recognized. Visitor orientation is always to the sea, yet the mauka side of the coastal highway, especially in West Maui, shows frightening, deeply carved, foreboding canyons of immense proportions and mountain skyscapes alongside. The forests and the very appealing middle and upper slopes, especially on Haleakala, support a wide range of landscapes which so far have been little used for recreational and tourist purposes.

In listing visitor industry resources, limited attention is given to the everyday aspects of human life on the Valley Isle. These, I believe, are of major consequence to the visitor. The cosmopolitan community is both attractive and interesting to outsiders: Japanese, Hawaiian, part-Hawaiian, Filipino, Portuguese, Chinese, and Puerto Rican all have contributed to the composition of the population (table 5). Each group retains at least something from its source culture in speech, song, dance, food, or clothing. Although in many ways each group is distinctive, their common island history and heritage have welded them into a relatively coherent community, not without internal differences, but nevertheless completely distinct from the mainland or newly arrived haole.

Economic activity, apart from tourism, includes major sugar and pineapple plantations, mills and a cannery, cattle ranching, truck farming, papaya and macadamia nut raising, and the only vineyard in Hawaii on a portion of Ulupalakua Ranch. Although tourism is now the major activity, visiting Wailuku, the county seat, is still like going through a prosperous country town with few signs of visitors. Nevertheless, Wailuku and its southern twin, Kahului, support a large number of agricultural, food processing, retail, and government workers (table 6) and three major shopping centers. It is as though the west was the island's flashy front of hotels, condominiums, and entertainment spots. The eastern towns and settlements house the fundamental behind-the-scenes support activities. And if you lived on Maui this is where you'd buy a car, license it, see a lawyer, consult an architect, buy furniture, go to the dentist, or attend the community college.

On the slopes of Haleakala, increasing altitude results in the unfolding of a variety of different landscapes. Puunene, an aged but

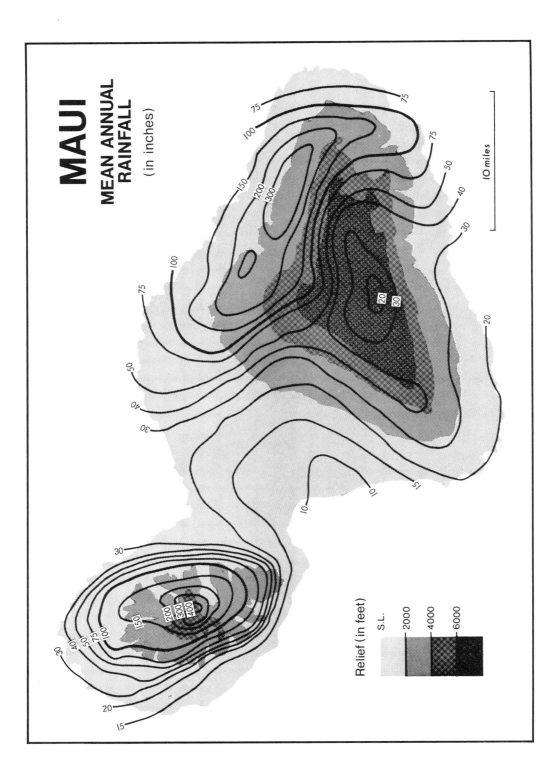

MAUI
MEAN ANNUAL RAINFALL
(in inches)

Relief (in feet)

S.L.
2000
4000
6000

10 miles

TABLE 6. *Maui Civilian Labor Force*

	1964	1969	1975	1980
Agriculture	2,850	2,710	2,850	2,950
Food Processing	2,350	2,010	1,700	1,600
Retail Trade	1,540	2,280	4,000	6,200
Hotels	760	1,400	2,350	4,550
Government	2,000	2,330	3,050	3,700
Other	4,720	6,440	9,000	8,550
Unemployed	720	630	2,100	1,500
TOTAL	14,940	17,800	25,050	28,150

SOURCE: Hawaii State Department of Labor and Industrial Relations; figures for 1980 are preliminary estimates.

appealing sugar mill center shaded by huge monkeypod trees, lies among sugar cane in the dusty valley bottom. At higher levels, sugar gives way to pineapple and here one finds the settlements of Haiku, Makawao, and burgeoning new Pukalani set in luxuriant tropical vegetation, the result of increased rainfall at higher elevations. With altitude, temperatures decrease. Higher still the landscape changes to the lush pastures, hedges, fine cattle, magnificent plantings of eucalyptus, and the functional yet picturesque buildings of the Haleakala Ranch. Farther west are smallholders— vegetable and flower farmers and the residential dwellers of Kula. Continuing along the contour, one finds the open space of Ulupalakua Ranch, formerly the famous Rose Ranch and Makee Plantation, with its tree-shaded buildings and the relics of the old sugar mill. With its many historical and social resources to enhance the sea, sun, and mountains, it's easy to comprehend the appeal of Maui.

Situated between Oahu and Hawaii, Maui has benefited from air fare price structures which make for relatively inexpensive and easy visits. At present there is no satisfactory alternative to air transportation. For a short period a hydrofoil service plied between the islands. A ferry service has been discussed for many years but has not progressed beyond that stage.

Roads on Maui, by Pacific island standards, are very good with good connections between the airport, resort areas, and places of major interest. A major highway, opened in 1971, made travel from the airport to Lahaina and Kaanapali considerably easier. Several attractive areas are not served by major roads, but people with the inclination to get away from crowds and the perseverance to do so will not be disappointed. This, though, is not likely to last forever. A good north-south if not a circum-island road is bound to come. In a highly visited area like Maui, bad roads can sometimes be a blessing in disguise. Hana and Kipahulu in the southeast of the island retain their unique charm, rural industries, and higher Hawaiian populations largely because the area is so remote.

If not now, certainly in the near future, educational and cultural facilities will play an important role as essential resources. The island is rich in historical assets and the museum at Wailuku is charming and first rate. The historic buildings of Lahaina and Lahainaluna serve a similar historical function. There is an excellent state library system with attractively housed branches at Wailuku, Kahului, Makawao, and Lahaina. In addition, there are several secondary schools and Maui Community College which offers university introductory courses and vocational programs.

Contemporary Trends

During the 1960s, Maui's hotel inventory grew by over 835 percent from 290 to 2,720 (table 3), an increase of over 2,400 rooms. The success of this radical development was itself a spur to further development. Although Maui did not escape the effects of the economic slowdown at the end of the sixties and during the early seventies, the next decade saw a total of almost 9,500 rooms, a spectacular increase of 6,500.[2] These were periods when Maui had a decisive hold on the state tourism market and as construction grew to accommodate increasing numbers, occupancy rose appreciably. Early estimates often underestimated what seemed to be taking place. One early forecast saw visitors to Maui at the end of the 1970s being greater than the 1971 total for the entire state —actually a prediction not far off the mark. Similar estimates in the past had always been equalled or exceeded.[3]

The 1980s may see 2 million visitors arriving annually on Maui, a figure which probably would have appeared horrifying to observers in the late 1960s or to people who made the island their home in the expectation of long-lasting peace and tranquility. What people seldom take into account is that those same characteristics which brought people in the early days are bringing 16,000 daily visitors now.

Most estimates assume hotel use by visitors from overseas. On Maui there are many Hawaii visitors who stay with friends or relatives. In addition there are those, a considerable number, who stay in their own condominium units or that of a friend, or one rented through mainland contacts. Few of these people are likely to be accounted for in statistical surveys. Condominiums on Maui outnumber hotels 4.0 to 1. It is not inconceivable that in a decade this will become 5.0 to 1. Condominium blocks have an average of about fifty-seven rooms and are small—hotels average about 210 and are getting larger.

An analysis of owners in a well-established Kaanapali condominium complex shows the significance of Hawaii-based ownership. Of owners 35 percent is from Hawaii, mostly Oahu, 44 percent from the Pacific Coast, and the remainder from elsewhere. New condominiums have a much higher out-of-state ownership, perhaps 75–85 percent. Condominiums have always been an important element in the development of Maui and although the county administration has misgivings about them in comparison to hotels, their share of the overall accommodation inventory is unlikely to lessen. The official unit total (table 7) is lower than it would be if all condominiums as well as hotel units were listed. Under these circumstances total hotel-apartment inventory would be no less than 11,800 (see table 8) and possibly as high as 12,500.

Condominiums are characterized by problems not found in hotels. Management is often spotty, owners' associations are frequently not prepared to put sufficient resources into management or toward maintenance and landscaping. Quality, mixed at any time, has a ready potential to deteriorate. After initial construction is finished, condominiums characteristically employ fewer persons than hotels and again, in comparison with hotels, may make less of a contribution to the local economy. From the view-

TABLE 7. *All Visitors Arriving on Maui and Maui Accommodations*

Year	Entire State	Maui	Percent	Daily Visitor Counts	Units
1966	835,456[b]	222,411[a]	27	2,000[c]	1,497[b]
1970	1,746,970[b]	447,985[a]	20	3,645[a]	2,720[b]
1974	2,786,489[b]	852,201[a]	30	7,541[a]	5,506[b]
1978	3,670,309[b]	1,414,867[b]	39	14,492[c]	8,941[b]
1980	3,939,275[d]	1,379,528[d]	35	15,831[c]	10,521[d]

SOURCES:
[a] State of Hawaii, *Data Book* 1978.
[b] Hawaii Visitors Bureau, *Research Report*, December 1978, and *1978 Annual Research Report*.
[c] State of Hawaii, *Data Book* 1980.
[d] Hawaii Visitors Bureau.

TABLE 8. *Rental Accommodations, May 1981: Hotels and Condominiums on Maui*

Area	Hotel Units	Hotel Establishments	Condominium Units	Condominium Establishments
Kapalua-Lahaina				
Napili Area	196	1	677	14
Kahana Area	—	—	528	8
Honokowai Area	—	—	773	17
Kaanapali Area[c]	3,041	5	1,276	9
Lahaina Area	120	3	292	3
TOTAL KAPALUA-LAHAINA	3,357	9	3,546	51
Maalaea-Makena				
Maalaea	—	—	225	8
Kihei	227	2	1,662	35
Wailea	950	2	200	3
TOTAL MAALAEA-MAKENA	1,177	4	2,087	46
OTHER	495	11	46	1
TOTAL ALL AREAS	5,029	24	5,679	98
TOTAL RENTAL HOTEL & CONDOMINIUMS				10,708[a]
ESTIMATED TOTAL ALL CONDOMINIUM UNITS			6,800	—
TOTAL ALL HOTEL & ESTIMATED CONDOMINIUM UNITS—ALL AREAS				11,800[b]

SOURCE: *Hawaii Business*, May 1981, with modifications.
[a] The total for Maui differs from that used by the Hawaii Visitors Bureau. Some condominium complexes listed by HVB have a variable number of units in a rental pool. The actual number offered can vary from week to week.
[b] This is a conservative estimate using actual hotel totals and making an assumption that only 80 percent of condominium units are available. Numbers of small, more exclusive complexes are omitted from the source list and some larger ones on well-known developments have not been enumerated. The actual count for Maui could be higher, e.g., 12,500.
[c] A detailed and slightly different Kaanapali estimate is noted elsewhere.

point of the owner, a condominium provides a relatively moderately priced home in an area where land values are so high the purchase of a house may be prohibitive or inappropriate. As a second home, the condominium is primarily a rental investment and a vehicle for capital appreciation. Owners and developers alike benefit materially. This type of housing has been exceedingly popular with developers so that it is not surprising that overbuilding has taken place from time to time.

Although thousands of tourists breeze through Maui, visit the Iao Needle and Lahaina, and do not stay overnight, the average stay on Maui is over 3.5 days.[4] From a pre-1960 average stay of less than one day, the length of stay has increased consistently. We might justifiably predict that in certain areas like Kapalua, Kaanapali, Wailea, and Makena the average period of visit will increase to five or more days. The better developments can be expected to keep visitors even longer.

Land Use Planning

In 1961 the Hawaii legislature passed the Land Use Law which established the State Land Use Commission (LUC) and instructed it to classify all land in the state and to determine rules for the regulation of land use within the state. The first "Rules of Practice and Procedure of State Land Use District Regulation" were established in 1964, and the first of a continuing series of quinquennial reviews took place in 1969.[5] The entire state, as the result of the law, was divided into agricultural, rural, conservation, and urban districts. In 1970 the state instructed the LUC to establish shoreline setback lines. Subsequent legislation, to be discussed in later chapters, has been designed to regulate development in the coastal zone. The specific zoning of residential, commercial, resort, hotel, and apartment areas within urban districts is the responsibility of the county. If a landowner feels there is justification for changing his classification to urban, he may petition the State Land Use Commission, after which, if successful, the county will exercise its zoning powers.

Within an urban district, the County Planning Commission delineates the precise use for each parcel of land.[6] Along the west coast where the special case study areas lie, the drawing up of zones was done through an urban planning grant awarded Maui County by the federal Department of Housing and Urban Development under the provisions of Section 701 of the Housing Act of 1954. The County Department of Planning, outside planning and economic consultants, interest groups, and the public were involved in various ways and to various degrees. As a result, general plans for the Lahaina and Kihei districts were drawn up and published in 1968 and 1970 as the Lahaina 701 and Kihei 701 plans.[7]

In determining the direction of these plans, certain assumptions were put into play—for better or for worse. They had the potential for making a positive contribution to the orderly and rational development of Maui until 1990, the end of the planning period. I say "had the potential" because obviously many people do not think the results have been admirable. In a later chapter I discuss the Kihei plan and some of its effects in greater detail. Areas covered in each of the plans have been cited by critics with justification as examples of some of Hawaii's worst planning.

Major assumptions of the plans were that by 1990 Maui would receive about one million visitors annually (a figure already exceeded); the average length of stay would increase from three to five days; and rather than 25 percent of visitors being local island people, there would be only 4 percent. Finally, the dramatic increase in hotel and visitor-support employment would be matched as dramatically by the drop in agricultural employment. On the contrary, agricultural employment remained remarkably steady (table 6). In West Maui this would mean that almost two-thirds of total employment would be concerned with visitors and an insignificant percentage with agriculture.[8] The plans seriously underestimated the numbers who would arrive and overexaggerated the allowable accommodation units for those who did. The function of condominiums was not clearly understood then, nor was there any real link established between hotel/apartment units and employment needed locally.

The goals of the plan—the enhancement of the land for human use, the coordination of both large and small developments, the improvement of environmental quality first for permanent residents then for visitors, the preservation of openness, and the creation of sight corridors—were admirable. But one has only to travel by car from Napili to Kahana and Honokowai and then from north Kihei to the gates of Wailea, to see the harsh disparity between intention and actuality. The major development projects, used as case studies, are now embraced by the two general plans —Kapalua and Kaanapali in the Lahaina 701 and Wailea in the

Kihei 701 plans. The Lahaina 701 plan covers what the State Tourism Plan calls the Kapalua-Kaanapali resort area and the Kihei 701 plan, the Maalaea-Makena resort area. Within the general plans, the four large projects each have their individual master plans which they follow under the planned unit development concept.

Kapalua-Kaanapali Resort Area

By far the bulk of tourist development on Maui has taken place in the Kapalua-Kaanapali region, a narrow fifteen-mile strip from Kapalua in the north of the island south to the old whaling town of Lahaina. The area, commonly known as West Maui, has the greatest concentration of accommodation units on the island (see table 8)—approximately 6,130. Kaanapali, farther south along the coast, was the first major planned resort area on Maui. In 1980 it had four large hotels and two more in the construction or planning stages. Smaller-scale development has taken place at Lahaina and between Kaanapali and Kapalua where it forms an almost unbroken ribbon of wall-to-wall condominiums. Whereas Kaanapali boasts grand expanses of an open golf course and middle- and high-rise hotels all in landscaped surroundings, Honokowai-Napili is characterized by both small and larger apartments and condominiums frequently set cheek-by-jowl with minimal landscaping and of mixed quality. Close to forty condominiums are found along five miles of coast.

At Alaeloa, an area zoned residential, are two small well-planned, elegant settlements. At Napili much has been done voluntarily and by special ordinance to control development and maintain higher-than-normal standards.[9] Napili Kai, a resort area in miniature, attempts to offset with beautiful manicured landscaping and low-set buildings what it loses in crowding along a restricted side of Napili Bay where, as the result of economic inducement, local people sacrificed their pleasant surroundings and allowed good quality houses to be demolished for further condominium expansion.[10]

Kahana to Kaanapali has short stretches of beach somewhat similar to Kihei but with greater maturity. Density of settlement together with higher rainfall gives the coastline a lush and busy appearance. The hilly backdrop, relatively close to the coast, is green and forested; on the lower slopes are plantings of sugar in the south and pineapples and patches of beautiful exotic trees further north. The coast is fretted with interesting coves and rocky headlands which provide shelter to an extent not found in the Maalaea-Makena area.

The focus of the area has for many years been on the settlement of Lahaina, a town of several thousand residents. Many of these are families of the approximately 650 workers employed by Pioneer Mill as sugar plantation laborers and process workers.[11] Many family members work for hotels in Kaanapali, about four miles away, and for visitor-related industries nearby.

Within the general Kapalua-Kaanapali-Lahaina area are over 9,000 persons or roughly one-seventh of Maui's population. Of these almost 40 percent is Caucasian, 22 percent Japanese, 21 percent Hawaiian or part-Hawaiian, and 11 percent Filipino. This represents a Caucasian component almost 60 percent higher than the Maui average.[12]

The area has much to recommend it. There, within a small area, is a variety of attractions. Mountains, sea, historic sites, simplicity, and sophistication lie side by side, and the coastal lands are well occupied. Compared with Kihei in the Maalaea-Makena region this is a lush, softer, and more heavily settled area.

Maalaea-Makena Resort Area

The Maalaea-Makena region is about three-quarters of a mile wide and about twenty-two miles long. Wailea is about midway between Kihei and the extreme south point of La Perouse Bay (see fig. 3), a little beyond the Makena development. In comparison, this region, frequently referred to by its core—Kihei—is dry and stark, especially where new developments have yet to be blended into or softened by landscaping. From the *pali* (cliff) at McGregor Point at the north of the region, the majestic sweep of coastline around Maalaea Bay is a fitting visual foundation for the bottom easy slopes, scrub-covered, which rise over 10,000 feet to the Haleakala summit. Within the region, there are thirteen miles of white coral sand beaches which are used by local residents and visitors alike. The best of these beaches front the Wailea project, smaller-scale operations at Kamaole, private residences at Keawakapu, and numerous parks.

When development was well underway in West Maui (Kapalua-Kaanapali) at the end of the 1960s and the beginning of the 1970s, construction was just starting in this region. By the end of the 1970s, the change was amazing. The population tripled, from less than 2,000 to around 6,000. Its greatest concentration is between the south end of Kealia Pond and Wailea (see fig. 3).

In 1969, except for sections of the shoreline makai of Kihei Road, settlement was sparse. On the mauka side, widely spaced homes interspersed with overgrown unused land and abandoned houses were the remaining signs of former homestead subdivisions. There were a few small farms growing vegetables or raising chickens and a scattering of unkept mango orchards. Today this feeling of spaciousness has disappeared. The major coast road is heavily used by construction vehicles, private automobiles, and rental cars. The area has moved from rural lethargy to a state of apparently never-ending freneticism and exuberance. The beachside bonanza arrived, bringing with it inevitable change and staggering costs which will not be realized for twenty years.

The 1970s was a decade of unbelievable activity. Signs appeared with monotonous frequency proclaiming the future site of a "luxury seaside condominium" grandly named and selling at the drawing board stage at "10 percent down and no closing costs." Every month a new crop of real estate salespersons took up residence in the area. Not a day went by, it seemed, without bulldozers clearing land with frightening ease. Kiawe trees from another century were nosed over to lie dejected, if only temporarily, in a heap of wind-blown sand. After the bulldozing, the sandy land was consolidated and stabilized by constant watering. Construction then started, and gradually a condominium, stark in its bare surroundings, rose where kiawe forests once stood. A golf course emerged from the scrub and dun-colored grass of the semi-desert; and, on the larger developments, teams of gardeners prepared new man-made landscapes of tropical shrubs and trees to adorn the newest clubhouse or swimming pool. This pattern was repeated, with remarkable sameness printed in every tourism region of Hawaii: it was the condominium landscape.

The region is primarily a holiday place for mainland and international visitors, a declining bedroom suburb for Wailuku and Kahului, and a center of retirement. The outward signs of tourism dominate: three major hotels and over forty condominium projects. The condominiums range in quality from subminimal to outstanding, from several units to two hundred to a block. In 1972 the region launched itself into the tourist business; in 1973 it took off and, except for a short lull mid-decade, it never looked back. By the last quarter of 1979 and into 1980 despite a decline in visitor arrivals, construction continued.[13]

During the 1970s, the infrastructure attempted to keep pace with development. New sewer lines were laid but the provision of water was a constant difficulty. With the help of two major developers, the county brought water to the area from central Maui. This provided temporary relief from a moratorium on building due to unavailability of water which had been in effect from 1978 to 1979. In mid-1979 the moratorium was invoked for all new buildings except those planned by Alexander & Baldwin (Wailea) and the Seibu Corporation (Makena), codevelopers with the county of the new water line. Moratoriums of this nature are to be expected in an area which, when I visited first in 1965, had one post office, two general stores, one hotel, a condominium under construction, and a scattering of local population. No initial infrastructure of any consequence existed in 1965 and development has been so fast that it has been unable to keep pace with hotel-apartment construction.

The human resources of the area have changed considerably. The Hawaiian component, 56 percent of the population in 1970, was twice the island average; Caucasians represented less than 20 percent; and the Japanese and Filipino populations were low. Five years later I estimated the composition of the population at 30 percent Hawaiian and perhaps 40 percent Caucasian. By the end of the decade the Caucasian element had increased to 55–60 percent, a typical effect of tourism development.

From south to north, the area is flanked by rough grazing land on its inland margins. As a traveler nears the central Maui valley, grazing gives way to the growing of hybrid corn seed and sugar. The connection between the people and agriculture is weak, almost nonexistent. One does not expect agricultural workers to be living in the area. The region's obvious potential as a desirable place to live has been rapidly tapped. This was not the case in the early 1970s. Then, unhurried Hawaiians lived simply in modified Polynesian style in the relative isolation conducive to retaining something of the past. With them, often in beachfront rental housing, were professionals, semiprofessionals, or the retired. This apparently amicable arrangement held within it the seeds of conflict but they seldom reached fruition, for as change occurred and resentments grew the population changed. The indigenous voice was diminished.[14]

Along with the barking Polynesian dogs, the junked cars beneath the kiawe, the No Trespassing signs, and the annoying wind and blowing dust were exquisite, sunny, rainless days, magnificent beaches, and a vast openness. This was a place for the discerning visitor. With a lack of ready-made places of interest, it was not a place for the package tour. Now that it is, the area has lost much of its fascination. But the steady prevailing winds, the climate, the seascapes, and the mountains never change.

Although the inherent appeal of the land remains, it must compete with development—the good restaurants, fine hotels, golf courses, as well as shabby small-scale development. Wailea, on a larger scale and in its early stages, is as elegant a development as one could wish for—a bonus for what has been lost in the condominium corridor which parallels the coast and leads almost to its front entrance. Today the population is greatly increased, mostly haole, and well educated. Signs of dissatisfaction with development are few, but the "Save Makena" movement cannot be ignored or passed over lightly. About this I will say more in chapter 12.

Wailea

Wailea is the shining tourism star of the Maalaea-Makena region where human ingenuity is creating a first-rate resort-residential destination area on 1,500 acres of dry savannalike woodland of *kiawe (Prosopis pallida)*, *wiliwili (Erythrina sandwicensis)*, and prickly pear *(Opuntia megacantha)*, and a terrain of beach sand dunes and gently sloping lava rock (see fig. 5).

Alexander & Baldwin (A&B), a venerable old Hawaii company, is developing its property in association with the Northwestern Mutual Life Insurance Company under the name Wailea Development Company.

Until ground-breaking in the early seventies, the Maui community wondered if anything would ever come of the property at all. When work did start the project became a battleground of controversy. Public groups alleged that the county was providing services for the area not provided elsewhere on Maui; and they took up the battle in earnest when the much beloved coastal dirt road was to be relocated on the mauka boundary of the resort, thus restricting previously unrestricted beach access. In a compromise, the road was given a middle position that paralleled the makai boundary of the golf courses. The county entered the fray insisting

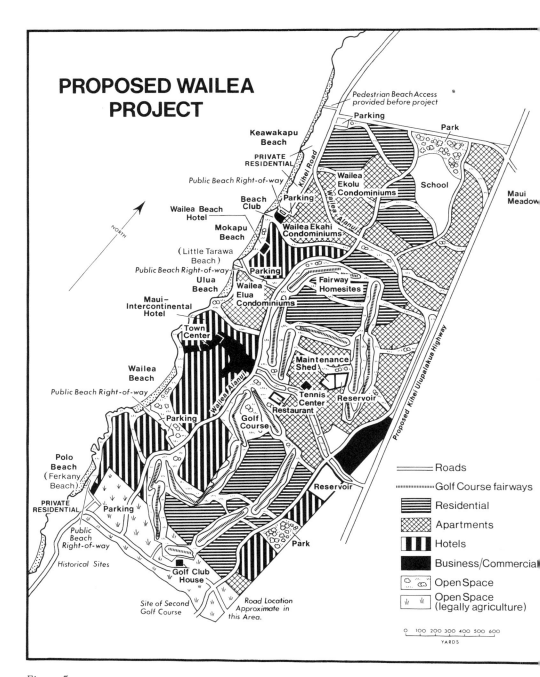

Figure 5.

Hotel Intercontinental Maui, Wailea, after development. The Hotel Intercontinental Maui, the first of two hotels to use Wailea beach, is in the background.
(Hotel Intercontinental Maui photo)

adequate beach access be provided for the public in the facilities
which had been planned but not yet submitted by the developers.

Some of the outward turmoil reflected conflicts behind the
scenes. Corporate management changes were taking place and
during this period of readjustment, no permanent representative
of the project resided on Maui. Until this situation was remedied
there was no one on Maui to reassure residents during this period
of growing concern that many of their wishes would be met by the
company.

Before the mid-seventies, resistance and controversy had all but
disappeared, the company bent over backwards to repair its image, and Wailea became a model for new planned areas. Further,
A&B, through gifts of land, parks, assistance with the county Kihei sewage plant, and its part in the Central Maui water system
with Seibu and the county, became a pioneer in cooperative projects with the county; it paid its way in return for what it was get-

ting or anticipated getting from Maui. The project contributed to a new development mode—the joint venture—which became the stamp of Maui and a pattern for the rest of the state.

The Wailea resort faces some of the most beautiful sandy beaches in Hawaii behind which are located two hotels providing something less than 1,000 rooms and several condominium projects with a total of nearly 700 units (table 9). Two further condominium blocks are to appear soon, L'Abri, next to the Wailea Beach Hotel and another facing Polo Beach. A further hotel is to be constructed overlooking Wailea beach.

Inland of the Intercontinental Maui, the anchor hotel, lies the attractive Town Center and paralleling the mauka boundary of the property are two magnificent golf courses.

So far the present expenditure on the property is over $200 million not including the value of the land. By 1988 when at least three of perhaps five hotels will be operating, it is estimated that $500 million will have been invested in the property. A permanent area population may approach 10,000 persons, five times that at the end of the seventies. By the nineties, perhaps 6,500 persons will be employed.

That many in the public sector appear to have accepted Wailea is confirmed in a May 1978 article in *Hawaii Business* called "The Wild Wild World of Wailea." It records a bizarre gathering in April 1978 when 1,212 names went into a lottery to produce 148 winners whose rewards were a chance to buy a condominium by paying on the spot 10 percent of the $125,000–$230,000 selling price of ocean-view units. Some winners were approached within the hour by people offering up to $40,000 more than the original price—par for the Wailea condominium course. Resales of two-month old condominium units with a $100,000 mark-up have been successful. Although there were $50,000 plus sales in the

TABLE 9. *Wailea Units in 1979*

Hotel Intercontinental Maui	Hotel	600
Wailea Beach Hotel	Hotel	350
		950
Wailea Ekahi	Condominium	294
Wailea Ekolu	Condominium	248
Wailea Elua	Condominium	152
		694
TOTAL		1,644

SOURCE: Various Alexander & Baldwin publications.

middle of the decade, by the end of the seventies nobody thought of a unit selling for less than $250,000. By 1981 the higher value units at L'Abri were being offered at almost $900,000!

The entire built-up area is beautifully landscaped. If the deeper ramifications of the monumental impact along that coast are being ignored (see chapters 8–12), it can be said in all honesty that Wailea, compared with similar other areas, is a credit to imaginative minds and corporate persistence. A moderate to low profile oasis has been created on an otherwise dreary desiccated land surface behind a shoreline which has always been exquisite.

Big Owners, Little Land

To an outsider, the value of land in Hawaii is horrifyingly high. One reason for this is that little land is available for purchase. In Maui thirteen owners have rights to 97 percent of the land. Eleven private owners have 48 percent—the most valuable areas. Most of the rest is in the hands of the state and federal governments.[15]

Three of the four major developments on Maui—Kaanapali, Wailea, and Kapalua—are products of major Maui landowners: Amfac, Alexander & Baldwin, and Maui Land & Pineapple Co. (table 10). At a time when many parts of the Pacific are fragmented with a multiplicity of owners, Maui and the other neighbor islands still have large tracts of uncluttered waterfront and mountain land—a situation resulting from land purchases starting in the second half of the last century, aspects of their history, and a former preoccupation with agriculture. This also set the stage for

TABLE 10. *Maui: Major Private Landholders and Associated Land Development*

	Acres	Associated Development
Alexander & Baldwin	74,600	Wailea
Ulupalakua Ranch Inc.	47,200	Sales of land: Maui Meadows, Makena Project
Haleakala Ranch	41,100	None
Maui Land & Pineapple Co.	34,200	Kapalua
Wailuku Sugar Co. (C. Brewer and Co. Ltd.)	26,700	None
Amfac	24,200	Kaanapali
Kaonoulu Ranch Co. Ltd.	16,696	None
Kaupo Ranch Ltd.	1,500	None
Hana Ranch Co. Ltd.	5,300	Hana Maui Hotel

SOURCES: State of Hawaii, *Land in Hawaii* (Honolulu: Department of Planning and Economic Development, 1970); Maui Land & Pineapple Co.; and Alexander & Baldwin.

ambitious resort development. Large-scale planned unit development under the control of one owner, rather than numerous small-
scale enterprises, has many added advantages—a point that is
reiterated continually in this study. In some countries with other
histories and values, this would be a subject of furious debate. The
fact that such land tenure still exists in an advanced industrial
country is remarkable, but within the Hawaiian historical context
where great economic inequality prevailed, it is understandable.
These circumstances provided the developmental advantages
Maui possesses now. With caution and careful planning the same
advantages, which should be considered a resource rather than an
ideological anomaly, should remain for future generations to
enjoy.

The Role of the Developer

The tourism achievements of Maui have resulted from the activities of developers guided or checked by planners and supported by
investors, many of whom reside outside the state. In the eyes of the
public, who really have had little to do with the present situation,
developers are by far the most influential group. Although some
developers see their roles as altruistic, others view themselves in
the way many members of the public do. As one former Maui developer said: "The role of the developer generally is that of a 'bad
guy' . . . motivated by the capitalist system to make money. For
him the possibility of profit determines every decision . . . The
first thing a developer does . . . is to conduct an economic feasibility study. If it looks like he can make a buck, then he will begin the
detailed planning . . . if the answer is no, the idea is generally
scrapped."[16]

After the essential preliminaries, with the exception of four notable large-scale projects, developers proceed to work quietly
within conventional ordinances. They talk informally to the planning department or the mayor and expect to gain approval for a
project which will bring them a 20 to 25 percent return on their
venture capital. In comparison with planned unit developments,
most construction is small scale even though it may involve an investment of several million dollars. Most follow the course of condominium developer Walter Witte of Kihei who, during a period
of spectacular growth and great expectations in the early 1970s,
said: "All I want is to get to work with no hassles, no special requests, and no variances."[17]

With large or small scale, economics is a prime concern. Entrepreneurs know they must at worst survive, at best make a profit. A knowledge of costs, land values, cost cutting, investor aspirations, and markets is a vital concern. So too are tax rates, political stability, construction costs, regional operating costs, demand, and knowledge of the ease with which a project can be sold in five, ten, or twenty years' time.

One phase is thought through and the next begins. What will be the development concept: luxury or budget hotels, condominiums, beach clubs, or second homes? The developer must find a site, acquire land, select a project team of specialists (planners, architects, engineers, hotel operators, marketing consultants); have a market feasibility study prepared; have plans and designs approved; arrange for financial analysis of the proposed operation; obtain financing in appropriate amounts and at reasonable terms; and arrange for the careful supervision of construction so that the job is done properly and on time.[18]

Developers' attitudes vary considerably. They are not necessarily those stereotyped by anti-development groups, though these can easily be found. Projects may range from shoestring, fast-return operations to those demanding excellence and a protracted period for a satisfactory return. Developers sensitive to the environment note changing community values and respond to questions concerning heights, materials, beach access, public use of setback areas, and shoreline protection.

A Development Ethic?

Across the state several plantation-owning developers have, at least in theory, an appreciation for the ways of Hawaii and an intuitive feeling for people's attitudes toward the land. But there are other developers who do not possess this consciousness. About these a Big Island planner says: "If standards are left completely to entrepreneurs . . . cheap exploitation of natural beauty and resources follows."[19]

There are many developers without a historic or sentimental attachment to Hawaii; they are more at home with oil, securities, lumber, or paper. For them island land is just a commodity, a useful hedge against inflation. In some ways they are not to be blamed. On the mainland, land as investment is as essentially American as the capitalistic system itself. In Hawaii such a system of exploitation ought not to be mindlessly put into play without modification. A sensitive, thoughtful knowledge of Hawaii would bring a much greater awareness of the worth of land and the economy and life-style that support it. The present situation is certainly in need of such.

To the insensitive newcomer who might say, "But that is our way," I would reply that our way is fine in its place, but in Hawaii unrestrained investment in real estate, tasteless design, and thoughtless development can destroy the physical and human resources on which tourism is based. It can destroy the industry itself. Respect and control can mean the perpetuation of an industry of excellence.

To provide for a healthy and satisfying environment, it is necessary to have at least a knowledge of the physical and biological processes of the tropics, an appreciation of social history, and enough understanding of aesthetics to allow building and design to be compatible with surroundings and in accord with the cultural traditions of long-time residents. Conservation, discussed later, I see largely as a philosophical approach to nature and society within a cultural context. In Hawaii the national context may be American, but the cultural context is not. Hawaii, as a special case, requires study and awareness beyond gestures and lip service to environment or life-style. I despair at the ineptitude of architects and planners who, trained elsewhere, are blind to the responsibility they bear, especially in small-scale developments. What does for Miami Beach does not automatically do for Kahana or Maalaea. Sadly, without strong opposition, without direction, such ineptitude often prevails.

On the more comforting side, there are several large-scale and impressive developments on Maui already (see following chapter). These are not alone. Good development can be found on every major island, created for the most part by large companies which have had an intimate connection with Hawaii's past. Although I may be challenged by the cynic who says, "What possible good does that do?" I would have to answer that in general it is better to have developers with a historical and social stake in Hawaii than those, other than financial, without a stake at all.

In many ways, one who sells land for development is as much a force for development as the developer himself—a *hapa* developer (part-developer), to coin a term. This is a person who makes land available for development and, consequently, bears as much economic and social responsibility as the subsequent developer. In a number of cases throughout Hawaii, large landowning companies have started or are planning to develop their own properties. The Campbell Estate, Alexander & Baldwin, the Lanai Company, C. Brewer, Amfac, the Bishop Estate, and Maui Land & Pineapple Co. are examples. But in other cases, *hapa* developers—agricultural companies, real estate brokers, estates, ranches, huis (consortiums), and individuals—have sold or leased land for development purposes. This category includes, the Robinson Estate on Oahu, the Parker Ranch on the Big Island, Princeville Ranch at Hanalei, the Knudsen Trust on Kauai, the Molokai Ranch on Molokai, and the Ulupalakua Ranch on Maui.

Ulupalakua is a classic case. Ulupalakua's first large sale, providing land for Wailea, was to the Matson Company in the mid-1950s. Pardee Erdman purchased the ranch in 1963, sold a large block at Kipahulu, then disposed of development land to George Hasegawa (Maui Meadows), Maui realtor Erling Wick, and through Valley Isle Realty to the Seibu Corporation (Makena Maui) to recover the $5 million purchase price in ten years.[20] These sales of over 9,000 acres represented about one-sixth of the total ranch area.

Legally, the owner of a parcel of land may sell it and there is no difference between one acre and thirty-thousand acres; but in practice, the scale of the sale and the purpose for which it will be used is critical. One owner may sell two acres of land for a fifty-unit condominium housing an average resident population of thirty persons. With appropriate zoning, this appears entirely acceptable. If, however, one owner sells 2,500 acres for development, the shared responsibility that person has is monumental. This is even more so if, before development, there is a further sale for purely speculative purposes. By these transactions, a settlement of 25,000 persons may ultimately grow in an area now occupied by 300. The economic and social impacts of the sale of 2,500 acres for resort-residential development is stunning in comparison with that of two acres, and the implications, as I describe later, are complex and far-reaching.

Relations with the Community

In the tourism industry, the developer is linked to the community in several ways. If it is an individual or a corporation associated with a particular individual, these links may assume great personal importance. Community members work on construction, later in the developed operations. Local companies may supply materials and service; locally owned shipping and local trucking get materials and equipment out to the site. The shape and design of buildings are discussed (but in no way determined) by the public; the quality, especially if development is within the coastal management zone, is examined by local government agencies and committees, and the finished project becomes a permanent monument, for good or bad, used by local people and visitors alike.

Of course, there is the developer who will buy resale condominium units at exorbitantly inflated prices so that the base price for units in his own proposed development nearby can be increased several thousand dollars, thus reflecting "current" values. There is also the practice of using illegitimate strawmen who will purchase condominium units and who will be replaced later by legitimate buyers; the effect is to create an immediate impression of stability and demand in order to influence genuine buyers, lending institutions, or government agencies.

Developers cater mainly to middle incomes, the rich, and the very rich. During the past few years even buyers in the middle income range have been eliminated by high condominium prices. During the buoyant conditions of fast growth development served, unfortunately, many local, modest income speculators. Because in general, in the most desirable parts of Hawaii, developers provide accommodation well out of the reach of the bulk of the population, great social distance may be created between resident occupiers who are most frequently in-migrants and local people or their families who, as the result of development, are often forced to live elsewhere in areas of lower land values or lower rents.

A Risky Business

A developer must not only make ends meet, he must survive—something of which the community is usually quite unaware. A knowledge of how to combat interest rates, where to get satisfactory financing, and how to select development partners in order to avoid power plays is essential. If a developer can answer the following, he very well may be on his way to success: How does one get a parcel of land zoned or rezoned? What are the local conventions and proven strategies for getting started and on the path toward approval? What attorney has the best success with the planning commission? Should one go into partnership with someone with local connections so as not to appear too greedy?

Development is a risky business. In all counties of Hawaii there are condominiums and hotels marginally surviving and major foreclosures are not uncommon. A recent statement by a developer noted that: "In the U.S., most of the developers who were in business two or three years ago [1974–1975] are now bankrupt."[21] This may not be the case in Hawaii; yet there are many who are forced to give up before the start. Developers of a moderate-to-large project may have to invest up to $10 million of their own money, depending on the size of the project, before loan commitments can be expected or other partners brought in. The working capital, front-end money, cannot be borrowed. Before significant investment takes place, the initial idea, with the aid of a private planner, must be translated into future costs and plans, and even something tangible on the ground is needed before a developer has real leverage. The risk factor is high; and for the developer this is a very nervous time.

Walter Witte says that a good project has something in it for everybody. The development hui must make money, the buyers must get a good return, and the general developer should be satisfactorily rewarded. As general partner in his own huis, his interest amounts to about 20 percent, at the same time that his limited partners, mainly Maui professional people, are assured of doubling, even tripling, their smaller investments by the time the project is completed. Their risk is limited only to the amount of their investment. The greatest risk taker in this formula is the general partner whose return reflects his added initiative and responsibilities. It is he who is involved in land acquisition, the development of a concept, procuring front-end money, and a whole host of other activities not the least of which is dealing with contractors, arranging for the timing of the project, and shepherding plans and documentation through legal procedures from start to finish.

The Power of Developers

Developers as individuals or groups of individuals exert tremendous power, much more than a corresponding number of citizens not in the business of developing. They have money and scarce land at their disposal; in Hawaii both mean power. Major resort developers have incredible impact. In numbers, they are a minority. In terms of individual projects, they have no equal. The major developers, already mentioned, all have large acreages at their disposal which could in theory provide for virtually indefinite tourism development.

This gives the large Hawaii landowner an immense advantage over developers who must buy land before they can start. The land they have owned for many years is often ridiculously undervalued. Other developers not associated with agribusiness would say, with good reason, land costs them nothing. Once development plans are announced and the land classified urban, the initial value skyrockets and the first costs of development are more than offset by windfall gains. Not only do landowners benefit from the immediate jump in land values but, also, from the heightened potential value of thousands of acres of company-owned land nearby, still classified agricultural.

Once development actually is underway, to protect his investment the developer relies on his team of experts. His public submissions must be efficient and well presented. By the time all materials are assembled for a large project the developer may then have a better understanding of the value of coastal resources than any other person in the community.

He then argues from a substantial position of knowledge and is usually more than a match for the general public and many community groups. The planning department and commission must constantly be on its toes and exert tremendous efforts just to keep pace with him and his battery of informants. Only by doing this will they be in a position to check proposed activities.

There is nothing sinister in development per se. On the contrary, indisputably, it has enhanced much within Hawaii. However, as a group, developers are no more or less ethical than any other group within society. They have tremendous power through economic influence; but their huge investments, which they always stand to lose, suggest that priorities in their struggle for survival and success may be narrowed to where they lose sight of the general community welfare. Consequently, the evolution of a Hawaii development ethic and firm, thoughtful regulation is necessary. Ability to achieve great advances for a community today is balanced by a similar potential for irreparable harm.

The Planners

Much of the detailed development work, the provision of creative design and technical expertise, and the moving of approval applications through the bureaucratic labyrinth falls to the lot of the private planner. He assesses trends, compensates for them, and acknowledges changing attitudes and values. In larger developments, as the physical planner he heads the developer's team. In overseeing a project like Kaanapali, veteran planner Adam Krivatsy sees six steps starting with essential intelligence and ending in implementation, the refinement and counterpart of development phasing already noted.[22] Simultaneously there is another parallel trend, responsive planning, involved with changing course or direction whenever necessary and bringing expansion of existing facilities into line with new travel trends, community values, and government legislation.

In principle the above is an ideal model; in practice it occurs only on larger planned unit developments. One searches, often in vain, for signs of the work of imaginative planning teams at Napili, Kahana, Honokowai and Kihei.

The only check on small-scale development—and before recent coastal zone regulations this was almost nonexistent—is through the county planning department. The public planner monitors developments, considers their compatibility with the general and community plans, and provides something of a gentle watchdog service. His is a life of frustration, treading the fine line between mayor, planning commission, council, developers, and the community. He not infrequently finds himself the adversary of his colleague, the private planner. Krivatsy feels public agencies in Hawaii should work closely with the private sector from the first phases of project planning to completion in order to eliminate lengthy evaluative and corrective processes which may be necessary later. He believes that involvement in the creative planning process would lead to a greater and different understanding of developers' objectives and ultimately greater public satisfaction with a job well done.[23]

In ideal circumstances, ideas generated in a planning office should move both upward to executive decision makers and downward to the community and its interest groups. Planners should be answerable to the public in two ways: first, through the mayor, the planning commission, and the council; second, more directly to public groups themselves. Developers are well served by both private and public planners. Similar services are infrequently provided the public. One notable exception is the Maui County planner who works closely with the residents of Lahaina.

In 1973, Donald Wolbrink prepared a set of tourism planning guidelines suitable for use in Maui or in other counties.[24] In it he draws attention to the unassailable importance of the resident who traditionally has received much less attention than the other two principals—the visitor industry and the visitor.

Wolbrink states bluntly that the major interest of the visitor industry is to make money. It is a simple economic fact that in order to remain in a competitive business, the visitor industry must maintain itself and produce a reasonable amount of profit for its supporters.[25] This being the case, and with the understanding that if expectations are reasonably met, little is heard from the visitors, then a tremendous responsibility rests with the residents and with their agents, the public planners. A few politicians are aware of what they might do but too infrequently speak on the people's behalf. Wolbrink's commentary continues: "Since the residents have a much greater commitment to islands than do either of the other groups [the industry and the visitor], a careful study of their needs is much more important than those of the others. The resident must deal with the lasting consequences of poorly planned development, while the visitors and the industry enjoy a mobility that would allow them to escape an unpopular situation. A careful analysis of the needs and interests of the residents must be developed and the mechanism for updating this information must be [found]."[26] It is unnecessary to analyze the entire document except to say that great attention is paid to citizen participation at every planning step including the initial one.

In this present study I frequently have observed that resident input has been ignored, called for halfheartedly, or has come into conflict with the views of forceful specialist resident groups. The public planner more than any other public official has an obligation to do much for this very important group. Previous or contemporary planning may ultimately bring the resident into conflict with industry developers. The developer wants his own plan to be flexible allowing for rapid changes after construction has started quickly to accommodate a new trend in general economic conditions. The public planner understands this as do many residents, but frequently both would like a binding contract for development to proceed on an approved course because of its critical impact on human habitation. In addition, local government must have adequate time to accommodate to demands in infrastructure made by a proposal and to plan for its implementation in an efficient manner.[27] The impact of the tourist industry can be stupendous allowing little room for unilateral action. Nevertheless, the developer's concern for flexibility is legitimate and another argument for the only sensible planning arrangement, that is, continuing dialogue between all groups—planners, industry, and residents—from the beginning.

What Now?

There is no doubt that some community members who sold land for development have never had it so good, but some are having second thoughts about the scale of development in their midst. In the last quarter of 1979 the number of visitors arriving on Maui dropped markedly. This led to a reevaluation of the character of past development as the November county election brought the message home to politicians, especially the newly elected Mayor Hannibal Tavares, that the "people felt Maui had grown too fast" resulting in "hodge-podge development especially in Lahaina and Kihei."[28] "Overdependence on tourism" is how Roger Knox of the Maui Chamber of Commerce describes it: "We've got a real problem on Maui."[29]

The beginning of the eighties saw new emphases on seeking solutions to problems inherited from the past: a monumental sewage system problem (which had not been disclosed), the provision of affordable housing, an adequate water supply especially for upcountry residents, a mounting level of crime, congested roads, and the problem of energy. Every item either stems from tourism or impacts on it.

On the question of growth Mayor Tavares says, "Maui has grown too fast. What we need now is quality growth."[30] At the time of writing, part of the problem had already been solved. As Kirk Spitzer puts it, "It was nice while it lasted but Maui's steamroller visitor industry has come to a screeching halt. . . . It slipped last year to a miserable 1.4 percent. Worse, visitor arrivals for the first two months of [1980] were down an unheard of 13 percent."[31]

Development growth in West Maui's Kapalua-Kaanapali tourism region has been considerable. Two case studies from the region follow. One study highlights Kaanapali, the first Hawaii development of major proportions outside Waikiki and one of the oldest planned unit developments in the state. The other study is of Kapalua whose developers feel is the creation of something quite unusual on Maui.

CHAPTER 4

Case Studies From Maui

Kaanapali: Hawaii's First Planned Resort
Study No. 1

KAANAPALI, a thriving, high quality resort, is historically important in the record of Hawaii tourism. Its creation was a turning point in the visitor industry of the state and in the economy of Maui where it was a revitalizing factor in the largely neglected West Maui region. Although to its developer, Amfac, it might be regarded "strictly as an earnings proposition,"[1] it has played many parts socially and economically above and beyond its primary cash flow role. It became a standard which subsequent large developments have sought to emulate (fig. 6).

Kaanapali, like Amfac itself, is a success story. In 1960 its original six hundred acres supported two hundred in sugar cane and the other four hundred in grazing land. There were three employees looking after the sugar and a payroll of $16,500. The gross income was $18,500, and only $1,400 was paid in property taxes. In the mid-1970s, the resort had more than two thousand employees, a payroll of $12.3 million, and a gross income of $45 million. Income taxes paid to the state were near $1.8 million, and property taxes paid to the county were just under $1 million.[2] By 1980 the operative area had increased to 1200 acres.

Profits went to Amfac, Hawaii's largest conglomerate, which started its history in an earlier century as H. Hackfeld & Co. and then became, along with Alexander & Baldwin, one of Hawaii's large factors serving the sugar industry. Besides hotel operations on all neighbor islands, agricultural operations in California and Hawaii, and sugar production, Amfac owns the Liberty House retail stores, and is one of the country's major wholesale merchan-

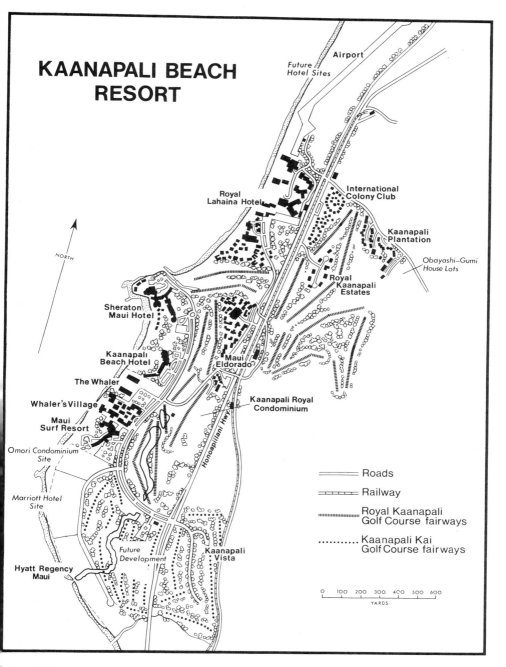

KAANAPALI BEACH RESORT

NORTH

Airport

Future Hotel Sites

Royal Lahaina Hotel

International Colony Club

Kaanapali Plantation

Obayashi–Gumi House Lots

Royal Kaanapali Estates

Sheraton Maui Hotel

Kaanapali Beach Hotel

Maui Eldorado

The Whaler

Whaler's Village

Kaanapali Royal Condominium

Maui Surf Resort

Omori Condominium Site

Honoapiilani Hwy.

Marriott Hotel Site

Future Development

Kaanapali Vista

Hyatt Regency Maui

Roads

Railway

Royal Kaanapali Golf Course fairways

Kaanapali Kai Golf Course fairways

0   100   200   300   400   500   600
YARDS

Figure 6.

disers. In 1977 the company's operations had revenues exceeding $1.7 billion. Thus, although important, Kaanapali represents only a small part of Amfac's activities. Recently, the giant United States conglomerate Gulf & Western, as a stockholder of Amfac, has taken an increasing interest in the company's activities. It has assured Amfac that its presence will in no way compromise internal policy.

For almost twenty years the area has been the hub of the Maui tourist industry. It was the first planned integrated resort area in Hawaii and initiated a major thrust by a neighbor island into the tourism market. With a larger area than Waikiki, wide open spaces, and few hotels, it became a restful and aesthetic antidote to frenetic Honolulu.

The development was begun during a gloomy period for West Maui when Baldwin Packers—Lahaina's pineapple canners—had closed, labor in both the pineapple and sugar industries was unstable, and employment in agriculture was falling drastically. Much has been achieved, and community values have changed. Now, as the community looks to the future and attempts to assess the benefits of the industry, voices are mixed. Inevitably there are some who see developments like Kaanapali as a panacea for all ills while others view them as objectionable, concrete symbols.

Nature and History

Well before Caucasians came to the Hawaiian Islands, Black Rock, the spectacular shoreline rock outcrop in the center of Kaanapali, was the site of an ancient Hawaiian *heiau* (worshiping ground). Later, in the mid-eighteenth century, when Lahaina was a whaling center, some of the activity associated with the industry extended to Kaanapali. Today through resort design, function, and advertising, this whaling theme has again come to be applied as well to Kaanapali, several miles north.

In the early 1950s, the undeveloped resort site on the low gentle slopes of the West Maui mountains looked very different. Winds and *kona* (south) storms had piled ridges of sand behind a wide and attractive beach both north and south of Black Rock. Except for two strips of cultivated sugar, much of the area was covered in thickets of low kiawe, an introduced, thorny, dry-land tree with delicate fern-like leaves. Both horses and cattle grazed the area.

There were few indicators of human use—the limited area of sugar, an access road, and a rudimentary air strip occasionally used for plantation spraying. Cattle fattening pens and a slaughter house occupied a few acres near Black Rock, and nearby storage tanks supplied fuel to the power plant to the north. Close by were some plantation residences and a club house built on the beach near the rock.[3]

The rugged dark beach promontory contrasted magnificently with the light-colored sandy beaches, and the rock itself helped form the sandy bay to the south while giving shelter for a deep-water landing from which barge traffic moved to and from Honolulu. Here the Pioneer Mill Co. owned two and a half miles of very attractive ocean frontage. As we would expect, the beaches are today a focus of recreational activity.

Unlike Wailea which experiences strong trade winds, Kaanapali is protected by the West Maui mountains. Skies over the coast are clear and rainfall is only 16 inches a year. Mean temperatures are in the mid-seventies which means that in the warmest part of the day they rise to the middle and high eighties, but dry air and welcome light breezes never allow conditions to become oppressive. Beach and climate are major assets to which may be added the constantly changing beauty of the often cloud-shrouded mountains, the offshore islands of Lanai and Molokai, waving fields of sugar cane, and the town of Lahaina.

Plan, Revise, and Plan Again

When new notions of other possible uses crossed the minds of Pioneer Mill directors in the early 1950s, the company controlled some fifteen thousand acres in West Maui. Of this, over nine thousand acres were in sugar. What eventually took place was not entirely a surprise. Since the 1930s, Lahaina residents had talked about the seafront potential of Kaanapali while the local depression and the financial difficulties of Pioneer Mill during 1948–1953 directed thinking toward widening the company's resource base.[4]

Kaanapali had some of its early experiences later repeated by almost every major resort development in Hawaii. Plan followed plan, modification was a constant procedure. Belt, Collins and Associates, which has probably been associated with more major developments in the Pacific than any other group of planners, started the process in 1953 when it evaluated the possibilities of the coastal lands. A later plan devised by Donald Wolbrink for Harland Bartholemew and Associates went further than the first, enlarged the scope, and looked closely at economic matters.[5] The owners were advised to move quickly before some other development stole the show and prevented the Lahaina area from realizing its full potential. The Royal Lahaina, the first hotel, was finished in 1962. A golf course and other hotels followed.

By the late 1960s, further reevaluations were made and John Carl Warneke and Associates was retained to prepare a master plan. It was on the basis of these plans and past knowledge that Kaanapali proposals were then incorporated into the county's Lahaina 701 plan. Then in accordance with the district plan, the Kaanapali master plan was revised at least three times.[6]

The Resort Today

Kaanapali now is the most extensively developed of any large-scale planned project in the state. By the end of the 1970s, it had almost 4,500 units completed or under construction. With almost 3,800 hotel units (table 11), Kaanapali has maintained a mix of hotels and condominiums which, in the eyes of many administrators and observers, is closer to the ideal than most resort areas in Hawaii. The ratio of hotels to condominiums is approximately 6 to 1. Although the first, it obviously did not provide the Maui model where the ratio is closer to 4 to 1 in favor of condominiums.

As one drives from Lahaina north to Napili Bay, Honoapiilani Highway cuts right through the resort. There is little break be-

TABLE 11. *Kaanapali Resort Accomodations, 1980*

Name[a]	Type	Units	Site
Royal Lahaina	Hotel	735	Beach
International Colony Club	Condominium	42	Mauka highway
Kaanapali Plantation	Condominium	62	Mauka highway
Sheraton Maui	Hotel	503	Beach
Maui Eldorado	Condominium	204	Makai highway
Kaanapali Beach	Hotel	430	Beach
The Whaler	Condominium	360	Beach
Royal Kaanapali u/c	Condominium	105	Makai highway
Maui Surf	Hotel	556	Beach
Marriot Hotel u/c	Hotel	720	Beach
Hyatt Regency Maui	Hotel	820	Beach
CATEGORY TOTAL	Hotel	3,764	
CATEGORY TOTAL	Condominium[b]	773	
RESORT TOTAL	All categories	4,537	

SOURCES: Amfac, Hawaii Visitors Bureau, *Maui News, Hawaii Business.*
[a] Listed north to south
[b] Condominium total is a changing quantity. It is usual for each condominium complex to have some units classified as hotel units. These are not shown as such above. Table 8, which relies heavily on *Hawaii Business,* lists only those condominiums available for rental. This table lists total capacity.

tween the last buildings associated with Lahaina and the southern-most extension of the newer Kaanapali Kai or Executive Golf Course. This golf course is one of the two 18-hole courses which are pivotal to the area, assuring the maintenance of large restful areas of green open space. The other course is the Royal Kaanapali farther north.

Most tourism activity is on the makai side of the road. Part way along the highway an imposing entrance, the first of three, leads to the new Hyatt Regency Maui, a slightly smaller Marriott Hotel under construction, and the older Maui Surf Hotel. The three are the last of a line of beachfront hotels starting in the north with the Royal Lahaina Hotel. Farther south, Black Rock is the site of the Sheraton Maui Hotel whose architecture blends appropriately with the volcanic configuration of the promontory. Farther south still are the Kaanapali Beach Hotel and the Whaler. At a higher elevation on the makai side of the highway is the Maui Eldorado, a condominium-type apartment hotel, while south of the Whaler, one of the high-priced condominium complexes of Maui, is the Whalers Village, an attractive shopping center and museum, both with whaling as a central theme.

Mauka of the highway, except for the Royal Kaanapali Golf Course, which straddles it, the area is essentially residential. From the highway at several places it is possible to look down and across the fairways of the golf course to the ocean. Three major open corridors, free from building, have been preserved to allow a spectacular unobstructed view of the ocean. In addition, fairways separate the hotels north of Black Rock from those to the south and also segregate one residential area from another. Not everywhere does the prospect please. At times the highway passes through cuttings where graded side walls present a less than attractive aspect, and to the north, openness is replaced by anomalous poorly planned clutter.

Beyond this point, the small planes of Royal Hawaiian Airlines and other small aircraft land on Amfac's airstrip thereby saving visitors an hour or more travel from the Maui airport at Kahului. As the result of heavy use and a need for the land, Amfac and Hawaiian Airlines have conducted negotiations which they hope will lead to a new and larger airport three miles south of Lahaina.

One of the greatest problems in resort operation now being faced on Maui is employee housing. The previous mayor made it clear that employee housing is not an extra—not a bonus—but an essential element in the costing of development. The county devel-

Two views of hotel design. Sensitive use of terrain was made at Black Rock, in the foreground. In the middleground, later construction reflects the greatest possible use of highly valuable beachfront property, at Kaanapali, Hawaii's major planned destination area. (Amfac photo)

oped a formula which must be followed: one housing unit for four employees.

Housing became critical with the Hemmeter proposal for the Hyatt Regency Hotel. Building was held up until Amfac and the developers worked out a scheme to build worker houses above Pioneer Mill at Kelawea Mauka. The same rules were applied to the Marriott Hotel.

Employee housing is critical. West Maui studio apartments rent for $400 a month, $700 for one- and two-bedroom apartments, $1,200 for three-bedroom units. Hotel employees are filling the lower priced units to the brim.[7] These are highly undesirable conditions for semipermanent mainland workers who are likely, because of this, to become disenchanted with hotel employment in the area. It is much worse for resident families who see West Maui as their permanent home. Housing, the county says, must be made available at prices workers can pay, either directly from the developer who is allowed a profit margin of 2 percent or, if this makes for too high a price, from the county who will buy from the developer and then institute for the employee a purchase-option rental program. Because it seemed impossible to build sufficient houses, employers recently were asked to hire only a limited, stated number of employees who would need housing. Those already living in the district were given preference. The former mayor, taking a tough stance, made it clear that housing was the developers' responsibility because they derived so much from Maui. The provision of housing could be considered a reciprocal act. "No housing, no development" was the theme at the time.

Implementation and Changing Goals

The ultimate master plan in the 1960s saw as basic a close relationship with Lahaina. It also viewed the entire region as a whole and Kaanapali as an integral part. An important question frequently asked was, "How can Kaanapali contribute to Lahaina and how can Lahaina enhance Kaanapali?"[8] Lahaina was considered so critical that a plan was drawn for the town but was never published.

Nobody can claim that Lahaina has been overlooked. The planned cane-haul railway connection between Kaanapali and Lahaina was implemented as a visitor attraction, but the close association between the two envisioned by planners never eventuated. Informants close to the scene indicate that Amfac lost interest in Lahaina when it sold its Lahaina shopping center. Amfac at the time said its actions were designed to create better relations with the Lahaina community. If most of its Lahaina properties were sold, the company felt it would lose its historic "lord and master" image in the eyes of the community.

The resort shopping center was a device to increase the average length of a visitor's stay at Kaanapali. But by paying special attention to the center, Amfac competed with similar shopping complexes in Lahaina; no effort was made to hide the fact that another reason for the resort shopping center was to create a self-sufficiency and lessen dependence on other areas.

Despite early notions about the relationship of Kaanapali and Lahaina, it is largely understood now that the resort will always remain separate from the town and, with time, forced togetherness means very little. The bulk of the town's population is made up of newcomers who have little interest in the past except as it reflects on their personal endeavors in Lahaina. Even if the marriage of the two areas did not work, Amfac Kaanapali managers have done much for Maui, and although the project remained separate, they personally were embraced as valuable and helpful members of the Lahaina community.

Although there was no symbiotic relationship between the resort and town, Kaanapali guests do shop in Lahaina, and Kaanapali employees do live in Lahaina. Townsfolk from time to time have a night on the town at the resort. Each group needs the other. The Lahaina community is not beyond basking in any kudos Kaanapali might receive from outside.

Some Future Changes

Amfac views the future in a pragmatic manner. It has recently sold several beachfront hotel sites to the Campbell Estate, the group from whom Amfac bought the property in the first place. The Kaanapali Beach Hotel has been disposed of and also the area occupied by the Kaanapali Royal condominium. Henry A. Walker, Jr., chairman and president of Amfac, said the sales are part of the company's ongoing program of harvesting values from its developed properties and investing the funds thus derived in other growing parts of Amfac's diverse businesses.[9] As the company is concerned with its own corporate future rather than that of Kaanapali, the threshold could be reached some time in the future when Kaanapali could not be considered an Amfac project. This could be the situation in other Hawaii projects and although understandable would not be at all desirable from the tourism viewpoint.

Amfac in the past has not been able to exercise the control over all aspects of development some planners felt should ideally be the case. Hotel management finds it difficult to serve two masters, its own and Amfac; consequently, the greater the control exercised by Amfac, the greater the possibility of conflict. In purely economic terms, conditions which allow hotel operations, within limits, to make the most profits also produce the most for the developer. Over the long haul such a situation can change the direction of tourism. Now, rather than the luxury clientele envisaged by planners, 40 to 50 percent of visitors are members of tour groups. This allows higher occupancy rates, makes the stockholders happy, but destroys the early paper image of the discriminating FIT maintaining a destination area of distinction.

Amfac has, however, achieved its aims albeit much less specifically than those of the planners: "The retention of a non-Waikiki aspect and the maintenance of views, vistas, a rural atmosphere, open spaces, and the old Hawaiian aloha spirit can still be maintained," said Peter Sanborn, former Amfac officer, "when the accommodation figure has reached 5,000–6,000 units." But to do this, all available hotel space along the entire Kaanapali shore would be taken up as well as other designated hotel sites inland.

Others have obviously seen the situation differently. In April 1979 when the 720-unit Marriott Hotel was announced, former Mayor Elmer Cravalho said, "It is my understanding that this is the last hotel scheduled for Kaanapali." When asked whether the hotel was needed, he gave the roundabout unexpected answer that from the point of view of the industry it was. "They're overflowing, booked up for the year." But he added, "I'm concerned about density in the area and the developers constantly criticize us because we're always at them to keep it down." Despite the mayor's assertions, hotel land is available at Kaanapali and I cannot believe that Kaanapali has seen anywhere near the end of development.[10]

The northern end of the development has been undergoing planning for several years and part of it will accommodate the "Hawaiian Sea Village," a $4 million "living arts center" on seven acres now occupied by the Kaanapali airstrip. The project, the brainchild of Amfac's Walker, will feature arts, crafts, dancing, and music of Hawaii. It had the encouragement of the mayor and leadership of Herb Kane, well-known Hawaiian artist and historian. "Although it is hoped that the village will pay its own way by virtue of its attractiveness to visitors, profit is not the primary motive behind Amfac's decision to go ahead with this development. Authenticity and excellence of presentation in a setting designed for demonstrating and perpetuating the Hawaiian arts and crafts provide the guiding purpose for this project," Walker said.[11]

The thought that traditional Hawaiian skills should be encouraged is admirable, but authentic it cannot be. To the Hawaiian, art was a part of everyday life. Spectators, not guests, unknown and uninvited, conveyed in canoes to view the activity is hardly part of "authentic" ancient tradition. Amfac is to be congratulated for going so far but that its creation could not be divorced from tourism is sad. What has been conceived is for visitors and only incidentally for the people of Maui.

In 1976 the Hawaii Resort Developers Conference met for a

workshop which, among other things, established the status at the time of all major developments. Kaanapali was then employing 2,250 workers, just half the number it projected for the completed project. The population of the area seen in terms of a daily visitor count together with permanent residents was close to 6,000. In the mid-1970s, private investment in the project area was around $150 million.[12] Thinking back to 1960, this was spectacular to say the least, but at the time of the workshop there was something of a hiatus in activity at Kaanapali. The Maui Surf Hotel had long since been completed, and the Whaler was brand new.

The lull was brief indeed. Before too long, at a time when the mayor was making public utterances to the effect that "enough is enough," Kaanapali was embarking on a period of activity the like of which it had not seen before. The Campbell Estate had just bought beachfront hotel land, and Ohbayashi-Gumi indicated its intention to develop houselots while a group proposed to develop the Kaanapali Royal condominium. Honolulu developer Chris Hemmeter started work on the Hyatt Regency Maui; its beachfront partner, Marriott, was drawing plans for another large hotel while a possible neighbor, Pundy Yokouchi of Maui's Valley Isle Realty, had plans for a condominium (Kaanapali Alii) on fifteen acres near the two hotels.[13] All this did not include Amfac's own plans for the northern part of the project.

This activity was taking place when employee housing seemed an impossible situation and the administration was practicing the politics of saying no. As perceived by its managers, investors, and developers, the industry had never looked better. This was before great energy shortages, a major airline strike, and a deteriorating national economy. So looked the situation as Kaanapali approached the eighties. By 1981 all foregoing planned proposals were completed or underway and the Amfac properties group considered that there was still room for worthwhile development.

Kapalua: Transformation of the Old Honolua Plantation
Study No. 2

Kapalua, along with Seibu's Makena development, is one of the latest major projects on Maui. As an entity it will be of moderate size and not on the scale of Kaanapali or Wailea. It is the stated intention of the owner, Maui Land & Pineapple Co. (ML&P), to create an area with such a distinctive character that when compared with other resorts the differences will be immediately apparent. In the words of Kapalua's master plan, it would be a "first-quality destination resort-residential community."[14] More than this, ML&P has been intent on developing a resort so elegant that it is thought of as "world class" rather than in merely local or national terms. To this extent, I feel it has gone a long way toward achieving its goal.

The Kapalua project area is part of the makai portion of Honolua plantation. The plantation proper occupies a pie-shaped wedge of land extending from peaks high in the West Maui mountains to a base which occupies much of Maui's northern coast. The center of tourism development is focused on Kapalua Bay (Fleming Beach) from which the project derives its name (fig. 7).

An Old Plantation Base

Kapalua is the development of the Kapalua Land Co., a subsidiary of ML&P. The parent company controls close to 34,200 acres on Maui. Of this, 10,300 acres are in pineapples—3,500 acres at Honolua. From Honolua, pineapples are hauled to ML&P's cannery at Kahului.

The plantation was originally part of the holdings of H. P. Baldwin, son of Dwight Baldwin and one of the founders of Alexander & Baldwin. After H. P. Baldwin's death in 1911, the plantation was incorporated as Baldwin Packers, Ltd. Thus, the present leadership of ML&P has roots deep in Hawaii's history. The story goes back to 1835 when the Reverend Dwight Baldwin arrived in Lahaina as a missionary, twelve years after the mission was started. Today Dwight Baldwin's name is associated closely with the Baldwin House, an impressive historical building and a focal point on Front Street in the center of Lahaina.

The Baldwin name, an essential part of Maui history, has been associated with sugar, ranching, the management of Alexander & Baldwin (A&B), and its pineapple producing subsidiary before the establishment of ML&P in 1969. At mid-century, leadership of A&B, which controlled the pineapple lands, Baldwin Packers, Maui Pineapple Co., and much of the sugar on Maui was in the hands of the extended Baldwin family. This included the Camerons who have provided the leadership for ML&P since its inception. Colin Cameron, grandson of Harry A. Baldwin was, at the time, general manager of the Maui Pineapple Co. As a result of increasing costs, Baldwin Packers merged with Maui Pineapple Co.

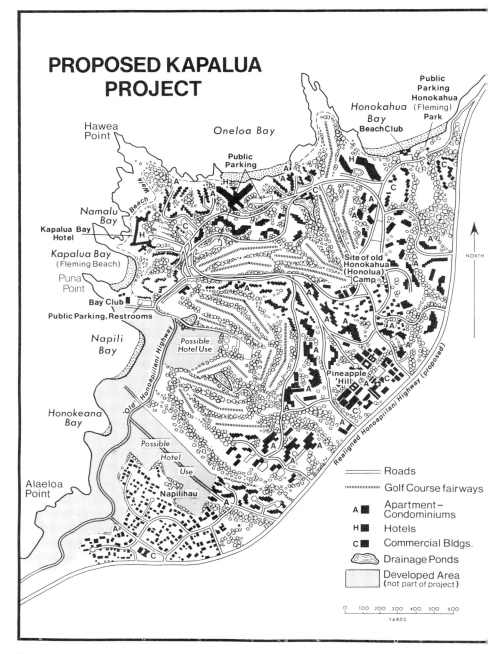

Figure 7.

in 1962, and Cameron remained as manager of the merged concern.

In the late 1960s, A&B felt it necessary to reorganize. This could have meant divesting itself of its pineapple holdings or buying out the interests of the Cameron family, the main minority shareholder in the company. The latter course was tried but abandoned; in 1969, after what Frederick Simpich calls "a bitter fight," the Cameron group arranged to take over A&B's interests in the pineapple business, and ML&P came into being as an independent corporation.[15] Colin Cameron resigned as a director of Alexander & Baldwin after he became president of the now autonomous ML&P.

The company today is a public corporation with Colin Cameron, his mother, sister, and children owning 52 percent of the shares. Upon the death of his father, J. Walter Cameron, Colin became chairman of the board and president of the Maui Publishing Company. His mother took over as publisher of the *Maui News*. Through its manifold activities including prominence in Maui communications, control of the fourth largest private parcel of land on Maui, and employment of more than five hundred persons, the family influences directly and indirectly a wide spectrum of island activities and people. The Kapalua development will significantly widen this sphere of influence in decades to come.

This brief history of ML&P and its relationship with A&B is appropriate here and is fundamental to an understanding of both Kapalua and Wailea as, up to 1969, much of their administrative histories were held in common. Both projects have relationships with individuals who have spent lifetimes in Hawaii, especially on Maui, and assert they feel a responsibility toward the land others do not. Although this and similar assertions do not guarantee responsible developments, the conviction is critical, nonetheless, as many projects have but a tenuous and superficial connection with Hawaii. The smallness of ML&P allows for a personal touch and an intuitive feeling as to what Mauians will approve. The personal concern of a local family, in particular of Colin Cameron and his determination to succeed, has had much to do with the public's response and distinction the project has so far achieved.

Brooding Mountains and Exciting Seascapes

The area planned and known as Kapalua is close to 600 acres and extends from Alaeloa northeastward to the most distant end of Honokahua Bay (fig. 7). Along this coastline are three golden coral sand beaches, rocky volcanic headlands, and the beautiful rock-girt tiny indentation of Namalu Bay. These are the places the project will emphasize.

Most Hawaii developments focus on beaches, and one-fifth of Kapalua's coastline is beach. The first, most southerly, and best known of the three beaches is Fleming or Kapalua Beach. It creates a distinctive 300-foot sandy crescent which slopes gradually inland and merges with well-trimmed grassy sward, shade-giving kiawes, and handsome *lauhala* (pandanus). Inland from the sandline is one of the most beautiful coconut groves to be found anywhere in Hawaii. It is here above the bay where the first hotel has been built.

The beach, well-protected and safe, has limited sandy patches beyond the waterline but always adequate for sunbathing. Both headlands are interesting for the diver but in the bay proper, especially in the north, there is much dead coral and at times copious plant life.

The middle beach north of Kapalua is Oneloa, perhaps the least known of the project beaches. Its 1,250 feet of sand is backed by an abrupt rise originally clothed with kiawe, scrubby koa haole *(Leucaena glauca)*, and ironwoods *(Casuarina equisetifolia)*. The beach has well-developed coral formations and deceptive swimming conditions. From a recreation point of view, it is the least valuable of three fine beaches.

Honokahua, the longest beach with 1,500 feet of sand, will eventually be as popular as the smaller and more densely occupied Kapalua Beach. Its size will ensure less crowding, and it has the only good surfing potential of the three. Its deficiency in comparison with Kapalua Beach is its lack of protection from both storm waves and wind. Its strengths are its good sandy bottom, its backing by one of the most impressive plantings of mature ironwoods found on Maui, and its beach park facilities provided by ML&P. Formerly this beach, because of its relative isolation, was little known except by local people of the immediate area, but it has become familiar to visitors.

Unlike the Wailea or Kaanapali projects, Kapalua is given limited protection by the inland mountains. Humidity can be high and, given the right conditions, the sweet smell of pineapple is evident downwind along with the pervasive hint of rotting vegetation. Again in contrast to the desert landscape of Wailea, the Honokahua and Honolua valleys are clothed in tropical rain forest interspersed with occasional shiny-leafed breadfruit trees or decorative exotics such as monkeypod or mango. Rainfall between thirty and forty inches is not high but higher than for any other major area on that coast.

More than half the project area was originally used for growing pineapples, and there is a lot of pineapple land left. Patterned parallel stripes decorate the remaining amphitheater-like Napili basin, the raised plateau areas mauka of Kapalua Bay, and the flattened interfluves between half a dozen deep valleys which radiate from the West Maui mountains. Over much of the first phase development area, the "original" cover is unattractive scrubby vegetation, kiawe, koa haole, and ironwood mixed with occasional aloe plants and other exotics. This was one of the first areas to be used for a golf course and for planting in a surface and landscape transformation about which few would complain. Part of the landscaped area terminates abruptly at the shoreline with stark clipped headlands below which white breakers crash.

In the project area and beyond are indigenous forest trees and enclaves of decorative exotics planted by former plantation manager David Fleming. The trees about the former Honolua village and near the old plantation manager's house on Pineapple Hill are particularly attractive, but the pièce de résistance is a magnificent double-lined Cook and Norfolk pine *(Araucaria excelsa)* avenue of giant trees leading from near Kapalua Beach to the top of Pineapple Hill with a branch to the site of the former Honolua plantation village—something which will always lend a distinctive character to Kapalua.

Hazards Natural and Human

Not long ago, guests of the Napili Kai Beach Club just south of Kapalua felt they were about to be swept out to sea as water in russet-red torrents cascaded down the slopes, flowed through the hotel lobby, across the landscaped lawn, and out to sea. It took weeks to remove the ravages of red topsoil stripped from pineapple fields. What was not swept out to sea was dumped unceremoniously anywhere water velocity was checked.

Without a doubt the major natural problem affecting the area is its potential for flooding. Over twelve major floods have been recorded during the past twenty-five years. Cropping has affected soil moisture retention, and clearing of the natural vegetation for sugar and pineapple has increased runoff. Before more intensive settlement, the major damage was coastal siltation. This still occurs to an extent and the flood hazard is now exacerbated by further clearing, landscape change, and heavy coastal settlement.

Kapalua management is very much aware of the possibility of flooding and damage. Constant attention has been paid to engineering; and the project design is integrated with the *Honolua Watershed Work Plan,* a scheme sponsored by the West Maui Soil and Water Conservation District, Maui County, and the Soil Conservation Service.

Great care is also taken to manage properly adjacent coastal waters. With this in mind, ML&P has commissioned a number of marine surveys. Perhaps the major step taken was the creation of a marine life conservation district in Honolua Bay by the state, the result of prior investigations, an application, and finally a presentation by the company. The motivation was straightforward and admirable. The marine life and ecology relationships of Honolua Bay were worth preserving. Population in the area was increasing, coastal waters were being used more intensively than ever before, and soon the Kapalua resort would be responsible for adding more pressure to a rather critical environment. It would be true to say that without the initiative shown by the company, the bay would not be protected.

A Concept Develops

In 1966 ML&P, while still a subsidiary of A&B, asked Western Management Consultants to study the economic feasibility of turning Honolua Plantation into a resort destination area. This was four years after the first building at Kaanapali, and at a time when it seemed obvious that tourism on Maui would be a successful venture.[16] The Matson Navigation Company was contemporaneously planning for Wailea.

Belt, Collins and Associates Ltd. of Honolulu simultaneously drew up a preliminary engineering study and later a physical plan. By 1968 the possibility of doing something with Honolua Plantation was plausible enough for its inclusion in the county's plan for West Maui. ML&P's subsequent planning showed commendable caution. It proceeded at a rate appropriate to its financial capacity which allowed time to learn something from the mistakes of others and to develop its own distinctive philosophy.

Unlike other projects on Maui, part of the area had been settled for decades. At the northeastern end of the area, Honokahua Village (Honolua Camp) of around eighty-five houses supported a small community of four hundred persons. Houses were old and needed constant repair, and services such as sewage disposal were a continual problem. Because of this, and after approval by union representatives, the company made a decision to relocate the camp to a nearby site now known as Napilihau. As a result, the new housing development and Kapalua were planned with both in mind.

Consistent with its conservative approach and to inform potential financial supporters of the project, ML&P organized a series of workshops in May 1970 at the Napili Kai Beach Club. Eighteen specialists in planning, architecture, development, and finance were invited to discuss problems of front-end and overall project financing, fiscal arrangements in tight money situations, managerial policies, minibus transportation systems, and strategies for preserving environmental quality. Four months later, Real Estate Affiliates, Inc., of Aspen, Colorado, started a comprehensive marketing research study.

A year after the first seminar, a more specialized design workshop took place. Members' roles were to challenge positions, analyze concepts, and evaluate designs concerning Kapalua. The Belt, Collins general plan, now completed, was used as a vehicle for discussion; philosophical questions as to what Kapalua was and why it should be visited were asked and the answers minutely scrutinized in what participants recall as an almost encounter-group atmosphere. Design objectives and policies came under fire in an all out effort to refine the first phase of the plan and to draw up a critical time path for this and later phases.

ML&P, its subsidiary Honolua Plantation Land Co. (now Kapalua Land Co.), its physical planners Belt, Collins and Associates, architects and planners Leitch, Kiyotoki and Associates, and architects and planning consultants Ernest J. Kump Associates were all represented.[17] From this meeting concepts were crystalized, and although many details were changed and the philosophy modified, most of the main points emerged as fundamental in the Belt, Collins–Charles Luckman updated master plan publicly submitted in May and June 1973. This document represented the distillation of thought and study and liaison work with the staff of the Maui planning department.

I shall not attempt to present an exhaustive list of the procedures which followed. The point here is to indicate the colossal task that confronts a developer before and during development. First, when the land was virtually all classified agricultural, it was necessary to make submissions to the State Land Use Commission through the County Planning Commission to have land designated as urban. Later, it was necessary to present plans for the consideration of the Maui County Planning Commission to modify the original Lahaina 701 plan. This amendment was approved by the County Planning Commission in 1973 when the master plan was submitted. Step I of Kapalua Planned Unit Development (PUD), written description and concept, came in 1974. In 1975, Step II, detailed site approval, was authorized. Others followed. Simultaneously, the Napilihau project for the resettlement of the occupants of Honolua village underwent review with various categories of plans. Every important planning step in both Kapalua and Napilihau had to be approved by the planning commission and this meant presentations, public hearings, and approval by the planning department. Napilihau needed approval by Hawaii Housing Authority, the Federal Housing Authority and, before money could be released by the governor, an environmental impact statement.

Several other important independent studies of Kapalua were made. These included a second economic assessment by Western Management Consultants; evaluations by the two architectural firms already mentioned; financial and marketing projection monitoring by the Omnimetrics Corporation, Los Angeles; a golf course plan by Arnold Palmer and architect Francis J. Duane; a marine environment study by Environment Consultants Inc., Honolulu; a geological study by Dames and Moore; and the Kapalua master plan by Belt, Collins and Associates Ltd. and architecture and planning consultants Charles Luckman Associates. The master plan also used more generalized studies by Western Management Consultants, U.S. Soil Conservation Service, and the Hawaii Visitors Bureau.

The above list did not take into consideration ML&P's assessment of the community, which expressed little if any hostility, and company frustration in trying to find development money. In June 1973 the Ogden Development Company, slated to be a partner in development, cancelled its agreement with ML&P; ML&P immediately searched for another suitable source of financing. In July 1975, as the result of what it decided was inappropriate design, ML&P scrapped its plans for the first hotel, lost $1.6 million and cancelled its contract with the architect. A decision was made to settle for a smaller, less ostentatious, low profile, but nevertheless elegant hotel complex. There are few persons who would not empathize with Colin Cameron who said at a press conference, "This is a high-risk business. I've learned that unless you already own the land and own it cheaply as we do, it's almost impossible to afford the time to develop a major resort of this kind. The front-end costs are so high no one can afford to buy the land too."[18]

In the middle of 1973, Colin Cameron and Maui Mayor Elmer F. Cravalho jointly announced the company gift to the county of the D. T. Fleming Beach Park at Honokahua. It included all facilities, well designed and set in four acres of landscaped gardens. In making the joint announcement, which has become a Maui convention, the mayor said, "I am deeply pleased with Maui Land & Pineapple Co.'s decision to dedicate Honokahua Beach Park to the County for public use. This gesture reflects the outstanding cooperation between the private sector and the County of Maui in achieving quality development and providing for increasing recreational needs of our community."[19] In Maui County, a wise developer does well to acknowledge the county and the public in a tangible way.

Despite the fact that the general plan of Lahaina district permitted 9,600 apartment and hotel units in the area, the Kapalua master plan asked for only 4,740—2,570 apartment-condominium units and 2,170 hotel rooms. In addition 720 house units were requested. All requests were granted and the total units now constitute the maximum permissible. In making the requests, ML&P asked for more hotel rooms and fewer apartments. Shortly after this, Colin Cameron talked in terms of two hotels with a total of 950 units and less than 2,000 residential units as a ceiling. This would have the effect of lowering densities considerably, concentrating population, and because of the space occupied by condominiums per population unit, providing more open space with less crowding. By the end of the decade it seemed that company aspirations would not be reaching even this lowered level.

Philosophy Responding to Change

It is difficult not to be cynical when reading brochures, master plans, and advertising materials on major resorts. Most seem written by the same hand and, in all, expectations are high—at least so long as stated aims do not too seriously compromise the unstated and fundamental goals of any project. Kapalua seemed different. Not only were the intentions there but subsequent actions have already seen the realization of them. ML&P was serious when it talked about a planned first-quality destination resort-residential community—the finest in the State of Hawaii.

Before the project could start, conflicting claims of leisure and agriculture had to be resolved. Whereas Kaanapali and Wailea had had only an incidental connection with agriculture, Kapalua had to compensate for the loss of 350 productive acres. This it did by making up the loss with land elsewhere on Maui.[20]

Throughout the 1970s, Kapalua management watched changing public opinion and changed themselves with the times. Very early it seemed the project was to be rigidly exclusive, perhaps even to the use of the beach; but management was quick to sense community change and, without direct outside pressure, changed too. At Kapalua it was a period of adaptive sensitive philosophical growth. When yielding was necessary, it yielded. When neighbors at Puna Point complained about plans for nearby buildings, both heights and densities were reduced.

On some points management would not give ground. The operation as a whole would be exclusive in the sense that it would be oriented toward independent travelers—the top 10 to 15 percent of the visitor market. Tours and conventions would be out. From the start there was an aversion to what company executives still refer to as the "name tag crowd." Heights of buildings would be adjusted to terrain, low buildings would not obscure views from above, and there would be no space made for high rises. The whole aspect would be one of unity despite differing densities where guests lived in a climate emphasizing a slower than usual pace of life within a planned environment. No through roads would be built; internal roads would be narrow and designed for interest and not for roadside parking. A key word in Kapalua philosophy is still corporate control—control of landscaping, architecture, general appearance, community character, in fact the total environment.

Making Best Use of Surroundings

The plan emphasized development of several attractive natural areas together with some newly created points of interest. There are Kapalua Beach and the Bay Club at the north end of the beach; Namalu Bay, the Kapalua Bay Hotel, the tennis center, the flanking Bay Villa condominiums, and shopping facilities; the Oneloa Beach apartments and shopping node; the Honokahua Beach with the existing park, beach club, and associated hotel and neighborhood commercial facilities. Other emphases are the golf clubhouse, the Honokahua Village site and Pineapple Hill where apartments, shopping, commercial, and service facilities are designed to create a community center bordering the proposed new highway. There are within the plan other developments but these I will omit. The specifics of master plans are always changing and Kapalua is no exception. When major resorts first started planning, ambitious plans were standard. As times changed and money got tighter, the tendency seemed to be to simplify planning rather than to set unrealistic goals.

And like all major projects, an eighteen-hole golf course is central and was the first unit completed. On Maui, a well-patronized golf course is not only good advertising, it is also likely to be a very good money maker. The course was designed, so company promotional brochures claimed, "for maximum enjoyment . . . [bringing together] larger land masses . . . [and creating] a dramatic green belt of significant visual impact . . . for the entire Kapalua community." The intent was not to spread the golf course, a common strategy to create sites for condominiums. The philosophy here, which obviously works, is to create quality and the cash flow looks after itself.

In 1979, after some bad setbacks, Kapalua had constructed some major components and as if to compensate for earlier experiences, these met generally with the greatest success. This included the first hotel—the Kapalua Bay, a beach club, a tennis club, and several condominium complexes.

The golf course, in operation since 1975, was followed by another, the village course, also designed by Arnold Palmer. The Kapalua Bay Hotel was designed by Ed Killingsworth of Killingsworth, Brady & Associates, architects of the Kahala Hilton Hotel. The 196-room luxurious $30 million unit is managed by Regent International Hotels. For a short period previously it was managed by Rockresorts, former operators of the elegant Big Island Mauna Kea Beach Hotel, the prototype, so many people believe, for the Kapalua Bay Hotel.

The Bay Villas and the Golf Villas were among the first completed condominium blocks. These were followed by the Ironwood and the Ridge condominiums. The unbelievably high prices and the way these last three complexes were sold made real estate history. The 140 Bay Villa units were sold in 1975–1976 for $16 million at prices ranging from $84,000 to $130,000. Of the 186 Golf villa units, 170 were offered for sale while they were still on the drawing board. All were sold on the same day in a lottery which brought in $22 million at an average price of $135,000 a unit. In the summer of 1978, 250 invited jet setters came to bid on the 40 Ironwood units. Then the 135 Ridge condominiums made national headlines when they were sold sight unseen in four hours for $28 million—an average price of $207,000. There is no point in continuing. By the time this is read, Ironwood units may very well have increased considerably in value beyond their $400,000 price despite the 1980–1981 economic slowdown.

Colin Cameron's concerns of some years ago turned to unabashed delight. "ML&P is essentially an agricultural enterprise and Kapalua is simply diversification," he said in an interview. But "Kapalua," he went on, "is really just a money factory based on the tourist industry."[21] Money factory indeed. Colin Cameron could afford to smile, but the accomplishment was a personal triumph as well.

Windfall Benefits As Well

It is well known that if a development has to start with the purchase of land which is well-situated but not superb, the haul may be long and heavy. But if the developer has held the land for decades and the site is superior, one can expect an initial struggle, but it will be just a matter of time before the money starts flowing. The implications for local society and agriculture may be tremendous. The Kapalua Bay Hotel site of thirteen acres is carried on ML&P books at the pre-urban zoning agricultural worth of $100 an acre. A recent estimate of the value of the parcel was $9 million, almost $700,000 per acre. Near Kapalua Bay itself are a number of homesites which may be put on the market in ten years. It is considered a wise move to place land on the market in small lots infrequently, a lesson learned by some other Hawaii developments the hard way. Tom Rohr, president of Kapalua Land Company, says, "Even now it would be impossible to put a value on the half-acre parcels. Their value ten years from now when Kapalua is expected to be fully developed defies imagination!"[22]

The Kapalua Land Company not only strictly controls development, but it still holds all the land by lease. "The impact of the

plush hostelry [Kapalua Bay Hotel] on the value of future development at Kapalua will be considerable. At every escalation, the
company will gain. In time the money machine becomes almost
an automated juggernaut.''[23] Exceptionally high prices for land
and condominium units, good for the company, bestow doubtful
benefits on local residents. What has happened is significant. The
robust sale of units at Kapalua has allowed an upgrading of the entire project. The company is now able to build lavishly, cut densities considerably, and still profit handsomely. In this way the community can at least indirectly benefit. Tom Rohr is reported as
saying that one recommendation was to put two hundred units on
the site of the present Ironwood complex which would have been
the standard conventional way of approaching the situation. Instead the company chose to build forty lowrise units with a density
of five units per acre rather than twenty or thirty.[24]

There is a serious side to the matter not yet mentioned. If a very
nice balance is struck between resort development and agriculture, an admirable formula will have been worked out. The Kapalua operation, for a long time subsidized by pineapple growing
before real cash flow began, will be in a position to reciprocate.
The valuable resort could underwrite and buffer the vagaries of
pineapple price and production, and, it is hoped, thereby maintain
indefinitely the open pineapple growing spaces and the associated
rural life-styles. If this could be achieved, ML&P would be doing
much to preserve what has long been identified as the best of
Hawaii, not the least of which is the greatly valued aloha spirit.

Lessons Learned

A study of Kapalua teaches much. It demonstrates the long and ar-
duous path one must tread to put together quality resort development. It indicates the risks involved, the setbacks which can be
expected, the work that goes into the creation of a resort, the frustration of navigating the bureaucracy, and the ultimate rewards to
the company that may eventuate.

ML&P started with fine natural resources: its singlemindedness,
tenacity, and slow pace served it well. At every step, Colin Cameron and his senior officers talked in superlatives about the project. They stressed respect for the environment, careful control of
every facet of development, and, above all, low profile, elegance,
and consummate taste. The Kapalua mystique was developed
even before anything was on the ground, and it developed without

hype and, from the company point of view, at the right time. It developed, I believe, because of the confidence people had in Colin Cameron. They thought he would deliver and he did.

Cameron often pretends Kapalua is just a business proposition —diversification—but this is merely a front. Kapalua is the product of the personal creativity of one who would not let go the concept of excellence while being yet willing to acknowledge changing public attitudes. To be a member of a respected local family helps, but to be in his position and continue to demonstrate a genuine concern for the people and the land is rare indeed. It is a quality worth nurturing in Hawaii tourism.

CHAPTER 5

State Relationships

THREE levels of government—federal, state, and county—and those special values associated with politics all play important parts in leisure land development in Hawaii. The fundamental details of planning, direct forms of regulation, overt and behind-the-scenes activities together with personal interaction are significant to the basic level of government—the county. Resulting land development reflects the county—its administration, agencies, and council—more than any other level of government, together with the investors and developers they attract.

The state, for its part, exerts a general degree of control; sets guidelines; attempts to maintain a statewide perspective; encourages redistribution and a balance of population and economic activity; coordinates overall planning; influences development through taxation; allocates capital improvement project funds; maintains relations with the mainland; and, above all, within broad areas, says where urban development should and should not take place. The state, through land-use decisions, may encourage the development of a particular island or region and, by withholding its authorization, may prevent development in otherwise attractive areas. Within state-designated areas, the county supervises details which, as far as the community is concerned, constitute a major concern. Within certain constraints, the county may be as creative as it wishes. Conversely, it is responsible for inferior development.

In the discussions which follow on the function of the state and the counties, I must, as an introduction, pay attention to some of the important relationships which exist between the state, the federal government, and the nation as a whole. A number of these relationships existed when Hawaii was a territory but this was accentuated and extended when Hawaii became a state. For the citizen, much of what I say is taken for granted and the question is even likely to be asked "How is Hawaii any different from other states?" For outside observers or Pacific watchers it may help explain some of the differences which exist between Hawaii and other Pacific island groups that physically are so similar. The differences are largely part of the "American connection" both a notion and a fact which is central to many of the interpretations I make. The following key elements should be kept in mind.

Hawaii is a multicultural society with its own values and attitudes, sometimes strongly influenced by its founding cultures. With political affiliation to the United States, the constitution, court interpretations and federal legislation introduced guidelines bound to drastically affect existing ways of life. These introductions were automatically associated with fundamental philosophical questions such as democracy, individualism, and the acceptance of a particular pervasive economic system. From the first to the present, local values to a greater or lesser degree sought ways, not without stress, to accomodate the introductions.

Close and stable political relationships with the United States provided a magnificent market for tourism, heavy in-migration, and a further strengthening of mainland values and mores. Federal funds in large quantities provided for strategic national defense and in various ways for the support of a growing population. But along with military reserves came wilderness preserves on a scale unknown elsewhere in island Oceania. The association meant also the introduction of federal cost-sharing programs, the support of agriculture, and the development of a geographic personality unique in the Pacific.

The physical framework for tourism was always there, trade relations with the United States created a fascinating plural society, while federal activity resulted in recreational reserves and open agricultural spaces both of critical importance to tourism.

The State

The state plays an extremely important role concerning land: establishing policy, enacting legislation, implementing its own and federal regulations, examining growth, maintaining openness and quality, and planning for the future. One major difficult role of the state is to interpret federal policy and integrate this with both state and county endeavors. Dr. Shelley M. Mark, former director of the Department of Planning and Economic Development, voiced a pressing need for federal agencies to coordinate activities before imposing land-use regulations unilaterally on the state. He noted that "the State must abide by land-use requirements embodied in the National Land Use Policy Act, the Coastal Zone Management Act, the Water Quality Act, and the Better Communities Act while the United States Environmental Agency, the Department of the Interior, the Department of Housing and Urban Development, and the Department of Commerce are all seeking to participate in the land use game."[1]

Certain legislation, reflections of overall philosophy, and policy concerns of the state have a great bearing on local planning and development. There is an understanding that the range of resources is limited; that land is owned by few owners, including the state (776,000 acres or 19 percent); that growth in the economy must be shared by all islands and not concentrated on Oahu; that support of agriculture is essential; that diversification of primary production, especially agriculture, is now essential; that greater efforts should be made toward self-sufficiency in food and animal feed; and that employment must rest largely, but not entirely, on a controlled visitor industry.

Much of the work of the government and its departments revolves about legislation and policy emerging from an updated and continuously revised state plan covering social, economic, environmental, administrative, and financial affairs. The multi-volume plan was prepared initially by the State Planning Office, now the active Department of Planning and Economic Development, which with the Hawaii Visitors Bureau monitors, though differently, the visitor industry.

The first general plan of 1961, introduced by legislation four years earlier, was widely praised and a source of governmental pride. In comparison with other states, it demonstrated progressive thinking. But a plan and its implementation are different matters.

In 1967 the general plan had need for revision, and because of changing economic and social conditions, numerous studies were embarked upon. These studies would provide the basis for another thorough revision of the plan in the late seventies. To help pave the way for farsighted action, in 1970 the governor initiated a Conference on the Year 2000 bringing local authorities and experts from across the country to make exciting forays into the future and to stimulate as well practical thought.[2]

Economic growth has always been a central concern for the state. In 1974, as part of the general plan revision program, a volume on practical economic growth policy and alternatives for use through 1984 was produced.[3] This study presented the consequences of rapid growth, medium growth, and low growth. No action was ever taken on these recommendations, however, as it was published at the beginning of the first significantly slow economic period since World War II and legislators believed no legislation was necessary.

The Governor's View

Policies of the late Governor John Burns carried over into the administration of George Ariyoshi, the first locally born governor of Hawaii. Both men had strong union endorsement, a fact necessary to understand better their views. In the 1978 election, Governor Ariyoshi had the firm support of the International Longshoremen and Warehousemen's Union, the Hawaii Government Employees Association, and the Hawaii State Teachers Association.

His policies, with slight changes each year, are predicated on the status of agricultural health, on the status of unemployment, and on the delicate balance between agriculture and tourism. A particular concern has been the buildup of population pressure and the possibility of limiting in-migration to Hawaii. This and similar issues peaked for the first time in 1976 when a residency law was passed requiring a year's domicile in Hawaii before a person could be employed by the state. This has since been overturned in court, but the population issue is far from dead.

In addressing county delegates at the 1976 conference, the governor clearly indicated his feelings. This was at a stocktaking period when the economy was sluggish. He first called attention to the disproportionate area of land preempted for federal use in an already land-poor society. "We do not get our fair share of federal grants," he said, and pointed out that the economic growth rate had slowed and the entry of investment capital had lessened. He noted that the construction industry had fallen on hard times, and tourism had been noticeably checked. The sugar industry was in deep trouble and, he continued, a "creeping urbanization, particularly on Oahu, is systematically and relentlessly . . . chewing up our prime agricultural land for subdivisions and shopping centers . . . my administration has invested heavily in capital improvements projects . . . to prime the economic pump . . . Our role is to keep our construction industry alive."[4] Ironically, only a year earlier, the governor had talked about "hyena crazy urban development." But all this gives some clue to attitudes toward the visitor industry: acceptable if finely attuned to public feeling but always vulnerable.

Throughout 1977 the governor's public statements showed marked concern for a number of problems. This concern was applauded by some, condemned by others. His State of the State speech received some approval while causing consternation. The population theme was again brought to public notice with an assertion once more that population growth was too great in Hawaii: "If we have no say over who comes here and in what number, we might as well abandon any thoughts of a Hawaiian tomorrow. Too many people can spell disaster for this State," he emphasized.

The governor called for, first, a constitutional amendment to allow the state to establish residence requirements; second, federal legislation to channel foreign immigrants to other states; and, third, federal aid to help Hawaii deal with its high migrant population. These issues later appeared in the Hawaii State Plan. Aliens in Hawaii comprise 8.1 percent of Hawaii's population, the highest percentage of any state. In the 1960s, Hawaii's population grew by 2 percent per annum, twice the national average, but not anomalous in the wider Pacific context.

The governor won little immediate support from legislators, nearly all of whom, like Ariyoshi, are children or grandchildren of immigrants. There was a degree of sympathy and understanding, but generally his views were regarded as unrealistic. His restrictive views were considered unconstitutional, illegal, a handicap to plantations which depend still on imported labor, and a destroyer of the unique ethnic mix characterizing Hawaii. What was not said was that to single out aliens mostly from Asia and elsewhere in the Pacific within part of the proposal would be legislatively to support an even greater haole influence in the future, a situation which would be anathema to large numbers of local voters.

But Governor Ariyoshi was not easily deterred. The 1978 legislative session saw further administration-sponsored bills aimed at controlling overpopulation and related maladies. His 1979 State of the State address reiterated his previous views and called for

greater self-reliance through the development of a range of indigenous energy resources and the extension of diversified agriculture.
Community security was also an important theme. Rampaging
crime, he said, must be suppressed before we are forced to live,
"behind barricaded doors and windows." In his quest for indepen-
dence over dependence he stressed another Ariyoshi theme,
Hawaii's role as a cultural and economic link between Asia and
the Pacific. Virtually all major issues were closely linked in some
way with tourism.

In the context of what the governor called Hawaii's "preferred
future," he called for curbing the growth of immigrants (aliens)
and of in-migrants (new residents from other states) who would be
unlikely to find work and thus become a burden on welfare. He
asked for inquiry into the possibility of taxing newcomers at a
higher rate than others in order to cover the extra services that
would have to be provided for them. He successfully asked that
able-bodied in-migrants under the age of fifty-five be denied state
welfare, and he submitted a measure, later to become law, to give
preference to Hawaii residents applying for state and county jobs.
Immediately media spokesmen were debating whether or not such
measures would stand if challenged in court.

By January 1980 in his sixth State of the State speech, Ariyoshi's specificity, unlike that in past years, was less well drawn. The
themes he had been hammering on were not clearly expressed, but
his views were well known. With something of an ominous economic cloud over the state he could, in principle, count on a broad
consensus of support. He again stressed self-sufficiency, diversified
agriculture, the need for agricultural parks, aquaculture, and the
importance of promoting Hawaii as a Pacific regional center. The
promotion of diversified manufacturing including an electronics
industry, marine education in elementary schools, and a Hawaii
fisheries development plan was new. Although little was said
about the visitor industry it was in the mind of every listener. The
industry was foundering in difficult times, it was obvious, and
every item called for would be complementary to it, providing an
insurance policy if it were to falter seriously.

State Policy

As a result of examining the less desirable aspects of exceptionally
fast economic growth on its own doorstep, the state has chosen a
policy devised to ensure better all-round quality—a worthy, nebu-

lous, and illusive goal. The economic health of the Islands still remains important. Growth must be sufficient to provide jobs for the locally born, thus preventing out-migration, but not with such speed as to encourage rapid in-migration, speed environmental degradation, or militate against good coastal management.

State policy avers that every effort will be made to promote agriculture, to diversify it, and to promote clean industry which will diminish the present dependence on tourism. The ideal, the maintenance of the life-styles of Hawaii with reasonable rewards for all residents within the context of a strong, steady, developing economy, will not be easy to attain. Development brings with it social problems which, during slower economic periods, are more obvious. As such, the 1974–1976 recession can be seen as something of a blessing in disguise—a time for the state to take stock quietly of what was happening. The same can be said for 1980–1981.

The moving of Hawaii's visitor plant away from Oahu has resulted from past state policy which will continue despite the objections of some counties. When the proposed Hawaii State Plan was presented in Kahului in November 1976, officials and citizens were vocal in their reactions. "Don't screw up the other islands [outside Oahu]. Don't shift the burden of Oahu over here," said Maui County Water Director Shigeto Murayama. Planning Director Toshi Ishikawa was quick to add that he did not think "the problems of Honolulu could be solved by shifting that problem to the neighbor islands." A member of the public added, "We don't want no cement jungle over here on Maui." Not only was population dispersal the subject of debate but also county rights. Officials felt that counties would have limited say in the way future plans were likely to affect them.

As all neighbor islands have large planned unit resort developments already approved by counties and as implementation of these projects except Kaanapali has barely begun, the population center of Hawaii is likely to move away from Oahu whether the State Plan directs attention to this fact or not.

Past diversion of economic activity has been achieved in a number of ways: by the encouragement of development on neighbor islands with the lesson of Honolulu in mind, by judicious enforcement of land-use regulations,[5] and by the skillful use of capital improvement projects. During the period 1960–1970, over one-half of the state's capital improvement budget went to the Big Island of Hawaii, approximately one-fifth to Kauai and Maui, and only one-twelfth to Oahu.[6] In the 1970s, capital improvement project pol icy changed the reorientation, giving a much greater emphasis to Maui, slightly more emphasis than previously to Oahu, and commensurately diminished emphasis to the other island counties.[7]

Classifying the Land

Details of the function of the Hawaii Land Use Law and the Land Use Commission (LUC) have already been mentioned. The state, guided by its plan, uses this law to determine where urbanization will take place in the future. The purpose of the law is to eliminate public costs associated with widespread and scattered subdivisions, to achieve equitable real property taxation,[8] to preserve prime agricultural land from encroachment, and to preserve space for future growth, whether residential, industrial, or leisure.

A developer may wish to use land differently from that suggested by the state's classification (agricultural, rural, urban, or conservation). The usual request is from agricultural to urban. The developer must prove that the land is needed for the new use and that it is *either* usable or adaptable for that use *or* that conditions of development have so changed since the adoption of the present classification that the proposed classification is reasonable.

If this is supported by the planning department of the county, the state, through the LUC, may change the classification. It may also deny the application. During the first decade of operation, requests for urban classification were received for one hundred thousand acres of land. Of this land, less than one-third was classified urban.[9]

Although many applications are denied, some are approved, but when this happens there is no policy of removing a similar area of land from an urban classification elsewhere. The urban classification is alleged by many to be far too extensive already. By developing what lawmakers saw as a tough law, it was hoped that the law would stabilize agriculture and be a deterrent to unnecessary, capricious applications for urban zoning. This, indeed, is the intent of the legislation, but legislation is administered and interpreted by people for people. Values change as does the composition of the commission whose members operate within the paradigms of the group they represent and, as public figures, are subject to innumerable pressures. One may expect decisions which appear on the surface anomalous and others which, when checked into, reflect a degree of humanity where justice is done without cost to the community. There is, however, a possibility that the law can be made too flexible, thus allowing barely justifiable re-classification. Within an admirable framework, there seem to be questions meriting further attention for which the public deserves explanation.

If it is possible to "upgrade," it is also possible to "down-grade"—this too is a function of the LUC. The actions of the last few years indicate that the philosophy of the LUC is changing. Au-thoritative informants suggest there is now the feeling that too much land has been classified urban, resulting in a "get tougher" policy tying development down to a time period and imposing conditions which continue from titleholder to titleholder. This does not prevent, from time to time, surprisingly large areas being reclassified from agricultural to urban.

By the end of 1974, after a boom decade of tourism develop-ment, the LUC conducted its second quinquennial district boun-dary review; the first had taken place in 1969.[10] The commission heard well over one hundred applications for change in land use classification, apparently from those wanting a piece of the tour-ism pie. Applications requesting reclassification of 14,000 acres from agricultural to urban were heard. Of this, all but 5,400 acres were denied; in addition, downzoning took place in a few areas —1,800 acres on Molokai—to give a net increase of only 1,380 acres of new urban land.

In a doctoral thesis on the application of the Hawaii Land Use Law, from 1961 to 1976, Gordon Lowry found that the law, en-acted in 1961, succeeded "in reclaiming [for the state] land use au-thority that had previously been granted to the counties." The commission, he concluded, has had some influence on the rate "prime agricultural land has been converted to urban uses, but it has not prevented the conversion of 34,906 acres of agricultural land, 3,191 acres of which were rated as having high agricultural productivity." The overall impact on Oahu, he stated, is to permit urban expansion where prime agricultural areas are located.

The act allowed small farmers to benefit where land had been dedicated to agriculture, and taxation was lowered. Large land-owners and developers, however, also received advantages. Commission actions always ensured substantial reserves of unde-veloped urban land, much of which was in the hands of large land-owners. "This allowed the private sector more flexibility in de-termining the rate and location of new development." For some landowners, parcels were reclassified from agriculture on an incremental basis. Only land then which was needed for construction was rezoned and, consequently, taxed at a higher rate while the remainder awaiting development was taxed at the lower agricultural level. "The major argument for the Land Use Law (as it is now implemented) is that it bought time for counties and the State to fashion programs and policies for guiding urban growth on each of the islands and for identifying particular resources requiring special management."[11] Contrary to the purpose of the law, neither prime agricultural land nor the restriction of scattered urban development guided LUC decisions.

Lowry contends that more than 10 percent of petitions involving more than five thousand acres violated most of the commission's standards but were approved wholly or partly anyway. "Hawaii's . . . experience with a State Land Use authority suggests that much more than centralization of control is required to deal with problems of urban growth guidance, environmental protection and community development."[12] This seems to be understood, I believe, when one looks at the provisions of the Hawaii State Plan, a discussion of which follows. In 1980 a bill was introduced into the legislature to avoid past ad hoc case-by-case consideration of petitions without a broad regional approach. The bill required the LUC to consider State Plan goals, compatibility with surrounding uses, and cumulative impacts.[13]

A growing state concern, the topic of several items of legislation, is recreation and preservation. In addition to the maintenance of existing parks, attempts have been made to analyze the recreational behavior of islanders and to suggest strategies for reserving recreation areas for the future. These were included in the State Comprehensive Outdoor Recreation Plan[14] and its 1975 revision which, with federal approval, provided eligibility for the state to receive matching grants until 1980 for the maintenance, development, and preservation of Hawaii's outdoor recreation and open space resources.[15]

Preservation is achieved through shoreline reserves (tantamount to a seaward extension of beach parks), ocean parks in near-shore areas, wilderness reserves, and natural area reserves. The state had, in the past, determined beaches as public property and required building setbacks of at least forty feet from the shoreline. In 1973 (under Act 139 of 1970) the first Hawaii natural area reserve was designated. This was three square miles of land and ocean near Makena, Maui. Approximately 1,300 acres of land and

800 acres of sea at Ahihi Bay and Cape Kinau lava flow were included in this reserve of unique marine and terrestrial ecosystems. The public may enjoy the beauty of the reserves but only under stringent conditions. As the Ahihi-Kinau natural area, until 1974 relatively remote, embraces part of one of the Pacific's most beautiful beaches, and borders Seibu's Makena project, dedication of the area came none too soon.

This action on Maui followed the setting up of a full-time State Office of Environmental Quality Control, part of a thirty-item environmental legislative package of the late Governor Burns in 1970. There is no doubt that this legislation was hastened by the dramatic growth of tourism in the sixties. From this excursion into the environmental field came the Temporary Commission on Environmental Planning which in August 1973 issued a comprehensive document covering recommendations on the total environment—the Hawaii habitat. The focus of the commission, which took evidence from twenty-eight community and environmental organizations as well as several individuals, was as much on the quality of life as on physical and biological concerns. Dr. Richard Marland, director of the Governor's Office of Environmental Quality Control, called it the most important planning effort ever undertaken in the state which would provide policy guidance for state general planning. So that policy matters adopted would also be acceptable to the counties, major input came from influential county delegates on the commission.

Prior to the 1970s, general control of life and environment was exercised through the application of land use law and the activities of the State LUC. In 1972, Congress passed the National Coastal Zone Management Act, making it incumbent upon all states wishing to participate in joint programs to follow suit with their own compatible legislation. In Hawaii, this took place in stages: public and committee discussion, an interim act, more discussion and hearings, a substantive act, discussion, the preparation of a coastal management program submission to the federal government for funding eligibility, scrutiny and approval, and finally full implementation.

On 1 December 1975 the Shoreline Protection Act or the Interim Coastal Zone Management Act (Act 176), came into effect and, for the time being, gave sweeping powers to counties to control all major buildings and development in zones (special management areas) not less than three hundred feet from the shoreline.

The purpose of the act was to preserve, protect, and where possible restore the natural resources of the coastal zone in Hawaii as well as to ensure adequate community access to public-owned beaches, recreation areas, and natural reserves.

Although the wording sounded dreary, its implications were exciting. For the first time, the state had the rough outline of an instrument which, if used wisely, could do much to rehabilitate a coastal zone already showing the harsh ravages of unwise use.

From 1975 to 1978, many discussions took place for the purpose of drafting a final coastal zone management (CZM) act and of designing a workable program based on it. The Department of Planning and Economic Development (DPED) took the lead in its formulation assisted by public hearings, regional citizens' advisory committees, a statewide citizens' forum, the policy advisory committee, and the federal contacts panel.[16] Few legislative actions have had such public input, received such publicity, or been discussed so purposefully by interested groups and individuals. Local interest in CZM legislation followed a popular national wave of interest in the environment combined with a growing public interest in general marine and coastal studies. Tourism legislation in comparison, except by a few select committees, remained largely undiscussed and unanalyzed.

By 1977, Governor Ariyoshi signed the Hawaii Coastal Zone Management Act (Act 188) and the DPED was again busy working on a management program which was to reflect provisions of the legislation harmoniously. In theory the act was a giant step forward and, although tourism development occupied only a portion of its legislative concern, it was the first time real control could be exercised in a comprehensive manner along Hawaii's shoreline. It had, of course, been applied provisionally since 1975; it was now confirmed.

The act provided for preventive management in the best sense. Not only was there concern for ecosystems and areas of critical biological importance but also a consideration of prehistoric sites (to the extent of restoration), the design and placement of buildings, the preservation of open space, and the provision of adequate, accessible, and diverse recreational opportunities. Although tourism control was infrequently mentioned in coastal zone discussions, it was nevertheless understood that almost every clause within the act could refer directly or indirectly to overall tourism activity.

The act instructed that coastal development be concentrated in appropriate areas. Greater beach access consistent with good conservation practice should be provided and, above all, the legislation mandated that the public should be made aware of the potential impacts of proposed development early "and in terms understandable to the general public to facilitate public participation in the planning and review process."

One area of contention yet to be clarified within the legislation was the mauka boundary of the coastal zone management area. Federal legislation insisted each state seeking program approval had to define its own coastal zone. This zone must extend seaward to the three-mile limit and include all shorelands which "directly and significantly affect coastal waters."[17]

Counties wished to persist with the interim narrow strip, special management areas, rather than the broader CZM areas mandated by the act. Ultimately the state accepted the county special management areas (SMAs), giving up part of an effective instrument for control of development including tourism. This illogicality could be demonstrated graphically in relation to major resort areas. In Kauai, all major resort development fell within the SMAs. In Hawaii, only a portion of the resort areas were in SMAs. In Maui, the smaller independent developments were largely included but the mauka portions of Kapalua, Wailea, and Makena were excluded as were portions of West Beach, Queen's Beach, and Makaha, all on Oahu.[18] By December 1979 each county was instructed to examine its SMA boundaries with a view to embracing areas with higher incidences of unique and important coastal resources and with high potential for development warranting additional management control. The result was that all counties except the City and County of Honolulu extended certain SMAs. The greatest changes seemed to take place in Hawaii and Kauai.

The Visitor Industry

In order to prepare adequately for the future, the governor's office set up various committees, all of which were directly or indirectly concerned with the visitor industry. Along with the Department of Planning and Economic Development, the governor's steering committee was concerned with carrying out capacity studies. This committee in 1976 sought and received federal funds for water and sewer systems, flood control, and agricultural parks. It helped the counties work together for such capital projects with the Eco-

nomic Development Administration of the United States Department of Commerce and the Hawaii Economic Development District Committee. The governor also set up in 1975 the Tourism
Planning Advisory Committee to aid the Department of Planning
and Economic Development in its now completed task of formulating a tourism plan for Hawaii.[19]

This was followed in May of 1976 by the Interim Tourism Policy Act, Act Number 133—a bold step forward in view of the absence of a written policy on tourism. The policy stressed not only
the industry but also, as it should, it linked the people of Hawaii ir-
retrievably with the activities of the industry. I have added my
emphases to the preamble which states: "Hawaii is unique in its
combination of beauty in the natural physical environment, in its
people and their Aloha Spirit, and in its cosmopolitan mixing of
ethnic groups, cultures, religions and life styles. These facets of
beauty are to be preserved and enhanced, not only because they
are the basis of Hawaii's attraction to visitors but because *they are
the basis for Hawaii's attraction to its own people.*"

One of the Act's objectives is to "preserve and enrich the understanding, by visitors and residents, of our native Hawaiian heritage as well as the cultural and social contributions to Hawaii of
all of its ethnic groups and people and to sustain economic health
of the visitor industry *to the extent that such economic health is
compatible with the aforesaid objectives.*"

It is also interesting to read that agencies are instructed "insofar
as practicable" (which seems an unnecessary loophole) "*to regard
the interests of residents, including employment, as preferable
when attempting reconciliation of conflicting resident and visitor
requirements.*" In addition an attempt was to be made to develop
"an understanding among all citizens of the role of tourism in
Hawaii both in terms of its economic importance and *the problems it presents.*" Finally, to provide necessary advice and a
means of citizen input, a *Tourism Advisory Council* was established.

Since 1972 and the publication of the Hawaii Tourism Impact
Plan,[20] there has been a discernible change of attitude concerning
the relationship between tourists and residents of Hawaii. Aspects
of the change, part of which is summarized below, are analyzed
by Sommarstrom.[21] The greatest potential for change has come
with the Hawaii State Plan and the State Tourism Plan.

Whereas the Tourism Impact Plan paid scant attention to anything other than economic impact and the problems of the industry subsequent state-sponsored publications oriented the issues more strongly to the community.[22] The Overview Corporation's Study of Open Space in Hawaii of the same year, 1972, stated that Hawaii is first and foremost "a homeland for its permanent residents and that their environmental needs must be paramount in all decisions." The needs of the tourist industry must therefore be adapted to the indigenous amenities of Hawaii. It went on to say that the state should seriously consider how fast it wanted to add people, determine just what carrying capacities would be wise for various islands, and then decide how it wanted to stabilize permanent populations.[23]

In 1973 the report of the Temporary Commission on Statewide Environmental Planning, mentioned earlier, again addressed the issue of carrying capacity, noting several areas of critical overload. It stressed that the way of life and the accompanying aloha spirit were enmeshed delicately in the environment and that this balance would be quickly upset by needless population pressure. Population growth, of course, is very closely related to the rate of growth of the tourist industry.

One might despair at the speed at which a burning issue is officially confronted, but in this instance there is hope. Gradual changes in attitude are heartening, even if to some their appearance is inordinately delayed. At this point a reader not familiar with the bureaucratic literature of Hawaii should be warned. The annual production of reports, studies, briefs, and similar materials in Hawaii is stupendous. "Population pressure," "quality development," "quality of life," "aloha spirit," "critical capacity," "preservation of cultural heritage" are the motherhood issues and stock cliches of every printed volume. They have been falling easily from the tongue and flowing just as smoothly from the pen for well over a decade. The sincere sentiment is always difficult to separate from the casual.

Ceremonial publication may have some benefit. It does contribute in the end to changing attitudes, and when this is achieved, new notions must be transformed into action which may take the form of legislation. The crucial test is in the implementation of the law. In addition, unfortunately, it seems impossible even in law to get away from words like "critical," "quality," "aloha spirit," and "way of life"—all nebulous concepts of the fuzziest variety defying precise interpretation. Along with the letter of the law, there must be a universal feeling for the spirit as well. Rarely are the two applied simultaneously.

The Hawaii State Plan 1978

Several years prior to April 1978 an array of documents to aid the Hawaii State Plan was prepared on virtually all aspects of life in Hawaii. Some of these have already been mentioned. In addition, in the field of tourism and agriculture, legislation was enacted to help in the refinement and guidance of the 1978 Hawaii State Plan. The wide ranging Interim Tourism Policy Act paid special attention to the relationships of Hawaiian culture, life-styles, and environment with tourism. Another act established the Governor's Coordinating Committee to monitor all state-supported agricultural activities and "to develop a State agricultural policy to serve as a guide for future agricultural growth."[24] And finally in the 1978 legislative session, a step was taken which, curiously for Hawaii, had not been taken previously: the establishment of the Office of Tourism within the Department of Planning and Economic Development.

In 1976 and 1977 as part of the overall Hawaii State Plan process, several technical studies—staff and consultant reports—were written. These contributed to different levels of operation from the general to the particular. In theory, on the highest level was the State Plan, followed by state functional plans on specific topics, then the county general plans.

Numerous policy statements were used as a basis for the development of various sections. These included staff reports, (for example, that of the Interim Tourism Advisory Council), and massive documents such as the economic base technical study and the environmental concerns study. There were similar documents for other topics. To these were added other studies made by consultants whose input would continue until 1980.

By July and August 1977 a preliminary document had been prepared and discussed by individuals, public groups, and appointed committees.[25] There were no restrictions on submissions. Twelve public workshops were held on all islands. Oral submissions were recorded and DPED officers listened. This was the second of a series of public information workshops.

These were sifted, sorted, noted, or rejected by DPED. In consultation with the policy council, a revised plan was drawn up.

This advisory body consisted of eleven state agency directors, four county planning directors, and four citizens appointed by the governor.

The revised document was then distributed and public discussion meetings were held during late fall 1977. Finally, the Hawaii State Plan was submitted for legislative approval in early 1978.

The Hawaii State Plan provides guidelines and policies. It does not provide precision, specifics, strategies, or the delineation of exact areas for preservation or development. These are provided at the less general, more focused level through functional plans and by DPED and the counties. The department, in close conformity with the Hawaii State Plan, is required to have drawn up detailed state functional plans no later than two years after enactment of the State Plan.

At the same time counties went through similar exercises to provide county general plans and county development plans which conformed to state guidelines. In some cases this involved only modifying existing plans. During this period counties were expected also to develop plans for special local districts such as Kihei, Kailua-Kona, or Wailua-Kapaa. Here planning must be quite specific. Each county must plan for its own special problems, way of life, and economy. As it turned out, planning had to be completed more within rules and constraints set down by the state than counties had hoped for.

By far the weakest link in the Hawaii State Plan was public input, although on the surface the intent was admirable. A relatively small sample of the total population completed questionnaires and, in many cases, the public input at workshops was unrepresentative and inadequate. The interrelationship between federal, state, and county activities has been complex. The role of the Hawaii State Plan, the activities of such units as the State Land Use Commission, and the applicability of county plans were so uncertain and anomalous that the significance of effort was lost.

It was impossible to come to grips with the language of the plan which was characterized by issues of bureaucracy. To attempt to discuss it was like trying to contain a drop of quicksilver. Frequently public hearings resulted in cynicism, frustration, or in the riding of personal hobbyhorses unrelated to the content of the plan. One wondered whether the purpose was informational or merely therapeutic. Typical neighbor island comments were: "We don't want creeping Honoluluism here," "Leave us like we are,"

"Let us plan for ourselves," "Give us back our lands," and "The DPED has no sensitivity."

Public input *is* important and deserves better preparation and handling. There was no reason why citizens should appear so ill-informed about the workings of the state on such a vital matter as planning. A series of educational and informational meetings with resource persons over the course of a year, concluding in written thoughtful citizen input is what the plan deserved. Hurried encounters with uninformed and poorly represented citizenry were an insult to both the plan and the people. Both deserved better. In addition, there was little about the final version which was not the same as the first draft. I am left wondering why the workshops, public hearings, and so on? Despite a bad start on the main plan, some surprisingly good public contributions were made to functional plans.

In the main technical input into the planning process was good. What happened was another instance of the disparity between two groups—the governors and the governed. Sophisticated technical experts and decision makers adhering to the letter of the law, and often in frustration, attempted to communicate with ill-represented, somewhat less educated, intuitive, and frustrated citizens. By having well-selected citizens groups or neighborhood boards, the counties, in their planning, are at least theoretically better able to reflect the feelings of the people.

The situation as described above is not a black-and-white issue. Few of the questions in this book are. The point I am emphasizing is not that the DPED slipped up on the job. My point is a plea for communication—on both sides of the fence.

Major Provisions of the Plan

The governor's concern for population growth is reflected in the provisions of the plan, although these are much milder in contrast to gubernatorial statements made in 1977 or presented to the 1978 legislative session. The higher percentage of population growth rate in the neighbor islands in comparison with Oahu, the plan said, is to be encouraged and promoted by economic activities. Along with this were notions suggestions for development legislation and other means of lowering migration to Hawaii and encouraging the federal government to create a more balanced distribution of immigrants among all states. It was suggested that the federal government should provide assistance for states receiving a greater than average proportion of foreign immigrants. Although the state was to "foster an understanding of Hawaii's capacities to accommodate population needs," the finger was pointed elsewhere than the state itself for the solution to its problems.

The need to diversify the economy was noted. Export markets for home production were stressed as was the promotion of Hawaii as an attractive investment market and a service center for international activities. This latter point has since been expanded by the Governor's Committee for Hawaii as the Regional Center of the Pacific which sees Hawaii as an ideal site for the regional headquarters of multinational corporations.

The announced intention was to work toward greater stability in the sugar and pineapple industries and greater growth in diversified agriculture. Two policies meriting attention concerned fostering new attitudes toward agriculture conducive to its maintenance as a major sector of the economy and to increasing its attractiveness as a livelihood.

Specific policies such as those to assure the availability of agriculturally suitable lands with adequate water to accommodate present and future needs were stressed. At public hearings prior to approval this particular clause brought forth snorts of derision from farmers. Persons interested in small-scale farming have been confronted by staggering prices for land and in some areas equally staggering prices for water.

The visitor industry, the plan stated, would provide a major component of "steady growth for Hawaii's economy."[26] It did not say that in reality the visitor industry is expected to be the *major* component no matter the growth because there is no hard and fast policy for growth nor any definition of "steady growth." The plan went on to predict a slowdown in economic growth due to a decline in tourism, defense, and federal spending. This prophetic situation probably arrived sooner than any of the plan's writers expected.

Part III of the plan was concerned with policies and directions; it was prepared with little public testimony and no hearings on neighbor islands. Here the plan called for a "managed growth rate" which, imprecise as it is, suggests control rather than no control.

Other provisions direct that "future urban development [be] away from critical environmental areas" and encourages "the [accommodation] of urban growth in existing urban areas while maintaining agriculture land in agricultural designation." Further, to prevent the insidious infiltration by small residential "farmlets" into otherwise agricultural areas, another clause required "[exclusive] agricultural uses in agricultural subdivisions" and a close monitoring of their uses. In this provision there is the appearance of substance and direction. With further clarification, the plan can give much needed direction to the LUC.

Reaction to the Plan

The State Plan in draft form was discussed at public meetings on all the islands. Conflicts which ensued were concerned mainly with county rights as opposed to state's rights. "Home rule" was the catchword. There were allegations of imprecise wording and criticism of some notions so all-embracing they were meaningless profundities. It was alleged that the plan lacked any substance and that major principles of it were unenforceable.

On the surface the plan was an admirable piece of work. But upon closer examination, one wondered how such goals could be achieved. How was it that regulation would be implemented when regulation was absent before? Perhaps the plan gives a hint of possible changes in legislative attitudes. I am optimistic enough to think it does.

County planners, however, felt that the county general plans should be preeminent at the county level and that the State Plan should be tied to the county plan rather than vice versa. Essentially adoption of the plan meant a large schism in what many county proponents saw as their "home rule" prerogatives.

Neighbor island officials did not like the thought of their own growth, which they felt should be in their control, predicated on the growth of Oahu, nor did they enjoy the thought that possibly cherished county plans might ultimately play only a minor role in their counties' futures.

The approval of the plan was a cliff-hanger until the very end of the session and only by concerted effort did it pass the legislature by the 14 April 1978 deadline. Passage was near unanimous with only two objectors, both from Maui. There was trading, wrangling, and compromise in both houses. Critics stated that the final version stacked the law in favor of the state rather than the counties. The overall theme, goals, and objectives became the law to which all other state and county plans must ultimately conform.

Functional plans (for example, energy, agriculture, water resources, transportation), it was decided, must be submitted and if necessary resubmitted to the next legislative session until approval was won. This meant adoption by resolution which critics aver did not give them the force of law, the case of the State Plan proper. Nevertheless the State Plan set the direction of lesser plans.

The law calls for all county general plans to be used in drawing up the state's functional plans. In this way county wishes can aid and advise but can, if necessary, be overridden. Once functional plans are adopted, county general plans would have to conform. County planners were instructed to include in county plans matters concerning population density, land use, visitor areas, urban design, and all other development matters.

By mid-April the *Maui News* in an editorial called for a veto of the State Plan which "takes from the County and infringes on the charter."[27] Criticism was rebutted by Ron Kondo, State House majority leader, who said that during work on the bill, county planning directors wanted the county plans to be the basis of functional plans and "that's what they got." Nevertheless the bill said that county plans could be suspended by the legislature if it so wished. "If the county plan overrides the State Plan from the beginning, you don't have a State Plan," said Kondo. He went on to enlarge on a theme apparently in many minds, "Everybody wants some kind of growth, I don't think there is anybody against expansion economically . . ."[28]

There were some at the time, and more surfaced the following year.

State Tourism Plan

One of the required functional plans, compatible with the State Plan, was the ten-year master plan for tourism. By the passage of Act 133 "An Interim Tourist Policy" in 1976 the DPED was given the task of working on the plan. The resulting State Tourism Plan and its accompanying five study volumes were presented to the legislature in 1978 and, with modifications, again in 1979 and 1980.[29]

This massive and controversial accomplishment will be considered separately in a later chapter. As the concerns of Act 133 were extremely diverse, these could only be met by a series of technical studies: basically these were "economic projections," "physical resources," and "manpower." To this array were added volumes on "public revenue/cost analysis" and "executive summary."

In his address to the legislature in January 1979 Governor Ariyoshi spoke of the 1978 Constitutional Convention "as one of the most significant happenings of the past decade." In 1978, voters in the November election approved thirty-four changes recommended by the convention which represented over one hundred elected members of the public. Several of the changes have a direct relationship with either development or the contributive impact tourism has on the environment or society.

One amendment was concerned with gathering together all similar functions and activities with a related purpose under one executive department—a move which gives encouragement to those persons struggling to achieve a worthy goal yet who are thwarted at every turn because of overlapping jurisdictions. Control of the taxation of real property was placed exclusively in the hands of counties. This included exemptions and deductions for a special purpose with tax assessment levied for that use rather than for the "highest and best use." It was recommended that the state develop the cultural and creative activities of all ethnic groups. Amendment 18 required the state and the counties to manage the growth of population.

Amendment 23 fundamentally required both state and counties to "conserve and protect the natural beauty and natural resources of Hawaii." Finally an amendment on land management required "the State to conserve and protect agricultural lands, promote diversified agriculture, and increase agricultural self-sufficiency."

Many of the amendments have yet to have enabling legislation so that they can be taken beyond the publicly approved recommendation stage. Some confirm under the constitution what the state is already doing, what is already in legislation, and what is an integral part of the Hawaii State Plan. Some amendments represent however, a radical departure either in fundamental concept or in their specific detailed implementation.

Conclusion

Critics will solidly maintain that government agency publications are symbolic rather than practical, rhetorical rather than truly reflective. In the past many sound reports appear to have been ignored, their recommendations remaining unimplemented. Those which eventually are incorporated into an act are so legislatively watered-down, so say the critics, that they felt that the legislation might as well not have been enacted. There is some validity in the assertion that there can be great disparity between what appears initially to be a good bill, the final act, and that act's implementation—interpretation and enforcement.

There is a positive side to government business. The fact that many reports and much legislation move in a direction toward greater community welfare is on the credit side. They have the effect, if only very slowly, of changing public attitudes. Some consolation may be gained from the fact that a weak law may, at a later date, be strengthened when initial views have been changed and later attitudes are more responsive.

Unlike on the U.S. mainland, many levels of government in Hawaii are dominated by non-Caucasians. These people have some of, but certainly not all, the characteristics of national minority groups. Much however remains unique. There is obvious ambivalence to the values associated with the culture of origin and to the learned (rather than always experienced) values of mainland United States.

A historical factor is considerable. It is not long since these groups were viewed as aliens rather than true citizens, second-class citizens only once removed from the plantation. Their insecurity largely resulted from and was fortified by resident or incoming haoles who sometimes presented a less than admirable model of the American way of life but who, in comparison, were nevertheless powerful.

The solution to this predicament must have seemed clear: gain self-respect and integrity through achievement. That meant work hard; value education for what it will bring; learn the ways of business, commerce, and the professions; and if the great economic niches are already full, gain at least partial satisfaction and power of another sort through political activity. These strategies will at least bring some of the rewards, for so long beyond the reach of those of non-Caucasian background.

To understand what is happening in Hawaii, it is necessary to understand these aspects of Island history and the common personality themes of Hawaii legislators. Under such circumstances, no one would expect radical solutions to Hawaii's problems. One might expect pragmatic solutions, expedient compromises and an emphasis on growth and development. This seems to be the case. Some recent laws are essentially good and with time their implementation may change hearteningly.

As a state Hawaii is young and its politicians lack a long tradition of experience drawn on by mainland counterparts most of whom do not have to operate in a bicultural world. Yet, despite this local politicians are called upon to cope with arguments concerning traditional U.S. business practice, no growth, advanced coastal zone management, and ecological strategies—all conceptual notions originating from outside the state. Some of these ideas are new on the mainland, often need refining, and are still not well understood. That a group of local politicians (state or county) should not embrace them as wholeheartedly as some might wish is no surprise. Local lawmakers have their own priorities and agendas and what has already been achieved is a credit to them.

The state now has a comprehensive plan; its provisions are wide ranging. It has something for everybody. There are provisions which have the potential, if applied assertively, for taking care of virtually every conceivable problem. Annual reviews allow for special consideration and greater specificity to be given individual items. One encouraging theme is that in many areas special emphasis is given to the needs of Hawaii's people. The implication is that the needs are those of *all* Hawaii's people and not those of a particular, powerful group. Although in reality one group frequently has more economic leverage than the other, the plan pays attention to all.

CHAPTER 6

The Counties

IT could be claimed that the state sets the tone and the county through personal contact, attention to detail, policing, leading, persuading, and cajoling, gets the work done. The county, too, receives the reaction of the community if what is done is not to its liking. An attempt is made to bridge the gap between state and county by having county representatives on most of the governor's advisory committees. Close liaison between state and county is maintained through these numerous committees together with the State Policy Council, which includes the governor, his cabinet, and the four county planning directors who keep the lines of communication open between the state and the counties.

Though the counties are mentioned after the state in the organizational hierarchy, this should not indicate an inferior status in any way. Whereas the state may appear aloof and the federal government remote, the county government is closely identified with the people. Because of infinite and manifold personal interchanges, the county's contribution is difficult to analyze. Its relations with the community are frequently on the basis of feelings and emotions. This is understood by a good politician who knows that the hopes of the community within the county fasten firmly on the office of mayor and the elected council.

Each community within a county has its actions prescribed by a number of elements: the law of the land, the law of the state, the law of the county and its specific charter, physical and human resources of the county, external markets, the economy of the county, the attitudes and representation of the council, the mayor, the influence of the large companies and land holders, and the pressures exerted by developers and interested individuals inside and outside the county. But this is not all. Other factors must be taken into consideration such as the strength and range of activities of local interest groups, the ratio of visitors to residents, the attraction the county has for investors and outsiders, and the awareness of the citizenry concerning the impact of these activities on community welfare. Within the counties some of these elements are strong and others pitifully weak. Procedures of governance are set out in individual county charters, but recent experience has shown that these can be revised and changed by referendum and then appear counter to state law.

Because of the diverse elements making up a county, each county has a personality of its own, parts within it differing markedly from the whole. This uniqueness is reflected in the economic and human situation of each county and in such recognition given by the state in its planning. The City and County of Honolulu, with its large population, has views which are probably closer to those of the state than those of any other county. A large percentage of state decision makers live in Honolulu and because of greater input and some more pressing problems than those found on neighbor islands, such as population growth and visitor activity (a four to one visitor-to-resident ratio), these concerns are more likely to be reflected in Honolulu policy than in similar policies for neighbor island counties.

That Honolulu has more than its share of problems is obvious. It has had more than a century and a half of development. It is the service and industrial center for the state, the seat of government, and the hub of all tourist activity. The resultant crowding, the high number of in-migrants and aliens, and the urban concentration pose the county's (and the state's) major problems. Many approve a strategy of dampening growth in favor of accelerated growth elsewhere. This could bring the county into conflict with other counties, but because the county seat is also the state capital, the thrust of the other counties' hostility is directed toward the state rather than toward the county.

The County of Honolulu has problems unique to the capital city and major port. In many ways, the county provides a service function to the rest of the state where reciprocal services by other counties are not provided on the same scale. Over three-quarters of a million people live in Honolulu and many of them are responsible for entertaining and providing services for approximately four million visitors a year.

There are the inevitable problems associated with large numbers. An efficient transport system is essential as is the availability of adequate, moderately priced affordable housing. This has been achieved by extensive downtown redevelopment which has made central Honolulu the focal point of highrise residential condominiums.

The hub of the tourist industry, Waikiki, many feel, has surpassed its carrying capacity, and limits have been placed on the expansion of hotels and apartments in the area. Waikiki's magnetism, mystique, and easily accessible location has had its effect in dampening what might otherwise have been the success of other Oahu destination areas.[1] In addition to limitations placed on Waikiki, it is county policy to provide public services and to encourage private efforts to improve the state's major destination area.[2] Some disagree, saying that the state has continually been forced into this role which properly should be the county's.

As in other counties, attempts are being made to support the continuation of major crops and to encourage agricultural diversification. Population growth and related problems are so concentrated in the county that even in comparison with some "problem" neighbor island counties, Oahu's economy is considered weak.[3]

Although for many things County of Honolulu and State of Hawaii are coincident, this does not mean that one works hand in glove with the other. On the contrary, there was for a long time conflict between a feisty mayor, Frank Fasi, and a powerful governor. The conflict was seen in the withholding of funds voted by legislators for work in the county, the visitor industry, Waikiki redevelopment, and the distribution of capital improvement funds. Fasi's conflict with the state started with the late Governor John Burns and reached a climax mid-1977 in court when the state charged the mayor with bribery-related activity in what was popularly called the "Kukui Plaza scandal." The mayor, an unsuccessful gubernatorial candidate the following year, contended that this and other state actions were politically rather than judicially motivated. The case was eventually dropped. The new mayor, Eileen Anderson sees working with the state for the upgrading of Waikiki, a top priority.

The neighbor island counties are very different from Honolulu, more rural, less urbanized, and far less sophisticated. Kauai and Hawaii have from time to time been in poor economic shape.

Maui has been an exception. Mayor Herbert Matayoshi of the Big Island and former Mayor Elmer Cravalho of Maui both understood the importance of agriculture to the county economies and both mayors played important parts in making the state and the country aware of Hawaii's mid-seventies' sugar crises. The counties have in the past welcomed capital improvement projects directed toward them by the state, but now these projects must be seen as a two-edged sword helping to draw economic activity as well as unwanted population away from Oahu.

In 1964 the County of Hawaii was asking, "How do we catch up with the rest of the state and get our slice of tourism's pie?" The pundits answered loud and clear, "Build an overseas airport, increase your stock of hotel units, promote the island."[4] In 1969 the mayor's rather apprehensive question was "How do we guide the tourist industry?"

By 1974 a policy of controlled growth was an essential part of the Hawaii general plan. This entailed environmental impact statements before development, the provision of shoreline access where appropriate, historical site surveys, capital improvement contributed by developers, on-site housing for employees, and limited amounts of what realtors delight in calling "vacation house lots."

Then recession hit the state, and in particular the Big Island. Hotels were half full, worse hit than those anywhere else. Exactly the same questions were then asked in 1976 as were asked in 1964: "How do we get a greater share of the tourism pie?" But take note. In 1976, Hawaii did have an international airport, it did have more than 6,000 units of tourist accommodations, and it had had its tourism promoted. The sugar industry was worse off in 1976, and tourism, as a buffer, provided employment for former sugar workers. Economic factors had provided effective if undependable control to growth, but these factors were to some very frightening. With increased development even a mild recession can cause repercussions through a wide sector of the community. There is thus the temptation to advocate increased visitor growth as a hedge against unemployment and underused facilities. But very successful promotion calls for the further expansion of facilities with the possibility eventually of even greater recessional impact. The whole process, if not managed wisely, can be a vicious circle.

Hawaii County in 1976 was at the wavering and somewhat erratic interface between burgeoning development and the slow de-growth of recession. There was great concern that the county may never return to the more prosperous days of the early seventies. There was the growing realization that tourism as conventionally practiced elsewhere was not necessarily a certain success, nor was the Big Island a conventional case. Some political figures believed promotion should counteract de-growth, especially promotion that emphasized the unique qualities of Hawaii: its rural industries, enclaves of Hawaiiana, and its active volcanic areas. The pressure was placed on Mayor Herbert Mayatoshi to do what he could to improve the island economy. The state-county task force in Kohala, formed to take up the slack in unemployment after a sugar mill closed, largely came to grief. In 1978 after seven years of operation and a budget of $6.5 million, there was little to show for its activity. Unemployed sugar workers had found work in the tourist industry, thus rendering the mayor's efforts to stabilize the sugar industry useless. The mayor was a representative of all too small a group in the state who felt the need for a balance between agriculture and tourism. Sugar was viewed as an island economic mainstay both as an agricultural crop and as a provider of open space.

The county has suffered economically, and because of the importance of sugar to the island's economy, it will always be particularly vulnerable. Cattle raising, because of its rangelands and past tradition, would seem on the surface to have an obvious potential. Yet competition from the mainland, Australia, and New Zealand would make a livestock industry marginal. An obvious strategy is to find means to keep tourist capacity full while hoping sugar will rebuff further retrogression. Great efforts are being made with diversified agriculture; the prospect looks better each year but is not without problems. Forest products and geothermal energy are on the agenda for the future. Energy already seems to have had a good start.

The mayor sees locally generated energy as a future growth point for the county. It will be necessary first to prove feasibility, second to find organizations willing to generate energy, and third, in the case of geothermal energy, to understand to what extent it is dependent on groundwater. Geothermal power then has an exciting but nevertheless hard-to-predict power potential and future. A drilling program is in operation at Puna and the Department of Energy is working on the possibility of transporting surplus energy to Oahu by undersea electrical cable.

The present energy situation is exciting. During 1977–1979, progress was made in preparation for the successful August 1979 operation of the Keahole Point ocean thermal energy conversion (Mini-OTEC) project. This is a theoretical system long known in the energy business where the differential in temperature between warm surface and cold deep water nearby is exploited for energy production purposes. Some considered the 1979 breakthrough a Hawaii equivalent to the moon landing.

A consortium representing the State of Hawaii, the County of Hawaii, the Lockheed Missiles and Space Company, Alfa-Laval Thermal Inc. (Sweden), and the Dillingham Corporation participated in the $1.5 million project whose goal was to construct and operate a fifty-kilowatt floating OTEC plant off Keahole Point, Kona. This was not the only project. In late 1978, Global Marine Development Company, Newport Beach, was awarded a $42.7 million federal contract for a floating test platform as part of the OTEC-1 project, a more extensive three-year study due for completion 1983.

Also the U.S. Department of Energy and the State of Hawaii announced funding for a $9.3 million Seacoast Test Facility, a land-based support unit for OTEC test plants "to experiment with nutrient-rich sea water for mariculture studies."[5] Almost simultaneously the State Board of Natural Resources granted rights to four acres of land at Kapoho to the Research Corporation of the University of Hawaii on behalf of the state, county, the university, and the Hawaii Electric Light Company. The group, with a contract from the U.S. Department of Energy, was expected to design, operate, and test the feasibility of a geothermal electricity generating system. All going well, a geothermal-supported industrial park, electricity generation, or manganese nodule processing may be in the offing. By 1981, however, federal retrenchment clouded the future of energy programs.

While other places in similar economic straits might automatically have looked to tourism alone, this is not so easily done in Hawaii. The same promotion has not worked as quickly as it did on Maui. Like Kauai, Hawaii County is a little off the customary beaten track. It does not have the same tourist excitement of Waikiki or the beaches of Maui. But by late 1978, some change from the prolonged slump was in sight. Thomas Hitch, economist at First Hawaiian Bank, saw the recovery led by tourism and helped by millions of federal dollars allocated to energy research and other development.[6] Observers in 1979 felt his prediction was right. But by the end of the year the county was feeling the effects of a visitor industry economic downturn. Economic conditions by 1981 were considered to be the worst in a seven year period.

But past development has already taken its toll. Of 331 miles of shoreline, only 19 miles are actually sandy beach; of this, some prime beach areas have already been foreclosed to the public because of ecological damage. Nevertheless, despite limited beach areas, the landscape is diversified and attractive and has great appeal.[7] It is frequently said that a different island image needs to be developed and promoted. The Big Island does indeed have much going for it. In some ways, its riches are more subtle than Maui's. In others, it, like Kauai, is a residual bulwark of Hawaiiana. Gentle country conservatism together with "ruralness" are elements essential to the Hawaiian life-style (see chapter 9).

Kauai is different. From a transportation and psychological point of view, it is more remote than elsewhere. It is not on the way to another island. Critics will point out that it does not have the tourism infrastructure of Maui, there are few places to eat, limited entertainment, and little to do. To the outsider it is very Hawaiian and has some of the characteristics of Molokai. In comparison with Maui, it has not been such an easy place to develop as Princeville, and its subdevelopers, to their disappointment and dismay, found out.[8]

The present Kauai mayor, Eduardo Malapit, considered less development-oriented than his predecessor, found himself in a conflict triangle with a council at one corner and developers at the other. Mayor Malapit claimed that the council exceeded the power given it by charter and he wanted some of it back. To do this, he brought suit against the County Council, and his complaints were upheld in court.[9] But this was not the worst of his worries. County finances were in bad straits. Bill Wood's editorial in the July 1977 issue of *Hawaii Business* reads:

> The hardiest source of new revenues is to encourage expansion of Kauai's visitor industry and some politicians are now talking of doing just that. Embracing tourism has paid big dividends for Maui County and given it what is probably the soundest economy in the State . . . But on Kauai there has now been a marked reluctance to open the door to tourists. Preservation of Kauai's rural life style has become a popular and politically potent issue. Changing that image

would require not only political courage but much more than just talk if it is to be convincing to potential developers. Kauai's Mayor . . . speaks of encouraging both resort and agricultural development. His dual approach may make sense politically and even in the long run economically since he has some justifiable qualms about the future of tourism. But Kauai's financial problems are immediate. Fostering agricultural development is a long-range proposition and one, by the Mayor's admission, that is largely out of the hands of the county government. Resort growth is available now . . . But Kauai has a choice . . . less palatable politically . . . That alternative is to slow the upward trend of County expenditures, allowing exciting revenues to catch up with the outflow. It's a novel notion nowadays and painful to accomplish, but it seems the only real choice if Kauai is to go on having its environmental cake and eating it too.[10]

By 1978 the economy had made a real turnaround, construction was again at a high level, and unemployment was way down. Visitor expenditures were up 20 percent, farm sales 28 percent, and during 1978–1979 real estate values soared as investment dollars poured in from all directions. By the end of the 1970s economic buoyancy had arrived. The time had come, said another editorial, as hotels overflowed, for the people of Kauai to decide clearly whether the available growth is to be met enthusiastically or otherwise. It was time, the writer felt, that Kauai "got its act together" in providing a climate which "citizens can live with and others can rely on."[11]

In the eyes of some, the economic turnaround had come none too soon. The First Hawaiian Bank, in October 1976, stated that the key to increasing job opportunities, income, and even government revenues lay with the island visitor industry. The alternative they predicted would be "stagnation, out-migration of youth, and deteriorating government services."[12] This was a strange situation indeed when a reason frequently given for the establishment of the visitor industry in the first place has been that "it creates jobs" and "keeps the kids on the island." After almost four thousand units had been built, it was again predicted that unless development took place, younger people would be going to Honolulu or to the mainland where there are more job opportunities.

As a purely economic statement, this was eminently true. *Hawaii Business* editorials saw the situation within the context of the current Hawaii business paradigm. There are some on Kauai who might agree, but a growing body of them have voiced different feelings. Kauai maintains a local life-style which its people hold dear. It has a conservatism which has served it well. It has demanded low-profile, high-quality development. While others have raced forward, Kauai has held itself in check allowing public citizen groups to assess the direction of the island. Kauai's remoteness, in this regard, probably worked in its favor. A large number of residents work the land. Urbanization is limited. Rural life characterizes the whole county. If some of the older people are reticent and nonverbal, they are well served by younger community members. All ages however joined forces in fruitlessly expressing their disapproval of the contentious Nukolii project (see chapter 12).

A Maui County Case Study

Maui County has been touted by the media and its former mayor as the best-run, most economically viable, and most successful county in Hawaii. Like all counties, it has a strong home rule element eschewing centralized state control. Many of its citizens would still like more of the heady development of the past; others think differently. Some say, "Leave us as we are. We like the simple life. We want no change"—a sentiment hard to understand when the ratio of visitors to residents runs 20:1. The administration's view has been to preserve the unique life-style. This may be vain hope as the three major resorts under construction could easily increase the population by 60,000–70,000 affluent, Caucasian, sophisticated urbanites.

During the seventies no single person was more influential, or controversial, in county affairs than Mayor Elmer F. Cravalho. Obviously, the office provided him with clout, but it was as much the Cravalho mystique. In July 1979 he resigned after twelve years in office and after having been the single most important person in Maui tourism development.

His views of the importance of the county role were well known. "The biggest help we can get from the State is the help of noninterference." This was his continuing attitude on highly centralized control which never varied while he was in office. "Quality development" he told planners at Kaanapali "characterizes Maui because of local decisions and controls . . . Maui doesn't need someone in Honolulu or Washington determining what is best for Maui.''[13] Cravalho was unwavering in his distaste for greater state involvement. The State Plan received no praise from him although the county was charged with bringing its plans into line with the master plan two years after its adoption. In August 1977, he said that adoption of the plan as it then stood "would spell disaster for the State and the Counties."[14]

The Mayor and His Policies

Even today, Elmer Cravalho is perhaps the most widely recognized name on Maui. As *Hawaii Business*' "Man of the Year" for 1978, he was one of the best-known and well-regarded politicians in the state. He was commended for his work with youth and his housing program for the elderly.

He was definite about what he wanted, and what he wanted, he often got. He is alleged to have said to advisory committees concerning the general plan for the county: "There are certain things we are going to do with you or without you because I believe them to be right. I hope it will be with you."[15] He insisted on keeping a finger on the county pulse and having lagging departments move along at his pace. He liked to know what was going on and, in some matters, virtually insisted on placing his signature on the bottom line.

The outside developer expecting county help and cooperation had to jump through a number of hoops. "What's expected of private developers," said Teney Takahashi of Amfac, "is not in the rule books. To do business here you've gotta do this and that . . . You're not going to do business here unless you do."[16]

Proposals had to be checked by appropriate county offices. There was a way of doing things on Maui and an outsider had to tow the line. His behavior was carefully observed. Any major proposal which would affect the welfare of the county and tax county resources had to be discussed first with the mayor. Only after arriving at an amicable understanding would it be prudent to make a public statement. A substantial project warranted a joint announcement introduced by the mayor. Woe to the company developer who tried to circumvent this protocol.

There are charitable and less charitable ways of interpreting this insistence on procedure. The mayor was never a lover of powerful companies, especially those of Hawaii. He recalls keenly their historical impact on the people of Hawaii. The expected joint announcement of a new project was thus a symbolic gesture. It indicated that the company had done its homework. It had not arrogantly come into the county expecting gratefulness while dispensing largess. It had approached the matter with care and a joint announcement dispelled any suggestion of unilateral imposition. It suggested a cooperative venture in which appropriate reciprocal tribute was paid to the county for the use of public resources upon which a large part of development enterprise always rests. The tribute may have been in the form of a public park or a contribution to a water system. It also indicated willingness to conform and a degree of respect for the people of Maui.

Cautious developmental growth with stringent controls was always part of Cravalho's stated policy; one can be excused for wondering whatever happened then to Kihei and Kahana, areas often cited as examples of poor developments. Several years ago he said: "We can afford [growth]. We're twice the size of Oahu with 6 percent of the population. Our population is 30 percent below what it was in the 1930s. Ours is a growing community—the hottest place in the State." In a special edition of the *Lahaina Sun*, 13 June 1973, on alternatives to the present Maui economy, he challenged anyone to suggest an industry rivaling tourism as an immediate builder of the local economy and offering jobs and revenue. It is the short-range answer to stabilizing the economy but "only a fool," he maintained, "would say that the visitor industry is a panacea."

At Kula, on the slopes of Haleakala, Cravalho raised pigs. He saw farming as a useful conservation measure, as an alternative and worthy counter to too great an emphasis on the leisure industry. In the early seventies, he saw a diminution in the importance of agriculture; he scorned those who with little knowledge of the land advocated diversified agriculture and mixed farming as a substitute for tourism development. This view he supported with the results of a Molokai Task Force questionnaire. By the end of the seventies when development was concretely engraved onto the landscape, one could perceive a several degree shift in his views —softer toward farming, harder on development.

The views of the former mayor concerning development are clearly reflected in a statement called County Growth Policy, submitted to the mayor-appointed planning commission in July 1973. Planning Director Howard Nakamura summarized preferred goals and attitudes. The statement suggested caution and a growing concern with the cost of development. Development was referred to as "a runaway juggernaut." The underlying principle was that "land must be treated as a limited resource rather than as a marketable commodity."[17] These guidelines formed a basis for the Maui central plan discussed later.

The Cravalho administration, in the open and behind the scenes, had been the single, most potent force in Maui development. It encouraged growth as the mayor often did, it initiated policy recommendations, and it could check development through recommendations to the legislative branch of the county. It could also exact tribute as it did with the major land developers, and it could smooth the path of approval. By the imposition of restrictions of county services and facilities, it could make the road to development very rough indeed. There is no doubt that Cravalho's no-growth policy for Hana (a small rural village based on cattle production and limited tourism) and his determination not to facilitate any development which would change the Hana life-style were instrumental in terminating negotiations to sell the Hana Ranch at a price which would have necessitated a high degree of development to justify its purchase.[18]

The County Planning Function

Because of the extreme importance of the visitor industry, planning for increasing urbanization in all its facets is a major county focus. This is not a matter of purely county initiative. Many of the efforts made are in conformance with both federal and state legislation and completed often with matching state planning grants and federal support. For example, the federal Urban Planning Grants (701) have been very useful in the past.

Besides day-to-day activity, more than enough work for the staff to handle, periodic tasks are concerned with the revision of regional general plans, the formation of rules and regulations for shoreline management, and the consideration and implementation of such legislation as the Open Space and Outdoor Recreation Plan, an outgrowth of the 1971 State Comprehensive Outdoor Recreation Plan.[19]

In 1974 attempts were made to have an architectural review board set up within the county. Opposition was so great that it was dropped. Such a board was not uncalled for, certainly, as examples of hideous design abound, but county government finally acceded that the board would but add to governmental bureaucracy. The vocal few brought pressure to bear and the board was discharged. Counties develop a great sense of apprehension when accused of controlling, even as this is their responsibility. To be charged with introducing further unnecessary red tape frequently brings a local government to heel. The reversal took place at a time discussions were in progress concerning implementation of the Shoreline Protection Act. It was known that the act would give wide-ranging environmental control to the counties and, within county-determined regulation, developers of proposed structures could be asked to submit plans to an urban design board anyway. Within the rules and regulations for the Interim Coastal Zone Management Act, Maui County made provisions for such a review.

The act, as it applied to counties, was a major step forward in the regulation and preservation of environmental and cultural resources (for an account of coastal zone legislation in the state, see chapter 5). Anything more than a single-family dwelling and valued at a minimum of $25,000, any man-made device or activity which might conceivably degrade the shoreline in designated special management areas required a permit. One could proceed only after plans had been closely scrutinized by the County Planning Department, the Planning Commission, and the Urban Design Review Board.

Maui took the matter seriously and proposed managing a greater area of shoreline under special management than any other county. Special management areas were designated in places where building was likely to take place in a zone at least 300 feet from the high tide mark. The law designated 300 feet, but if a county wished, it could extend the special management area 1,000 feet from the shoreline. A County attempt to go well beyond the 300-foot minimum met with such resistance from, among others, the representative of Alexander & Baldwin (Wailea Development), that the county yielded. It meant that for the long run, the county voluntarily yielded control of areas beyond 300 feet from the shore which it was legally empowered to control. The regulations came into effect 1 December 1975. Developers who did not wish their projects to be governed by the act were permitted to file for approval to commence development whether they were financially ready to begin projects or not.[20] There was a welter of eleventh-hour applications in all island counties. When the smoke cleared, a large number of beachfront projects had slipped under the wire of shoreline protection. Since then, the legislation has been superseded by the State Coastal Zone Management Act (see chapter 5). As the result of a 1979 amendment, Maui has considerably increased the inland dimensions of its special management areas at Kihei, Lahaina, and Kaanapali.

The purpose of the Shoreline Act was to prevent injudicious use of coastal lands and ill-conceived projects from despoiling the littoral. The December 1975 situation had the effect of encouraging projects of lower quality than would otherwise have been the case at a time when the spirit of the legislation was to encourage environmental respect and quality.

A Long-Range View

By far the most interesting, comprehensive, and formal statement of Mayor Cravalho's policy was the previously mentioned Proposed Goals and Objectives for a Long-Range Comprehensive Plan for Maui County (1977), republished with modest changes in 1979. The document provided a basis for the critical evaluation of the State Plan and a pilot study for the Maui general plan. It was without a doubt intended to mold the thinking of the citizens advisory committees who were to be charged with making recommendations for the general plan. It specifically included an environmental element which was a substantial change in direction. The visitor industry since the sixties was likened to "charging cavalry." In some parts of the state it had been uncontrolled. In Maui, the document stated, uncontrolled growth would meet with certain problems such as a critical lack of water, diminished open space, the expensive maintenance of access roads, large numbers of visitors becoming permanent residents and, consequently, increased burdens on county support services.

To prevent "helter skelter" development, the document proposed a guided development, continued excellence, and "resort development [that] maintained the social, economic and physical environments of the County and its people." Certain guidelines and strategies which it was hoped would achieve these goals are outlined as follows:

> Destination areas should be clearly defined to prevent overflow to undesignated areas;
> Obstructions to ocean views should be prevented;
> Landscaping should be required; lighting and heights would have limitations imposed;

An architectural review board should review construction to ensure excellence and quality;

No direct mainland flights to Maui should be permitted;

Construction should blend with the environment;

Education and training for the visitor industry would be provided residents; and

Charges and fees would be assessed on new development for the provision of water.

The above were considered necessary despite the tremendous lift to the island economy tourism had given. Nonetheless, tourism was acknowledged as having given extra income and attracting investors; "the multiplier effect of the visitor dollar . . . [had been] used and reused for the benefit of the community," stated the Proposed Goals.[21]

The future would set the tone for life-styles and amenities in community development. The industry's impact would be viewed in terms of Maui's life-styles—lives should not be styled to accommodate economic forces; rather the reverse should always be true. Resort destination areas were redefined and confined to Kaanapali-Kapalua, Wailea-Makena, West Molokai, and to a limited degree Hana.

It was unfortunate that the statement came after much coastal grandeur had been marred. The area's development, along with that of Kahana and Napili in the northwest, had discredited the county, challenging its sincerity concerning quality. Nevertheless, from a practical and political view, it seems unlikely that the populace would otherwise have comprehended what nonconfined mixed development could turn out to be.

Water supply was seen as the main problem. Today, the document said, this can only be provided by ad hoc joint ventures of the county and developers. No longer can a county be relied on to provide the infrastructure—indeed a healthy sign suggesting the county was in no way prepared to assume a subordinate role in the development game.

Water was crucial and an element which would limit new development—resort, residential, or agricultural. Water could also be used as an instrument of control as it was through 1978 and 1979. Although building permits were issued, it was on the understanding that connections would not be made until construction could be appropriately serviced.

The proposed policy direction, although somewhat discriminatory, promoted the large, well-planned major development which could contribute substantially to the infrastructure and be controlled in greater measure by the county. It assumed that the community members would be happy to settle for such development which would provide the greatest benefit to the community.

Soon after the mayor's views were made known in the first document, Cravalho appointed nine committees made up of 246 persons from 28 Maui districts for the purpose of advising the preparation of the Maui County General Plan. The draft plan was distributed 28 December 1977. Two and a half years later, after numerous revisions, it was approved.

Through 1978, 1979, and 1980, the general plan underwent scrutiny by the General Plan Subcommittee, the Council's Planning and Economic Development Committee (PEDC), the public, the Planning Commission, and the Council itself. Changes were made by the chair of the PEDC, Councilman Rick Medina, and the unclear and fuzzy language of the draft was polished by an employed consultant. With an obvious eye on the mayor who, with the advisory citizens' committees, fathered the plan, Medina made clear that the plan's wording had been carefully analyzed because "the Council did not want to give the Administration any extra powers."[22] Here was a statement with deep meaning, no doubt indicative of some of the circumstances which ultimately led to the mayor's resignation.

Cravalho was highly critical of the county council. He admonished it for slowness. He took it to task on several matters: agriculture had been downplayed and the word quality omitted as an adjective with reference to the visitor industry. The committee explained that adjective was inadequately defined and thus left out. The mayor responded: "All the major developers in the County have stressed they are going after quality. They sure as hell know what quality is. Does this mean we're to go the route of the numbers game? Quality is the FIT [free and independent traveler] . . . the carriage trade . . . low density . . . open spaces . . . not maximum density . . . or another Waikiki."[23] In the final version the word quality was put back in.

Like the Hawaii State Plan, the Maui County general plan had its share of weasel words and buzz phrases. Planning cliches, it propounded, had been stated time and again in planning documents throughout Hawaii. Two stated themes, the encouragement of individual ownership of land and housing and the maintenance of agriculture were specific by comparison. But nowhere did it state plainly, rather than imply, "the major problems" or "set forth the desired sequence" of development, as the county charter clearly mandated. A vague and flexible plan can as easily reinforce the machinations of the corrupt as it can support the thoughtful and responsible.

The citizens advisory committees did arrive at specific recommendations concerning particular programs and facilities but these were omitted from the general plan presumably to appear later in community development plans. Despite the use of vague terms, there were some encouraging, straightforward statements, many originating from the mayor's initial formulation. No one could contest the plan's views on compatible urban design, discouragement of land speculation, and land taxation tied to the "most reasonable and beneficial use" as opposed to one geared to "the highest and best" use of the land.

In the tourism section, resort destination areas were finally omitted before plan approval because "it should be left up to individual communities to decide whether or not they want resort areas in their neighborhoods." Councilman John Vail in the same report is recorded as saying that "it isn't right for the plan to arbitrarily tell people in Makena or Kapalua that they are going to be visitor destination areas . . . whether they like it or not."[24] This part of the exercise did not bear analysis and statements such as this had a hollow ring. Kapalua already was a destination area and the die was long since cast for Makena when the council gave the green light to development. It had also voted almost unanimously in favor of the Furhmann case and refused to consider the views of "The People to Save Makena" (see chapter 12).

There was no doubt about developers having to bear what was called a "fair" share of public service and utility costs. The plan also recommended the prohibition of direct mainland flights as well as the meshing of visitor industry growth with the availability of local labor and housing.

Agriculture recommendations were straightforward and were concerned with maintaining agriculture and making it more attractive. Agriculture's relationship to the tourist industry, however, was not suggested; and if public education were necessary, it might have been in this area rather than in indoctrinating the citizenry for the benefit of one sector of the economy. The tourist industry, of course, is important and so too is education, but the situation calls for a balanced awareness of the implications of the industry in all its facets (see chapter 14).

Although it has been stated that the county general plan does not identify means for resolving problems, it was agreed that the plan come closer to some of the major issues. With rapid economic growth, in-migration and housing were seen as important questions and the provision of new housing a critical problem. Like the provision of water to many areas of Maui, the lack of housing for employees could be a factor which dampens the growth of tourism depending on the extent to which the county is willing to implement its policies.

Fundamentally the county plan was like the Hawaii State Plan and all other county plans. There was the suggestion of reasonable satisfaction with the past and status quo, yet the need to improve. There was the inevitable resignation to the fact that the future would lie mainly with tourism. Planners hoped that tourism would not impair the environment, erode life-style, or make too many demands on local resources. Agriculture, a "major component of the economy," the plan implied, was ailing and in need of nurture. In the face of increasing development, it was time to reestablish local integrity, evaluating those things taken for granted but which would be lost without proper care.

External Relations

As far as relations with developers and with the public are concerned, the county makes every effort within the framework of busy staff schedules to be helpful. Much of the Planning Department's time is taken up with the evaluation proposals and preparation for both public and private meetings with the Planning Commission, the Land Use Commission, and the Board of Adjustment and Appeals. Innumerable requests are met, denied, or conditionally approved. During the Cravalho administration large landholders were manipulated, cajoled, arm-twisted, or merely encouraged to make concessions on behalf of the community. The relationship between Cravalho and Alexander & Baldwin was particularly interesting in this respect. In the exercise of interdependent strategies both parties hoped that they would gain.

In early 1978 the relationship between the mayor and the great landowners of the county was taken a step further and formalized. In the past, agreements had been less public, discrete, and arrived at on a one-to-one basis. Landowners met with the mayor for the first time together and eventually agreed to share lands to guarantee the continued production of sugar and pineapples and the expansion of diversified agriculture. There was also agreement for the provision of cheap or free land for the construction of employee housing. Under appropriate conditions, the county would be prepared, they learned, to negotiate cheap short-term money from the banks, as well as federal mortgage financing. To prevent speculation, it was arranged that, if during the first ten years the owner wished to sell, the developer should buy the house and property back at the price paid together with a 7 percent increase in equity.

"We cannot allow $250,000 paid for a condominium unit to set the value of real estate for residential use," the mayor said. "To compensate, the developer must make available land for local housing to offset the inflationary effect of the market in condos . . . Each developer gives a little and in the long run each is making a lot. It's a new approach talked about but never done."[25]

This was not altogether true as reported. It had been, in modified form, part of Elmer Cravalho's stock-in-trade for a decade. The latest at the time of the statement was a proposed land and water-sharing arrangement for the new agricultural park at Omaopio (Kula area) contributed to by the county, the Haleakala Ranch, the state, and Maui Land & Pineapple Co. (the developers of Kapalua Resort area).

Behind the Scenes at the County Building

In conversation with Mayor Cravalho, I found him to be the antithesis of many other informants: frank, forthright, and always to the point. There were times when his statements warranted careful analysis and occasions when the mind reeled in attempting to clarify a contrived obscurity or a carefully included allusion. The choice of one word could turn the unequivocal into the equivocal. It was here one had to admire his sense of public politics, and as much possibly took place behind the scenes as up front.

Elmer Cravalho prided himself on being champion of "the little man." In his dealings with many citizens he was private and intimate rather than public. "What's achieved at a public hearing?" he would say. "Who attends? The haoles. Who gets up and talks? The haoles. Public meetings are for haoles. This is not the Maui way. Our people have come up through the plantations and they've been controlled by the big companies. When a public meeting is over or an announcement appears in the newspaper, my telephone starts ringing. 'What they trying to do?' the caller asks. 'What you going to do?' They need someone to look after their interests and that's just what I do. These are the people we've got to protect. The little man from Keokea, Kaupakulua, or Wai-hee. It's my job to see that his life-style is not destroyed." A good sentiment, but not new in the Islands. One can draw analogies with aspects of colonial plantation paternalism and later union paternalism. It is part of the arcane, behind-the-scenes, subliminal activity of all local government. It's part of the workings of the planning commission, the council, as well as the mayor's office. This is not new in politics; in fact, it is an essential ingredient. But its use, perhaps, is more necessary in Hawaii than in many other places in the United States.

The Subliminal Factor

In prolonged discussions over many years in the Islands, it has become apparent to me that what goes on behind the scenes is tremendously important, influential, and a variable defying either measurement or substantiation. Out of dozens of individual informants, all felt that behind-the-scenes activity was a vital, inevitable, and an almost mystical element that did much to determine the course of development and frequently who was to make more money than somebody else. Very few people talked frankly, and although everyone knew (gravity enters the voice) "these things happen," few persons proffered tangible information. Some would brazenly say "If I wanted to I could easily 'nail' him." I sometimes felt that I was in the middle of a vast conspiracy. The intensity of mystery and excitement changed from group to group, depending on who the informants were and which year it was. At times, it appeared to be vintage years for covert activity. The more radical the informant, the more sinister the "plot" was made to appear —much more so in the late sixties than the middle seventies. The actors changed too. Some rabble-rousers of Earth Day 1969 miraculously appeared as staid conservatives in the electioneering of 1978. But there were many solid, nonradical informants who felt that they, or the community, had suffered injustices, perhaps from an area suddenly spot-zoned, a high-level position filled by an unqualified political appointee, or a magnificent road which appeared to outsiders to lead to nowhere. Many of the most forceful informants were those who alleged they had suffered through some sort of malicious manipulation of zoning or who felt some regional plan steering committee members contrived to rig the process and benefit monumentally from the plan. Others claimed open hearings a fait accompli, entirely devoid of public participation. When I tried to tie it down, asking "who is responsible?" the knowing reply, seldom if ever definite, invariably was "who else?" Depending on the conversation, this could have referred to the governor, the mayor, the planning director, the chairman of the planning commission, an ILWU representative, or the "governor's man" on Island X.

The reality of a large number of successful human (including business) relationships in Hawaii (and elsewhere) includes hearty handshakes, informal discussions, a nod of the head, tacit acknowledgment, the return of a favor discussed over a private lunch, outward pleasantness, and reciprocal and multi-faceted interchange. One cannot see that the situation could be otherwise or necessarily should be. Where public officials are concerned there are many persons who appear to view such behavior with distaste. In the corporate world the same behavior is usually acceptable, even admirable. The subliminal atmosphere is closely related to politics, always tinged with excitement and closely watched by self-appointed vigilantes alert for a scorching scandal or a reprehensible conflict of interest.

This aspect of Hawaii life—by no means unique to Hawaii—is difficult to describe or document but is nevertheless there. Few would deny that it is something one must be aware of, especially in relation to land development. It is difficult to write about and yet it has to be written about because it exists—vague, shadowy, illusory, good, and bad. The same situation is interpreted with different perceptions by different groups: one will see it as good, stable government for the people; another will perceive it as insidious corruption. A developer's visit with a mayor can be seen as perfectly normal by some, or reprehensible by others.

The subliminal factor then is difficult to assess, impossible to quantify, not easy to authenticate, but nevertheless extant. It embraces the informal and quickly dispatches business which otherwise would take much longer to complete. It provided me with much authentic and specific information not appropriate for citation here. It also provided information which was without a doubt erroneous. No one should ignore these very helpful informants operating in the thick of things who say frequently, and resignedly, in answer to apparently unanswerable questions, "It's politics," "It's Hawaii," "It's Maui," "It's Kihei," or "You're in Hilo." Like Woodward and Bernstein, one shouldn't ignore information confirmed by several highly respected informants who can never be acknowledged. Now back to the Maui case study.

The Maui County Council

Although policy is approved by the council, the council's views of land were less restrictive than those of the Cravalho administration which had day-to-day close relations with the people.

The council's concern can be great. When faced with the problem of people wanting homes but finding them impossible to afford in central Maui, they placed the blame squarely on speculation, a spillover from leisure land development on the west side of Maui and at Kihei. In the mid-seventies they made it perfectly clear to the director of planning that they would get tough with speculators working county-sponsored projects. They insisted developers require buyers to guarantee they would fill the role only of owner-occupier and that resales within a certain period would be handled by the developer. But performance was not always consistent. In 1976 the council was not prepared to support an anti-speculation recommendation made by consultants working with the Kula Plan. Anti-speculation strategies were essential with county-sponsored housing developments, but apparently feelings were not nearly as strong in the case of private projects.

Officially the council is the de jure policy-setting arm of county government. "It is they who decide the limitation or otherwise of an industry such as tourism," said Cravalho. It was he, however, supported by his cabinet, informally by council supporters, who was the de facto policymaker. It was he who said, "We're going to have quality growth," and it was he who, in answering a question concerning the reason for wall-to-wall condominium development north of Kaanapali (and later at Kihei), said "Every condominium built represents a small developer. Every one we allow to build diminishes the power of the great land companies. They have controlled everything in Hawaii in the past and they'd like to control development today. They have always held the little man to ransom. When I help the small developer, I weaken the large companies and I help the community. What is lost aesthetically through small-scale development is gained in greater freedom—a small price to pay."[26]

In comparison with the unified voice of the mayor and his direct staff managers, the council often spoke from diverse points of view, yet it, over time, gave the mayor much support. There have been in the council ranks hard core individualists who felt an owner or developer should be permitted to do whatever he wished on his own land—hardly a formula for the preservation of Maui for future generations. There have been attempts by the council unilaterally to modify regional plans and to bypass both the planning department and planning commission. When discussing Donald Wolbrink and Associates' Kula plan, to which reference has already been made, the council took a much more permissive view on controls than the consultants who had obtained considerable citizen input and based recommendations partially on that. But there was a hidden agenda behind the lines. There had been a feeling among council members that to mean something, the representatives of the people should be independent and should do more than concur with the administration, a difficult thing not to do if the administration does its work properly. In the past, the opposition alleged that the mayor controlled approximately half the council members. "Under these conditions," one councillor complained, "we are no more than just a rubber stamp." By 1978, a number of representatives were saying, "We've got the bit between our teeth. We're not rubber stamps. We must maintain this momentum." They never let go.

Rick Medina, a councilman, expressed another area of contention when he said: "A lot of people feel that we've spent a lot of money on the resort areas and ignored the other needs of the County. Had the non-resort areas been attended to, the County would be in a position to lower the unemployment rate."[27]

Mayor Cravalho insisted that development for leisure purposes could be controlled by denying permits for water, maintaining that the council controls by zoning. One may ask, "How?" In 1976 there were 3,500 persons in the Maalaea-Kihei-Wailea region. It had 2,800 condominium units, 800 or more of which lay vacant or unsold. Nevertheless (one might be permitted to gasp), zoning still allowed for over 30,000 units—thirteen times the 1976 inventory. On a conservative basis of 1.8 persons per unit, a 50 percent occupancy rate, and the State Tourism Plan formula for employment, the future tourism-related population of the area could be 60,000. This population is a highly speculative figure, but the number of units is not. To say that the council through zoning and general plans can control the industry is to a degree correct but hardly convincing even to the most naive. Existing zoning to most developers suggests partial if not complete approval. To have allowed for over 30,000 condominium units and to talk about control tests credibility to say the least.

Mayoral Politics

Much more can be said about the county and its administration but again it is necessary to return to the decisive, powerful figure of Elmer Cravalho, who as a political force in the 1972, 1974, 1976, and 1978 elections had little more than token opposition. His policy of quality growth with restrictions was well known and, if votes meant anything, overwhelmingly supported in all mayoral races.

Without a doubt, for a variety of reasons including administrative expertise and a remarkably strong personality, Elmer Cravalho kept the people of Maui in the palm of his hand. The mayor's third inauguration was attended by Governor Ariyoshi who was described by the *Honolulu Star-Bulletin* as having a "preferential regard" for Cravalho. He praised the mayor for his part in "guiding Maui to the position where it led the State in its program for quality growth."[28] "The seventies," said Cravalho, "will see a new era when the Neighbor Islands, to a substantial degree, will become masters of their own destinies and begin contributing to the State . . . instead of going to the legislature with outstretched hands. We promise to work for greater economic stability, wide employment opportunities, lessened government centralization and against the use of money as a development 'come-on'."

During 1978–1979 it was obvious that the mayor's relationship with the county council was deteriorating. For some time the council members had been sensitive about their belief that the mayor had manipulated past councils while he took the kudos for the success of Maui development. His handling of the proposed Kula Agricultural Park and certain federal grants were not liked by some council members. To the mayor's mind, the council had taken an intolerable amount of time approving the Maui County general plan. Council members accused him of using water restrictions to effect control when he found he could not have it through the council. The council made it difficult for the mayor to get budget approvals, and it seemed that the council was intent on tying his hands. It was evident that it intended to play a more important role than previously and that the mayor could not easily continue to operate in his accustomed manner.

It was acknowledged that no other person had done more for Maui development. He had the happy knack of making most constituent groups feel he was doing something for them even if this were not the case. His statements were well chosen and designed to cover most obvious contingencies, but he could point to Maui developments with considerable pride. In a future decade this might not be possible—something he may have tacitly understood. He was on the crest of a wave having made probably the greatest contribution any single person could have made in view of the diversity of forces at play. The character of Maui in all its ramifications at the end of the seventies was overwhelmingly the work of Cravalho.

On 24 June 1979, well before his term was through, he resigned; that same day, he left office. Eighteen candidates stepped up to take his place without the benefit of primary elections. The administration under Mayor Hannibal Tavares, who received more votes than the other seventeen candidates combined, is too young yet to have made a substantial mark. He has appointed former planning director Howard Nakamura as county managing director. Between the two of them some of the old policies concerning the importance of agriculture and quality development will certainly continue. But nobody knows what might be in store for Maui. To keep Maui at the level it has achieved will take all the strength expert leadership can muster. It is already showing the strains of too rapid growth. The Cravalho act, in places flawed, is difficult to follow.

CHAPTER 7

Tourism and Agriculture

DESPITE the fact that the bulk of the residents of Hawaii live in urban areas, mainly Honolulu, the economic and social roots of the island group's people still lie in agriculture and the land. The much-emphasized charm of the people stems not only from Polynesian tradition but also from an essentially rural background where simplicity is satisfaction and where friendliness is part of the behavior pattern.

I have discussed early agriculture and the fact that within the state large areas are controlled by relatively few people. Tourism in Hawaii is a comprehensive experience, an important part of which is rural areas where a particular life-style and open spaces free from crowding lead to a feeling of tranquility and contentment. Agriculture is the key. But reinforcement is mutual. The export component in diversified agriculture—high value crops and flowers—could not exist without the availability of relatively cheap air transport directly attributable to tourism.

Agriculture is an important prop to tourism. It is the third major contributor to the Hawaiian economy after federal spending and tourism. If economists were to devise a method for evaluating public good, social values, and the real worth of the countryside to the overall well-being of Hawaii, then agriculture would be close to the top where it was in traditional economic terms immediately prior to World War II.

The agriculture issue is critical. Traditional economics and urban business notions are powerful attitude makers which can blind decision makers to the broader, more human picture. In this case, it is the relationship between agriculture and Hawaii society.

The narrower view is easy to understand. Before 1967 the income derived from agriculture was in excess of that reported as "visitor expenditures." From that year onward, tourism receipts were ahead of agriculture and remained that way. In 1973 tourism surpassed federal defense and nondefense expenditures and rose to the top. Agriculture remained well down but still important. By 1980 receipts from agriculture were almost $1.0 billion, a little less than one third of the total federal expenditures (defense plus non-defense spending as one category) and a similar fraction of the visitor industry expenditures for the year. On this basis tourism appears overwhelmingly important and the dependence on agriculture considerably diminished. But the situation is more complicated than this. In the past two years agricultural income has grown considerably. Sugar receipts can only be described as volatile, having increased 100 percent from 1978 to 1980.

Agriculture in the 1970s: Sugar

In the mid-1970s, agriculture was doing better than it had at the beginning of the decade. This was due to a somewhat enlivened market for both sugar and pineapple, but this was only a temporary bright spot. Neither of these crops is strong, and although immeasurably important to the economy and way of life, in no way does the future for agriculture look certain. In the late 1970s approximately 220,700 acres were in sugar, 44,000 acres in pineapple, and 28,700 in diversified crops. At the same time there were an estimated 1,150,500 acres in various types of livestock grazing.[1]

In 1974 sugar prices hit an all-time high and production brought in $685.2 million in sales. For a time agriculture production looked good and company profits soared. Retail prices skyrocketed. Mainland manufacturers then found cheaper substitutes for cane sugar, using corn-derived fructose sweeteners which now account for over a quarter of the total sweetener market.[2] Manufactured products with a high sugar content rose steadily in price, and consumer resistance to higher prices steepened. The anomalous high price for one year did much harm to the industry at a time when it was competing with other cane areas in the country as well as beet and corn producers. Hawaii sugar found itself for the first time on a world market without the protective legislation which had buoyed it up for many years. The 1975 sales dropped to $365.8 million despite increased production. The total for

Puunene Mill, Maui. Tourism in Hawaii is closely related to agriculture, which provides tranquil open space, rural villages, and work for a large immigrant population. All are resources essential to the visitor industry. (Alexander and Baldwin photo)

1976, $252.0 million, was lower still, reflecting lower production, the result of poor weather conditions. Most growers made little from their sugar acres. By 1977 production costs rose well above sales. By 1978 conditions improved slightly with receipts close to $285 million but by the last year of the decade these had risen to $346 million, and by the following year, with world sugar prices soaring, to over $600 million. Producers were elated with these gains after four years of losses. By 1981 prices were down again but still above the dark days of the 1970s.

Since 1946 land devoted to sugar has with minor fluctuations amounted to 220,000 acres.[3] Today's acreage is higher than the 1940s or 1950s. In the past few years this acreage has declined but has been compensated for by increasing yields, an important factor over the past thirty years.[4] Earlier, land was available for cultivation, but world production outstripped consumption and militated against expansion. In the United States, protection was offered the industry by the Sugar Act which ensured that costs would be covered and a profit made.

The U.S. Sugar Act, first legislated in 1937, gave quotas for the protection of mainland beet and cane grown in Hawaii, Puerto Rico, and the Virgin Islands. It set a sugar price which would keep United States sugar production alive, allowing the industry to be maintained in Hawaii.[5] However, at the end of 1974, the Sugar Act lapsed and Hawaii sugar found itself on an open market. Because of temporarily high world prices, the industry continued to do well. From the traditional surplus which had formerly characterized the industry, a deficiency had developed. During the early 1970s, world consumption was ahead of production, the International Sugar Agreement terminated, and Hawaii had its best year in history. But this was short lived as will be seen later. The future appeared unstable, and no one viewed it with any optimism.

In 1979 about 5,000 persons worked in sugar growing and another 4,600 in processing.[6] Processing took place in fourteen mills and two refineries. For a long period during a world surplus of low-cost sugar, the Sugar Act, stringent economic measures, reorganization, research, and new techniques kept the barely viable, marginal Hawaii industry above water. One aspect, admirable in one sense, proved a problem in another. As the standard of living in Hawaii raced ahead of many other sugar-producing areas, the wages of agricultural workers kept pace. In the mid-1970s, sugar workers were earning $60 a day including fringe benefits ($43 in direct earnings), perhaps the highest in the world.

To combat unfavorable economic conditions several courses of action were taken, some of which resulted in Hawaii having the highest average sugar yield of any world producer. Poorer producing land was let go, a number of mills were closed,[7] sugar lands were consolidated for more economic management, and every possible improvement was incorporated into sugar growing technology. As a result acreage, labor force, and some production expenses declined but overall costs are still great and increasing.

Relief for Sugar: Band-Aid Style

After two years of unprotected American sugar and sales of the cheaper, imported product increasing 25 percent, the Department of Agriculture announced the administration would act against sugar dumped on the United States market.

The years 1976–1977 were critical. From all countries, groups gathered to support an onslaught on Washington. The Hawaii Sugar Planters' Association, the State Department of Agriculture, the media, the county delegations, and the Hawaii congressional group threw themselves into the job of saving sugar. The market price was dropping dangerously, and the costs of production had soared well above the break-even point.

The 1975–1976 harvests were bad. C. Brewer's four plantations in 1976 had costs above the average and made a loss before taxes of $8.5 million; in 1975 agricultural losses were $9.5 million.[8] Alexander & Baldwin, whose subsidiaries run the viable Matson Shipping Line and the new Wailea resort, had no sugar earnings in 1976 yet it usually counts on sugar providing two-thirds of its earnings.[9]

The effect of the 1976–1977 sugar crisis was to sound the alarm to the state's major farming industry. There was no room for long-term optimism. The writing had been on the wall for years, but only now was the whole community assaulted with the real situation rather than a scenario.

On the Big Island it was feared that lack of support would threaten the survival of the five remaining plantations. The county council passed a resolution asking Mayor Matayoshi to draft alternate plans to cope with the closing of plantations resulting from the sugar price crisis. The jobless rate, the resolution said, would skyrocket and tax receipts would fall off sharply if plantations closed.[10] A *Maui News* editorial on 15 July 1977 called it "Zero Hour for Sugar."

The 1976–1977 crisis was only a start. After that, representatives of all related interests worked untiringly to establish a substitute for the defunct Sugar Act. It was not easy. The Carter administration, congressional committees, and the United States International Sugar Commission were solicitous, but the situation was not that simple. Other elements had to be kept in balance. There were the signatories of the International Sugar Agreement, other American sugar producers, nonsugar agricultural producers, producers of sugar substitutes, and consumer groups all with their own agendas and different perceptions of the situation.

For Hawaii, until 1979, the critical elements were these: sugar was overproduced, prices did not allow for any profit by Hawaii producers, sugar substitutes were making greater inroads into sugar markets, and drought conditions had lowered yield drastically. Direct subsidies, reduced quotas, increased tariffs, international agreements on floor prices, and voluntary reduction of foreign sugar exports to the United States were considered. What was agreed upon was a combination of tariffs and subsidies. These were stop-gap remedies and by the end of the 1970s, nothing long term had been worked out. In 1978 and again in late 1979 the administration instituted a price-support system to tide the industry over. But by the end of 1979, although no domestic sugar policy had replaced the old Sugar Act and opposition to protection had grown, two events took place. First, as the result of poor crop years in some other sugar-producing nations, both demand and price increased markedly. Second, Congress ratified the International Sugar Agreement by which sugar prices could be maintained internationally at levels aimed at covering production costs. Prices rose and by international agreement, enough surplus sugar entered the market to maintain a satisfactory price level —not too high but high enough to be gratifying. By 1980 conditions looked much better but the state still did not have a secure formula for the future. Despite short-term gains there is no room for long-term ease.

Another use for sugar, likely to grow in importance, is cane fiber bagasse as a source of energy and furnace fuel. Already this bagasse produces about 15 percent of the electrical energy generated in the state. It was argued that when oil is at $34.60 a barrel, its value could equal that of Hawaii's 1976 sugar and molasses production.[11] A spokesman for the Hawaii Sugar Planters Association forecasts that "the time could come when sugar would be a by-product of energy farming—electric power would be the primary product." This statement was made before sugar's value skyrocketed. With a return to mid-1970s prices the assertion could undoubtedly become true as sugar is one of the best possible crops for converting solar energy through biomass into heat-producing fuel. This can be done by converting a substantial portion of the crop into the raw material for methanol and ethanol, a distinct possibility in the not too distant future especially with increasing oil prices.

Should the conventional harvesting of sugar disappear, the ramifications will be many. Remove sugar and you not only remove agriculture, you destroy the delicate rural structure built around it. This constitutes "ruralness," which I believe is a partial but nevertheless important basis of the so-called "aloha spirit."

Sugar has always been a prime reason for the rich cosmopolitan plantation population—a major attraction of Hawaii tourism.

During the sugar crisis of 1976–1977 and even into the next decade, few persons saw the connection between sugar, tourism, and the Hawaii way of life. The problem was seen almost solely in terms of unemployment, corporate health, and future economy. To my knowledge, no visitor industry spokesman publicly supported agriculture and, sadly, few within the visitor industry saw the monumental impact a dead sugar industry would have on the quality of tourism. Maui Mayor Elmer Cravalho was one who understood the connection. Making a public statement about the sugar industry, he contended, "It is a component which maintains both our economic stability and our way of life."[12] He backed up ideology with action. He refused "to countenance the removal of even an acre of cane land from production except under the direst of circumstances." He insisted that "lost acreage be replaced elsewhere on the island, tit for tat."[13]

The demise of sugar as a food crop could, with nothing obvious to take its place, deal a monstrous blow to the resources on which tourism rests. Many essential wide open spaces could be lost to the tourist industry if landowners successfully pressured the state to allow subdivisons or resorts in areas formerly in crop. What was not taken up in this manner for tourism, retirement, or second homes could well be in grazing. But much would depend on the health of tourism at the time, the status of diversified agriculture, and the use being made of crops for energy purposes.

Pineapple

As a crop, pineapple is a significant income generator possibly more reliable, but not as important as sugar. Like sugar, it suffers from a variety of ills. Most of the crop is harvested on Maui, Lanai, and Oahu from 44,000 acres, a decline of roughly a third of the area planted in the late 1950s.[14] Although acreage and tonnage have fallen dramatically by a similar factor over the past decade, the value of the crop has almost doubled through higher prices and an encouraging fresh pineapple market. It is estimated that 5,800 persons are employed in the cannery and the field. In summer, labor peaks to around 11,000 as harvesting provides an important source of employment for students and other summer workers.[15] This number drops to 3,500 to 4,000 by fall.

Statistics tend, however, to mask the changes taking place. Twenty years ago ten companies were in the business. Today, three companies operate the industry: Dole, Del Monte, and Maui Land & Pineapple Co. In the immediate future Amfac may be in the business. Dole (Castle & Cooke) on Lanai indicated that it believed pineapple too dominant and the island would benefit if the company turned to other sources of revenue. On Molokai where over 10,000 acres were in production, Dole has phased out its operation, and Del Monte will do so in 1985. Both companies have new overseas operations more economically feasible than those in Hawaii.

Hawaii as a producer suffers from high costs of production, in particular labor. There has been a decline in the demand for canned pineapple, competition from other fruit, cheaper producers elsewhere, and high transport costs especially from Molokai. There are points in favor of pineapple. It is a low water user in comparison with sugar, the demand for fresh fruit (as opposed to canned) has increased considerably, and in 1978 pineapple constituted 14 percent of the market. The 1980 receipts of $229 million for all types of pineapple were 3 percent higher than in the previous year. Pineapple producers have had some good years recently, starting about the time of sugar's successes, but whether this will continue indefinitely is yet to be seen. In a number of quarters there is optimism.

In 1973 the last pineapples were grown commercially on Kauai until in 1979 Amfac's Lihue sugar plantation decided to diversify and planted ten acres as a pineapple nursery. This will provide plants for 500 acres near Hanamaulu, and if "the sugar industry falls apart," says Tony Faye, president of Lihue Plantation, "we can't rule out the possibility of [putting] half our best sugar land in pineapples."[16] This is a staggering possibility for a plantation now occupying 17,500 acres.

An upswing for fresh pineapple came as new markets opened in the mainland United States, Canada, and Japan. The United States mainland market was given a lift by relatively cheap air cargo space available on the routine flights from Honolulu on Boeing 747s and other large aircraft. At the same time during the seventies, Taiwan, Hawaii's number one competitor, drastically reduced production because of land and labor shortages. Production was also reduced in Malaysia.

Along with Dole and Del Monte, Maui Land & Pineapple Co.,

the only purely Hawaiian producer of the three, has done reasonably well recently but is diversifying to tourism. As a marginal crop at present, pineapple may at times have the edge on sugar but its future is clouded. As with other agricultural crops, costs have mounted for such items as fertilizer, transport, fuel, and labor. Future demand is an unknown quantity. Like sugar, pineapple production is essential to the economy especially through its role as a diversifier.

The maintenance of both the sugar and pineapple industries in Hawaii is essential, well beyond purely direct economic consideration. They are essential to the Hawaii life-style, they maintain open space, they help maintain an ethnic mix which would otherwise become overwhelmingly Caucasian, and workers' families have the opportunity if they wish of providing labor to resort areas. The ethnically mixed population is as vital a tourism resource as warm temperatures, clear water, and attractive tranquil scenery.

Ranching and Diversified Agriculture

Persistent efforts are being made to explore other agricultural pathways. This is given the blanket label of "diversified agriculture" and considered by some to be the panacea for struggling rural industries. Diversified agriculture includes the production of macadamia nuts, coffee, papaya, vegetables, corn, and cattle. Other alternatives included in this discussion will be forestry and aquaculture.

During the past decade the economics of ranching in Hawaii have improved only moderately. Unlike export crops, cattle ranching has at least a potential for supplying a local Hawaii market, but the response of local people to local products has been less than encouraging. The only stable spot is dairying.

There has been a shift from grass-fattened to grain-fattened cattle. Imported feed grains may be expensive, but cattle are fattened by grain in half the time taken by grass—eighteen months as opposed to three years. Quality too is better although nutritionists would debate this point. Feed lots have been established at various parts of the state to which cattle are shipped, and it is not unusual to ship cattle to the mainland for fattening. The future for competitively produced feed grain then is great, and efforts have been made to produce local feeds.

The greatest problem of the Hawaii meat industry after the high prices for feed is that the large food stores import great quantities of mainland meat by air, and this has competed successfully with the locally produced product. To convince the consumer to buy island-grown beef at the supermarket is the issue, states an article in the *Maui News* concerning the upgrading of local beef and the dilemma of local producers.[17]

Mainland tastes, which dominate retailing in Hawaii, have determined that the most desirable, tender, and flavorful beef is from a mainland corn-fattened animal. That these consumer tastes exist is not to be denied but they are not without cost, the least of which may be harmful fattening additives.

Sugar is unlikely to dominate Hawaii agriculture forever. If it goes something must take its place, and the only activities which equate with sugar's occupation of thousands of acres of land are livestock ranching and forestry.

Milk can be provided easily on a local basis. From several thousand acres, Haleakala Dairy, which has the production monopoly in Maui County, can satisfactorily supply fluid milk to 60,000 or more persons, including visitors. Dairying alone, although worth $27 million, cannot be a viable alternative to sugar.

State-county task forces and large landholders are pursuing diversified agriculture so far with limited success. The possibilities for protein produced by grass-fed livestock are being investigated. One might be through the use of highly productive crossbred animals, ones which are efficient converters of both natural and planted pastures and have the edge on traditional breeds in terms of nutrients per pound and rate of growth.

Recently there has been a trend toward fresh, home-grown, chemical-free vegetables in North America. With promotion similar to that for pineapples and California oranges a generation ago, one can foresee Hawaii as a leader in grass-fed, organically produced, low-calorie, low-cholesterol, health-oriented beef. The details may be a bit awry, and the scenario farfetched, but the principle remains—a well-organized approach to extensive ranching in Hawaii could vitalize the agricultural economy.

Despite inherent problems, diversification of agriculture has long been a major state goal. Its earnings grew from $16 million in 1967 to $91 million in 1980 for crops other than sugar and pineapple. The production from livestock farms during 1980 of meat, milk, and eggs approximated $81 million, an increase of 4 percent over the previous year. Diversified agriculture's total value, crops and livestock, for the year 1980 was $172 million, 11 percent higher than the previous year and gradually catching up to pineapple.

Diversified agriculture is not yet dominated by export crops but that seems to be on the verge of occurring. Today the balance between export and the local market is about even. Most vegetables and half the flowers from Hawaii are sold locally. Macadamia nuts, papaya, nursery products, and flowers such as anthuriums and proteas are exported. Macadamia nuts declined markedly in the decade before 1975. In the 1976–1977 year, production climbed 22 percent over a previously good year to give an all-time high production worth $7 million. The following years were even better with production for 1979 over $15 million. This reflects maturity of some of the new acreages. Other areas are under development to meet a potential demand yet to be reached. On Maui, C. Brewer's Wailuku Sugar Co. is in the process of converting 2,000 of its 5,000 acres of sugar land into macadamia nut production. The process will be completed by 1984.

Papaya plantings have increased. Ninety percent of production is from the Puna district on the Big Island. New plantations were established during the 1970s at Moloaa, Kauai (600 acres), and at Omaopio on Maui. Papaya, with its 1979 production worth around $10 million, is growing in importance. Major but uncertain markets are Honolulu, California, Japan, and Canada. The future looks to have some promise, but already some enterprises have had disappointing results from shipping and marketing.[18] The Japan market looks encouraging, yet the total market, including the mainland, is limited and readily oversupplied. A&B on Maui discovered this after an expenditure of $4 million and seven years of work. The protracted United Airlines strike in early 1979 also wreaked havoc with marketing dependent on air transport.

In local food production only milk is meeting 100 percent of demand. Hawaii produces 42 percent of its fresh vegetables, 34 percent of fresh fruits, 18 percent of poultry, and 35 percent of red meat. It would be true to say that local food production could double, perhaps triple without glutting the local market. Except for ranching usually at higher altitudes, diversified farming does not occupy large land areas so that its open space function, as well as its economic function, is much less than that for sugar and pineapple.

Good quality vegetables can be grown in Hawaii but not without strong local support. Items like Maui onions have developed a reputation and a following. The State Department of Agriculture and local hotel associations have worked closely together to use more local produce and to promote local items on Friday menus.[19] A significant percentage of vegetables used in hotels is locally produced. Much more could be done and local promotion might persuade residents to pass by imported foodstuffs in favor of strengthening the state's economy.

New Areas of Diversification

Forestry as a source of income to Hawaii has been studied sporadically over a number of years. Trial plantings often haphazard, some with success, have been made for a century. No serious study has been made of the economics of forest products versus sugar and pineapple—something which might be of value. Formerly forested areas can be reforested, areas with less successful species can be replanted with more useful species. The time has arrived for a break from a two-crop fixation to something more all-embracing.

Aquaculture has been attempted in several places on Oahu, Maui, and Kauai. There are obvious advantages the state has for the production of aqua-food (seafood) which can be produced competitively both for export and internal self-sufficiency. Kahuku Seafood Plantation grows oysters on Oahu's north shore in a matter of only months compared with a much longer natural maturation elsewhere. Catfish has been farmed with success at Kihei, Maui, using the Kealia Pond which is now producing baitfish for tuna fishing boats. In Kilauea, C. Brewer has been operating a Malaysian prawn farm while Lowe Aquafarms Inc. has started production of giant prawn from the initial 110 acres of a 400-acre project at Kahuku. More recently it was announced that the Coca-Cola Corporation and the F. H. Prince Company would construct a 100-acre shrimp farm also at Kahuku. Aquaculture is an area which has considerable appeal and appears to be moving rapidly in Hawaii.

Any healthy economic activity which will extend the economic base beyond what has become dangerously narrow would be welcome. Metallic marine nodules is a largely unknown but nevertheless fascinating possibility for the future. But before this, the critical issue is energy for processing. Geothermal energy may be the marginal answer. Some authorities believe there is a fifty-fifty chance of nodules providing the basis for a future Hawaii industry. A small but growing group of Pacific watchers feels that the twenty-first century will see the highly populated nations of the Pacific Basin clammering for access to the ocean's resources. At that time Hawaii may be in the thick of things.

Finally it would be unrealistic not to mention marijuana, an important but illicit crop potentially very important if legalized in the future. *Pakalolo* (marijuana in Hawaiian) is already grown on all major islands. Its estimated contraband income is very high and could exceed the present legitimate income derived from all crops other than sugar and pineapple.

Task Forces, State Programs, New Ventures

At a time when sugar plantations were regrouping, mills going out of business, land being consolidated or ceasing production, and pineapple operators leaving Hawaii, the state in cooperation with the counties stepped in with financial support. They formed task forces to provide substitute land use and alternative employment. These task forces were set up on all the islands affected by agricultural change—Molokai, Kauai, and the Big Island (Kohala Task Force).

The groups were composed of representatives of the state, county, and local people. That the results were not rousingly successful can be attributed to the reasons why diversified agriculture is not yet flourishing. Critics allege that, especially on the Big Island, millions of dollars of task force monies were recklessly drained off into local boondoggles and that a number of groups and companies backed by the task forces lacked necessary experience. Despite setbacks, experience was gained in economic areas with possible potential. Perhaps by the late 1980s initial failures will be forgotten and there will be substantial gains.

But state programs for diversified agriculture still continue as they must. Individuals, cooperatives, and companies—including the big established agricultural companies—are getting into and out of the act. There have been some significant successes, but the struggle has not been easy. Other than the more traditional minor crops of coffee, macadamia nuts, and flowers, attempts are being made to launch programs for papaya, guava, passion fruit, alfalfa, sorghum, seed corn, sweet corn, potatoes, bananas, wine grapes, and aquaculture. An encouraging task force–supported venture has been the production of nursery-raised ornamental plants and flowers. The ornamental plant and flower industry, the fastest growing component of agriculture, in 1977 earned more than $14 million. In 1979 it earned $20.8 million—a 50 percent increase.

Small operators are saying the big guys with hundreds of acres are ruining the market for them. As in tourism, the big guys, often representing corporate attempts at diversified agriculture, already own the land and have extensive capital to fall back on. International Utilities is not about to fold if C. Brewer's guava patch in Kilauea is a failure. Nevertheless, if one looks at the present situation in terms of achievement, making allowances for scale, large companies are not showing any more success than individual farmers. There are bright areas but the overall progress has been spotty. The fate of Alexander & Baldwin's papaya orchard on Maui is evidence that the going is rough even for those with the greatest resources.

In the mid-1970s, C. Brewer & Co., at Kilauea, Kauai, was desperately attempting to put to productive use land which had lain idle for over five years. It planned for 600 acres of guava, 300 acres of Malaysian prawns, 53 small farmlets, and an agricultural park. Calling the effort Project 150, the company expected to spend $3.5 million on macadamia nut expansion. It was not a newcomer to diversified agriculture. Its Mauna Loa Macadamia Nut Corporation with holdings on the Big Island is the world's largest grower, processor, and distributor of macadamia nuts. Brewer was prepared to incur operating losses of $2 million up to 1981. By mid-1978 $2 million had been invested in the Kilauea operations with much more development to come. But in mid-1980 after unacceptable yields and poor growing conditions, a decision was made to abandon the prawn project. None of this can provide a very hopeful model for the independent farmer with capital amounting to only several thousand dollars.

Functions and Problems: Diversified Agriculture

There are inherent difficulties in diversified farming. It is usually considered small-scale farming, yet it need not be. The optimum size for a farm in Hawaii is not known. It will vary with crops, methods, and area. It has long been associated with family farming; now large corporations are trying their hand at it. It is spoken of as an alternative farming operation in Hawaii but it cannot be conceived of as a ready substitute for the large-scale commercial agricultural pursuits which have operated for over a century.

Much has been written about diversified agriculture and more has been spoken on the subject. A mystique has developed around it. Alternative agriculture it is sometimes called by enthusiastic activists with nontraditional life-styles and city dwellers yearning for the arcadian romance of being sustained by the land, Mother Nature, and the *Whole Earth Catalog.*

One would only wish that diversified agriculture could result in the alternative use of approximately 270,000 acres of land and the employment of 14,000–15,000 persons should sugar and pineapple disappear. The above illustrates the extreme case: where declining sugar or pineapple production has become critical on Molokai, in the Kohala district of the Big Island, in the Kilauea district of Kauai, and at Kahuku on Oahu, diversified agriculture has not stepped in and taken up the economic slack. Nor has it been a startling success. But diversification does have a function to perform and a very important one at that.

Diversified agriculture is associated with great disadvantages despite numerous advantages. It has the blessing of the governor, the lieutenant governor, and some highly placed officers such as the director of agriculture and the director of the department of planning and economic development, but up until the late 1970s, along with sugar and pineapple, it had no plan for long-range development. Perhaps this situation will be remedied by the newly adopted State Plan and the yet-to-be approved functional plan for agriculture. Diversified agriculture has for years been overwhelmed by sugar and pineapple, large-scale companies, and heavy capitalization. In the past its small, undercapitalized family-run units, managed mainly by Asian Americans, have had little political or economic clout. Considered as marginal units, they have not had the ability to hold families together. Children from farm families graduate from high school and move to cities in the hope of finding economic opportunities not available in the country.

Country parents, whether independent farmers or plantation workers, support their children's efforts to attain higher economic rewards and jobs with higher status, jobs available in town or on the mainland. As a result of this, an area which should be socially and economically attractive to its people is not, and when new farming areas are opened up a pool of experienced workers is not available to support them. There is then, frequently but certainly not in every instance, lack of planning, lack of capital, lack of experience, and lack of a sympathetic climate in which diversified agriculture can operate. There is no end of moral support but there is a need for a coordinated approach from many quarters including the big companies. It should include an educational program emphasizing the necessity of rural maintenance and a strong agriculture to perpetuate the health and survival of Hawaii.

A prevalent way of thinking for those for whom upward mobility is important is to equate all farming with self-limiting plantation labor. For so many people, for so long, plantations have been a baseline from which the only worthwhile move has been upward and out. In distinct contrast a growing number of younger haole, urban mainlanders, influenced by what for them is a novel mode of activity, despite their inexperience in farming, look to the land for solace, spiritual satisfaction, and redemption. One can find in these newcomers the entire economic-social-philosophic gamut.

The Administration and the Legislature

Although Governor Ariyoshi and the state director of agriculture avow their commitment to agriculture, some state officials and legislators have shown little sympathy to diversified agriculture. For the past decade, many decision makers and politicians have regarded diversified agriculture as trivial.

Agriculture is invariably emphasized in Governor Ariyoshi's policy statements. At the twenty-eighth convention of the Hawaii Farm Bureau Federation, the governor told farmers he felt lonely in a state "that has gone hyena-crazy for urban development." He told farmers he was not only prepared to preserve agricultural lands but also to expand them. He insisted the state move forward toward self-sufficiency in food production. War would be waged on speculators. Farmers should not be forced to compete with urban developers for land and he promised "to keep agricultural lands out of the hands of speculators including pushing for a price ceiling on farmland."[20] Pre-election statements in 1978 were virtually the same. After the election the newly elected Lieutenant Governor Jean King echoed some of the same sentiments.

Former State Agricultural Director John Farias maintained his opposition to the urbanization of fine agricultural land. He showed concern with the fact that state laws are inconsistent and that agricultural land, unless counties step in, may be subdivided by law into one-acre plots on which a residence is erected and from which no further agricultural production emanates. Public agencies, he felt, should be restrained from funding urban-oriented construction projects in rural areas without thorough public scrutiny. He would have liked to see red tape cut concerning ordinances that might affect agricultural parks and the judicious use of environmental impact statements to help secure farmland from urban encroachment. In addition, like other groups in Hawaii, the Department of Agriculture is frequently in conflict with the State Land Use Commission. Farias was quick to point out that his department had almost always "come out the loser" when it had gone before the LUC to oppose the redesignation of agricultural land to urban use. One major problem the administration avers is that rather than see the broad picture in terms of areas already designated urban or the relations of agriculture to industry, the LUC views its mission "on a case-by-case basis and has been reluctant to take a broader regional approach."[21]

There is no doubt that something decisive must be done if agriculture is not to remain in the doldrums. Unlike a cyclic setback to tourism, the agriculture condition appears to be chronic.

One of the recent tasks for agricultural planners has been the preparation of the draft functional plan for agriculture.[22] In it concern is shown for getting farmers onto affordable land and into nine agricultural parks, only one of which—Pahoa on the Big Island—is operational.

The Department of Agriculture sees the possibility of selected self-sufficiency in vegetables, the potential of nursery products, and papaya as a growth crop, the last despite the poor results of independent growers on the Big Island and Alexander & Baldwin on Maui.

Apart from measures to help park farmers, the plan advocates increased availability of water, improved disease control programs, and revitalized agricultural training courses. In an article critical of the plan, *Hawaii Business* points out that out of seventy "implementing actions . . . only a dozen innocuous suggestions [dealt] with marketing," including a marketing potential study. "Why wasn't such a study," asks the article, "part of, and basic to, the plan itself?"[23] Why indeed? Associated with the plan is an industry analysis program initiated in 1978. Each analysis starts with the potential of the particular activity such as papaya or macadamia nut growing. Although many analyses had been completed, the plan was desperately short of policies and strategies related to markets, especially those dependent on other countries or the mainland. Even the advisory committee to the plan recommended that "market potentials of commodities should be identified." One hopes such fundamental information is included in the plan when it is approved.

No Room for Choice

All successful tourism developers should know that without a reasonably viable agriculture, the climate for development and a healthy cash flow is seriously impaired, the much-touted open spaces and tranquility are endangered, and the cosmopolitan demographic mix is lost. Unemployment would be high, and the Hawaii life-style and aloha spirit could quickly become things of the past. Together these could present a socioeconomic environment which would be an embarrassment and disappointment to the tourist industry and its clients; and, like its counterparts in areas of the Caribbean, it could founder badly.

Not only is it difficult to farm in Hawaii but greed and expectations of huge returns from the tourist industry, related development, or both, make farming even harder. In 1977 the 9,700-acre Huehue Ranch near Kona on the Big Island was put on the mainland market for $16 million and advertised in the *Wall Street Journal.*[24] The names of the southern California owners were unknown and it appeared there was little if any consideration given to having ranch ownership return to Hawaii. A small part of the area was in urban classification because the ranch had, in the past, signified its intention to develop. Development plans were shelved after a presidential study mission recommended that a park be created in the area. No action was taken but the mere fact that a recommendation had been made seemed a sufficient deterrent to development. Part of the acreage borders a white sand beach not far from Kona's airport and the Kona Village resort in an area classified conservation. The ranch, the advertisement said, could be bought in increments for $19 million or as a going concern for $16 million. The main agricultural portion runs 2,500 head of cattle. Around $19 million is a high price to pay for 6,000 acres which sustains cattle raising, a difficult business at any time in Hawaii. But this is a case of land being sold as a valuable commodity with potential. The sale of zoning and the sale of expectations permeates all rural activity in Hawaii and impacts in a devastating manner on the person who genuinely wants to buy twenty-five acres to farm or the small company which sees prospects for fifty or one hundred acres.

One of the least attractive impacts of tourism is the peripheral and windfall fortunes people feel they may make. Usually they are based on high expectations, land speculation, and unreasonable profits over a short period of time. The effect on the lives of rural people and those individuals or companies of modest means who want land for farming is devastating.

The art of those who govern should be to acknowledge the necessity for both activities—tourism and agriculture (even uneconomic agriculture)—and to determine a balance between the two so that society, life-styles, and spirit survive rather than the wealthy few. Such a balance does not come by magic. The pressures on politicians and decision makers from the governor down are great. Large companies are represented in both agriculture and development. For these companies agriculture is an albatross around the neck of management whose first allegiance is to the stockholder. Alexander & Baldwin, for example, sees resort development after agriculture as the light at the end of the tunnel, Maui Land & Pineapple Co. sees it as "the money tree,"[25] and Amfac sees it as its most promising growth area.[26] All have moved from agriculture to some resort development on land which otherwise would have been used for farming. For them and others in Hawaii, the change makes very good business sense, perhaps the only sense.

In this century the pendulum has swung away from agriculture. Educational programs are necessary to bring awareness where it is absent and to explain the fundamental worth of rural industry not only for employment and tradition but also for the tourist industry. This will entail not only a change in the attitudes of politicians and bureaucrats but also in older people of the community, students, and in the educational system as a whole. The relationship between tourism and agriculture is emphasized by the governor, who in the summer of 1979 wrote in the introduction to a governmental document: "Agriculture contributes substantially to our number one industry, tourism, providing both open space

and the rural setting that so many of our visitors come to see."[27]
This is only part of a wide relationship which is emphasized in this
chapter.

Agriculture needs new status, organization, markets, and direction. Diversified agriculture, in particular, requires support and
imaginative programs. Research, expertise, and long-term financial backing is called for. The land and what it grows is something
to use respectfully and cherish.

The century and a half conflict which split haole and non-haole
concerning land as a commodity and land as a perpetual human
resource is by no means resolved. It lies at the heart of the matter.
Hawaii without the tourist industry would survive, in a manner of
speaking, for generations. Without agriculture it would most assuredly wither. Because mainland United States obviously values
the visitor amenities provided by Hawaii, and these can only be
secured by a strong agriculture, there are compelling arguments to
support substantial federal and state aid for all agriculture. This
support, I submit, should be in lieu of local tariffs, which under
other historical circumstances would have been levied, and as reciprocal payment for the benefits four million mainlanders get
every year from Hawaii. Government policy calls for a stronger
and more self-sufficient agriculture. This can be achieved only
with monumental effort, attitude changes, and, for some time to
come, continued federal support.

CHAPTER 8

Impacts on the Physical Landscape

THE impacts of the visitor industry on the people and land of Hawaii run the gamut from positive to negative. In this and the following four chapters, I call specific attention to major impacts on residents and visitors alike; on the biota, landscape, and coastal waters; on living costs, family structure, and on life-style—end products of tourism, good and bad.

Every activity of man has some effect on the physical and biological environment. I will spare the reader a long discussion of the fact that the scale of the activity as it affects the environment is crucial and that the United States, not a major part of the world's population, nevertheless consumes a colossal amount of the world's resources. This is an accepted and documented fact. The point here is that Hawaii development has been high technology growth, its environmental impacts worldwide. Although I propose to talk only about Hawaii, what goes on in the state nevertheless affects traffic patterns, congestion, and air pollution, agricultural resources, and oil resources not only on the mainland but elsewhere in the world.

A human activity cannot exist in a vacuum. For every occurrence there is an opposite occurrence, for every benefit, a cost; the *yin-yang* syndrome, the zero sum equation. A golf course cannot be created in Kauai without carving the land surface and destroying previous vegetation. Tourists cannot visit Hawaii and spend money without generating service, intensifying beach use, and bringing extra traffic. One set of circumstances is traded off for another, sometimes good, sometimes bad.

A system of human interaction which is reasonable and ordered, treats both land and people lightly, assesses resource use thoughtfully, and respects the community and the integrity of local life-styles, is likely to cause the very least trauma. Under such conditions, which are often difficult to achieve, successful and satisfying human activity may continue indefinitely. To pursue any other system is to court danger. Development within this context is called ecodevelopment.

Although impacts of tourism are both positive and negative, the connotation of impact suggests something less than beneficial. Tourism's effects, however, can seldom be drawn in white or black. Often they are in shades of gray between the two extremes. Here and later I propose to look at both the gray and the black areas of tourism. The black areas represent impacts that warrant immediate attention.

By now it should be clear that tourism is a subject about which the public is ambivalent. The advantages of tourism are not always acknowledged—something which representatives of the industry are incensed about. "I resent it," said Rudy Choy, a director of the Hawaii Visitors Bureau, "when someone . . . says tourism is creating a vast pool of servants. Local residents enjoy the tremendously efficient interisland air service because of the tourists, and the amenities of Honolulu restaurants. The cultural revival here is a luxury we could not afford without tourism. The tourists started it with their vast interest in anything Hawaiian."[1]

Although there are harmful impacts, knowledge of which is widely disseminated, the majority of the Hawaii community is no more than mildly roused. Nevertheless, a smaller and growing percentage is hostile. Various degrees of ambivalence characterize the public; in surveys it has responded favorably to what it sees as positive benefits. Sommarstrom, who studied stress in relation to the tourist industry in Hawaii, has this to say: "The most obvious private reaction to the growth of the tourist industry has been acceptance. Some individuals have profited mightily by real-estate speculation and many more have come to depend on it for employment."[2] In a mid-1970s survey of public attitudes to tourism in Hawaii, three-quarters of those questioned felt tourism was "good for Hawaii."[3] The survey was of slightly higher-than-average income people representative of the professional and managerial group. Four years later, by 1979, the scales were perceptibly tipping in the other direction as communities saw rural life-styles threatened by too much growth.[4] This is the subject of later discussion.

The Perception of Impact

There has been no end of organizations and individuals willing to instruct the state, counties, the visitor industry, and anyone who will listen on the dire and disastrous effects of development on the environment of Hawaii. There has been a wide variety of public warnings ranging from the early flamboyant statements of interest groups such as Life of the Land to the much milder urging of the Hawaii State Plan and most county general plans. Each group has its own peculiar strategies and messages. Although few groups would say their expectations have been met, their voices have not fallen on deaf ears. If I compare the situation today with my first serious observations in 1961, I see public opinion and action have moved a discernible distance in a positive direction. Today among citizens, influential legislators and administrators, planners and major developers, there is a collective consciousness concerning impacts, a number of which are either already or potentially serious. There is now greater acceptance that some regulation is in order.

Environmental impact is a matter of perception. The understanding of the threshold at which a situation becomes critical may vary markedly between groups or individual observers. In addition, the course between identification and solution is studded with wayside impediments. There are essential steps between start and finish. These include the identification of a problem; assessment of the degree of its severity; problem solving decision making (including legislation if necessary); acceptance of the gravity of a situation by relevant agencies, developers, and users; implementation of decisions or policies; and enforcement.

It is difficult to predict how individuals will perceive change or associated criticism. Financial interest in an activity will frequently alter the perceiver's view. The resulting viewpoint will tend to be in harmony with the dominant objective. The greater the reward, or the greater the possibility of intervening economic opportunity, the less critical the perception of impact will be. Sometimes those depending most on the environment for income such as a developer or a hotel operator may paradoxically appear the least sensitive. Those furthest removed may be most vocal and least informed. In comparison, natural scientists (social scientists, too) who work within another paradigm lack an adequate understanding of the economics of development and hotel operation with which to refine their views. Their perceptions may be completely different from those within the visitor industry. Change which is most obvious is viewed as most damaging (outside intrusion, alien architecture, or crowding). Change which is less obvious is virtually ignored (cesspool seepage or cultural dilution).

In addition, for dissimilar reasons political decision makers, industry managers, a large, upwardly mobile component of the population, and the media may wish to present, above all else, an unblemished image of Hawaii to the nation. For these reasons perceptions are appropriately tailored to accord with views, and numerous environmental or social questions may be downplayed or ignored in consequence.

Photographer Robert Wenkam is a veteran campaigner for environmental causes. In 1975, as president of the Federation of Western Outdoor Clubs and representative of Friends of the Earth, he insisted "paradise must be rationed. It would appear," he said, "that the Hawaii Visitors Bureau and the Hawaii Hotel Association are guilty of misrepresentation under the guise of economic growth and job opportunities . . . They are destroying our environment, our island culture, irreplaceable scenic resources, and threatening the multi-billion dollar investment in tourist facilities already built and operating in the name of absentee owner profits and jobs for mainlanders . . . In my opinion it is a rip-off of the Hawaiian Islands . . . [the HVB] causes most of the damage renting and selling beaches and scenery . . . highways and airports are ruining Hawaii."[5]

Thomas Creighton, less sensational in comparison, has published a thoughtful study, *The Lands of Hawaii*, essential reading for those concerned in any way with the changing Hawaii landscape.[6] His views, fundamentally the same as Wenkam's, are stated less dramatically. "Environmental overloads in a human society," he says, "are caused by one major factor—uncontrolled population. The State of Hawaii . . . will have to stop pussyfooting on this issue. No prognostication can foresee and no scenario can invent a future where land is handled with respect if the number of people who must use it are not limited . . . Hawaii's land surface is limited in [area, and] . . . the population the State can care for [has] a limit which can . . . be computed."[7] This view, stated differently, represents the essence or the governor's public statements and a central theme of the Hawaii State Plan. State policy, while theoretically acknowledging the problem, is reluctant to talk about it directly and prefers to hypothesize: "Due to Hawaii's limited supply of useable land, an increasing population can result in a decline in the use of lands for agriculture, open space, and scenic purposes. It can lead to crowding, and congestion on streets and highways, parks and beaches."[8] So says the State Plan. Despite the fact that official wording seems to draw attention to problems yet to come, the writer cannot believe this to be the case.

Sea and Shore

No part of Hawaii is more than a few miles from the sea. Its islands have two major physiographic and settlement components —the inland mountains which are sparsely settled and the shoreline lands, the littoral, which in places are heavily occupied. The mountains in Hawaii, easily seen but infrequently experienced, are a spectacular backdrop to the tropical lowland habitat. The coast, in bureaucratic jargon the "coastal zone," accommodates most of Hawaii's population and all its visitors.

The coasts embrace warm, clear, well-stocked waters and reefs, living marine communities, spectacular surfing areas, coral sand beaches, romantic avenues of coconut palms, historic buildings, taro plantings, archeological sites, and patches of strand vegetation and rainforest. Population is concentrated in ten urban nodes and about fifteen scattered, discontinuous ribbons. In terms of surroundings, resources, and facilities, the area suffers the excesses of heavy population. It is here that environmental and human stress is at its greatest. Half of the nodes are strongly tourist-oriented as are the majority of the fifteen coastal ribbons. The entire population is related in some way to tourism.

Tourism operations affect the land in two ways: first, the major direct effect occurs through the influx of visitors and the actual land area which is prepared and used for building, landscaping, and recreation. Destination area hotels and small condominiums may together occupy from one to one thousand acres. Roads join the living spaces with airports, recreation facilities, and scenic vantage points. Large land areas are used for supporting activities —restaurants, entertainment areas, shopping centers, U-drive headquarters, airports, beach parks, cultural centers, and parking lots. Second, there is an indirect effect, which occurs through the small percentage of those who buy second homes and become semi-permanent seasonal residents and others who return as retirees. More important by far are the many who are attracted to

Wailea Beach prior to development. In the process of providing for the tourist industry, wild seascapes are changed into sophisticated tamed landscapes. Wailea
beach is now the core of the Wailea resort. (Alexander & Baldwin photo)

Hawaii and who seek jobs directly or indirectly related to the industry. This, together with other economic activity, results in in-
migrants (mainland migrants) and immigrants (alien migrants) arriving in droves. To some extent, all respond to the mystique, the
advertising, the experience, the opportunities, and the high expectations.

There are four million tourists who visit Hawaii annually. To
serve these visitors, many thousands of people are employed in the
labor force. The tourists, the workers, and the workers' families all
contribute to the impact of tourism. No group escapes. Impacts
occur, of course, with other types of economic activity which
bring population to Hawaii, but in these cases effects are usually
localized and not nearly as widespread as for tourism. In Hawaii
there is no other activity with such vast reaching linkages. The
fact that this all takes place on a tropical island group makes these
impacts extraordinary.

During the past decade or more, numerous environmental issues have been brought to public attention in Hawaii through court cases. Hawaii, like other states, is accumulating increasing numbers of environmental laws. On the other hand, social separation, erosion of life-styles, and human maladies, because of their subjectivity, are rarely covered by law even if they are frequently referred to in policy guidelines. For this reason, environmental law in Hawaii has been used to slow or stop what is obviously an environmental manifestation of a human problem. The case of Hulopoe Bay, which follows later, is one such example.

Raymond Dasmann writes that "the most beleaguered group of ecosystems on this planet [are] those that form the interface between land and ocean."[9] One need look no further than Hawaii to find classic examples of his assertion. The problems and issues, however, are not unique to Hawaii, but can be found throughout the Pacific.[10]

The idea of environmental change lacks in perspective. Nowadays, with somewhat presumptuous human chauvinism which Lewis Thomas in *The Lives of a Cell* so ably demolishes, we continually talk of "fragile" environments.[11] This is true only in a human context where many environments are fragile. In a geological context, they are not. The environment is tough and resilient and keeps on going. The physical environment provides continuity. Societies may come and go, appear and disappear, but the environment forever continues. Let me demonstrate this with reference to Hawaii. Its island surfaces were created then changed by stream erosion which dumped huge amounts of sediment, greater and more threatening than any development could contrive, into surrounding seas. But as the level was reduced, volcanism simultaneously added to the surface, volcanic smoke "polluted" the air worse than any canefield fire, and extruded lava rolled seaward destroying every vestige of terrestrial and marine life in its path.[12] This happened repeatedly and during the intervening periods of relative quiescence, organic processes worked toward balance and adjustment before being thrown into disharmony again by another accident of volcanism or changing sea level. It happened in the past and it will happen again. Human habitation has little effect on the long-term course of nature. What has gone before is an episode in geological time. In terms of human survival, our activities are crucial; in terms of environmental history, they may in the long, long run be of little account.

In a context of human history, the twentieth century, especially the past two decades, has seen amazing changes. Changes have been instigated for, directed by, and oriented toward the short-term gain of only the human occupants, only one of a number of living communities, all of which have a right to reasonable existence. Another pattern has been that not only are other living communities largely ignored but newcomers seem to have similarly disregarded the older settled human communities. Unlike change due to natural causes which we have just discussed, human-instigated change, sometimes little short of cataclysmic, is antagonistic to natural ecological processes. When uncontrolled, it results in the long-run deterioration of the area occupied by the instigators—the human habitat. Some damage done today can last as far as we can see into the human future.

As opposed to a geological time context, our time frame is strictly limited. Within this context the more thoughtful, responsible, and humane must assume our obligations as trustees for future generations so that they will be able to enjoy a quality of life equal to, if not better than, that enjoyed now. This being the case we must ask the question, "What has been done about this obligation?" Sadly the answer must be that beyond some good intentions and some recent encouraging attempts to develop guidelines for future behavior in Hawaii, virtually nothing has been done. The implementation of welcome legislative action is likely to be countered effectively by the purposeful accentuation of the problems prompting legislation. Probably never before in Hawaii's history has such a heavy population load stressed island resources so critically. Still, state and private plans are designed to result in a considerably increased labor force. Immense sums are being spent by developers, hotel operators, and real estate interests for purposes which will ensure greater population pressure. Planning, beset with the pressures of conflicting values, can only reflect this conflict: the provision of a worthy habitat for future generations, the provision of future employment opportunities so that limited unemployment prevails, and the creation of a climate in which investment opportunities are readily available and entrepreneurs are provided for in a way acceptable to the American free enterprise system.

Of the great development areas only one, Waikiki, is considered to be approaching full development. Yet it too can legally go much further than it has. It already has 28,600 units which exceed the 26,000 room ceiling proposed by various advisory groups.[13] Kaanapali, the second most developed area is still a long way from completion and most other resorts are virtually in their infancy.

Each development, depending on prevailing pressures, has the potential to become another Waikiki complete with constantly raised ceilings for development. This may not occur immediately but the possibility is there.

As a result of coastal development, changes will take place and problems will evolve. Their severity will change with time from place to place. The importance of a particular class of problem may change as more information becomes known and as human perception of the problem changes. Now perhaps only the tip of the iceberg of coastal deterioration is perceived. As Dasmann points out, "The first law of the environment today seems to be: no matter how bad you think things are—the total reality is much worse."[14] Such has proven true during the long process of this study.

The Sculpturing of a Resort

To illustrate some major physical impacts, I will use the preparation of a new resort area. Land surfaces are graded, drainage patterns are changed, soil and vegetation cover is removed, and new air circulation corridors are created. Runoff, if only temporarily, is increased dramatically, and the wind, previously of limited consequence, may become a matter of concern. The immediate effects, although shattering, are usually justified in terms of income, financial investment, jobs, or prestige the completed project will bring to an area.

Wind damage, if watched, can be minimal, except at the construction stage where it may be a source of irritation to local residents. At most sites developers are quick to replace the vegetation removed with something more to their liking. But it takes time for new plantings to become established and in the meantime runoff occurs. Even after the new vegetation is established, runoff will be different. The amount will depend on the dominant cover. Soils will change to reflect new organic components and processes including reactions to fertilizer. Infiltration, leaching, and illuviation rates together with water-holding capacity will all change with the new vegetation and, in drier areas, with irrigation.

Simultaneously with this activity other grading must take place for roads, building foundations, parking lots, and tennis courts. After this, even under the most controlled circumstances, a considerable amount of natural debris and introduced pollutants will enter the drainage system on their way to the sea, first perhaps by

sheet wash and unintentional gullying, then through newly laid
drains or natural waterways. Without the greatest of care a major
impact may be felt close to the area which prompted development
in the first place—the beach. Virtually nothing is ever known
about the severity of a once-in-fifty years flood—nothing about the
once in a century disaster.

What I have said until now concerns the initial phase of resort
construction. Imagine the site ten years into the future. Several
hotels with a combined total of 1,500 rooms, three condominium
developments, two low-density residential developments, two golf
courses, a shopping center, and a tennis complex have been constructed. New construction continues because resort areas are
long-term projects and ten years old may still be young. Convention extensions to an existing hotel are being made and a new hotel
is being built. Plans are about 40 percent completed. The estimated daily population at Christmas is 5,500 people, but when the
project is finished the district population may be close to 25,000.

The hotels have their own sewage treatment plants while the
lower density residences have cesspools or septic tanks. The resort
has two water wells, one major water pipeline serving the community and, as well, recycling equipment to reuse water to supplement golf course, lawn, and garden irrigation. Already the signs
are obvious that a new source of water will have to be found before the project is much further along. If it is not, a building moratorium will have to be imposed.

The effects of large quantities of artificially applied water are
often spectacular especially where development has taken place in
a desert region such as at the Mauna Kea Beach development and
Wailea, both examples of tourist oases in the middle of dry, stark
lava fields. Everyday, from nearly all major developments, large
quantities of irrigation water enter the ocean where formerly limited amounts flowed from springs or from streams, and then only
after a rain.

At this hypothetical resort large quantities of fertilizer are applied to the golf course and landscaping and there is little way of
knowing how to apply the exact amount without waste or damage
elsewhere. With constant watering and heavy rain, soluble salts
from the fertilizer and fine sediments removed by illuviation enter
the sea by surface streams or through groundwater seen as springs
at low water. Some seepage will unfortunately make its way to already fertilizer-rich aquifers or to the Ghyben-Herzberg fresh
water lens underlying the islands, both of which are essential

Mauna Kea Beach Hotel. Long considered the standard setter for elegance, the Mauna Kea Beach Hotel, overlooking Kaunaoa Point, also has established a reputation in terms of environmental adaptations. It was the first development in the South Kohala area of the Big Island. (Mauna Kea Beach Hotel photo)

sources of Hawaii's drinking and irrigation water. Such chemical seepage, including some mainland-banned insecticides, already results from agricultural use.

Other water seeps from treatment plants and cesspools to reach the sea as unnecessary nutrients. This is a problem in many coastal places. In 1976 at Kealakekua Bay on the Big Island, developers planned to service a 400-acre residential subdivision with cesspools. "Any more cesspools in this area," said the director of the Institute of Marine Biology at the University or Hawaii, "will result in the deterioration of the bay and the destruction . . . of the coral."[15] In some places elsewhere in Hawaii dry chemical toilets are being used but with unpleasant side effects.

Water from streets and parking lots highly contaminated with pavement materials, oil and gasoline,[16] sewer and cesspool leach, fertilizers and detergents in solution, and other pollutants together with sediments all do grave damage to sea water quality. Sediments increase turbidity; pollutants and sediments smother and kill coral reefs; and fertilizer and sewage enrichment encourage certain marine organisms to the serious detriment or destruction of others. Deteriorated water rich in nutrients has been associated with increased algae growth, offensive beach sand smells, less pleasant swimming conditions, and a marked diminution in the richness of marine life.

I can take the story further. Beach litter is always present although well controlled on beaches fronting larger developments; this also has the ability of changing water quality. Marine erosion is an active factor in changing the morphology of all unprotected beaches and in an attempt artificially to provide a more stable beach, decreased water clarity and greater turbidity have resulted. Beach improvement projects are popular in numerous Hawaii coastal areas and are achieved with varying degrees of success and damage.[17]

Talks with old-time residents indicate that development and other related activities have resulted in a deterioration in fishing. As a result, local people have had to abandon favorite areas formerly used for line fishing, netting, and crabbing. In many areas, especially those which have been popular over a long period, coral reefs show signs of depredation by snorkelers who remove live coral without penalty; until recently, when legislation was enacted, undersized fish and occasionally another diver were speared.

Always in a development, no matter where it occurs, there are changes involving use, vegetation, and landscape appearance or pattern. Although occasionally developers with some justification may throw up their hands in despair over public unenlightenment, there are local people who mourn the passing of an open forest and its replacement by a golf course and hotel landscaping. These changes do not so much represent economic advantages as they do, in this regard, a major transformation from wilder to tamer landscapes, from open space to developed land, from rural and agricultural to urban and tourist.

Threat to Wetlands

Development including reclamation and drainage threatens the existence of remaining wetlands—coastal marshes, swamps, and freshwater lagoons. One of the most ingenious reclamation-drainage projects now closely associated with tourism is the Ala Wai project. A major canal was constructed to drain a large area of swampland, part of which is occupied now by Waikiki. The project, the brainchild of Lucias E. Pinkham, was completed early in the century. Almost three decades later a less ambitious but nevertheless spectacular scheme took shape. During the construction of Honolulu's Ala Moana beach park a wide swath of coral from the fringing reef was taken out to deepen the water and to improve swimming conditions. As compensation for the work, the contractor used the dredged coral and sand to fill neighboring swampland owned by the company. When the project was completed a huge white dazzling rectangular lot occupied the swamp just mauka of the beach. For years the vacant lot was known as Dillingham's Folly until the 1960s when, on the former swamp site, the Dillingham Corporation built its huge Ala Moana Shopping Center, popular today with tourists and local people alike.

It is interesting to reflect that with today's attitudes and the environmental opposition that could be mounted, no contemporary developer would dare contemplate such projects as the Waikiki and Ala Moana reclamations. Although not possible today, these projects provide functional space for the heart of Hawaii tourism.

On Maui the Kanaha Wildfowl Refuge fronts the Kahului airport, a local terminal bursting at the seams from tourism-related flights. The danger from the presence of birds in flight paths is real, but conservationists and others have fought successfully for the retention of the reserve. No one wants to see it go but economic pressures are always present.

In 1972 developers Foremost-McCormack submitted an ambitious proposal for a housing development to occupy Heeia marsh near Kaneohe and the adjacent Heeia fishpond as a settling basin. The project planned for five thousand houses, a population of seventeen thousand, a shopping center, and a dredged lagoon. When completed it would have increased the area of Kaneohe by one-third. "From a development point of view, the marsh is ideal. It's got a good view, clean air, and it's flat," said developers' representative Harvey Gerwig. Obviously the county did not feel the same way, and approval was denied.

Local groups, the Department of Health, and the state legislature gathered forces. The state appropriated funds to acquire the pond (now a National Historic Site) and surrounding areas to build a cultural center. By 1980 much had yet to be done. The marsh—some thought it could be a future taro patch—remained a natural runoff basin and habitat for endangered waterfowl. The pond remains, says Marion Kelly of the Bishop Museum, "a living artifact of Hawaiian culture . . . one of the few remaining on Oahu."[18] When the Kaneohe Outdoor Circle has finished its appointed tasks, it will have restored an ancient Hawaiian pond and created a cultural park and a wildlife refuge—valuable cultural and natural amenities and a fine antidote to nearby urbanization.

Coral Reef Problems

Damage done to reefs has been considerable, a serious problem in view of the wide use made of this resource. Not only is the living reef a fascinating resource every visitor and local person can share but also it is the source of livelihood for glass-bottomed boat operators, for professional divers, and for aquarium fishermen. These are diverse uses which, if not watched, can easily become incompatible.

One of the most conspicuous modern examples of reef destruction has been the construction of the three-mile reef-runway extension to the Honolulu International Airport, much of it over an existing reef. Dredging, filling, and general construction in the interests of increased tourist traffic have had serious ecological impacts.

Until 1976, only three-quarters of a mile offshore at Sand Island, a major sewage outfall discharged into thirty-five feet of water, inflicting damage on adjacent coral.[19] The outfall has now been moved two miles offshore in water 225 feet deep and in conditions where dispersal is better guaranteed. Here, in the airport area, an environmental loss, the reef runway, is partially offset by a mixed environmental gain: relocation of the Sand Island outfall and less aircraft noise over the built-up area stemming from the use of the new runway. Both environmental problems are closely related to tourism development. There must always be trade-offs in the process of extensive development of the land Hawaii has experienced. It is for the people of the state to decide which are worthwhile. If we assume that the present Hawaii visitor industry is a necessary and legitimate enterprise, then we must ask as well what dislocation is reasonable in the handling of four million visitors annually on an island with limited flat land. With both military and commercial airlines using the same area and with tourism increasing steadily even in some less encouraging economic times, new runways for future use seem necessary. The runway became a cause celebre and several organizations fought hard to halt construction. Its construction was a major price to pay and being on Honolulu's front doorstep, a symbolic reminder for all thoughtful people of the environmental cost of tourism.

One of the most spectacular cases of reef damage is found at Kaneohe Bay where over the past years sediments originating from land development, freshwater runoff, and sewage outfalls have done untold damage to the ecosystems of the bay. Silt from the land built up faster than it could be removed and eventually covered the reef flats. Extra nutrients from primary treatment effluents and raw sewage caused great blooms of undesirable phytoplankton. As a first step toward solving some of the problems, the Kaneohe Bay Sewage Relocation Project, sponsored by the Environmental Protection Agency and overseen by the Hawaii Institute of Marine Biology, diverted sewage to the open ocean off Mokapu Peninsula. Beneficial results are being observed now, but in the enclosed waters of the southern part of the bay flushing action is not effective and nutrients are still being released from past residue sludge. The concentrations of phytoplankton brought about by enrichment are still the main problem. They have the effect of force feeding other organisms (including the one-celled algae, *zooxanthellae*) which then become so numerous and vigorous they eventually overwhelm the coral. *Zooxanthellae,* "bubble" algae *(Dictyosphaeria cavernosa),* and sponges, after systematically killing the coral, dissolve what remains of the reef, destroying fish refuges and eliminating steps in food chains.[20] Fish populations diminish quickly. Rich organic sediments are digested by microorganisms that leave toxic wastes a few centimeters below the sediment surface in oxygen-depleted strata which, when disturbed by currents, release gas which also kills the coral. These complicated processes continue despite the removal of a major cause of water quality deterioration. Dr. Andas Laws, oceanographer at the University of Hawaii, believes that the recovery of normal coastal water conditions in the bay may take many years.[21] Tourism did not create the situation at Kaneohe Bay. Population resulting from tourism-related activity, however, contributed significantly to the change.

With further development, efficient well-regulated sewage disposal becomes increasingly critical. Sewage-related crises have not been uncommon in Waikiki and now as a result of increased population pressure, major problems have arisen at Lahaina on Maui and at Poipu Beach on Kauai, both prime tourism centers. These are not just environmental and health problems. They represent the possibility of monumental economic problems for the counties, for the responsible parties, and especially for the industry if tourists ever become repelled by the continuation of these undesirable conditions.

To preserve precious reefs and marine areas of great value, several legislative devices, national and state, are available. The case of Hulopoe Bay is mentioned later and the Natural Area Reserve of Ahihi Bay has been discussed in an earlier chapter. In 1978 steps were taken to protect Honolua Bay, a marine area of great distinction close to the emerging Kapalua resort area. In this case it was the developer, Colin Cameron of Maui Land & Pineapple Co., who initiated proceedings. Such protection is not unique. Underwater preserves have been set aside in the Bahamas (Exuma Cays), the Palau Islands, and in the Galapagos group.[22]

Problems of Beach Access and Use

The most prized parts of the Hawaiian landscape are its beaches. Tourist literature assumes this and so does the siting of every major destination area. Only Volcano House, a small specialized hotel in Hawaii's Volcanoes National Park, is away from the sea. The primacy of the beach can be explained by the fact that near the littoral, comfortable warm sand, rocky coastline, clear water, waves and surf, coral gardens, coastal plant communities, mountain and seaward vistas, recreation possibilities, and picnic facilities are all possible.

The experience of the beach is public, available to anyone who can be there. Legally, the public cannot be deprived of the beach. Its boundaries were determined by the State Supreme Court in 1968 when the extent of publicly owned beach in Hawaii was tested. Privately owned land, the court decreed, legally extended to a boundary known as *ma ke kai*, the "upper reaches of the wash of waves usually evidenced by the edge of vegetation or by the line of debris left by the wash of waves."[23] In comparison with a number of other places, this is a very liberal definition.

To have public ownership of the beach is one thing, to be able to exercise this right is another matter entirely. The de jure and de facto situations can be very different indeed. Access through government land, through leased state land, through recently subdivided land, or land set aside for coastal planned unit development is reasonably well assured. Nevertheless there are many choice areas from which the public is precluded sometimes by only a twenty-yard strip posted "no trespassing." Until the early 1970s there were resorts proposing to prohibit the public from beaches (which are still advertised as "our beaches"), but this is largely a thing of the past with few exceptions. This does not mean, however, that there is enough beach access. Present signs suggest there will always be demand for more access to Hawaii's beaches.

There is no need for beachfront home ownership to result in private preemption of scarce beach areas which with increasing urbanization are absolutely essential for public recreational use. No longer can beaches be considered preserves for those who can afford them. They are now a social necessity for all. This is particularly important in Hawaii where 90 percent of the people participate in some outdoor recreation. In a recent survey, nearly 70 percent of these followed an activity related to the sea such as swimming (23 percent), beach going (21 percent), picnicking (12 percent), fishing (8 percent), surfing (5 percent), or beach camping (3 percent).[24]

Over the past two decades on the mainland, courts have applied public use doctrines and displayed "a growing judicial recognition of the need to preserve beaches for public recreation." If natural barriers or private owners restrict access, beaches are de facto private beaches. Thus, the courts recognized the "substantial threat posed to public recreation by private development [which] has probably been the decisive factor in tilting this balance to favor the public claim."[25] Such legal opinions have vastly aided in opening up Hawaii beaches.[26]

In 1975 when InterIsland Resorts applied for a permit to make renovations to the Kauai Surf Hotel at Nawiliwili, it was informed by Kauai Planning Director Brian Nishimoto that at least two new beach accesses would be a necessary condition for the issue of a permit. InterIsland's attorneys contested this condition (one which is fairly general in all counties now) and referred to an agreement for beach access reached with the County of Kauai in 1960. In a letter, the attorneys wrote "We believe that InterIsland has been reasonable in its efforts to provide for the needs and concerns of the Planning Commission . . . the access rights agreed to [in 1960] as reasonable by the parties should no doubt be reasonable now . . ."[27] The fifteen intervening years between 1960, when any access was reluctantly given, and 1975 saw the greatest growth in the visitor industry Hawaii had even seen, and the consequent changes in public attitudes to access and awareness of the beach as a public resource were dramatic. Whatever may seem reasonable today is unlikely to be exactly so in fifteen years' time.

With development, access is often not as free as it was before development despite the fact that there might now be a path labeled "beach access." Resorts, unless instructed to do so, do not make the locations of public access clear. With smaller developments, it seems a common practice to disguise an access by landscaping it in the manner of adjacent land so that the public or other visitors have no knowledge that a public right-of-way exists. Sometimes guests are led to believe that they are occupying a private preserve that from time to time is transgressed by local interlopers which true noblesse oblige tolerates. There are some interesting examples of poorly identified public lands between Kihei and Keawakapu on Maui where state land occupies a strip between the sea and the first row of buildings. In places, the state has allowed developers to remove sand dunes to provide condominium owners with better sea views. The state also allowed this and other intervening state land to be landscaped in the same manner as adjacent hotel and condominium lands.

At some resort areas, former coastal roads have been relocated —or relocation is planned—to a position considerably inland from the former coastal access road. Wailea, Kaanapali, and Kapalua, all on Maui, are such examples. In the name of better and safer transportation to a nearby resort, previous access to the coast has been replaced by more difficult public road access with limited parking space. In the case of Kapalua, free access to a beach beyond the resort was provided in lieu of more restricted use of beaches previously used. Removal of a coastal road allows resort landscaping to the beach's edge without interference.

At Wailea, the public access is physically limited by the placement of access roads and the number of parking spaces associated with each access. In contrast hotel guests without the need for parking have unrestricted use of the shoreline. The public is restricted and can no longer drive close to and parallel to the beach while choosing where to park. When such accesses are completed the public use noticeably declines with the effect that the beaches for several years might be less crowded than they were. The impacts are never all on the debit side. The beaches, now backed by resorts, are probably clean and free of the masses of litter characterizing numbers of free access beaches in Hawaii not associated with beach parks.

An application for realignment of a coastal road was made by the Makena project. At a public meeting held by the Kihei Community Association in May 1978, the need for realignment was explained by Felix Pascua of the County Public Works Department and Carl Murota, a consultant. It was explained to the public that there was a "need to build the road to 'design standards' for thirty-five mile an hour traffic as indicated by the Kihei General Plan." "You realize," said Pascua, "that the general plan calls for a certain amount of growth [see later discussion on the tyranny of law and planning, chapter 12]. We have provided the sewers, we're providing the water, now we have to provide the road system."[28]

The Community Association's reaction was that the need for any change from the present road alignment would have to be proved. Most of those who spoke were against any change in the alignment. Individuals whose property value might rise were for it. The general feeling was summed up by a spokesman who said, "The developers are getting all the beachfronts and we're miles away. We can't even get our boats in the ocean any more. We don't want beach accesses, we want the road open so we can see the ocean. What can you see from Wailea? Nothing. You guys are giving the whole island away to developers."[29]

Middle-class spokespersons seldom speak in this strong and forthright manner; nevertheless, here was a sentiment shared by many. On the island of Maui, realignment or the equivalent has been virtually part of every major resort design. In the past, county planners felt they had done well by the public insisting on alternative access. But the alternatives have never been acceptable substitutes for what was lost. Perhaps in a decade we will understand the sheer folly of not only diminishing physical shoreline access but also reducing visual access.

My argument is one largely of design. By all means, divert the bulk of traffic but retain an alternative which allows local people who treasure the view and the access to proceed, where it is physically possible, along a two-way limited speed road where the view is unimpeded by large masses of concrete. I agree it will make a less tidy plan in terms of a development oriented toward visitors, but we are quickly learning that quality tourism depends as much on the satisfaction of the hosts as well as the guests. If developers are expected to contribute substantially to sewers and water lines then, in their own interests, they should be listening intently to new viewpoints. Acknowledgments of public feelings could turn social costs into social benefits and ultimately economic benefits. This is a matter which should be a concern of both the counties and the state. It is better to act now than have a situation in the future, as in Britain, where huge sums of money are being spent in creating public thoroughfares around the entire coast so that the public can enjoy views which are rightly theirs.

The real dilemma concerning access is that resort development rests largely on the use (including the viewing) of public resources —the beach and the sea. Consequently the community contributes substantially to an activity catering exclusively to a small number of people in relation to the total population. Local people, whose moral rights due to permanent residence should be greater than visitors and whose legal rights are equal to those of visitors, are in terms of beach access nevertheless restricted by comparison. Some argue this is a trade-off local people make for jobs in tourism and a higher standard of living.

Several recent problems concerning beach access have occurred on Maui, Molokai, and Lanai. Often beach access controversies arise for symbolic political reasons. Always it involves human conflict between the transgressors and the transgressed, between groups who see themselves as the manipulated and the manipulators. Although the cases do not involve tourism directly, they are related. On Molokai a local group tried to gain access to a number of beaches before one was opened up primarily for the use of outsiders. At Lanai local residents protected their local beach from a growing number of outsiders making inroads into their privacy and, by the use of environmental legislation, they attempted to keep it the way it was.

The Hui Alaloa March, Molokai

In the mid-1970s the people of Molokai experienced frustration in attempts to gain access to beaches fronting portions of the 75,000-acre Molokai Ranch whose policy was to prevent beach visits except by permit. This was tested by a local group, Hui Alaloa which on 4 July 1975 organized a march through west-end coastal ranchland over what was claimed to be a traditional Hawaiian trail. The use of the unspoiled west-end beaches and fishing grounds were at the time restricted to three hundred ranch shareholders (many from Hawaii's kamaaina, old guard, families), ranch employees, and guests.

Aka Hodgins, the ranch manager, is reported to have said to representatives of the marchers, "After the march, hikers on the public beach will not be stopped but once they cross over into Molokai Ranch land we will take the attitude they are trespassing. Our policy . . . of controlled access will continue to be maintained and violators will be . . . prosecuted."[30]

The confrontations between residents and the ranch were taking place at a time when Molokai pineapple companies had either pulled out of the business or had threatened to do so, unemployment was high, and the county felt the situation called for emergency action. To this end, the long-planned Kaluakoi resort project using former ranchland was officially encouraged. Already the Molokai climate of opinion concerning the decline of agriculture, unemployment, and Navy bombing of the island of Kahoolawe (a Hui Alaloa cause) was tense. A denial of beach access together with a resort project rumored to involve six hotels and an additional population of 30,000 persons aggravated the situation.

The public was informed that coastal access would be granted by the ranch at the site of the resort if and when the Kaluakoi project got off the ground. The pressures which gathered within the small island community and especially in the Hawaiian group Hui Alaloa were immense. The group was striving for community and Hawaiian integrity while feeling impotent at the hands of powerful companies. Those concerned with pineapples were denying them jobs, the ranch which symbolically represented Hawaii's elite was not only preventing them from using their own recreation and fishing grounds but in the eyes of the activists, it was threatening to mount a venture capable of overwhelming them demographically and culturally—using tourism as its instrument.

There is of course another side to the story. The resort turned out to be low-key, attractive, and unobtrusive, with its fair share of community support. And for the ranch, as any farmer well knows, free public access can mean broken fences, damaged cattle, poached deer, shoreline litter, squatters, and range fires—just a few of the problems which can be associated with unsupervised access through a livestock-ranching operation.

The example from Molokai along with a similar occurrence at Kuiaha Bay, Maui, show the possibilities of conflict and hostility when people are denied access to areas rightfully theirs. Both cases are linked with tourism and related to growing local populations demanding increased beach use and the blatant removal of what is perceived as right, a reminder of plantation times. The following example from Lanai is interestingly the reverse of the above. Local people were determined to establish their own privileged position in the face of imported tourism which introduced issues of privacy, crowding, and intrusion of primary territory—conditions previously unknown.

Hulopoe Bay, Lanai

During 1978 a controversy arose involving the residents of the island of Lanai, the charter boat operators and boaters of Lahaina, and Castle & Cooke, the owners of most of the land. For some time, the Lanai community had complained about Lahaina yachts and charter boats landing passengers at Hulopoe, White Sand Manele Beach. The bay, they alleged, was being polluted by visiting boats whose passengers were arriving in increasing numbers. Since the arrivals began several years previous, local observers alleged that beach litter, floating debris, and ecological damage were resulting. Official complaints were laid. The Department of Land and Natural Resources (DLNR) responded with the creation, in 1976, of the Manele-Hulopoe Marine Life Conservation District, an area of particular concern, in need of special management protection under the Hawaii Coastal Zone Management Program. The DLNR proceeded to regulate fishing, water pollution, shoreline construction, and conservation, and the Department of Transportation, boating activities. The issue of Regulation 40 aimed to bring about the creation of the district, prohibit fishing in the bay, and prevent boats from damaging marine life and geological formations in the area.

Lanai economically is oriented to pineapple growing and next to Niihau is the least tourist-oriented island in Hawaii. Visitors are incidental. Hulopoe is a major recreational area for the island's twenty-two hundred residents, most of whom work for Castle & Cooke or a subsidiary. Its beautiful white sand is shaded with picturesque palms. Restrooms, tables, and barbecue broilers are provided by the company which has several interests in the area. Not only does it own adjacent agricultural land, but also, on some future occasion, it hopes to build a resort focused on the controversial bay. Because of increasing pressure on the facilities, the company has policed the area and has charged outsiders a fee. Yachtsmen and charter boat operators from Lahaina have been arriving in greater numbers and have estimated they pay the company $4,000 to $6,000 a month for the use of the beach. Because of complaints by local residents, charter boats do not arrive on weekends.

The specific issues of the 1978 controversy were that Lanai's residents, not happy with Regulation 40, alleged that although there were signs of more marine life in the bay, water pollution and misuse still continued. The agencies responded with further regulations. Portions of one read "that no person shall operate, anchor, or moor any vessel within the boundaries of subzone A (Hulopoe Bay)."[31] At this suggestion, more than Hulopoe's floating garbage hit the fan.

Sparks flew. Heated discussions and acrimony set the tone. Lahaina boat owners cried discrimination, while Lanai residents replied that the boats must go. A side issue, strongly denied, was an allegation that Castle & Cooke was working behind the scenes to create an exclusive reserve for its future resort guests.

The situation was much more complicated than presented here. The nature of Regulation 40 turned attention to an issue, the pollution of the bay, which really was not central to the controversy. Pollution was denied by marine biologist Dr. Lawrence Read who, in his own newspaper column, bemoaned the fact that as an objective scientist, he was caught in the politics of Hulopoe Bay.[32] Of course it was politics of a very real kind. What was happening on Lanai, in microcosm, is happening to Hawaii as a whole. Local residents resented the incursion of large power boats and affluent tourists into the simple and treasured life which was theirs. In desperation they saw the inexorable erosion of their particular way of life. A boat owners' representative, Don Anderson, president of the Hawaii Boating Association, at one of the public hearings met public pleas with a question directed at them: "Think about what you're doing to my life-style." Pleasure boaters, charter operators, and divers saw the bay as just another resource which they, as residents of the state (or the county), had every right to use. The conflict was not just a series of legal and political maneuvers. It was economic and social as well, while the pretext for presenting the matter for open discussion was environmental law. At the time of writing, DLNR is still considering the evidence and an appropriate course of action.

The Maintenance of Beauty and Natural Areas

Crowding of inappropriate places can be a genuine source of annoyance and an instrument of destruction of the very things that cause the visits in the first place. In order to see the Hawaiian village of Hana and the exquisite Seven Pools, hordes of visitors travel the picturesque winding road south from Kahului, Maui. The small, charming, unhurried farming center is now overrun by visitors seeking to capture on film the town's tranquility before they "do" Seven Pools, where traffic appears so congested one is reminded of the passenger pickup zone at the Honolulu airport after the arrival of several 747s. The two issues are a real source of resident annoyance. To some extent, but I would say only temporarily, residents are protected by winding narrow roads and quite inadequate parking at the Seven Pools. I can only see the situation deteriorating. One possible solution is that private cars park on the Kahului side of Hana and the occupants travel by bus to Seven Pools.

On Kauai the two most revered wilderness areas are the Na Pali Coast and the Kalalau Valley. The Department of Land and Natural Resources is working out a program to protect the thirty miles of stunningly beautiful uninhabited coast. Campers in the area complained of low-flying helicopters traversing the same area fifteen to twenty times during an afternoon. One pilot, Jack Harter, noted that helicopters were landing people at remote spots every fifteen minutes. "The Na Pali Coast is becoming another Yosemite, a place of breathtaking beauty overrun by sightseers to the point where its intrinsic value is buried under a mound of debris."[33] Like Hana, the Na Pali Coast presents something of an insoluble problem. How can increasing numbers of people be accommodated in areas whose great attraction is not only fabulous beauty but also the absence of human activity?

At times residents are at a loss to identify clearly a problem which is causing concern. Various facets of the environment, natural and social, become inextricably intertwined, and it is difficult to separate the wish for the preservation of an unpolluted natural area from the maintenance of coastal beauty or from the preservation of a rural way of life. A late 1978 public opinion survey sampling four thousand households in ten Oahu areas made it clear, as Oahu's advisory neighborhood boards had done, that saving agricultural land was a prime objective. Rural residents of the windward coast reflecting a county consensus considered the need to protect scenic and natural areas to be particularly important. The vast majority of Oahu residents were concerned not only about their own water pollution problems but also with cleaning up all the polluted waters of Oahu.[34]

The perceived needs of the community have not been overlooked by the state. In his 1980 State of the State address Governor George Ariyoshi made it clear that "in Windward Oahu alone we have determined that the area from Waiahole to Kahuku should remain as rural and agricultural as possible. We have purchased hundreds of acres in that region . . . to assure that future generations may enjoy these lands as we have."[35]

This is a wise decision. The American penchant for real estate investment is well understood and in Hawaii has been facilitated by the building of condominiums in coastal areas for this purpose alone. Construction for this debatable purpose may destroy the aesthetic beauty of an area, facilitate additional in-migration and encourage further construction on choice coastal locations or on prime agricultural land.

Energy and Water

The end of the 1970s saw particular emphasis placed on new sources of energy for Hawaii—solar energy, wind, water power, ocean thermal energy conversion, geothermal power, biomass conversion, and the manufacture of ethanol and gasohol.[36] Both the Big Island and Molokai have embarked on comprehensive alternate energy packages. Until now, except for the use of biomass, an important energy source for electricity generation at sugar cane mills, great dependence has been placed on imported oil.

With pressure from tourists encouraged to consume and travel with little restraint, with a voracious energy-consuming population used to automobiles and air conditioning, and with spiraling oil prices, the state has made a central concern the Islands' power vulnerability. The state's frightening dependence on oil comes from the need to maintain transport links between the mainland and Hawaii and to keep visitors and local people moving on island roads where outside the City and County of Honolulu public transport is largely absent. To prepare for an all too obvious future, great efforts are being made in the direction of local production of fuel and energy. At the same time, these efforts will use island resources which have been overlooked, maintain a better state trade balance through energy import substitution, and strengthen the tourism multiplier effect by preventing some obvious income leakage. In the long run the costs and contributions of local energy production will be known. In the short run, increasing conventional fuel costs and uses as they relate to the visitor industry may weigh the state's contribution to the industry's infrastructure in favor of costs rather than benefits. Present high oil costs focus attention closely on local energy resources and at the same time on the potential oil pricing has for damaging Pacific tourism. This latter distinct possibility is mentioned later.

Greater population creates great demands on local resources. One of these is water, yet paradoxically now with large coastal populations there are occasions on which the roles can be reversed. Uncontrolled natural flow can make spectacular impacts on human resources. Every decade floods of great severity have the potential for doing more and more damage as coastal areas become increasingly populated in response to tourism.

Removal of any vegetation, forest, or scrubland for agriculture or construction increases run-off. On an island group capable of fifty-five inches of rainfall in four days—the case on the Hamakua Coast in January 1979—the situation can get frighteningly out of control as lowland areas, no longer settling basins or sparsely inhabited flood plains, are covered with carpets of condominiums. There was a time in the past when flood water influenced only the marine life and then sporadically without more than minimal damage. Now flood waters on the rampage can cause hundreds of thousands of dollars of property damage, threaten lives, and cause environmental despoliation. This was certainly the case in Maui in January 1980 when tourist districts became disaster areas.

A much greater problem than flooding is the compound problem of water deficiency associated with competitive consumption by residential, industrial, and agricultural users. Despite the possibility of heavy rains, even in dry areas, the state during many years has suffered damaging periods of protracted drought. Low storage facilities, deterioration of artesian water quality, increased competition for use, limited reticulation facilities, high price, and dwindling supplies are all problems of the highest order.

The pressure on water resources is everywhere. In July 1977, the Honolulu Board of Water Supply was scrambling to meet the needs of the fast-growing population of Oahu's wet windward side. It was then suggested that supplies be augmented from the Punaluu stream, the first ever public use of surface water on Oahu. To that date all water had come from underground aquifers. Edward Hirata, Board manager, went on record as saying, "We're telling anyone who needs water—agriculture, housing, or industrial entrepreneur . . . they'll have to provide their own water source." The situation was typical of present day conditions in Hawaii: drought which left underground reserves low, demand by a growing population, wells overpumped and turning salty, and water development projects yielding less water than expected.

During 1978 and well into 1979, development in most major areas of Maui from Kaanapali to Makena, from central Maui to Kula were restrained by a moratorium on building brought about by the lack of water. In central Maui, new subdivisions were prohibited until the completion of the central Maui water transmission line. And then only certain projects were allowed. The non-availability of a natural resource provided restrictions to growth the county was not otherwise prepared to implement. Lack of water very neatly got the administration off the hook and uncompromisingly solved the dilemma of growth versus conservation. The validity of the strategy certainly did not have universal approval.

The 1978 Oahu public opinion survey to which I have already referred attempted to identify the most pressing planning problem on the public mind. The protection of the island's water resources was the top planning objective. Over two-thirds of the respondents felt it "very important." Other items listed were low- and moderate-income housing, the solution of traffic problems, as well as the preservation of agricultural lands.[37] All problems could be tied to population pressure and this in turn could be related readily to the ramifications of the state's major industry.

With increasing population, permanent and temporary, with new uses in diversified agriculture and aquaculture, with the completion of resort projects already started, water has become, along with energy, a most critical resource. Both can disastrously curb economic endeavors from which the state expects so much and provide a serious unlooked-for dampener to the growth of the state's major industry—tourism. No-growth supporters, on the other hand, may see the setback as a blessing in disguise as they did in Kauai in March 1980 when a water moratorium brought construction at Poipu Beach to a halt.

Mapping and Monitoring

The state of the art for defining and delineating physical areas for attention or preservation is spotty and inconclusive. No consensus of a fragile resource or, for that matter, of what is in need of attention is available. Understanding comes slowly, but it comes. More is agreed upon and acknowledged today than ever previously. Some institutions and agencies have made efforts to map and monitor, but nothing yet has been accomplished in a systematic manner. What has been done is useful and at least a basis for further work. A valuable service has been provided by the technical studies contributing to the Hawaii State Plan and to the State Tourism Study. Despite its imperfections, persons interested will find a useful document in the physical resources volume of the latter study.[38]

Although it is difficult to differentiate environmental tourism damage from that of agriculture or other activities, much more work must be done to evaluate the status of coastal lands, to measure change, and to do something about it. The laying of specific blame is not as important as problem identification, thorough evaluation, and finding an appropriate remedy. What has been important in the past is that "fragile resources" have been usually protected at public expense and through public programs largely because of the difficulty of establishing public value. This has been a source of irritation and has resulted sometimes in conflict between developers, public agencies, and environmental groups over "whether a resource has sufficient value to be preserved and warrant denial of development of property on or near such resources."[39]

CHAPTER 9

The People of Hawaii

WITHOUT a doubt one of the most valuable tourist resources of Hawaii is its multi-ethnic population. However, the major conflict that divides this population and bears on the extent and direction of future tourism is the degree to which individuals and groups identify with local integrity, the conservation of the essential character of Hawaii, and the degree to which local people feel they should be guided by their perception of mainline, mainland Americanism.

The founding group was of course Hawaiian; but now except for a tourist industry-reinforced mystique, the number and economic clout of Hawaiians—let alone their history and culture —render them virtually powerless. Former colonialism and its present-day counterparts, all of which foster inferiority, have aggravated this complicated matter.

During the first half of the nineteenth century, the Hawaiian people, like Polynesians throughout the Pacific, came into close contact with sandalwood traders, whalers, missionaries, and adventurers from many parts of the Western world. The seeds for change were then sown; they produced, as expected, social dislocation. During the second half of the century, plantation labor recruiters ranged widely in the Pacific basin. In 1850 the Royal Hawaiian Agricultural Society was formed to recruit workers for Hawaii sugar plantations, and from 1852 when the first few hundred Chinese arrived until 1930, approximately 400,000 men, women, and children were transported to the plantations of Hawaii.[1]

Aliens arriving on plantations were usually housed in camps according to nationality. Plantation labor came from China, Japan,

Portugal, the Philippines, Korea, Puerto Rico, Germany, and Scandinavia. Each camp was separated from the others by physical distance, custom, and language. Housing, food, pay, and medical attention were provided by the haole-owned plantation, whose manager was always haole, and the *luna* (foreman) usually was Caucasian as well. In fact, well into the nineteenth century most of the residents who were born in Hawaii or who had newly arrived worked for a haole.

Cottington describes the situation pre-1900 as oligarchic paternalism, followed by a subtle shift she calls "employer welfarism."[2] This meant loyalty to the interests of management, a situation which frequently still persists inside and outside the plantation. Plantation labor was not expected to show leadership or entrepreneurial mobility. Limited education only was the worker's due.

This new economic paternalism existed alongside the old-style Hawaiian feudalism, which it replaced. Few would debate that chiefs and commoners still existed but in a new form: chiefs were haole and commoners were represented by the various ethnic groups.

After 1900, contract labor for plantations was no longer legal. However, there was minimal change for the worker population. The well-defined master-servant relationship remained. Only its quality and intensity changed throughout the years. The communication handicaps of workers who spoke little English, the language of management, and the low level of worker education impaired their ability and effectiveness as a social or economic force. These deficiencies caused the majority of the population to be vulnerable to any who wished to manipulate them. This was not unusual elsewhere in the Pacific, also.

In 1946 unionization reached the plantations. Slowly conditions improved. More persons with plantation backgrounds moved into town and started to gain commercial positions of responsibility and influence. However, despite the fact that wages were now higher, the old life of dependency, deprecation of ambition, and a meager education remained. Dependency was still there but less concentrated in a single source.[3] Strangely, in some ways unions started to assume former roles of plantation management. Plantation workers as a group were an ineffective force even for their own change. After unionization they readily transferred their dependence from plantation to union management.

While slow changes were taking place on plantations, spectacular changes were taking place in developing urban areas, especially Honolulu. Since the 1850s haoles had controlled great land areas, and their early companies had exerted tremendous influence on both land ownership and commerce.

The haole had the edge on all other outside groups by being on the scene early and by being able to manipulate the situation through advising and finally terminating the Hawaiian monarchy. After the distribution of land in 1848, all major parcels fell into haole hands, and, after a process of consolidation, most ownership rested with relatively few individuals and companies. These were also the people who dominated the government.

However, there was always a flow from plantations to towns by dissatisfied, contract-expired plantation workers who saw themselves participating in a future quite different from that of the plantation. They left the plantations only to be replaced by a new intake of laborers with little or no local language who became quickly dependent on management, the union, or both. Those who went to town frequently had better language competency and more motivation in comparison with their fellows.

Relative population figures for all ethnic groups have changed through time as has the statistical reporting system, which has not only changed but has varied from agency to agency. Present data do not allow for either precision or statistically-backed generalization, nevertheless, I have from time to time made estimates based on the figures available. One can understand how difficult it must be to classify ethnic mixtures which, by one tabulation, amount to almost one-third of the total population. Of almost 900,000 people in 1979, 26 percent were Caucasian, 25 percent Japanese, 11 percent Filipino, and 1 percent Hawaiian. These four groups are called unmixed. If mixed and unmixed Hawaiians are added together, they constitute 20 percent of the total population and the fourth largest group in the state.

Chinese and Japanese

Outside the plantations and with the knowledge that plantations provided their major work alternative, both Chinese and Japanese worked assiduously and single-mindedly for their own betterment. From an early date in keeping with their homeland tradition, Chinese had filled a middleman niche in commerce. They were also in a position to give concerted help to countrymen who were in trouble or entering commerce for the first time. Ultimately, Chinese became very successful in their urban occupations, and their economic clout prepared the way for their assumption of a respected place as solid members of society, in business and the professions.

The background to Japanese success is interesting. Throughout the early history of the plantations Japanese laborers, who became the essential strength of the workforce, were treated with little if any respect. When they rebelled, as they did occasionally, the inhuman treatment meted out to them was shocking. Reciprocal hostility became acute. It was the memory of plantation mistreatment, the experience of haole racism in the 1932 Massie case, and the wartime attitude of white Americans toward Japanese that colored Japanese-American activity and thinking during World War II and as the territory approached statehood.

They have much to escape from and much to gain by harnessing their inherited cultural characteristics of hard work, thrift, family cohesion, and obligation for the purpose of channeling emotional and physical energy into constructive achievement rather than activity guided by hostility. A recent study of Americans of Japanese ancestry (AJAs) concludes that, "In three generations descendents of poor immigrants have entered the American middle class, economically, socially and in many ways emotionally . . . they are an example of the American dream. In doing this they have maintained their own identity and critical mass."[4]

Education, the key to success for the Japanese, was gained through the professions, by employment in education, and through government as staff members or legislators. High points for Asians were reached in 1959, the mid-1960s, and the mid-1970s. In 1959 Daniel K. Inouye of the famous 442d Regiment was elected as the first AJA in the U.S. House of Representatives, and Hiram Fong, son of a Chinese immigrant, became one of the first two Oriental senators in Washington, D.C. By the mid-sixties Spark Matsunaga and Patsy Takemoto Mink (a Japanese-American woman) had joined an entirely Oriental Hawaii congressional group, Inouye having moved to the Senate. Then, gaining non-haole representation in all major political offices, in the mid-1970s upon the death of another immigrant, John Burns, George Ariyoshi was elected to the state's highest post as the first Hawaii-born Japanese-American governor.

In 1975 the Hawaii State Legislature of seventy-six persons had thirty-five Japanese and sixteen Caucasians. A survey by Michael Haas of the University of Hawaii (1975) produced interesting findings: Not only did AJAs dominate the civilian work force, but in nearly every department and including top jobs there was a concentration of Asians, especially AJAs, even in the Department of Hawaiian Homelands. In this department, the report says, "Japanese males are over-concentrated at the top and preponderant among the professional staff."

For these non-haole governmental decision makers along with their counterparts in business and the professions, their upwardly thrusting mobility had put significant distance between them and the bulk of the population—especially rural dwellers and plantation workers. In a survey of all ethnic groups within today's corporate, political, and bureaucratic power structures, Japanese, Caucasian, and Chinese are well represented, possibly in that order. The AJAs did more than any other group to break what at times seemed the almost overwhelming hold haoles exerted on both the economy and the society.

Smaller Ethnic Groups

Over the past several decades, other groups were not faring well. Newcomers were arriving all the time in search of rural or urban opportunities. In some ways the situation had not changed much from the early days of contract labor. From the Pacific Islands, Samoans entered in larger numbers than ever before, now high enough to constitute part of the greatest Polynesian migration of all time. The net situation for the entire population was somewhat obscured by the fact that they were also leaving in disproportionately large numbers. In recent years Filipinos, who for decades have been the backbone of the plantations have been arriving in great numbers. They are followed numerically by Koreans, Chinese, and Japanese.

None of the non-haole groups has done as well economically as the Japanese and Chinese. The Portuguese, traditionally considered a separate group, fill a middle niche as they did during plantation times, and the Filipinos still occupy many of the low-paying jobs.

The present Filipino population is close to 100,000, or more than 10 percent of the total population. A third of them are aliens making up about half the total number in the category and constituting the most important alien immigrant group today. A larger percentage of Filipinos are in the labor force than any other major group and many of them, because they are recent arrivals and have a low level of education, have lower-paying, lower-status occupations than they otherwise might.[5]

The extended family is, for the Filipino as for the Samoan, the main means of support to the immigrant. Labor and good fortune are shared with relatives while there is a feeling of indifference to those outside the family. Where the biological family has not been present, Filipinos have substituted alliance systems of members with common interests, and this like the extended family involves regular and predictable exchanges of goods and services.

The Filipino is extremely conscious of personal wants and, being exceptionally sensitive, will employ "elaborate means . . . to avoid giving offense . . . [and] desperate efforts [are made] to avoid direct confrontation, disagreement or criticism."[6] This desire for frictionless relationships is called *pakikisama*, a characteristic which "favors avoidance of direct confrontation that could lead to open and violent aggressive behaviors."[7]

Present conditions are not as many in the group would wish them to be. In the assimilative process determined by the dominant culture, older children reject traditional priorities and place economic productivity and financial status first, thereby increasing individualistic and materialistic acquisitive goals to the detriment of affiliative networks.

In terms of conventional values Filipinos and Hawaiians are similar with stress placed on group appreciation and interpersonal harmony. The traditionalists in both groups see the older values under siege as some of their members give preference to assimilation and individual gain.[8]

Caucasians: The First Aliens

The haole group is difficult to classify. Its members have been arriving in increasing numbers during this century. In the two decades 1960–1980, the Caucasian population probably doubled. Total in-migration, including military, averages about 50,000 persons a year. Of this possibly about 35,000 are Caucasian. This included in 1976 about 20,000 military personnel and their dependents. If military personnel are excluded and out-migration is taken into consideration as well as live births, it can be estimated that the haole population increases at about 12,000 a year.

Toward the end of the 1960s, the Caucasians became the dominant group numerically. Approximately a decade later, they numbered over a quarter of a million persons. Although the Caucasian is the largest individual group in absolute terms, nevertheless the group is far from dominant. It is outnumbered by others approximately four to one. Slowly and steadily, the Caucasian component is growing. This comes mostly from in-migration from the mainland and is countered only by substantial Asian immigration and natural increases from local non-Caucasian groups.

The haole arrived early in the century, introduced alien technology and customs, Christian religion, diseases, land speculation, commerce, racism, and numerous other foreign practices that had the effect of changing the local life-style. Such introductions included transportation, which ranged in time and complexity from horse to airplane, Western medicine, Christianity, hymn singing and musical instruments, public utilities, cloth and alien building techniques and materials, commercial agriculture, and formal education.

Haoles have in the past been very influential, and some haoles through land and corporations wield an inordinate amount of power. Some Caucasians whose families have been represented through many generations of haole control look on the people of Hawaii and the land with respect and benevolence rather than with demeaning paternalism. There are many, without doubt, who see themselves as admirable models, a credit to the system which their forebears initiated and through which they have risen.

But such families are now few in number and may be looked upon as the vestigial remnants of early colonial Hawaii. Onto this vestige is grafted the bulk of the haole group. Some came later; most of them are relatively recent arrivals. As an entity, they run the gamut from rich retirees to young welfare recipients, from the overeducated to the ignorant. Many are permanent, some are seasonal residents, and some are transient. Part is a military group of 125,000 personnel and dependents—almost three-quarters Caucasians, and definitely not all affluent. On Oahu in 1976 the median civilian income was $16,100; for military families it was $10,300.[9] Haole values, local and mainland, form one of the themes of this book. In some manner they are featured in every chapter in conjunction with the dominant culture. This section, then, is purposely brief.

Hawaiians: The Founders

Ethnically Hawaiians are Polynesian and consequently have a lot in common with the Polynesians of Tonga, Tahiti, the Cook Islands, and New Zealand. The Hawaiians' common heritage and similar past history to a number of other Pacific islanders is largely overlooked by the majority of residents of Hawaii who see Hawaiians as a separate, discrete group comparable with Japanese, Filipinos, or haoles, unrelated to the rest of the Pacific.

Many Hawaiians perceive their lives as simple, oriented toward children and family, celebration, ceremony, the land, the sea, and the church. By grasping firmly to all but the last element, which was introduced and replaced an ailing indigenous religion, increasing numbers link themselves with antiquity in an effort to preserve and develop an integrity essentially of Hawaii.

Each ethnic group within Hawaii obviously stereotypes the others, but along with this stereotyping comes a prevalent status hierarchy based largely on perceived socioeconomic levels. Although there are outstanding exceptions to this order, the consensus now sees the haoles, Japanese, and Chinese at one end of the spectrum, the Filipinos, Okinawans, and Samoans at the other end. The Portuguese are somewhat down from the top, while the Hawaiians and part-Hawaiians are somewhat elevated from the bottom. This describes the situation only partly. It does not account for the "working" (as opposed to business and professional) Chinese and Japanese, ethnically mixed persons who might find themselves anywhere on the scale, or those Portuguese, Hawaiians, or Filipinos who have done exceedingly well in economic terms.

Through the activities of a demographically dominant group at home and through political connections on the mainland, the life of all Hawaii residents is inextricably linked with the customs and mores of white Americans. The bulk of investment capital is mainland Caucasian. Much mainland money comes to Hawaii from the sale of tourism services, federal grants, and spending and receipts from the sale of produce from federally supported agriculture. The educational curriculum is mainland-haole oriented and so too are architecture and the legal system, if not appointments to the judiciary.

Not surprisingly then, the haole has been stereotyped as the controller of Hawaii's affairs, affluent, business-oriented, paternal, an efficient organizer, aloof, superior, and mindful only of his own concerns—some say self-centered. Haoles bring in mainland values which are not necessarily from a wide spectrum of society, often from the center rather than the periphery. Like many mainlanders in the past, some, despite their already influential positions, still feel they have something of a mission to fulfill—to bring enlightenment. Many are delighted with Hawaii, and as relative newcomers often take a most proprietorial view of land and life despite the fact that they may be ill-equipped to say anything about either.

Such a state of affairs is frequently irksome to kamaainas (natives of the land), haole and non-haole alike. There was a time, which may now have passed, when it was chic to talk disparagingly of educational and social services, while waiting for the time to "get off the rock." This may have had its origins with military families assigned to Hawaii for a specific tour of duty. It was, however, not confined to the military.

The Hawaiians have suffered, as many Polynesian groups have, from early and similar stereotyping and from the insensitive and distorted perceptions of those in more dominant cultural positions. In the achievement-oriented, acquisitive, urbanized milieu of the West, they were patronized as likable but irresponsible.

Hawaiians are frequently seen as friendly people who have developed numerous strategies to avoid confrontation but who can eventually be sparked to action by oppression or mistreatment although potentially explosive situations are frequently suppressed.[10] They are outstandingly hospitable, a cultural characteristic of all Polynesians.

In the 1930s and 1940s the stereotyped Hawaiian not infrequently lived up to others' expectations of him—a good-natured surfer, singer, and dancer. Maybe this was something upon which to capitalize. The Hawaiian religions had gone, the land had gone, persons of pure Hawaiian stock were rapidly dwindling, the language was going, the monarchy had gone, the social structure had disintegrated, and several other ethnic groups had usurped power that was formerly exercised by Hawaiians alone. Why not do the expected? Live like happy natives and sing film versions of Hawaiian songs written in English so that a few affluent haoles, traveling to Hawaii by ship, might see for themselves what they had been led to believe existed in a tropical paradise.

An aspiring Hawaiian parent then might have told his children: "Forget the ukulele, the fish and poi, wear shoes, don't talk pidgin, learn English, and get a good job like the haole." At the time, in many ways a low point for the Hawaiian, the successful haole seemed the only obvious model to emulate. Success in terms of economic opportunity did, at that time, often mean cultural abandonment.

Unfortunately in Hawaii only the haole can operate in the mainland culture and feel perfectly at home. For all others a sometimes uneasy adjustment is required. But to have Hawaiians holding high-level executive positions some feel would require transforming them into the sort of people they characteristically are not. This has already happened to a degree both in Hawaii and elsewhere in Polynesia.[11] It has been done at great cost, destroying the very way of life which, together with ruralness, described elsewhere, contributes largely to the precious Hawaiian aloha spirit. Few truly culturally directed Hawaiians can ever get to the top of the haole totem pole, a reward perceived as the acme of attainment by many non-Hawaiians.

To other groups Hawaiians may develop a special mystique. They alone "belong" and have roots here in Hawaii, roots which are an integral part of the Pacific island world. Because of this, persons from other groups may relate closely to the Hawaiian heritage. Some, perhaps, relate more closely to Hawaiian custom than they do to their own ethnic background, and for them to talk of "our Hawaiian heritage" is not anomalous. Indeed it seems absolutely necessary that in this and other ways a neo-Hawaiian culture develop.

Social Conflict, Education, and Speech

In any multiracial society the potential for conflict is great; if the gaps are great, the potential is greater. The disparities, social, educational, and economic, are sometimes wide in Hawaii, and reaction to them is manifested in a variety of ways. It runs the gamut from the ever-present unstated uneasiness to displays of violence. From time to time mainland newspaper articles and books give special emphasis to a growing militancy purporting to reflect a significant part of the state's population. Often this is a sensational mainland-perceived militancy as experienced elsewhere. But it is not without some foundation. On a more reassuring note Harry Kitano of the University of California, Los Angeles, paints a different picture. He says "Every Hawaii AJA should spend some time on the mainland to get to know what it feels like to be in a real minority. And for the mental health of every AJA on the mainland, I recommend they come to Hawaii and spend some time here to experience what it means to be comfortable in their ethnicity."[12] To a degree what is said applies to all ethnic groups, but one must not become too complacent.

Early socialization takes place in the family, the neighborhood, and at school. Here children learn to live together, in conflict and in peace, and also learn about the socioethnic pecking order. Some learn to patronize or despise the latest immigrants because of their poor language ability, unusual dress, or strange customs. It is not unusual to be victimized by one's own ethnic group. Children reflect the views of parents who may resent the intrusion of outsiders, even newcomers from their own ethnic group, who will compete with them for jobs.[13] Attitudes formed in elementary school continue into high school and beyond.

The United States educational system of which Hawaii's is part is oriented toward middle-class Caucasians. Working-class students, "minorities" in the mainland sense, are, consequently at a distinct disadvantage. The curriculum can easily become a disincentive to motivation. I am told of students graduating from high school with barely any ability to read or write. As a result their career expectations can be only minimal.[14] If they are successful in obtaining employment, it is menial. Only those persons who have worked at assimilation or biculturalism achieve in the accepted mainland sense. For most students the physical possibility of being in close contact with the dominant culture is impracticable. A substitute, contact through television, is probably already responsible for an undesirable and distorted view of that culture.

It is no secret that in terms of standardized tests based on mainland norms, the Hawaii educational system appears to have shortcomings. The 1978 Stanford Achievement Test scores for Hawaii tenth graders speak for themselves. For the United States as a whole, test score distribution was 23-54-23 where the first number is the percentage below average, the second the percentage average, and the third the percentage above average. In Hawaii the distribution for reading was 34-51-15, for English 31-56-13, for mathematics 26-52-22. On Maui, Molokai, and Lanai, not one school came close to the national average.[15]

With diverse language ability, cultural disparity, and varied home backgrounds and attitudes, this is expected. And although deprecation of a system which already produces more than 25 percent functional illiterates in public schools is aired from time to time in Honolulu, the inappropriateness of a "traditional" mainland education does not receive the attention it should.

The educational system geared to middle America is something of a caricature. It neither trains students for a mainland vocation nor has it relevance for the life one would lead on Oahu or a neighbor island. It is a transplanted system, not unlike those in other parts of the Pacific, which emphasizes events and values of little meaning, much less understood or practiced. As elsewhere in the Pacific, it predisposes those with mainland educations, those with one or more haole parents, and mainland in-migrants, toward a greater degree of achievement.

If nothing else, the public educational system accentuates the separation of haoles and non-haoles. This separation has been reinforced by language and its intonation. Popular communication within the diverse non-haole group is in local pidgin. This is something which is essentially theirs, not to be shared with outsiders. For many local people to succeed in their own terms—socially and economically—it is necessary to be bilingual, in some cases, trilingual. The intonation carries over into "standard" Hawaii English. Both the pidgin and the way it is spoken are prized. Both are "of the people" and both provide an effective social separation between haole and local non-haole.

When attempts are made to learn a more standard, less parochial English, local persons suffer a degree of disparagement from their peers: "Why talk haole?" "You've become haole-fied!" The same happens when a locally born person returns from college on the mainland. The attitude seems to be that the user of non-pidgin English is pretentious and deserving of a degree of contempt. Mainland Asian-Americans have suffered some embarrassment when visiting relatives in Hawaii. "It was the first time they had ever heard a katonk [mainland-born AJA] speak. They said, 'You talk like a haole,' " reported a Japanese-American mainlander to me after staying with his cousins in Hilo. A large percentage of the public listens to haole speech constantly on the radio and television, but there the use for such speech ends. Talking "haole" has its circumscribed place.

Some Coping Strategies

To depart from the fold by using speech identified with the more educated, "superior" haole is a serious threat to local cohesion. A strategy to avoid this situation is to be "bilingual." To visitors or haole friends, one speaks standard English; to non-haole friends or local people, one speaks pidgin. The switch from pidgin to standard English is as the circumstances demand.

Hawaiians might very well question whether their culture in its essential form is compatible with what has become the public culture. If it is not, and they wish to retain and cultivate what they have retained of it, coping strategies will have to be developed. Such strategies should allow at least an increase in their material resources as well as easy accommodation of the Hawaiian life-style by present institutional structures, including the schools. Alan Howard suggests a culturally pluralistic strategy might work but it must be up to the Hawaiians to choose.[16] To the Hawaiian it may be preferable to assimilate than to resist. It would not be easy, and rough times would characterize the long period of changing attitudes on all sides. Ideally a life-style and cultural patterns would eventually be accepted by all and open to all—biological Hawaiians and "Hawaiians at heart" equally. It would allow movement in and out of the group and for members to have a foot in a number of camps if that were their wish.

Leilehua Omphroy sees a somewhat similar but more one-sided strategy—"the situational process of acculturation." In this, individuals and groups become bicultural to varying degrees. This allows behavior and values to be determined by the cultural setting of the moment. This she feels removes the mental health problems of rapid overt acculturation and prolonged covert internal conflicts over traditional values and beliefs that she sees as the usual pattern for Hawaiian migrants to the mainland.[17] The situation in Hawaii then, would be one of scale only.

Hawaiians must always be to a degree bicultural, but I believe there are few people able to distinguish themselves in two cultures simultaneously while receiving great cultural satisfaction from each. The extent to which a Hawaiian is bicultural will always be up to him. Howard finishes his study with this observation: "We

... believe ... that successful coping requires the initiative of Hawaiian-Americans; that no matter how benevolent the guises of the power elite, the stakes are wealth, power, prestige, and admiration. For Hawaiian-Americans the stake is much higher. It is human dignity."[18]

Given the number of ethnic groups in Hawaii and the possibilities for conflict, the situation, far from ideal, is surprisingly harmonious. There are several organizations which work on behalf of native Hawaiians, and recent legislation stresses the virtues of the Hawaiian heritage. In 1976, as Hawaii's contribution to the bicentennial celebration, a reconstructed giant sailing canoe, the Hokulea, with a crew from Hawaii retraced the route the original Polynesians had taken from the South Pacific. Again in 1978, the Captain James Cook bicentennial displays, celebrations, and activities brought the study of Hawaiiana to the forefront of public attention.

Courses in Hawaiian studies are being taught in schools, community colleges, and on university campuses. On all islands, encouragement is given to the study of local Polynesian culture. There has been a revival of ancient hula and chant. The thought of becoming a custodian of past art is powerful motivation indeed. Teachers of chant, song, and dance have emerged from remaining enclaves of Hawaiiana on the Big Island, Kauai, and Oahu; some refuse to teach in any language but Hawaiian.

However, these circumstances have also engendered some problems. The Hawaii community of all ethnic groups has so far followed a mild-mannered "Hawaii Way," preparing to face situations resignedly, having faith in the basic good will of their legislators, talking in small groups, and rejecting public display unless it is felt to be totally justified.

The attitude of not rocking the boat is statewide. Every island is to a degree affected. It has been alleged that persons closely associated with or employed by influential landowning conglomerates with interests in every avenue of Hawaii endeavor are careful not to speak up on matters of public interest, sometimes for fear of victimization, sometimes because that is "just our way." Long periods of cultural conditioning have their price, which on some neighbor islands is especially high. "The landowner/employee is the dominant factor in ... [the] power hierarchy. Government recognizes this dominance and unconsciously supports it."[19] Even if the possibilities of retribution were unfounded, the fears and the

historically founded self-subordination are a reality. It also tends
to be common knowledge that hearings on public questions, of
which there are many, are largely for haoles whose mode of operation is perceived as argumentative and verbal. Few non-haole individuals contribute.

Cooperation, Affiliation, and Assimilation

The situation, then, found in Hawaii today, a product of history
and conflicting values, is in many ways restrictive and not conducive to local involvement. Although the numerous social disparities are critical to democratic debate and decision making, the
important deliberation is conducted by a group of relatively sophisticated, well-educated, high achieving, business- and system-
oriented, elite decision makers. Their decisions affect a large
group of somewhat retiring, nonverbal, traditionally dependent
local people occupying the lower socioeconomic levels of Hawaii
society. A group such as this is vulnerable to manipulation by the
powerful, the articulate, and the arrogant. State policy might do
more to encourage its own agencies, counties, and developers to
involve local people in discussion concerning county and regional
development. The above is essential if local people, developers,
and visitors are to interact cooperatively to the advantage of all
concerned.

To deal with the changing socioeconomic milieu, various coping mechanisms have been adopted by Hawaii's people. Analysis
indicates two paths: one, affiliative in character turns inward
toward locally based cultures, evolved life-styles, and Hawaii as
the true home of its residents; the other welcomes assimilation and
the symbols of the dominant mainland culture ranging from the
trivial to the fundamental. Antidevelopment and development
forces in Hawaii, in a very general way are related to these two
different orientations and so too is dissent. Affiliative versus assimilative approaches provide the conditions for local conflict.

Antitourism hostility is a complex issue. Tourism may trigger
what is really fundamental and deepseated disquiet. For the time
being, at least, most hostility is directed toward the industry in the
abstract and the tourists who symbolize it. Although there is resentment on the part of some residents against companies and individuals within the industry, hostility toward the large number of
Hawaii's people who either support or operate the activity has not
yet developed.

Later I discuss social dislocation and the centrifugal forces that can lead to it. In this chapter I have indicated some centripetal influences which may prevent conflict: ethnic strategies directing potential hostility toward achievement, cultural patterns of conflict avoidance, local concern with the maintenance of the status quo (not rocking the boat), high individual expectations associated with upward economic mobility, and a perception of the significance of development. The forces which dominate the future will play an important part in determining the character of Hawaii's tourism development. Greater assimilation may help remove the gap between the decision makers and the governed, while increasing the antagonism of those not wishing to follow that route. Greater affiliation will preserve local integrity and a resource vital to tourism and not close the gap. An alternative which may, could be strong local organization and greater unity providing greater equality while maintaining local distinction.

Analytical discussion masks the tensions that exist between groups which are simplistically called "the haves" and the "have-nots." This implication of exclusively economic reasons for disharmony between two groups is patently not true. There is a great gap between the affluent and the poor. The tensions also exist between haoles and non-haoles, between immigrants and oldtimers, among ethnic groups, and among "locals," in-migrants, and the military. Tourism not only provides irritants but also emphasizes and brings into sharp relief a host of social and economic ills initially unrelated to it but attributed to it by many. The situation now is so bad that perceptive long-time observers see conditions as volatile and dangerous.

CHAPTER 10

Tourists and Residents Meet

ATTENTION has been given to problems rising from increasing population and from construction and resort operation. I have also dealt with the issue of beach access—a human conflict concerning a major environmental element. In this chapter, I concern myself with the human conflict that appears when two groups —guests and hosts—come together in close proximity.[1] The obvious questions arise: how does the visitor behave in the new environment, what are the hosts' reactions, and what are perceived as the main impacts of outsiders visiting Hawaii.

Host and Guest Interaction

In the presence of tourists, human impact is in its rawest form. Here relationships have the potential for warmth, hostility, or something in between. Fortunately, friendliness has characterized Hawaii tourism for a very long time. There are, nevertheless, unfortunate occurrences which could degenerate into ugly incidents if allowed to smolder or escalate without attempts to identify and remove the fundamental source of antagonism. Opponents of tourism point to many areas of conflict and it is true that in some places and groups, tourism is discussed with acrimony. This is not unusual in an area where tourism has become the dominant activity. Hawaii is lucky. In general from the outset of tourism a good-natured, harmonious, and controlled rapport with tourists has prevailed. This should not engender a sense of false security. All conflicts should be considered seriously as social danger signals. The corollary to this is that social signals are always early economic warnings about problems requiring attention. Hawaii has an excellent reputation for fine human interrelations and stability but this is not maintained without constant work. Not reacting to warning signals could result in situations like those in the Caribbean where visitor-resident relationships have been at the lowest possible ebb. Elements making for such a situation of course differ in every place. Trouble usually emerges from the role of tourism in the overall social and economic mix not necessarily from tourism per se, a point which is frequently overlooked.

The Visitor Experience

Every tourist arrives in Hawaii with a preconceived idea of local life and tropical landscape. Elements making up this mental picture come from persons who have previously visited the state, television, films, and magazines. This is the pre-contact level, where the mystique of the Pacific, if not specifically Hawaii, gathered from artists such as Gauguin or LaFarge, writers such as Stevenson, Twain, or Michener, and articles from the *National Geographic* or *Sunset* magazines help color the imagination.[2]

Doubtlessly, some travel brochures have assisted in creating the initial images. Some information is probably good but much is misleading and second-rate, stressing color, sensuousness, and romantic ambience, a small part of the total picture. Even articles in the nation's most reputable magazines fall short. Although promotional agencies do their utmost to arrange feature coverage with top publishing companies, planted articles still do little to resolve the difficulty.

Promotional advertising and travel stories emphasizing sights, events, and leisure activities while downplaying but not excluding the foundation of the state—its people—leave much to be desired. Travel articles unfortunately are usually promotional and while no one expects dry-as-dust expositions always pointing to social difficulties or economic ills, one would expect professional writers to acknowledge intelligently and respectfully the multi-cultural integrity of the state with greater realism than they do at present. Substantial topics are largely ignored in favor of the single-minded pursuit of luring visitors to a destination area.

For many visitors such mixed information including stereotypical descriptions of their hosts is their only preparation for a foray into a very different society. With this mental map, an inadequate and haphazard preparation, the tourist experiences his first on-site contact. He is bombarded with unusual stimuli to which (unless he is encapsulated in a package tour or by a thick padding of his own values) he is potentially receptive. He now experiences the natural environment—mountains, water, sounds, warmth, or chill —together with stimuli stemming from buildings, busy streets, quiet rural areas, local people, and other visitors. This is all added to the already existing personal picture of Hawaii.

As a result of propinquity and insecurity, a tourist relates easily with other tourists and includes them inside his ego boundary, a new mental map, a small organized territory around himself, his family, and others from the tour group, together with a few local people whom he feels he has already come to know. This boundary can be thought to separate security from insecurity, self from others. Gradually, the ego boundary is extended to encompass other secure things, for example, persons extending friendship and further elements of a newly found world. In other words, the original and the newly forming conceptualizations attempt to accommodate each other. Sometimes they symbiotically merge, in other cases they may be in conflict.

The tourist often dresses in a manner which is strange, incongruous, or laughable to local residents. He may have bought clothes in California or South Dakota, but he may have been advised what and where to buy by his local tour guide on the first day in Honolulu. This can be given a curious psychological twist. In this way, consciously or unconsciously, local retailers, for a significant percentage of visitors, determine what is worn. This is ideal for Hawaii's economy but it contributes toward the creation of social distance between hosts and guests. Clothing, if not bought locally, may seem to be of a pattern or style which is unusual in the eyes of residents. No matter whether clothing is bought in Honolulu or at home, it will likely be brighter or bolder than local wear. Essentially there will always be something identifyingly different about the clothing visitors wear.

Often the new mental order encloses a very small world beyond which nothing else seems to exist. For this reason some self-conscious tourists appear to view the local people as objects outside their world, or as though they did not exist. Some assume an arrogant stance as a cover for insecurity. Others, through a feeling of superiority, do the same thing. But frenetic activity and excessive travel on the part of a tourist can cause stress and an unfriendly way of dealing with local people who in turn might respond in a similarly negative manner. Some adventurous tourists try to extend the boundary widely, sometimes clumsily, and as a result are rebuffed. Others with more finesse are successful and welcomed and experience the most rewarding aspect of Hawaii travel, a reassuring response to offered friendship. Satisfaction comes from a similar exchange in reverse—the genuine offering of aloha by local people. With the pressure of mass tourism the generation of aloha can become a difficult performance for some, easily replaced by curt offhandedness.

By now the visitor has done a lot of checking back consciously or unconsciously to the original internalized model, the precontact mind picture. If there is too much conflict between on-the-spot perception and the model, and if the visitor is reluctant to accommodate the disparity, he might express disappointment about the trip. This does not happen too often in Hawaii. A high percentage of repeat visits support this contention. Nevertheless, better preparation concerning the realities of Hawaii could overcome this disappointment. To facilitate this situation mainland travel agents could be more careful to brief prospective visitors. A beneficial result could be a minimization of the difference between the precontact and on-site mental pictures and a satisfied visitor willing to stay longer or to return to Hawaii.

Between arrival and departure, a whole array of interacting experiences occur to link one with the next. The first may enhance the second and so on in a very pleasant and satisfying activity. This is the very stuff of travel. Each visitor in interaction with his host determines the quality of his own experience. I am not concerned here with motives for travel which will range from the escapist to the spiritual or cultural. Some have already been discussed. Local people will not evaluate motives. They will evaluate respect for the people of Hawaii and their land. Respect is the key to rewarding individual experience.

A visit to Hawaii does not stop as one leaves the Honolulu airport. A sensitive tourist, by selective reading, conversations, and the viewing of movies and slides, can keep recapturing and enlarging his or her tour experience indefinitely. The total tourist experience then is at least previsit, on-site, and postvisit, all of which contribute to the traveler's ordinary consciousness. A bonus, too, may be increased awareness of the visitor's home surroundings, if only temporarily, upon return. I have tried to make these interchanges sound uncomplicated. Physical travel is straightforward.

Human interaction on the other hand is a worthwhile but complex activity.

The Resident (Host) Experience

Although all residents have seen tourists, relatively few meet them frequently. The tourist stereotype then is an image derived from those residents who are in contact with tourists or who feel they know them. It has a very shaky basis but is, nonetheless, a genuine perception of the host group. Just as local people become stereotyped by promotional material, word of mouth, and sometimes living out the stereotype, so too are tourists devastatingly stereotyped by the Hawaii community. Who has not seen at some time, laughed at, or derided the typical tourist—cigar, camera, bermuda shorts, and a loud voice or blue-tinted hair, polyester pantsuit, and an irritating voice.

The manner in which mass tourism is processed by members of the host group and representatives of the mainland and international tourist establishment makes it possible only for those local people working directly in the industry to meet many outsiders. It is rare then that the tourist has the opportunity to rid himself of his own stereotypes to become an individual. For the short-stay tour group member, pressures inherent and imposed all but prevent this situation. Unlike the independent traveler who has the opportunity to move beyond the beaten track where the social rewards are greatest, the tour group member may have to be satisfied with meager contacts with a tour leader, a bus driver, a bartender, or a store assistant. Where are all the local people, they ask after experiencing the briefest of contact in a local hotel.

The resident, too, must have a mental map based on experience, hearsay, and conventional stereotyping. The pressures working on him are possibly more effective than those working on the visitor. The boundary which includes many other local residents is frequently readjusted when a communications channel with a tourist is opened for a special reason. A pleasant personality on either side works wonders at the outset of the contact and offsets restrictions of time and the fact that each communicator is a member of a somewhat psychologically bounded group. Channels are often opened when there is the possibility of direct monetary reward to the host. Residents employed within or close to the industry have traditionally served the visitor well. The realtor man, the bartender, the lei maker, or the restaurant maitre d' may all be expansive toward potential clients at a particular time for a particular purpose, but beyond that time and purpose the same people may close off communications. This is understandable. However, along with monetary gain an associated social gain may develop which in time leads to a fuller and more rewarding exchange.

A channel may be opened by residents proud of their Hawaii background in response to visitors showing a sincere interest in local culture. The economic or social bonds, limited by a short period of contact, may at best be partial. A Hawaiian realtor may be charming to a visiting potential client in a Wailuku office, but truculent to a tourist harassing him with questions as he nets fish on Sunday at Makena. A special channel of rapport is opened for a particular purpose. McKean describes these as "narrow bands along which interaction can take place," which he and other anthropologists have called "partial equivalence structures."[3] The channel provides a virtually ready-made line of communication, a potentially useful addition to intercommunication in an activity where worthwhile understanding on both sides is achieved by too small a group. In Hawaii, the positive side of host-visitor interaction for which local residents are internationally known and which embodies easily accessible channels goes under the name of aloha or aloha spirit: words commonly used to refer to a number of very positive personality traits about which I have already spoken and will say more later.

Employment and the receipt of wages from tourism by no means ensures loyalty to the industry. This has been noted by Knox who says that in Hawaii, conventional wisdom sees a resident dependent on the industry as a person most favorable to tourists. However, "our tourism research project survey found little or no difference between emotional attitudes and behavioral inclinations of those who had a tourism job in their family and those who did not."[4] Another survey question asked whether each respondent felt their family income from any source depended on tourism. Those who felt it did were "slightly more likely to dislike tourists" than those who felt it did not. Knox concluded that perceived economic dependence could well result in resentment rather than gratitude. Nevertheless, there is some evidence to suggest that in Hawaii, as researchers have discovered in Tobago, employment in tourism has tended at least to soften negative tourist stereotyping.[5] In a mature area with more aware residents, it is quite possible for visitors to be assessed with understanding while the residents still view certain characteristics of tourism with suspicion. In an area where hostility to tourism has developed, residents may resort to stereotyping to reinforce prejudices (which may have partially stemmed from stereotyping in the first place).

After a long period of working with tourism in Hawaii, I am convinced that in general those who stand to gain markedly from tourism have developed a different consciousness from those who do not. This needs some qualification. If by some chance employers in an area treat workers badly and thus disrupt the local community, industry employees and others occupationally close to them are unlikely to be sympathetic toward tourism. On the other hand, if there are limited areas of dissension, local persons in middle management or above, those with land for sale, relatively well-paid entertainers, taxi owners, tour bus operators, local bankers, rental car firms, automobile agencies, and retail store and restaurant owners will be supportive, even enthusiastic about the activity. These persons would be tourism's advocates and I will reiterate a previous point that the greater the return from tourism, monetary or otherwise, the greater the recipient's positive response.

Friendly Interactions

Local personal reaction to tourism can be both positive and negative. In the paper just mentioned, Knox has this to say: "In some destinations. . . the major concern is whether friendliness or apathy will prevail, hostility is not a concern. In other places . . . the key question is how to prevent polite tolerance from degenerating into hostility." He notes what is essentially an area of friendly interaction which exists beneath a critical threshold. "Above this [threshold] mass institutionalized tourism is a powerful force for impersonal interactions."[6] I will take this further. Scale is overwhelmingly important. Within a Hawaii community, whether or not tourism enhances or is subversive largely depends on the scale of activity. Most persons and communities can tolerate tourism on a modest scale. Once the scale exceeds a limit, which will vary with the type of tourism, the ratio of tourists to local people, and the extent to which tourists financially support the community, tolerance becomes another matter.

Should information about the residents of Hawaii and their lifestyles be used as an essential part of Hawaii travel advertising, it would be possible that a much larger percentage of visitors would display interest in and respect for the local society. If the stay were longer rather than just less than the eleven days average, there might be time to cultivate a sympathetic interest in the host group. Two major attractions of the state, the Polynesian Cultural Center and the USS Arizona are undeniably educational. An argument which suggests tourists are not interested in educational or intellectual matters cannot be sustained in the light of the facts.

In Hawaii there is evidence that when there is time and visitors evince an interest in local people, local people in turn reciprocate with a friendly response.[7] The same may be said about tourists who actively and genuinely seek information about district history and the land on which local residents live. In a short trip of five to eight days which includes several islands, most stimuli including those conducive to friendship are lost as a result of sensory overload.[8]

The indigenous people of Hawaii, like all Polynesians, have a traditional sense of hospitality. Many local people, while still being proud of their own ethnicity, have added this Hawaiian tradition to their personality traits. The welcoming and entertaining of strangers is part of the Hawaii way of life. With large-scale tourism or constant exposure to tourists, hospitality may easily wear thin especially where tourists exist only as faces in a crowd or symbolic sources of income. The predisposition to amicability, nevertheless, remains, but the question is for how long? It is a valuable asset in need of nurturing. It does not just appear and stay indefinitely. Like all relationships it needs working on and the application of respectful reciprocity. I have discussed aspects of this question before as the aloha spirit. John Knox adds an interesting comment when he says, "Native Hawaiians . . . are skilled in the art of hoomalimali [buttering up, giving strokes]—a talent that may be responsible for some of Hawaii's reputation for 'aloha.' "[9] Strokes or no strokes, sincerity is the key, and this I personally have always experienced.

Upsetting the Local Population

We have already seen where friendly and warm channels of communication can be opened up but just as easily local residents can be bruised by encounters, incensed, and finally goaded into taking action. These are all points on a path leading toward alienation.

The sense in which alienation is used here is that something is wrong and it is difficult to be in tune. Estrangement is a key concept. Wyckoff puts it in an equation which, with slight modification, can be stated as follows: "Alienation = oppression + mystification."[10] When mystification becomes awareness, anger may be the result. Awareness plus contact may lead to action and attempted resolution. People in Koloa, Kauai, broke through the mystification barrier concerning development, planning, investment, and the law when the citizens' interest group *Ohana o Mahaulepu* was created and put into action by local people. The group submitted evidence to governmental bodies, and two large corporations, at least temporarily, had tourism development plans thwarted in the interests of what appears to have been the community will.[11]

Oppression in the tourist context of Hawaii, wherever it is felt to exist, could be more correctly described as exploitation (a sense of being used, manipulated, or having something imposed). In this connection I would like to bring out two important elements. First, the islands of Hawaii are distinct, completely circumscribed parcels of land on whose shores visitors from the mainland and other countries arrive. To some extent, consciously or unconsciously, they are seen by some local people as violating local territory. This is the primary territory of the environmental psychologist who would describe the entry coldly, in clinical terms, as intrusion, violation, and invasion.[12]

Second, the past relative remoteness of Hawaii has developed a special homeland cultural coherence, a mixture of numerous cultural traditions and internalized values derived from early mission and plantation activities, visits to the mainland, past visitors, and from schooling and the media. All island populations are peculiarly vulnerable to sudden change, and inroads made by outsiders can readily be interpreted as a cultural threat. Significant numbers of representatives of Hawaii communities are likely to be most sensitive to this invasion, more so than representatives of mainland communities which are invaded each summer by tourists usually from the same society. The situation described, without a doubt, contributes toward alienation.

Another source of alienation has to do with the visitors' leisure behavior. Local residents (many of whom may have been raised in a morally conservative work-ethic environment) see only the carefree attitudes and lessened responsibility of visitors during their leisure travel. Sometimes the difference of attitudes and values jars local people. This is professed as a cause of discontent in literally dozens of books and articles concerning the Pacific as a whole. Then, to feel that one is also viewed as an "object" by such persons hurts. Of course there are many residents who do not feel put upon in this way. There is enough evidence to suggest, however, that the number of disaffected local residents is increasing and it would be folly indeed to ignore local reactions without further investigation and analysis.

Leisure travel is based on discretionary income and local persons serving the visitor during his leisure may never see, in their lifetimes, sufficient surplus income to do the same thing elsewhere.[13] Rich mainlanders appear to flaunt their affluence in the face of less fortunate residents. This situation has a basis in fact. Tourist industry employees are not well paid and comparisons are made between their income level and the incomes of the affluent who visit Hawaii. Herein lies another source of irritation, an argument which is frequently quoted but may not be too compelling based on statistics alone. In 1977 the median family income of visitors to Hawaii was around $22,000, that of Hawaii residents one-fifth lower, while that of Hawaii visitor industry employees 12 percent less still. The income disparity then between visitors and industry employees taken along with the high cost of living, high land values, and the necessity for several persons in the same family to have jobs is enough to provide a predisposition toward discontent. The perceived income disparity alone is not the problem. What is a problem is the disparity exacerbated by the marked differences between two societies.

One potent force leading to alienation is the feeling by residents that the local way of life is being whittled inexorably away by unacceptable outside influences. This I will talk about in greater detail in the next chapter. Nevertheless, changes that are seen as a consequence of outside interference are viewed as assaults on local integrity. One must be careful to distinguish between acceptable and unacceptable change. Unacceptability is almost invariably associated with what is seen as imposed change, or with change which is so rapid it shatters the gestalt of the local person, or both.

Possibly the most telling source of alienation in Hawaii lies in history. Attitudes and values engendered in colonial times, now with contemporary counterparts, still remain the most influential factors. Only the role players have changed. Some people call this situation neocolonialism, a not inappropriate term if you conceive of a new breed of colonizer: the developer, the hotel operator, the tourist, and the mainland entrepreneur. The analogy may be too strongly applied to those persons trying their best to make both social and economic contributions. Nevertheless, behind some of the new colonizers one finds to a degree the same patronage, exploitation, and paternalism found earlier in the century and before.

I would like to take the colonialism analogy a little further. Berne has, for the purpose of psychiatric analysis, identified harmonious and disharmonious modes of communication among three major personality states of adults. These he calls the judgmental parent, the mature adult, and the ingenuous child. Extending this model, one conceives of comparable group states. In healthy interchange, adults communicate with adults; otherwise, it becomes a crossed transaction and, from the mental health viewpoint, unsatisfactory.[14]

In colonial times, the crossed transaction, parent to child, was the prevalent mode of communication between the haole missionary and an indigenous church member or the plantation manager and a Japanese employee. I will call this the colonial transaction. Today, with statehood and greater political equality, the group transactions are more frequently adult to adult but, nevertheless, colonial transactions still exist. The mainland-oriented decision maker, the plantation manager, and the representatives of the big company are still there. Even the company names may be the same. Other substitutes for the old-time figures of authority and sources of irritation may now be local bureaucrats, the new local elite, an outside investor, or a tourist. The point is that the tourist is only one of a number of apparently possible exploiters.

For a significant but thankfully decreasing number of people —and similar situations are true across the Pacific—the manipulator who must be shaken free is the white, haole, shadow of the past. What some writers interpret as hostility toward tourists, found to some degree in all areas, can be a much more deepseated malady than simple antagonism to what may be perceived as an unattractive outsider. Of course, a tourist (and the structure built for tourists) does cause change, but no more than the in-migrant developer, the newly arrived military family, the young transient, or the couple who has arrived to start its own business. The real objects of some or much hostility, for which the tourist is blamed, may be influential large land companies, associated old established kamaaina families, or the ever-increasing streams of new mainland migrants. Other reasons for possible disquiet are outlined in following chapters.

In concluding this section I can do no better than to quote the late Dr. Thomas Hamilton, a thoughtful observer of the Hawaii visitor industry who, over the past several decades, saw many changes either from a view inside the industry or very close to it. Most recently he served as chairman of the governor's Advisory Council on Tourism, and in this or any other capacity he never shirked from confronting the industry or the community with critical situations as he saw them. In the overall tourism activity the most important factor of all, he would say, is the relationship between guests and hosts. Where this attitude is characterized by mutual respect, friendliness, and helpfulness, the satisfaction of the visitor is well nigh guaranteed and the life of the resident is infinitely more satisfactory—an invaluable observation lest we believe tourist-resident friction inevitable.

CHAPTER 11

Human Impacts

SO far I have looked at the physical impacts of tourism and followed these with a discussion of the things that happen when tourists and residents meet. There are other impacts, some of which I want to draw attention to now, but before I do so I would like to reiterate that these are impacts that are perceived. There will always be some people who will say, "that doesn't worry me," or "I've never heard of that in forty years of living in Hawaii." I understand this but contend that if a sufficient number of people feel that untoward things are happening to them or to Hawaii, then these alleged happenings may constitute problems even if some do not see these as such. The perception of an activity or a set of circumstances as a problem, if perceived as such by a significant number of people, is a reality and, for all practical purposes, is a problem which must be resolved even if evidence points to the fact that the reason for the perception lacks foundation.

Relatively little has been written about the human impacts of tourism. In one way or another over more than a decade I have experienced many of the things about which I write. In other cases, I rely on literally scores of informants from every island. No observer is neutral. Methods that take this into account, thus, are needed to quantify the severity and extent of problems, that is, to place elements into some order of priority or degree, in order more effectively to monitor human reactions. The deficiencies in this area are now beginning to be recognized by the state, as seen in the State Tourism Plan, which calls for a social impact assessment, and by some members of the legislature.

What follows is a discussion of irritations, some of which, under particular circumstances, have the potential for or already have caused alienation or overt hostility. Some of these nuisances may seem trivial, but they seem so only if one's orientation is to the benefits of tourism. Minor nuisances may be part of multiple packages that, when taken together, are perceived as a symbol of fundamental disagreement. Given the right circumstances open hostility may be engendered, triggered by something which on its own might be considered of minor importance.

A discussion of impacts is never clear-cut. Perceptions vary; virtually all Hawaii residents will admit to benefits of tourism ranging from few to many, but no one I met, even the most enthusiastic supporter of tourism, was so incautious as to say there were no deleterious effects. Unanimously they suggested the need for prudence.

At the University of Hawaii, the Tourism Research Project (TRP) is underway, a joint project of the School of Travel Industry Management and the Social Science Research Institute. Its first publication by John Knox classifies resident attitudes to tourists and tourism and is a valuable step toward the type of analysis that is essential.[1] Several studies in the early 1970s addressing isolated aspects of the overall topic were published by the Hawaii Visitors Bureau, the Visitor Industry Education Council, and the Department of Planning and Economic Development.[2] The TRP study is the basis for a systematic continuing approach to the topic. Knox developed six lists designed to illustrate residents' beliefs and perceptions on tourism's impacts, residents' perception of mainland tourists, and residents' emotional and behavioral orientation toward tourists.

A list of 100 impacts was derived from questionnaires sent to opinion leaders of various ages, ethnicity, income levels, tourism/ nontourism employment, and places of residence. The impact list was divided into fourteen different categories such as crime, vice, and morals, and culture and arts. Twenty-five percent of the observations were decidedly positive, most of the remainder were viewed as negative, and several were conditionally neutral. In this category I place such observations as "[tourism is good because] more mainland businessmen are investing in land or business here."[3]

It was interesting to note that positive comments either dominated or were prominent in such categories as culture and the arts, entertainment, social and cultural exchange, and outdoor recreation (with the exception of closed beach and trail access).

There were no two ways about the negative feelings of respondents concerning crime, vice, and morals, human relations, population and crowding, and land and environment. Of the twenty or so impacts listed as economic, only six appeared favorable. This is not really surprising. There is a probability that respondents would expect a research questionnaire to be seeking problems.

Hints, and only hints, come from the listing where for instance there is apparent consensus or unanimity in a particular direction. I will speculate that anti-tourism forces find numerous ways of expressing their distaste while tourism supporters might predictably stress a more limited number of well-advertised benefits. In consequence, one must consider with great caution my statement that 25 percent of the listed impacts were positive. This is true, but it does not mean that only 25 percent of respondents were in favor of tourism. This would not be correct. None of the impacts was evaluated in terms of importance. The minor appeared alongside the critical. As Knox is quick to point out, the value of the list is not in the questions answered, "the value is in the questions raised."[4] It does, however, provide information of value if considerable care is shown.

Wages, Jobs, and Health

Does tourism lead to a servant class? Radical critics, many old and newly arrived social missionaries, and now a growing number of thoughtful residents believe it does. Tourism supporters consider the entire question deserving of little consideration.

The 1978 State Tourism Study's manpower section looked into the question whether or not jobs in the tourist industry were demeaning. From the study it appeared that the majority of informants were happy in their work. On a satisfaction scale of one to ten, two-thirds of those questioned ranked their jobs eight, nine, or ten. This information must be used carefully. It does not say that for some people in some areas the work is not demeaning. In some activities it certainly has the potential for being so. Comparable studies are not available for other industries and about all that can be said is that like other occupations those with the greatest hostility may have left and of those who remained most were satisfied.

There are a great number of variables which contribute toward the perception of visitor industry employment as demeaning. Many are the same elements which have the potential for contributing to resident hostility. Many are interdependent and few are mutually exclusive. The following I see as important: the ethnic identification of the employee as haole or non-haole; the employee's perception of tourists and their attitudes; the local community's views of tourism; the socioeconomic aspirations of the worker's family; the degree of specific anti-tourism influence exercised by peers, parents, or teachers; the social, economic and cultural disparity between visitors and workers; and the manner in which workers may be treated by industry management. The wage question is but one element of several influential factors.

Further aspects of labor are discussed as a characteristic of the industry in a later chapter but its nature does have social impact. It is true that average wage levels in service industries are lower than in other economic sectors and this is helped by the large number of people who want to live in Hawaii and flock in as in-migrants (9,000 in 1978). Because of fluctuating hotel occupancy, the nature of some hotel jobs, and the desire for short hours by certain groups within the community, much work is done on a part-time basis and the overall average hours worked and, therefore, wages earned per week is low. The average weekly wage of hotel workers is exceeded by just about every other group except laundry workers. The hours worked per week average about thirty-two which along with those in the retail trade is about the lowest.[5]

Job availability with low wages and short hours may appeal to a semi-transient Caucasian worker who might welcome more time for beach recreation and surfing. Part-time work may allow more members of a communally living group to contribute to the cost of food and to rent. But for a local busboy with several children whose motivation is survival and not recreation, low wages and short hours may be disastrous.[6] Contrary argument is not lacking. Tourism work is seen as being clean, interesting, and relatively easy. One alternative in the past was tough, backbreaking agricultural labor.

A result of low wages is the view that industry jobs are therefore devoid of status or exploitative. Because of this, many local people are reluctant to be employed in tourism. An increasing number of local people who do work in the industry have two jobs and in larger families several members may work to support the unit. Competition for employment is with other local people, some of whom already have one job and are seeking a second, and with mainland in-migrants. The flexible life-style and limited family responsibilities of some recent arrivals make this particular competition, to an extent, unjust. The other side of the coin is that because of some local resistance to tourism work, competition in certain places is not too fierce. At the Kapalua Bay Hotel most employees are newly arrived outsiders. Local people are not convinced a long commute is worthwhile. At a number of other places personnel recruiters complain their operations are only partly staffed.

There are some decision makers who believe that low wages are an illusion and that a basic wage is more than offset by tips and fringe benefits. Such conclusions were brought to the attention of the industry largely by a report by Touche, Ross, Bailey and Smart who analyzed hourly hotel wages for 1968 on behalf of the Hawaii Hotel Association and the AFL-CIO Local 5.[7] The analysis found that in addition to an average hourly compensation of $2.36 an hour, tips amounted to $0.56 and fringe benefits to $0.60. In other words, from a total compensation of $3.52, one third was from a roughly equal split of tips and fringe benefits. Within the categories analyzed, individual wages varied widely and depended on the class of hotel, the location, and the actual job performed.

Another analysis of hotel-worker wages was a 1972 study of the Commission on Manpower and Full Employment which asserted that hotel industry employee earnings were in line with the earnings of sugar workers and that hotels were not a unique substandard-paying industry. Three years later in December, the *Monthly Labor Review* noted that "according to the union's chief negotiator [Hawaii] workers are now the highest paid hotel employees in the nation, except for those in Alaska."[8] There is no need to point out here that both states have notoriously high costs of living and that residents carry the state and county tax burdens for around 100,000 tourists a day and an unknown number of seasonal condominium residents. Under these conditions survival requires a much higher than minimal wage especially with the state and local tax load the fifth highest in the nation. We might also note that although family wages have improved over the years, the wages of specific groups have declined as communities shifted from agriculture to tourism.[9]

"Our visitor industry wages are as high or higher than any city in the country except [Las] Vegas," said Irving Baldwin, executive director for the Council of Hawaiian Hotels.[10] Under Hotel Workers Union and ILWU contracts, workers in several categories pastry chefs, for example, can make up to $6.72 an hour. Laundry attendants can make $4.00 an hour. But there are bonuses, it is said, over and above basic wages. "Take waitresses in a top-flight tourist-oriented restaurant in Waikiki. Theirs are the most sought-after jobs in town," said Baldwin. "They make a minimum of $800 to $1,000 a month and I have a hunch that they are making much more. At the Hilton Hawaiian Village Dome, waitresses," he asserts, "are 'guaranteed' $1,200 to $1,500 a month." In the same interview, he maintained that Sheraton bellhops are said to receive $40 to $50 a day in wages and porterage, not to mention tips. This amounts to "upwards of $800 a month. In good times the paycheck for a typical bellhop could top $1,000 a month."[11] All this sounds encouraging but there are many not in the better paying categories and frequently those who receive tips are employed at a wage no higher than the minimum notwithstanding the fact that a large portion of any tip obtained must be shared with numerous behind-the-scenes workers. A starting front office clerk takes home $190 a week and a cafeteria hostess $166. *Hawaii Business* comments that "given the generally low wages in town for similar jobs in other industries, the wages in tourism appear not too bad at all."[12] The unspoken message is that workers are really much better off than they imagine themselves to be.

The quoted examples, from the top brackets of hotel workers, give something of a skewed view of the visitor industry. There are many persons in the service industries including retail clerks who receive few if any tips and only minimal fringe benefits. The specific technical element on manpower included in the State Tourism Study shows the median weekly income category (hourly rates are not quoted) for the average visitor industry employee at $126 to $175 per week, a category in or below which 58 percent of all visitor industry employees fall. No comparable figure is available for the state as a whole but household income is. The median household income of those surveyed was $14,000 in 1976 compared with $15,770 for the state as a whole. This is only useful as a rough guide. All working members of a family are included and the distribution of industry versus nonindustry employment in the families of both groups is not known. The number of workers in a family and the amount earned by them change from year to year, yet during several years the industry wages may remain stable.

There are other ways of looking at job status and income. Between 1969 and 1977 during a period of marked growth in the

state, two things happened: employees in the two top income earning occupations, federal service and construction, dropped by 5.2
percent while numbers in the two lowest paying categories, services and retailing, increased by 35 percent.[13] The latter are the
groups containing the bulk of the visitor and related industries'
workers. In addition two other relevant facts must be considered.
In 1977 wages in the service industries were 19 percent below the
statewide all-industry average and those in retailing, 37 percent
below. With the growth of tourism likely to remain ahead of other
industries, by the end of the century, the extra weighting at the
lower end of the economic scale may have greater social ramifications than it does now. In 1980 with cost of living exceeded only
by that in Alaska, the average worker in the state made only
$12,400, twenty-sixth in the nation.

In the six years under review, Hawaii's per capita income rank-
ing in the United States fell as the result of adding considerable
numbers of workers. Recent studies of the operations of the state
economic model made by the state and East-West Center researcher Eleanor Nordyke show that increased growth in tourism is associated with decreased per capita disposable income. Tourism
growth as planned for the rest of the century (see chapter 13) is
seen to be associated with a considerable population increase
brought about by in-migration. A higher per capita income would
be achieved with a tourism growth which would cause a population increase exactly offsetting outward migration. There is a positive correlation in the model's output between tourism growth and
in-migration.[14] This could mean that one causes the other or that
both respond predictably to a third force.

Tourism wages are likely to continue as a perceived problem
unless in the future considerable attention is given to training, education, status, wage rates, and in-migration. The problem is not
only one concerning economic survival, it has the potential too for
increasing social conflict. Wage levels may legitimately be considered a symbol of the industry's, and by implication the state's,
view of the worth of those thousands of employees who concerted-
ly hold Hawaii's major industry together.

There are other implications. If status and the lack of middle
management jobs remain a continuing source of irritation, a chain
reaction may set in. More persons may become disenchanted with
the industry, fewer local people would seek tourism-related jobs,
and, to keep the industry going, in-migrants would have to fill the

gap. This would contribute further to crowding and would exacerbate the perception of exploitation. Attention to this question is crucial.

The presence of the tourist industry has encouraged subsidiary and related activities which have consequently affected occupational structures. The number of persons in service industries, security systems, restaurants, and fast food outlets is particularly high. Hawaii has an inordinate number of real estate sales people, large numbers of persons working in retailing and transport, and more than its share of small entrepreneurs in specialty businesses catering to the tourist. In 1977 the former sleepy village of Kona had fewer than two hundred real estate agents. At the end of 1979 this settlement supported four hundred real estate sales people working for thirty-three brokerage firms.

The rapid rise of tourism has without doubt created stress and introduced physiological life change problems to areas previously rural and now highly urbanized. I would include as examples Makaha and Kahuku on Oahu; Kailua-Kona and South Kohala on Hawaii; Lahaina on Maui; to a smaller extent Poipu Beach and Hanalei on Kauai; and now Kaluakoi, West Molokai. I have talked to Dr. Dwayne Reed who has been interested in this question for some years and who, with a team of medical practitioners, has studied the health effects of modernization elsewhere in the Pacific. The team found change had been characterized by increased geographic and occupational mobility, new patterns of physical activity, altered diet, and differences between generations in attitudes and education.

The same conditions with modification may be applied to Hawaii.[15] In the most changed study area, Koror, Palau, it was found that modernization was associated with higher body weight, greater percentage of body fat, higher frequency of chest pain, high blood pressure, general health problems, and activities limited by sickness. Similar conditions characterized Hawaii during the past twenty years, and similar physiological changes can be assumed. Dramatic changes took place within essentially rural areas where small homesteaders sold their lands and became rich overnight, or plantation workers with minimal education went to work in sophisticated hotels catering to a national and international clientele.

There have been few mental health studies surveying the social psychological effects of change in Hawaii. One by psychiatrist Dr.

Frances Cottington focused on the impact of the introduction of tourism to the Big Island: specifically, the impact after 1965 of the building of the Mauna Kea Beach Hotel on the neighboring communities.[16]

Big Island rural areas at the time lacked economic opportunities and few persons had enough language competence to take advantage of an opportunity should it arise. Pidgin was the universal language. The male breadwinner was family boss. His wife occasionally had a part-time plantation job. Men drank, gambled, hunted, and fished. Women did not. Young women expected little respect and "settled for a life of low esteem." The community was unaccustomed to "aesthetic or polite behavioral values" and was reserved. To "make waves" was considered bad form. It was under these conditions that the first hotels entered Hawaii's west coast.[17]

The Department of Education instituted numerous how-to courses for waitresses, barmen, maintenance men, chambermaids, and so on, but it neglected language. Once on the job, local people did not speak in their own dialect for fear of being ridiculed; worse still they guessed at what visitors said to them because they could not understand mainland accents. An immediate communication gap arose.

Hundreds of rural women became hotel employees and, against a tradition of not wanting to talk like a haole, they practiced English and developed notions of corporate efficiency, smarter dressing, and changed manners. New skills were learned and transferred to the children. To get to work many local women commuted considerable distances daily. Often this required the purchase of another car. Although some of the men obtained hotel work large numbers continued with their previous employment.

Back home with increased family income, home improvement took place, new appliances were bought, and the standard of living was raised. In 1959, the median family income was $4,400. By 1970, it was $8,400, a considerable upward swing due largely to tourism.[18] Some women left the island seeking opportunities available in Honolulu—opportunities for which local hotel work had given them initial training. Some males questioned their own adequacy and masculinity. Many men became suspicious of the better grooming and appearance of the women, some of whom had evening jobs in places where they would be in contact with other males. Women insisted on making money decisions, some families overspent wildly, many couples argued over money or debts and ultimately divorced. From 1963 to 1970, the Hawaii County divorce rate increased 180 percent while the state rate increased only 52 percent.[19] One serious side effect concerned child care which ultimately fell to grandparents and older children, but a survey showed that in 1971, over 20 percent of children school age or under received no after school care whatsoever.[20]

What I have mentioned here is an oversimplification of a complex situation. Other significant changes have been omitted. All benefits were achieved at great cost. Probably neither the costs nor the extent of the benefits were anticipated by planners, the public, or development groups. Few investors could predict or would indeed be concerned about the manifold impacts of their activities when development makes dramatic inroads into a well-established rural community.

In preparation for the state tourism study, a health survey of Waikiki and Lahaina was completed and compared with the remainder of the state. There were flaws in the survey which were well recognized; nevertheless, it provided some evidence that parts of the state were being affected by modernization in the same way as other Pacific islands. The survey compared the two resort areas with the rest of the state. This showed the resort areas having a higher incidence of ulcers, higher blood pressure, and more heart complaints than the state as a whole. To what extent weight might be placed on these observations is not known. The sample was small and unusual. The fact that the Pacific pattern seems to have been followed is interesting.

Real Estate Values, Taxation, and Living Costs

When accelerated tourism came to Hawaii, not only did the large landholders make windfall gains, being part of or close to developing areas, but also small landholders and homesteaders gained similarly. They saw their land rise astronomically in value. Expectations were high and not a few saw themselves as potential tycoons. This situation was not without foundation. By the mid-1970s, simple rural people who had bought or whose families had bought waterfront land of fifteen to thirty-five acres found themselves near millionaires. The man who frequently fishes off the point could be worth $500,000 to $1 million. He could own a small motel, drive an old jeep, and still be an employee of the local sugar mill. Others' aspirations take other directions—large outboard motors or big sleek cars.

Kihei provides a good example of extraordinarily high and still rising land values. It is one of the most recently developed areas of the state. In the 1950s, buyers of smaller lots paid five cents a square foot for good property, ten cents a foot for waterfront. Lots ran about $3,000.[21] In 1969 when I first did field work in the area, I lived in a small beachfront house and paid $400 a month rent; I rented it from the owner who bought it for $45,000 the year before. By 1977, its value was $130,000 and the rent close to $1,100; by the end of the decade, after improvements, its value was $250,000.

Condominium units have had an even greater increase in value. A unit at Kamaole One condominiums on Kamaole Beach was $45,000 in 1974, $110,000 in 1976, and close to $200,000 in 1979. In 1972 residential lots at Maui Meadows mauka of Wailea sold for $15,000 to $17,000 for areas ranging from one-half to almost an acre. By 1977 these lots sold for $32,000 to $52,000, and a few modest houses were selling in excess of $250,000.[22] By 1979 the same houses were $325,000. Non-beachfront properties in Lahaina which sold new in 1974 for $46,000 were $90,000 in 1977.[23] These were no more than basic everyday houses. This was at a time when residential beachfront lots had spiraled to $10 to $15 a square foot (100 to 150 times the price in the early 1950s). Property zoned for apartments or hotels, depending on the allowable density, was valued at $25 a square foot and up.

A discussion of land and building values would not be complete without mention of the truly astronomical prices paid for lots and condominiums on Maui at Wailea and Kapalua from 1977 onward. *Forbes* magazine, with justification, entitled an article "Madness on Maui." Both Wailea and Kapalua have held public lotteries "whose only prizes are to buy $200,000–$400,000" condominiums still unbuilt.[24] The annual outgoings on high-priced units could be $20,000 to $24,000. In 1975 to 1976, Kapalua's Bay Villas sold at $84,000 to $130,000. By 1978 some resales of Bay Villas were at $350,000 to $500,000. Over and above the price, owners pay $400 a month leasehold. During the same year, the Ironwood project, forty units with views of the ocean, had sold at an average price of $425,000. "You've got to earn at least $72,000 a year to put your foot on a lanai at Kapalua," says Bob Sullivan of Kapalua Realty.[25] The situation is not unique. Similar conditions may be found at Aspen, Colorado, or around the shores of Lake Tahoe.

"There are certain spots in the world where people want to be and Maui's going to be one," so pronounced Pundy Yokouchi of Valley Isle Realty, Maui developer, real estate broker, and businessman. "Why would a guy from Australia come all the way to Maui . . . to buy a $200,000 condominium? Well, they say why the hell shouldn't I? These guys are in their forties and fifties and in the top 3 percent of income."[26] The year 1979 saw individual houses for sale at Wailea at well over $1 million. The next project planned for Kapalua will be three-bedroom houses on leased land at $200,000 to $750,000 each.[27] By 1981 high value condominiums in new developments ranged from $350,000 to $900,000. The day of the $1 million house has already arrived, the $1 million condominium unit is just around the corner.

In the same year other records were set. The market was sluggish and the developers of Kaanapali Alii condominium after one year sold only 45 percent of their 264 units. These included $718,000, two-bedroom, top floor units. To sell the mountain view, $319,000 and upward, one-bedroom units the developers launched a $1 million television promotion campaign, the largest ever in the state.[28]

The apparent irrationality of the rich is an advantage for the developers of expensive, high-class condominium units, but how does the local family fare under these circumstances? Low and moderate income families and young people suffer immensely. This is something considered a major local economic and social problem by many responsible persons. Although per capita income in 1978 was 8 percent above the national average, the cost of living was 24 to 30 percent higher.

When land values are rising so fast and when taxation is based on the highest and best use, owners of attractive property try to retain it as long as possible. Notwithstanding, their days are numbered. If the property is attractive and the zoning high density, it may be difficult for an owner to withstand the blandishments of a very rich buyer or developer. Such sales have taken place over the past two decades, good perhaps for the seller, but particularly hard on young adults. Younger people with modest incomes live in apartments, move to the edge of town, or migrate to the other side of the island to areas considered less attractive and cheaper. Another unhappy aspect of this situation is that some people selling for high prices or speculating have forced their own grown children and other local people out of the district. This process has taken place but is not completed at Kailua-Kona, Napili-Lahaina, Maalaea-Kihei, Wailea-Makena, and Poipu. The same principles are at work on Oahu but in a less exaggerated way where disparities are less and per capita incomes are higher—20 percent higher than on the Big Island.

Bruce Edwards, a retiree whom I met, lived in a fine house on a lot with over 200 feet of waterfront overlooking Napili Bay, Maui. His neighbors all had very presentable houses, some new. Sometime in the 1960s a petition circulated requesting an upward change in zoning to a higher use. A few people around the bay were thinking in terms of apartments and a small hotel at the head of the bay. This all sounded quite acceptable so he, like many others, signed. Eventually approval for a higher zoning than residential was given.

I talked to him in 1971, and by then he was a bitter man. He was now paying taxes as though he had already constructed a block of condominiums on the property where his house stood. Developers had come into the area. "Mostly Canadian," he said derisively. "You're not a Canadian developer's spy, are you?" he said within the first few minutes.

Napili Bay was then surrounded by hotels and condominiums. All the houses in the immediate area had gone save Bruce's. "Greed on all sides of me," he despaired. "The assessed value of this place has just gone up a shocking 115 percent. My taxes are 43 percent higher than last year. Emma Kunui's doubled last year and she is on the mauka side of the road down at Kahana. She won't last long on that site. But there's no point to complaining," he said. "I've done my share of it. The whole situation's ludicrous. The offers are too much for weak men to resist. I've got the money. I don't need more so I'll just wait it out."

He told the story of neighbors who had built houses for $12,000 to $15,000 and had sold them to developers for removal at around $35,000. The land was valued on behalf of the owners at $6 a square foot and 55-year leases were drawn up at interest rates of 6 percent. This gave owners a substantial return from leases for as long as they were going to be around. Once they received payment for their houses, some bought condominiums which were, of course, likely to increase spectacularly in value. That's just too much for former plantation people to pass up." Bruce said.

"They've never been prosperous. Now they find themelves with a potential fortune." While we talked the air was filled with dust and cement trucks shook the ground. It was a constant losing battle against dust which covered the furniture inside the house. He showed me cracks already developing in the chimney. At times the noise was unbearable. Bruce was a fighter and I understood when he said he was not about to be pushed around.

In 1973 I visited again. This time Bruce Edwards was dead. The house had gone and a formerly pleasant tree-lined street was now lined with condominiums serviced by the nearby hotel and occupied by Canadians, Californians, and wealthy business people from Honolulu together with a few former owners. The last building—another condominium—was going up, this one where Bruce had formerly lived.

Four years later similar discussions on taxation and development were taking place at Makena where Seibu was starting to grade its initial golf course. Sam Garcia talked about how his taxes had gone up 600 percent and he wasn't getting a "damn thing for it." But this meeting, run by the Aloha Aina Land Use Project, revealed what could be a change of attitude. Mrs. Chris Crockett said, "If we sell our land here, where else are we going to be able to buy the same kind of beachfront property we love so much? Nowhere!" Isaac Hall of the sponsoring group led the discussion around to the dedication of land for residential use.[29]

Just as farm land in urban-zoned areas can be dedicated to agriculture for a specific period of time to lower the taxation paid by the owner, so can the same case be made for devoting land to single-family residential use; but few people know much about it. Those wishing to preserve the atmosphere of single-family homes deserve to be protected from those who contrive higher zoning and from planning commissions who make it possible while giving little thought to the consequences. Act 171 of the 1976 legislative session finally made provision for tax relief through the dedication of lands for residential use—too late for Bruce Edwards but a distinct possibility for some Makena residents.

An encouraging sign which can bring this option more to the attention of the public flows from the 1978 constitutional convention and subsequent amendments which were approved by referendum. One amendment concerning "County Power to Tax Real Property" states in part that provision shall be provided for the "dedication of land for specific use for assessment at its value in such use." Without too many delays these provisions could go into effect soon.

Taxation can be a potent force to control land use. At the time Bruce Edwards' neighborhood was being built up so rapidly, the Internal Revenue Service was allowing condominium owners to consider rented vacation homes as businesses. This allowed for large write-offs on losses which inevitably followed. Not so now. A unit must be either a vacation home or a business but not both. Taxation based on actual rather than potential use seems both logical and realistic. At least it would favor a slower and more purposeful development with the continuation of low intensity where that is wanted.

In reference to a related issue, Dasmann advocates the use of federal taxation "to put the brakes on land speculation and the inflation of land values that lead to the misuse of coastal lands. It would be necessary to tax profit from land sales at the same rate as earned income. To pay at the lower rate of "capital gains" rewards "investment in land and land speculation."[30]

There are various well-known anti-speculation devices. They have been tried on the mainland and in Hawaii with varying degrees of success. But the results of speculation and similar activities are so exaggerated in Hawaii that the time has come for a statewide study to find a means of dealing fairly with the practice while discouraging it as an unacceptable activity in view of complex human impacts.

Hawaii is remote and transportation costs are a large component of the total price of commodities and foodstuffs. Huge quantities of food, manufactured goods, and raw materials are imported, thereby reducing the multiplier effect of major economic activities and contributing to a cost of living roughly 25 percent higher than the average for the mainland. The cost of housing is a quarter to a third higher, and personal income taxes for families are 66 to 100 percent higher.[31] But this is only part of the story.

I have already discussed the highly inflated values of land and other property. When leading business magazines say that the romantic ambience of Hawaii successfully seduces the visiting rich and otherwise cautious entrepreneurs so that they throw rationality aside, then the effect on the local economy and the local consumer is dramatic. A degree of financial recklessness always exists when purchasers are on holiday and, out of familiar and restraining surroundings, they unquestioningly will overpay for items ranging from a candy bar to a penthouse. Although this can have a definite social or environmental impact, it does not affect every transaction. In a very few areas such as clothing or dining, living costs are reasonably competitive or not so markedly higher than the mainland. Nevertheless, the presence of high-spending visitors without a doubt contributes to the character of the market in which local people on relatively low or marginal incomes must compete.

Strains on the Quality of Life

The trade-offs for economic success are numerous. Benefits never appear without counterbalancing costs. Construction and early development close to an occupied area can be very unpleasant. In the case of a large development, disagreeable conditions may last a decade or more. During this time, residents must endure noise, drifting dust and sand, lowered water pressure, fast, noisy, heavy vehicles, broken roads, heavily polluted air, and greater police, fire, and ambulance activity. Not only do local people have to withstand these conditions but also they are subject to slowdowns and delays as the two-lane road flow is slowed by greater activity, excavations for new water lines, and later for sewer pipes.

In Hawaii during one decade including part of the major tourism boom (1966–1976), the number of registered passenger vehicles increased from 250,000 to 463,000. On Maui the numbers more than doubled from 15,100 to 37,600. Highway traffic is slowed by a congestion of U-drives driven by visitors obviously enjoying the scenery, buses, contractors' trucks, and a few ancient World War II jeeps, a residue of pre-tourism Hawaii. Roads could be widened and in places straightened but again with possibly serious social and aesthetic costs.

As the first hotels or condominiums are finished in a new area, rental cars and tour buses are added to the already inflated traffic volume. On Maui, for example, where impacts are so obvious, 7,500 rental cars, about 20 percent of the county's vehicles, are on the road. When a new area is completed, there may be fewer trucks on the road, but this is offset by the spectacular increase of rental cars diverted to the area and, ultimately, tour buses. Sometimes a new condominium fills its parking lot with recently purchased cars, one for each unit. Imagine living in a suburban area when 150 more cars suddenly appear on the block or join the neighborhood! The first car rental agency opened on Maui in 1947. Today there are about fifty agencies in the county not to mention hotels or condominiums who rent their own. With a $5 excise tax fee, a car and an operator are ready for business.

On any island a good place to observe the impact of construction and new tourism-oriented activity is the old general store. By 4:30 P.M., sweaty construction workers in hard hats are downing their Primo or Oly on the edge of the parking area under the protection of a pleasant spreading flame or kiawe tree, condo courtesy cars and rentals fill a significant number of parking stalls along with private cars, jeeps, and pickup trucks. Inside the store which for more than a generation has been as much a community gathering place as a market, alien accents rend the air and loud insensitive conversations take place across aisles—"What are these? D'ya think they eat them? D'ya see the prices?" Everyone who has lived in Hawaii knows the situation. Never mind, despite strange changes and often because of them, the cash registers ring out a continuous merry incantation, and local realtors in aloha shirts and white Southern California shoes smile smugly recalling the day's sales and listings. This was the case at least in the 1970s.

While you stand in line, now twice as long as two years ago despite two new checkers, pink tourists pass by the clerk with their tubes of sunburn lotion, bottles of whiskey, Coke, and potato chips. In the delay as customers sign travelers checks, you may have time to think, and you know in three years' time, five at the most, this rather charming old rural emporium will be no more, a casualty to what many call progress. Nostalgia perhaps, but true.

Because building has been faster than needed and many local people have aspirations which do not include working in the tourism-development industry, large numbers of positions and short hour part-time jobs are filled by mainland haoles. In-migrants arrive in a never-ending flow. They inquire about work and business prospects or arrive in the advance party of a development company. Every year the ethnic mix becomes lighter and lighter. In time all islands will be dominated by Caucasians.

Relocation of Settlement

Although resort development has seldom displaced large numbers of individual residents, there have occasionally been times when residents thought it would. There are numerous occasions, some of which have been described, when economic lures, high taxation, or the expiration of leases have resulted in some small-scale movement. At Kapalua the inhabitants of the old deteriorating plantation village at Honolua were moved a mile or two to a modern subdivision, Napili Hau, on the outskirts of the new resort area. This was in keeping with the practice on other plantations where older plantation villages have been closed in favor of relocation in new developments close to town.

The situation has not been the same in nonresort residential projects which are nevertheless linked to tourism. One author, in a scathing critique of Hawaii development, draws attention to the defiance and strategies of Oahu Kalama Valley farmers who received eviction notices en masse in 1971 to make way for what he calls "luxury homes, golf courses, and elaborate plans for luxury hotels."[32] In the same year eviction notices were served to tenants at Niumalu near Nawiliwili in preparation for condominiums and a floating restaurant.

Several years later the residents of Waiahole and Waikane valleys, adjacent to each other on Oahu, gathered forces when they learned that Joe Pao and Windward Partners proposed a city of 22,000 in an area of agricultural land occupied by small farmers. Pao had recently purchased the land from Mrs. Elizabeth Marks, McCandless Estate beneficiary. The ensuing series of confrontations between developer and the local Waiahole-Waikane Community Association are well documented in newspapers from 1974 to 1978 and by Thomas Creighton.[33] The project was opposed by both the governor and the mayor. The state's position was that good agricultural land should be retained and the county contended that urban development was not appropriate in an area which should remain in agriculture.

The controversy dragged on for a number of years and resulted in the state enacting legislation to condemn and purchase the Waiahole Valley for $6 million from Elizabeth Marks in 1978. This at least would ensure that the valley would not be divided into minimum-sized farmlets owned by outsiders. A series of suits and countersuits were initiated between the state, Windward Partners, and Mrs. Marks. The residents who stood solidly together can for the time being feel secure again. At times the situation was highly inflammable, and it is understood a desperate situation was defused when the state stepped into the act. It was not the first time and it may not be the last that a similar occurrence takes place in

Hawaii. The conflict on each occasion tends to be actual or threatened displacement of long-term residents by development designed to accommodate a new, more affluent group, often made up largely of recently arrived in-migrants. The mood of local residents was obvious from signs along the Kamehameha Highway: "WE WON'T MOVE!"[34] In the Waiahole-Waikane case, the irony was that Windward Partners was made up of twenty-six investors with individual investments of $10,000 to $3 million, all local people, some very well known, who, had the project been allowed, would have displaced their fellow islanders.[35] Those who would contend that projects for in-migrants have nothing to do with tourism are referred to the studies linking the two processes and, mentioned earlier in this chapter.

Crime

There are new concerns about security and morality which never have been important in the past. With greater crowding and in-migration, the big-dog, high-fence, locked-door syndrome is now in Hawaii permanently. Honolulu is a big city with big-city problems, but what I am talking about now affects semi-rural resort areas where anyone should be able to walk alone at night. Even on Molokai where tourism is only a few years old, rape, previously unknown has entered the local scene. Although crime has now reached serious proportions, the feelings I experienced in the mid-1970s on Maui, Hawaii, and Kauai were reminiscent of the mainland in the 1960s when violence created violence and an aura of fear hung over many cities. From the big-city environment the atmosphere, if not the crime, came to Hawaii. It was not there in 1965. Neither was the high frequency of violent crimes nor the television program "Hawaii Five-O," which established its following on stories of violent crime. But this is only one facet of the question. Honolulu and resort centers in the state are somewhat similar to boom towns with some of the well-known boom-town pathologies: a high crime rate and a high degree of delinquency. And to all this is added the attraction of affluent tourists and the new pathologies associated with resort cities.

All county police chiefs talk about the increase in crime linked to the tourist industry. In a study completed early 1978, three University of Hawaii economics researchers concluded that tourism growth leads to marked increases in crime and imposes costs on society which must be taken into consideration by policymakers when evaluating net benefits of tourism.[36] The study, a computer analysis of crime patterns in twenty-five districts on Oahu, showed that given several regions with similar resident population densities and police protection, the incidents of violent crime tended to be greater in areas where a high number of tourists concentrated.

Although the few research studies done elsewhere showed that tourism generally increased crimes against property but not against persons, the Hawaii study showed that both categories were represented in Hawaii and that "tourists indeed generate a disproportionate amount of crime."[37] An increase in tourists, it was shown, increased crimes against property and violent crimes against persons such as homicide, rape, robbery, and offenses related to liquor consumption. The report was not welcomed by some in the industry. It did support those who perceived a crisis of crime as well as those like the police who dealt with some of its horrifying manifestations daily.

The results of the study showed that "if the average daily census of tourists increased by 1,000 [average stay of 10.8 days] . . . roughly 2 more homicides, 12 more robberies, 2 more rapes, 150 more burglaries, and 81 more liquor violations than a comparable increase in other population subgroups [can be expected]."[38]

In parts of the state at different times—no part seems immune— visitors may risk violence walking along the road, on the street, or in beach parks where crimes of violence have increased tremendously. Unfortunately a short-term visitor who has been a victim is loath to spend part of a holiday lodging complaints with police about a personal attack or having a car broken into. If a complaint is lodged and a wrongdoer apprehended, court appearances usually take place well into the future. Because crimes against visitors are anathema to the tourist industry, the industry will underwrite the cost for a visitor to return to Hawaii to testify in court. In seven years the Waikiki Improvement Association paid for the return of forty victims, thirty-eight of whom contributed to a conviction. Other organizations are following suit.

Crime must be linked to a very fast-growing population and a state in which opportunities to make money legally and illegally abound. There is no doubt that having a lot of people away from home looking like tourists with their pockets full is conducive to crime. Japanese, unused to carrying a wallet full of credit cards and a check book, travel with large amounts of cash and are particularly vulnerable. Prostitution is rife and from time to time the mayor of Honolulu and hotel organizations say they will take pains to sweep it from the streets.[39] Honolulu with a large local urban population together with its tourists has its share now, not only of tourist-related crime but also of big-city crime and organized crime operating on the fringes of the industry. The Yakuza, the Japanese organized crime syndicate, is said to have been associated with prostitution at several small hotels in Waikiki used only for that purpose.[40]

Organized crime and its relation to tourism is difficult to pin down. Local newswriters talk about the enormity of the problem; some close to the industry and government deny its existence. From time to time there are accounts of underworld vendettas in Honolulu and Hilo. A spokesman at an East-West Center workshop on tourism told of large numbers of mainland prostitutes, warfare between the local syndicate and its mainland counterpart, bizarre multiple murders, thousands of drug-abuse referrals, and wild west shootouts between independent drug dealers and the drug establishment. Organized crime, it is maintained, is deeply involved with hotel investment, prostitution, drugs, small-time gambling, and the multi-million dollar entertainment industry.[41]

In 1977, 7,400 crimes were reported in Waikiki—among them 270 robberies, 41 rapes, 63 assaults, and 2,200 burglaries.[42] This record in seven-tenths of a square mile makes up more than a fifth of the county's total crime. To combat this the Honolulu Police Department may have as many as one hundred officers in the area on a busy night. Few visitors understand the magnitude of the present situation. Only recently have residents become well aware of its severity.

In the neighbor island resort areas where the ratio of tourists to local people is exceptionally high, the increase in crime is directly equated with the increases in the visitor count. In the years 1963–1969 in the Lahaina area, next to Kaanapali resort, crimes increased 176 percent during a period when there was a spectacular increase in hotel rooms in the area.[43] During the same period there was a marked increase in the number of the town's transient visitors. In the annual report of 1939, the police chief of Maui County had boasted about the almost crime-free county he administered. Now, in all counties murder and violence are not unusual. In the

County of Hawaii the total number of crimes committed in 1964 amounted to almost 1,700; by 1970 after the first wave of hotels came in, the number of crimes had increased to almost 4,000.[44]

Today on all neighbor island locations, rooms are broken into, call-girl rings operate, visitors are robbed, campers are sometimes barbarously beaten, and rental cars, easily identified as such, are often vandalized. Although Hawaii's crime index is lower than that for the mainland in the violent crime category, for burglary, larceny, and auto theft, Hawaii is markedly higher. This should not be the point, however. A comparison has some purpose only if conditions are comparable. In Hawaii this is not the case. Diverse cultures and values and the tourist element make the state unique.

Change and deterioration have not gone unnoticed at the highest level of government. The growth and extent of crime in Hawaii is now a matter of critical concern for the state administration. In his 1979 State of the State message, Governor George Ariyoshi made it clear that one of his highest priorities was to make the Hawaii community safe and secure. He drew attention to the "astounding and disheartening" increase in crime in Hawaii affecting the day-to-day lives of the people. "I am referring especially to the alarming increase in murder, assault, robbery, burglary, larceny, auto theft, and similar street crimes," he said. "Unless we move quickly and forcefully, Hawaii may well become a place where merchants and homeowners can find security only behind barricaded doors and windows." He called for continued funding of the State Crime Commission and he assured his listeners that "we in the State government are not going to stand on the sidelines while our citizens are victimized by crime, are afraid to walk on the streets at night, are fearful of their lives and property in their homes, and are held at gunpoint at their places of work . . . We are declaring war on crime in this State."

By 1980 the *Advertiser's* Hawaii Poll showed that for 38 percent of Hawaii's people of every age, every educational level, every ethnic group and in every economic category, crime was the first and most pressing problem for Hawaii government to deal with, beating out inflation by 13 points.[45] In 1974 crime was sixth on the list of most pressing problems—six years later it was on everybody's mind and the major problem in every county except Kauai where it ranked a close second. By early 1981 the governor felt the topic important enough to call a statewide conference on the subject in an attempt to integrate the concerted actions of all mayors, the chief justice, and judges from circuit and district courts.

The Changing Life-Style

For hundreds of local people, there is no doubt that their most treasured possession is their island life-style, the fear of loss of which gives them grave concern. Indeed times have changed it drastically. Nevertheless, with justification, they feel there is yet much still to preserve. Today as the result of outside social intrusion and increased local awareness, its deterioration has become marked and obvious even to the minimally sensitive. Some have seen Kailua-Kona on the Big Island change from a friendly seaside village into a "miracle mile" of densely packed hotels, motels, real estate offices, and souvenir stores in an atmosphere characterized by drug abuse, violence, and other crimes, all marring what was essentially to Donald Wolbrink, "a place of gentle contrasting beauty, a place for peaceful relaxation."[46]

Tourists seldom consciously or directly destroy a way of life, but they do contribute. Economic development and its ramifications already discussed have had a profound effect on the "Hawaii Way."[47] As the tourist industry provides a major component to these changes, it must then be viewed as a potent factor in affecting local living. It is largely an alien and homogenizing force which does little to strengthen local ways but actively works toward their ultimate demise. This is not its purpose but it is its effect.

Homogenizing forces come not only from the outside through mainland visits, television, radio, movies, school curricula, visiting entertainers, and immigrants but also indirectly from the inside. One force, technology, may work in a very subtle manner. Air conditioning, for instance, allows the wearing of thicker mainland clothes at work and at home with a consequent deleterious effect on the local garment industry not to mention a loss of local color. Many professionals—local designers, architects, school teachers, planners and a varied group within the tourist industry —to a greater or smaller degree fill the roles of "culture brokers"; those who probably unconsciously, contribute to the introduction of methods, attractions, viewpoints and attitudes which would otherwise remain foreign without them.

Persons who believe tourism should be community oriented and uniquely of Hawaii might temper ideals with realism. Community viewpoints range from those who want to retain the old ways at all costs to those who wish to recreate the mainland in Hawaii. Culture brokers lie close to the leading edge of change along with great numbers of recent immigrants. There should be a realization that those who are drawn to the tourist industry and thoroughly understand international tourism are persons who have accepted the industrial society and understand its ways. They may not feel threatened by it or see the need to preserve the old except where it provides an obviously useful resource. Consequently to affect the momentum and direction of change, if this is what is desired, those at the other end of the spectrum must, I feel, acknowledge the significance of the industry and be prepared to become involved in it by thoroughly understanding it, offering constructive advice, working through political channels and training for its management. Hand wringing by those who feel they do not like change serves little purpose, nor does it achieve a balance closer to that of which they would approve.

One of the most graphic signs of change is introduced architecture. In the early part of the century, some obvious structural symbols of the outside were found in downtown Honolulu. These, in contemporaneous Spanish mission style—although possibly out of place at the time—now seem, as long as they last, an integral and tasteful part of the urban commercial heritage. Today, the importation of alien urban structures is occurring on all islands. Its impact is so visually obvious it hits with a punch. It is contemporary California and Miami hotel architecture and mid-seventies "mainland-suburban-shopping-center" form stamped out with monotonous regularity and punctuated from time to time with whimsical New England whaling village styles incongruous in tropical landscapes. "This," says Hideo Kono, director of the Department of Planning and Economic Development, "is the legacy of mainland-trained architects."[48]

This certainly does not mean that everything is distasteful. There are buildings which many may believe to be aesthetic in another context but strangely out of place and alien in Hawaii. The evaluation of appropriateness is a perplexing and subjective exercise. What seems to be much in keeping with environment and culture today may have appeared alien last century. Nevertheless, the more recent buildings, good and bad, tend still to be symbols of other places, instruments of a new cultural and architectural colonialism. Many of the better-looking buildings have been designed with elegance by outstanding and talented architects, but many make little concession to local authenticity or integrity. Few capture the real flavor of contemporary Hawaii.

Concession does not mean an instant overnight Hawaii architecture but there are indeed local or imported elements which could be and have been incorporated with success—a low profile, a high use of wood, lava rock facings, reflections of local ethnicity, adaptation to climate by design and not technology, and early historical architecture.

Warnecke sees several historical periods in Hawaii from which distinctive building styles arose and from which contemporary design could gain inspiration.[49] These were the missionary, whaling, Hawaiian monarchy, and the plantation periods to which I might add the merchant period characterized by the older buildings in the commercial district of downtown Honolulu—the Bishop Street, mission-type buildings. Houses like that at the Dillingham ranch or the manager's house at the Wailuku Sugar Company are models. The Pioneer Inn at Lahaina incorporated the Hawaiian broken-hip roof, Monterey-style balconies, Victorian scrollwork and is a blend well suited to its site. No one suggests duplication. I suggest that there are sufficient motifs—verandas, Hawaiian roofs, Japanese farmhouse styles, and so on that architecture might incorporate to fit into the environment.

Today not only are outside designs introduced but also mainland values, modes of nutrition, merchandising, and mores. Shopping centers, except those choosing to be purposefully different, are carbon copies of modern mainland centers. There are of course exceptions. Centers almost exclusively tourist-oriented are likely to be much more distinctive than those built to serve a burgeoning local population and tourists. Some have been innovative. After the closing of the Kahuku Sugar Mill, the more than century old building and its twelve-acre site lay idle until Blackfield Hawaii Corporation decided to transform the old complex into the new Kahuku Sugar Mill with shops, workshops, a museum, and a restaurant spread out across the property. The attraction rested in the historical ambience as much as in merchandising.

The influence of a shopping center may be shattering to the surroundings, the more so in a rural area. In 1969, Maui had one important small, low-profile shopping center at Kahului beneath the pleasant shade of spreading flame trees. This serviced local people, provided a place for plantation retirees to meet and play cards or checkers, and provided a shopping stop for occasional tourists. The land was owned by Alexander & Baldwin. In the early 1970s immediately to the north of the existing center, Maui Land & Pineapple made land available to the Dillingham Corporation to build a shopping center and to the south Alexander & Baldwin set aside more land for another complex. Two very pleasant, much larger, more sophisticated centers appeared and each brought with it not the essence of Hawaii, but the essence of mainline North America to an island which was rapidly becoming dominated by the tourist industry. Kahului then had three centers, each with a similar variety of stores. It was not too long before another, upcountry at Makawao, was completed.

On the west shore one was developed at Kaanapali, three at Lahaina, one at Wailea, one at Kalama Park, Kihei, and the latest in the heart of Kihei, Azeka Place Shopping Center. Azeka's started as a community grocery and butchery adjacent to the Kihei Post Office. Here at Kihei, smiling Bill Azeka, who had always presided over the small meat department, has now completed the first phase of his own shopping center, a purely local enterprise designed by a local architect. Azeka's Market will be anchor store but with a difference. The two old gas pumps out front have gone as have Baby Tusco, crates of empty soda bottles, and the local community bulletin board on the veranda. It is pleasant to look back. Inside was casual disarray. Much of the stock was still in cardboard cartons always on the floor, and despite efforts of after-school workers, no one ever seemed to keep pace with the sales. It had not always been busy like this but this was the situation during the 1970s.

Today the picture is scarcely recognizable. The battery of new freezers is almost clinical. The whole area has been landscaped and transformed. There are businesses I never expected to see: a bank, a savings and loan, three realtors and a title and escrow company, shoe and apparel stores, a sporting goods store, a variety store, 31 flavors of ice cream, and—of all things—a bar and disco! Rural Hawaii to urban mainland sophistication in a decade. Although a degree of development of this kind would have taken place without tourists, tourism encouraged it to survive and determined the scale of activity.

Maui is not unique. The impact of shopping centers has had its effect on all major islands. Shopping centers have proved to be a potential agent of change which, because they usually house branches of Honolulu and mainland stores, have the effect of exporting economic benefits from the same areas suffering social loss. The ability to export benefits is by no means of course limited to shopping centers.

The impact of the outside is just as strong in Honolulu as it is on the neighbor islands where the outsider-insider disparities may be more marked. The sheer size of the city tells that change has been going on for a long time and masks what would be obvious on a less populated island. In Honolulu as the average price of a house climbs astronomically, increasing numbers of people live in condominiums. In 1979 the average house in Hawaii was selling at over $143,000. For the nation as a whole the price was close to $75,000. In 1977 less than 15 percent of families on Oahu earned enough to qualify for a conventional loan to buy a median-priced condominium; less than 10 percent could qualify for an $83,000 single-family home.[50] After New York, more people rent in Hawaii than in any other state; in 1977 it was 65 percent. In late 1979 if one had chosen to buy a condominium, it would have cost an average of $87,000, $20,000 more than the year before. If a minimally priced $60,000 housing unit for a family of four had been available, 70 percent of visitor-industry households would have been unable to afford it.

Of thirty-nine acres between the Ala Wai Canal, Ala Moana Boulevard, and Kalakaua Avenue, the 1970 population was 3,300 persons; in 1977 it was 10,000, half of Waikiki's permanent population.[51] Discovery Bay with 667 units has as its occupants 50 percent local people and the remainder outsiders—California 20 percent, and 10 percent each from other states, Canada, and foreign countries. Chateau Waikiki with modestly priced units (originally $39,000 to $58,000) is two-thirds owned by local people in their mid-thirties to mid-forties, many single. Canterbury Place, on the other hand, is a haven for the international traveler and is owned by the affluent from Hong Kong, Canada, Japan, and the mainland.

The condominium started largely as an Oahu phenomenon to accommodate a demand for homeowner and rental units. Over 70 percent are still found there. They were, as well, very popular as investments. Neighbor island condominiums are much more oriented to investment, second homes, and rental units. Oahu responded to crowding and tourism, the neighbor islands mainly to tourism. All areas reflect the healthy regard both the mainland and foreign countries have for Hawaii as an area for investment. Increasingly developers have found that to sell units they must target markets in Chicago, New York, Dallas, Toronto, Vancouver, Tokyo, and Hong Kong. Condominium unit purchases are also made by vacationers who become absentee owners of rental units and ultimately resell or return to Hawaii to retire. Expectations for Hawaii are so high, constant resales of units do little but escalate prices which is great for salespersons and investors but harmful to those local people who cannot afford investment or as a matter of principle prefer not to contribute to astronomical property values. One in seven condominiums is listed for visitor use. By the end of 1979 there were 70,000 units in the state.[52] By 1980 largely as the result of condominium conversions the total was over 87,000.

Something has already been said about the rather homogeneous "condo culture" found at Kailua-Kona, Kihei, Kaanapali-Napili, Poipu, and Hanalei. At the present time it is possible to think of such settlements as being largely separate from local people. This will not be the case forever. As buildings start deteriorating and as some low-occupancy properties become high-occupancy retirement villages, as present owners become older, die, and units are sold, more and more local people will become part of the condominium culture and assume many of the values associated with it and its many in-migrant occupants.

Should condominium accommodations become more popular than they are now for visitors, so that the distinction between condominiums and hotels becomes blurred, then the characteristics noted above will become less obvious. Much more research needs to be done in both the economic and social aspects of condominiums. A recent study suggests that they might be considerably more important economically than the visitor industry formerly imagined.[53]

The situation is happening in Honolulu first not because of deterioration but because of population concentration and the high number of local people unable to buy homes. On the neighbor islands, this has not happened in the same way but may ultimately. What has happened is the development of a distinctive social separation. The resort areas with their impermanent, seasonal, and permanent residents have a style and stamp completely their own: homogeneous, uniform, white, and relatively well-educated (approximately only 61 percent of neighbor island populations have a high school education). Because of high land prices and taxes, young people who formerly lived with their families in the area now live elsewhere. The attractive resort areas are thereby serviced by local people—Asian, Hawaiian, and mixed—who may well live down the coast, inland, or ten to thirty miles or more away on another coast.[54] Many travel long distances daily to serve the affluent.

Tourism and Hawaiian "Culture"

There was a time in the 1930s to 1950s when, as a result of the impact of outsiders, Hawaiian culture reached a low ebb. One part of Hawaiian culture—songs and dances—had been featured as entertainment in several famous movies. The sonorous ringing of steel guitars accompanying hapa-haole hulas sung in English became well-known throughout the world. Local people with talent aspired to be part of the hotel-nightclub entertainment scene where the emphasis was "show biz" rather than Hawaiian authenticity. But the early entertainers were indeed Hawaiians deep down even if their audiences at the time were undiscerning. They were not to know that at purely local events offstage the Hawaiian entertainers still maintained links with old Hawaii.

Today attitudes have changed for both Hawaiian and haole. Contemporary Hawaii has an enthusiastic body of old-time professionals, many of whom take great pride in resurrecting, rehabilitating, and performing authentic songs and dances. In good hotels there are first-rate Hawaiian groups singing in the Hawaiian language to appreciative and discriminating listeners. Although in the earliest days of tourism Hawaiian performing arts were harmed, the industry created a group of performers many of whom are the great teachers of today.

All Hawaiian performers, young and old, have emerged from a period when Hawaiians in public lacked confidence and may have lived the stereotype expected of them. In a study completed over thirty years ago Hawaiians were seen by others merely as "musical, easy-going, happy-go-lucky, friendly, good natured, strong (athletic), and hospitable."[55] Present-day Hawaiian comportment has overcome much and brought respect which previous stereotyping failed to engender.

A matter of perception. Fun that will long be remembered by visitors in a hula class or the demeaning commoditization of culture, the view of some community groups. (Hotel Intercontinental Maui photo)

In the past two decades much greater pride and dignity have been developed by Hawaiians who have been helped in their task by other ethnic groups looking to Hawaiian culture as a central expression of the local way of life. This has been assisted by such organizations as the National Endowment for the Humanities, the State Foundation on Culture and the Arts, the Council of Hawaiian Heritage, the Committee for the Preservation and Study of Hawaiian Language, Art, and Culture, the Hawaii Committee for the Humanities, the Hawaiian Music Foundation, the Bishop Museum, a variety of programs at the University of Hawaii, the Hawaii State Library System, the Hawaiian Heritage Dance Company, and local organizations such as Waimea Hawaiian Civic Club and Na Mele O Maui.

Na Mele O Maui was founded on Maui in 1973 to preserve, perpetuate, and celebrate Hawaiian music, culture, and the arts. Interestingly, its most prominent organizers were Eddie Wilson, formerly of the Hawaii Visitors Bureau, and Peter Sanborn, at that time Project Manager at Amfac's Kaanapali resort. Wilson later spoke of the event as a "step in the right direction" in an effort to beef up special events "which could make the travel agents some money," so stated the April 1976 issue of the Hawaii Visitors Bureau *Maui Report*. Such activities by the HVB were not new. Through Aloha Week and special activities through the years it had made a positive contribution to Hawaiian culture.

Hawaiian performing arts have been a mainstay of entertainment in the state for almost half a century, and some Hawaii performers have gained national and international acclaim. The new currents such as Na Mele O Maui are taking performers in a different direction. Na Mele not only perserves, enhances, and enriches Hawaiian culture but also awards scholarships for studies of Hawaiiana. This organization and others like it have contributed to an exciting rebirth of Hawaiian tradition—not for tourists but for the local community.

Culture and, specifically, art are the basis for two major existing facilities and one which is being planned. At Laie, forty miles north of Waikiki, the Church of Jesus Christ of the Latter Day Saints established the Polyneisan Cultural Center in 1963. This has since become a major tourist attraction of Hawaii.[56] The Center, perhaps because of the strong religious and educational motivation of the workers, has proved to be exceedingly successful. Observers maintain that the program is frankly geared to tourists who come primarily expecting to be entertained, "not to be taught in any substantial or systematic sense."[57] Nevertheless, the potential for education and cultural enhancement is there, and, despite reactions of visitors, increased pride in culture is engendered among performers. In 1974 there were about six hundred persons of Hawaiian background at the center.

Wailea Art Center at Wailea Resort encourages local art without stressing it exclusively. Although initially started to encourage local artists, its range of interest has extended beyond this concept. In the past two years, it has also fostered local talent in outdoor concerts.

Other facilities are planned and at Kaanapali resort the Hawaiian Sea Village will be a project situated on a seven-acre site. Here guests will be transported by canoes through artificial ponds and lakes to view Hawaiians engaged in various arts and crafts as a replica of a Hawaiian village. At Laie, church motivation coupled with high income overcomes much possible resentment engendered by the scrutiny of visiting tour groups. In other parts of the

Pacific, indigenous people do not relish the prospect of being purposefully observed by visitors. Such an activity would have to be handled with skill and sensitivity to prosper. If it had this direction shared by the Hawaiians themselves, it could result in an authentic and highly successful enterprise. What is strongly evident in this discussion is something of which the industry should take note. Educational attractions can grow into multi-million dollar enterprises. Tourists are not mindless. They are willing to be instructed if it is done unobtrusively and with flair.

Symbols of the Outsider

Remove the tourists from sight, and some residents will still be aroused by symbols of tourism. Many of tourism's human impacts have some symbolic expression. Irritating symbols may take many forms and, of course, some may include inflated prices or crowded roads, the proliferation of golf courses or the deterioration of fishing, the noise of loud outboard motors or the sound of a Caucasian attempting to speak pidgin. These and many others may be capable of arousing considerable emotional response.

Irritation may come in the form of changed landscape— gardens in place of rural forest or familiar shrubs, or high or massive buildings, out of place in a Pacific setting and defiling a coastline. The absence of beach access to a coastline which was always freely accessible can be galling. So too can the "no trespassing" signs which say "guests only allowed beyond this point" placed on land which was an area where local children played ten years ago.

Circulation may seem directed, territory restricted. New primary territories are created and psychological barriers abound. A resort area, an enclave of outsiders, may be technically accessible to local people, but psychologically not. State law may say that beaches are public property, but if they are backed by alien buildings, the territories of their occupants effectively penetrate the beach and are an impediment to local use.

At times residents must feel incensed when they find themselves using place names that have been imposed by the tourist industry, by developers, or by real estate interests all attempting to create geographical images to their advantage and of no real advantage to local people. "Seven Pools" at Hana is not "Seven Sacred Pools," a flagrant use of false Hawaiiana. Little Tarawa and Ferkany Beach meant something to picnicking Mauians before the early 1970s. But now the same beaches have been renamed Mokapu, Ulua (Little Tarawa embraced two beach crescents) and Polo —euphonious yes, but not names previously used by the local people. And then to call the part of Kihei where condominium sales were faltering Waikapu-by-the-Sea is ridiculous when Waikapu is four miles away and well mauka of the shore.

The symbols of tourism are everywhere. Each may suggest another inroad into a treasured life-style. On the other hand, if such change is seen as bringing benefits, if it is locally encouraged by a well-represented constituency and not imposed, if the community has involvement in its management, then what might otherwise have been threatening symbols might be perceived quite differently. As many sources of conflict may be in the mind as in the landscape. The cognitive environment varies with time and with the attitudes of people.

Coping Strategies

Residents of Hawaii living close to tourist concentrations have a potential for habituation, the ability to tune out of consciousness constancies which occur over and over again and are predictable.

This is an important psychological coping mechanism which is put to work in development areas where the dust of construction, new hotel building, increased traffic, cement trucks, noise, tour buses, disoriented visitors, and strange accents of language are, after the five hundredth time, tuned-out of consciousness as though they do not exist. In this way, local people may become numbed to environmental or social change, especially if they feel the situation taking place is inevitable and beyond their control or convinced that such dislocation is worthwhile because it creates jobs, spending in the state, or keeps the children on the island. Visitors may be treated as though they do not exist, the counterpoint to visitors who see local people as objects rather than human beings. Habituation is the passive way of coping. When conditions become no longer acceptable and habituation does not work, the resident may respond to changing conditions actively. This may be the first overt step toward alienation.

Action may be called for when the impact of outsiders is so great and so worrisome that passive response is inadequate. This often involves competition with the visitor—getting even, chal-

lenging, winning, or in some way pitting oneself against the outsider. One strategy is to cause property damage to cars, to commit
criminal acts, to stone tourist buses, and to beat up tourists and
campers. This activity is not unique to Hawaii; to some degree it is
known in most Pacific islands. Regular reports of beatings and
stonings in Honolulu have been noted by several writers.

Knox writes of rocks being thrown at tour buses, an occurrence
which had been going on in parts of Oahu for over ten years until
it became serious enough for police to escort buses. Kent describes
teenagers stoning buses on Oahu's North Shore along the Kahekili
Highway and the picturesque Kamehameha Highway. He reports
bus stoning in Laie and a conversation with a local resident who
talked about the young rock throwers: "They're disenchanted.
They aren't sharing in the benefits of tourism. They feel insulted
by their jobs. The land is being stolen . . ." Sommarstrom adds accounts of violence to tourists at Waimanalo and talks of radio and
binocular-equipped police keeping parked tourist cars under sur-
veillance at a scenic Oahu coastal spot in order to apprehend
gangs of looters. The *Waikiki Beach Press* now warns tourists for
their own safety not to proceed beyond Barbers Point on the leeward side of Oahu. The towns of Nanakuli, Waianae, and Makaha, all sites of violence against tourists, including rape, should be
avoided at all costs.[58]

This behavior could reflect one or a combination of several
things: disregard for authority, rebellion against an authoritarian
upbringing, social problems of youth, and genuine hostility
toward outsiders. The direction of antagonism, however, toward
the tourist is a considered choice on the part of the perpetrator.
The tourist will have left the area within a few days, he is reluctant to report all but major crimes, and the perpetrators may hope
that those to whom a report is made may have the same attitudes
to the outsiders as the criminal being reported.

In areas where such behavior is characteristic there is probably
a strong awareness of social and economic disparities between residents and outsiders. Living close to the poverty line, yet observing
affluent tourists enjoying themselves, feeling that they have been
denied a rightful share of tourism's rewards, or knowing that in
the midst of imported affluence their own level of education is
well below a national average may contribute significantly to
group alienation. A reprinted *New York Times* article notes that at
Nanakuli where teenagers were accused of raping a Finnish stu-

dent and where beach park violence is common, "only 29.2 percent of the ninth graders [at Nanakuli High School] were able to pass a standard achievement test . . ."[59]

Another slightly less destructive reaction to outsiders is the commercial rip-off used while rationalizing that insiders as well as outsiders should receive a piece of the action—and profit.[60] An example would be local people buying half the units in a condominium block then selling them within a few months to mainlanders with a mark-up of 50 percent. This and similar strategies may combat feelings of impotence toward controlling tourist-oriented developments, envy toward those who seem to do so well financially from the activity, or compensate for past indignities imposed on a grandparent or a family name. This may be, too, a way of developing economic or even social self-esteem. It is certainly a way of maximizing a small or modest investment. Not all investors are small. In 1973–1974 a hui of Maui investors bought a parcel of land at Nukolii, Kauai from Amfac for $1.2 million. In a matter of months it was resold to Pacific Standard Life Insurance for $5.25 million.

A strategy for using tourism to project hostility toward the government has been used twice recently. Squatters evicted from the projected Sand Island Park handed tourists leaflets telling them how Hawaiians had been maltreated in the state. Later, in March 1980, leaflets from groups calling themselves the Ohana Makaala Kupuna and the Aboriginal Hawaiians threatened the safety of tourists after the month of May. The message distributed to visitors in Maui, Kauai, Kona, and Oahu as well as telling them to avoid Hawaii in the future asked "the help of all tourists to aid . . . in getting what rightfully belongs to us, the Hawaiian homelands . . . turned over legally [to us] . . . without State or federal interference."[61] Here activists were using the very sensitive and vulnerable tourist industry in an attempt to force the government's hand. The arguments historically were with the outsider and this time the tourist proved a useful agent for communication. This is a strategy likely to be useful again. It hits the state where it hurts most—its number one industry.

A fourth and most mature strategy is through education, political processes, business acumen, material possessions, entertainment talent, and even sports to prove to one's own satisfaction that the local person is quite the equal of the outsider and is not about to be pushed around by him. These strategies have been developed by people of Japanese and Chinese backgrounds with a great amount of success. They redress the balance. The result is a better trained business community and bureaucracy. Local persons who have distinguished themselves may have a feeling of great power. Although it does not necessarily result in immediately better relations with outsiders, it certainly sets the stage for the possibility of worthwhile relationships in the future.

An aware tourist, then, may feel a greater or lesser degree of hostility—some of which he earns, some of which he inherits from the past. Tourists per se may be singled out, but in reality it is largely, but not exclusively, part of a resident feeling toward the outsider. The feeling is not universal but there is no doubt it is there. Sometimes the mainland media refers to this as racism—a dangerous oversimplification.

CHAPTER 12

Interest Groups, Bureaucracy, and Conflict

DEVELOPMENT has many impacts not the least of which is the degree to which community organizations react to it or in some cases are motivated by it. These groups range from the specialized interests of the industry and the government supported Hawaii Visitors Bureau, to the public interest group Life of the Land. Between these are groups with outlooks as varied as the Sierra Club, the League of Women Voters, the Outdoor Circle, the Conservation Council of Hawaii, the Windward Citizens Planning Council, and the Council of Presidents. What they have in common is that all are concerned to a greater or lesser degree with the ramifications of developmental change in Hawaii.

The Hawaii Visitors Bureau (HVB), now over three-quarters of a century old, deals with promotion, facts concerning the industry, visitor reactions, and research.[1] Its statistical reporting service is universally relied on by the industry and all agencies of state government. Its dues-paying members include hotels, restaurants, newspapers, U-drive agencies, trade unions, retailers, and clothing manufacturers, but by no means are all groups or individuals deriving benefit from its activities members of it.

From 66 to 75 percent of HVB's funds come from the state and the remainder from membership. Its 1979–1980 budget was approximately $3 million. The question of its financial support is a contentious issue. When the economy is sluggish many within the visitor industry feel the time has come for heightened activity by HVB with increased support by the state. On the other hand, a number of legislators, reflecting those who pay taxes, believe that an industry which has always fought and beaten a tourist tax should put its house in order first by giving much greater support to an organization which has contributed so tirelessly to its welfare.

Public Interest Groups: Statewide and Local

The most well-known statewide public interest group pursuing environmental and social issues is Life of the Land (LOL). From rather radical beginnings it has, over a decade, changed its personality. In the late sixties and early seventies, with Don Quixote-like enthusiasm, it would challenge the state, a county, huge corporations, influential resort developers, or any group who would flaunt privilege in the face of the public. Tourism to its leaders was a symbol of the least desirable and most exploitive of human activities. Its court actions, still continuing, were sometimes successful, often not. As time progressed its views became closer to those of its old enemies—who in turn had also changed. LOL threw off some of its early more flamboyant trademarks and aided community groups. It advised involvement with politics and planning, especially at an early stage. As one leader said, "We are beginning a major technological shift in this country and all of us— environmentalists, businessmen, labor unions and government —need to deepen the terms of our arguments."[2] There was indeed need for a new awareness.

LOL had successes and failures. It pointed the way for a number of communities who were on the brink of taking action. Developers and government learned that to be challenged by a citizens' group was an expected and perhaps necessary occurrence, and because there was the distinct possibility of this leading to expensive litigation, special pains to plan for public approval and acceptable quality were taken.

There were spin-offs as persons who had gained experience with LOL moved to neighbor islands or turned to state or county politics. For all the criticism opponents leveled at it, and despite the frustrations it was subjected to, LOL was a pioneer in the area of citizen involvement in Hawaii. The state was better off for its presence. Whereas LOL was statewide, and included among its members numerous mainlanders, indigenous grass roots groups emerged in various counties. Oahu, with a high resident population, has been able to rally groups of articulate local experts, highly qualified and professionally removed from tourism to the extent they feel that their activities are neither anti-tourism nor antigrowth. Understanding well the role of tourism, they would regard themselves merely procommunity and realistic.

Such groups are underrepresented on the neighbor islands; yet, some with limited professional expertise do a remarkable job. This has been the case on Kauai. Here, during the seventies several enterprising groups grappled with environmental and associated issues stemming from development or proposals for development. The groups, in particular the Ohana o Mahaulepu were characterized by a number of unique elements: organization, leadership, and membership were largely in the hands of local people; leaders prepared and made submissions with skill; supporters represented a wide cross section of ages and occupations; their activities made the community a relatively powerful element in county affairs; and, best of all, they gained a good deal of respect from developers, planners, business, and the county.[3]

The focus of much of the group's activities was proposals by Leadership Homes and the Moana Corporation, both of whom, given their frame of mind at the time, would have developed lands which would have brought perhaps an additional twenty thousand persons to an essentially rural area. The Ohana aggressively maintained that its local district already had enough urban-zoned land to provide community jobs for a decade.

There were other groups before the Ohana and there have been several since it terminated its activities toward the end of the decade. Its fight against Island Holiday's (Amfac) proposed eight-story hotel at Poipu was successfully taken over by SHOK (Stop High Rise on Kauai). Amfac later asked for and was granted a height variance for six stories whereupon SHOK, using county charter procedures, had 6,400 signatures in two weeks to support an initiative preventing the planning commission from granting variances from the county's four-story limit.[4]

Faced with the possibility of a lawsuit, Amfac yielded and continued its negotiations within the framework of established county ordinances. This was yet another example of a powerful corporation in Kauai prepared to toe the line as the result of community insistence. Kauai public groups have not always gotten what they wanted, indeed they have suffered ignominious defeats, but they have overall been more determined, systematic, aware, and forceful than groups in any other county within the state.

By 1980, group organization on Kauai seemed to have taken a different, more positive direction. The days of the crisis-generated, transient interest group working exclusively alone seemed numbered. A larger umbrella structure, 1,000 Friends of Kauai with a representative board of directors and advisory board has been formed. It will provide permanent and continuing public interest, research, and educational services funded by one thousand members paying annual dues of $100. Its goals include a land-use policy which respects the environment, minimizes government services' costs, and insures a healthy economy; a diversified economy which avoids over-reliance on tourism; public involvement in government decision making; and the development of environmentally supportive sources of energy. Central to its activities will be the sound management of tourism.

The group will review revisions to the general plan with research, study, and testimony, present conferences on growth management and community participation, supply staff services including legal assistance to other similar-minded community groups, and have a full-time staff to provide the services. In some ways this is very close to the recommendations I make later in general discussion concerning the formation of community councils.

In the past public interest groups have been impermanent, ill-prepared, doctrinaire to various degrees, and frequently unsuccessful. Their actions have been symbolic rather than substantive. The changed orientation of LOL, the formation of 1,000 Friends of Kauai, and the formation of neighborhood boards on Oahu seem to indicate a positive change.

The neighborhood boards arose from the charter revision of the City and County of Honolulu in 1973. There are over thirty boards across Oahu with elected members. They are provided with a small budget for operating expenses. Their function is advisory only, but their recommendations are considered valuable especially to the current development plan revision. Their views on tourism and development have been found to be reliable reflections of community feelings on those matters. Despite this there is some question whether, with less-than-desirable attendance records, resident contribution to decision making is what it might be. A recent evaluation of the boards by private consultants concluded that "it [was] too early to verify the role of boards in City decisions."[5]

There are encouraging indications that public interest groups are starting to come of age. I hope that before too long one can look at these groups as an integral part of the visitor industry rather than as a hostile reaction to it which has so often been the case.

Their characteristic periods of quiescence punctuated by confrontations, legal or otherwise, cannot lead to either the economic or mental health of the wider community. There is an absolute need for some trust, though cautious, between the industry and the public. Each needs and must listen to the other. A development group must be appalled at community organizations and input concerned with some public controversies as they unfold. The developers have spent months, possibly years of planning, with investment already involving large amounts of capital. It has been assured by its own reference groups—the sellers of the land, real estate and financial interests, and sympathetic politicians—that the state and the county welcome them. Yet at this point, well advanced in the eyes of developers, they could be faced with a public-instigated lawsuit or confronted at a hearing with what may appear to be a motley group representing only a restricted constituency. Submissions from this group may be poorly prepared; homework, with exceptions already mentioned, is probably poorly done. The dress and stance of each party may create undisguised hostility in the other. The scenario is not invariably the case but it has frequently been so in the past.

The developer for his part operates in the conventionally narrow paradigms of his world which only minimally allows the consideration of human concerns beyond the small group of individuals intimately connected with the procedures, design, and construction of the immediate project. His paradigm stresses efficiency, sound business methods, logical thinking, and a knowledge of the extent of the law.[6] To the developer then, any unpleasant situation which appears to be emerging must have origins outside his limited ambit of operation and probably for some obvious reason unrelated to his own actions. This reaction directs attention away from the fact that what is happening may be a genuine expression of public opinion mounted only when a significant number of like-minded people become aware of plans likely to radically affect their personal surroundings.

Because of past history and the influence of the plantations, overt public action is still relatively new and certainly does not receive universal approval by many middle-aged or older persons within the community. Developers, feeling they know that the well-behaved island public does not protest, feel they can justifiably describe local objection as the obstructionism, or the irresponsibility of a small unrepresentative group. The basic assumption is that because a proposed project is perceived as bestowing benefit on the community, it must be approved. Anything which stands in the way of such action must clearly be a conspiracy.

Certainly at times in the past this has been the case. Now it must be understood that a great number of groups are serious, sincere, and prepared. Interest groups are becoming increasingly mature yet their behavior might still range from truly constructive to blatantly destructive. But even this latter approach can convey a genuine message which should not be ignored. I believe that members of many public groups in the seventies saw the developer as a rip-off artist, manipulator, and exploiter of the common man, unfeeling and mercenary.[1] The consciousness of each group prevented it from understanding the viewpoint of the other. In this country one strategy for conflict resolution has evolved—legal confrontation. Cooperation and arbitration, far more constructive, must be ways of the future—faster, and in the long run cheaper than litigation. Each group would learn to yield at the appropriate time—when the economic pump needed priming or when the carrying capacity or life-style was being strained beyond a reasonable limit. It might also be learned by one side that promoting small organic farms, unrealistic approaches, and a degree of self-righteousness do not guarantee survival in today's Hawaii; by the other that local people have pride, integrity, and sensitivity demanding respect. It would be unwise from any point of view, social or economic, to overtax the potential for genuine hospitable accommodation and good will—the aloha spirit.

The Tyranny of Law and Planning

It is not new for a developer or a hotel operator to complain about the red tape that must be cut to achieve something he perceives as a worthwhile end. When the management of invaluable environmental and human resources is involved, the amount of bureaucratic processing may increase dramatically. There is a plethora of legislative guidelines. Hawaii has its land use law, environmental law, coastal zone management regulations, county ordinances, county general plans, the state tourism plan, the Hawaii State Plan, and the Hawaii State amended constitution, to mention only some. Over and above this there may be ad hoc agreements between developers and a county or acts of reciprocal bargaining to be completed before a county grants a construction approval. These, of course, are outside conventional legal processes. Beyond what has been mentioned are still the normal step-by-step procedures, each to be accomplished before the next step begins.

I am in sympathy with the feelings of John B. Connell, executive director, Construction Industry Legislative Organization, when in a 1976 article he denounced the "proliferation of changes, regulations, and restrictions" making it almost impossible to provide for consumers at prices they can afford. Connell cited three illuminating case studies: Wailea (Maui), Waikoloa (Hawaii), and Kaiser Aetna's Hawaii Kai project (Oahu). He showed Wailea as having faced processing by the "State Land Use Commission, the County General Plan, zoning, planned development, three reviews, and twenty-two meetings with the Planning Commission, County Land Use, grading permits, foundation permits, Department of Public Works building permits, and approvals by the Department of Water Supply, State Department of Health, Federal Soil Conservation Service, shoreline protection permits, environmental assessments, etc." He went on to mention the need for further reviews under the Interim Coastal Zone Management Rules and Regulations. He finally noted that to receive various government approvals, it was necessary for the Wailea Development Company to assist the county by making a substantial contribution to the Kihei Sewage Treatment Plant and Sewer System and toward the central Maui water pipeline.[8]

This list, exhaustive as it may seem, is not exhaustive. Since the article was written, the list has grown longer. Nor is the list unique to Maui County. It takes place in every county. I must point out in all fairness that Wailea is just one of five major resort projects in the county served by a small unit of professionals who must deal as well with dozens of other projects, and who with regard to the resorts feel as the lawmakers did that the ramifications of taking a wrong path are colossal. Nevertheless, it is misleading to believe that to jump through an inordinate number of hoops guarantees quality as several notoriously badly planned areas in the same region prove. Multiple procedures must not necessarily be equated with good planning. One would also be mistaken to believe that procedures adequately protect the public, presumably their original raison d'etre. That this is not happening is an underlying theme of many of my discussions here. If neither the developer nor the public is served, who, if anyone, benefits? This is not a topic I have chosen but one which deserves considerable scrutiny.

To complete my explanation, design and construction at the places cited by Connell took place over a long period and at a time when environmental values and community awareness were changing fast. When planning began on the projects there were, for example, no coastal zone regulations and no design review boards. In addition, the planned unit development option chosen by the projects cited by Connell gave to developers much greater flexibility than any other means of completing the same task. There were benefits; yet what Connell points to is true.

Proliferation has added to development time, costs, and frustration. But it emphasizes one real impact of tourism and related development. With the passage of each year, the public and all levels of government see a growing need for careful regulation if the unique and marvelous resources of the state are to be conserved and nurtured. Some of the essential steps, uncoordinated it is true, have now been taken. The next task will be to consolidate and streamline procedures at all levels, putting substance in those regulations considered fundamental and devising guidelines (not more regulations) for the wise application of legislation. Connell makes some very good points worth repeating. "Hawaii's problem is not the lack of adequate laws, regulations or mechanisms to protect our shoreline and environment but the fact that we have too many which overlap and conflict with one another. It is our understanding that there are 130 separate programs just dealing with the Coastal Zone itself."[9] Fortunately, at the end of the seventies, there appear to be a sufficient number of laws and regulations already existing to deal with most major aspects of leisure development. All one can do is hope they will be used judiciously and effectively. Policymakers and administrators in important matters no longer have an out, much of the direction the future may take can be in their hands.

An essential part of planning is zoning. In 1979 a Hawaii court ruled that zoning duly approved as law had greater force than guidelines or policy. If my interpretation is correct, this situation needs immediate attention; otherwise, admirable statements in county plans may mean very little. Although much has been written about Hawaii's farsighted land use laws, they are far from perfect. Large areas (110,000 acres), but still less than 4 percent of the total, were opened for urban use, and since the initial classification, 30 percent more has gone the same way. After urban classification, counties zoned this land for various types of intensive use. This involved zoning sparsely settled areas, especially on the neighbor islands, in anticipation of what was to come. In some cases, although there was already ample urban classified land, counties optimistically went ahead and planned on paper future urban uses for land still classified by the state as agriculture. This later became the thin end of the wedge to extend urban land even further.

The Kihei 701 Plan is an excellent example of the use of this strategy where forward-zoning in anticipation of future urban classification by the state was widely used. In 1969, urban districts in Maui occupied 17,500 acres of which 10,500 acres were undeveloped and unoccupied. Despite this, local planners in the same year saw their problem as preparing "an almost totally undeveloped coastline with a population under 1,500 . . . to accommodate a possible fifty-fold increase in population within the next twenty years."[10] With this in mind, they pushed beyond state instituted boundaries. Granted, Alexander & Baldwin had announced plans for Wailea using mostly agricultural land, but the new Kihei plan went well beyond this, more than five miles farther south along the coast to include Makena and beyond.

Early in tourism's boom period, many county plans had minimal public input. Plans were often lines on maps drawn by people with limited experience. This was not to be wondered at. Citizens, communities, county public planners, or consultant planners from elsewhere had little or no notion of the impact of tourism in Hawaii. Sometimes questionnaires were circulated in planning areas but little notice was taken of resident views. "It probably got lost between offices," one planning director told me in answer to my asking why a questionnaire was not given more consideration than it was.

There was, too, a tendency for citizens' steering committees to see with a rosy glow the fantastic power up-zoning could have on the value of their own lands. "Why not up-zone it? What harm would it do? The roads are dirt, the area overrun by kiawe, there is little possiblity of anything big really happening quickly. Draw the map and it still will be the same pleasant place it always was. In areas supporting a few hundred poeple, does it matter if zoning densities accommodate 25,000 or even more people? Zoning represents lines on a map and these can be changed." Not every early plan was devised in this manner but some were. Since those days more sophisticated plans using solid citizen input have been drawn up.

The Kihei 701 Plan is an example of a bad plan. It is naive, formless, and ill-conceived. It determined the outline of tourism as it took place during the past decade and probably will for the next. Even when revisions were called for in the mid-seventies, the plan was given band-aid treatment only. County planners knew it was bad and a leading architect condemned it publicly, yet it still guides development today. The situation is paradoxical. The county expects superb private planning in the two resort areas, Wailea and Makena, yet where the county itself is responsible, it failed to give the leadership it might have given. There are many reasons for this. Inadequate staffing is one. Large private developers operating in Hawaii may have a planning staff as large as a county's or may be able to call on the nation's best designers—a tall order with which to expect counties to compete. The best many public planners can hope to do under existing conditions is to just keep pace with the scrutiny of actual development plans before approval rather than monitoring and supervising development in the field and spending adequate time on ensuring first-rate district planning and revision.

The Makena Example

Once a plan is approved, no matter how weak some portions might be, developers, the public, and even the county (who really know what it's like) imbue it with an unwarranted aura of authority. Studies of a condominium project at Poolenalena, Maui, immediately north of Makena Landing, and the Maui Makena project of the Japanese Seibu Corporation illustrate the tyranny of a plan (the already discussed Kihei 701 Plan), the pusillanimity of policy, the impotency of the public, and the power of a small influential group.

In 1970 John Carl Warnecke and Associates, nationally known architects and planners, completed a sensitive study of the Makena district, a few miles south of Wailea and Kihei. The Warnecke study found Makena a charming Hawaiian enclave remote from any other settlement. Its strong recommendation, among others, was to preserve Makena, its historical connection, and stunningly beautiful coast.

Here are some of the report's prophetic words written at a time before Seibu purchased its land or designed its Makena Project:

> Ten or fifteen years from now, the Kihei and Maalaea areas will have a great many more residents than they now have. And these

people will be in need of the very environment that attracted them to Kihei and Maalaea in the first place. This they should be able to find, in part, at Makena . . . Here they should be able to find wilderness that is as untouched as it is today. Here also they should be able to find the quiet, the solitude, the sense of spaciousness, the fresh air and sunshine that, while they may be plentiful in Kihei and Maalaea today [1969–1970]—will not be in as great supply ten or perhaps fifteen years from now . . . Urbanization of Hawaii will increase so long as tourism and population grow . . . Increased urbanization of an area creates a number of drives in a city-dweller —one which, ironically, is his periodical need to escape . . . Makena. . . [is a place] where one can go to fulfill these non-urban—or perhaps "anti-urban" needs. The premise of this plan should now be clear. Makena-LaPerouse must remain the natural recreational and wilderness treasure ten, twenty, or thirty years from now that it is today.[11]

In 1969–1970 the Makena area remained in the agricultural classification given it by the state. It was obvious that those who molded the Kihei plan were ambivalent. I have already discussed some of the questions which must have passed through the minds of members of the citizens' steering committee. The principal authors, however, had the same feelings as Warnecke about the area as a later quotation proves. Yet the Kihei planners drew lines of various colors around deserted or sparsely populated areas within the Makena district, ignorant of what tourism's impacts on Maui would be and of what direction public sentiment might take at the end of the decade.

In the early seventies, to accommodate the Wailea Project and Seibu's Makena project north and south of Poolenalena respectively, the State Land Use Commission upgraded sufficient agricultural land so that with county approval both projects could start the first phases of development. Wailea is now considerably ahead of the Seibu project. Between the two projects in the tranquil and beautiful coastal district of Poolenalena, commonly known as Chang's Beach, Rolph Fuhrman proposed a $24 million (now $50 million), 184-unit condominium development on fifteen acres of land. In 1978 opinion concerning the proposal was voiced by Maui residents and interest groups at meetings of the Kihei Community Association (KCA) and the State Land Use Commission (LUC). For two days the LUC heard testimony from the developer, government agencies, Life of the Land, and the Sierra Club. Fuhrman told the LUC he would be most willing to cooperate in any appropriate way with regard to a disputed graveyard, beach access, and archeological sites on the property. He also informed the LUC that "it was amazing the number of people who want[ed] a very nice condo well located on Maui" and that this was "the best piece of land on Maui available to a developer" to meet the demand of hundreds of people ready to spend $200,000 for a condominium unit (units now range from $290,000 to $625,000). Few people in Hawaii would have disputed the assertion but there were many at the meetings disputing the need.

Cathryn Dearden of Haiku after waiting nine hours to testify said that Makena was a unique and beloved area of Maui, and John Bose speaking for the Sierra Club told the LUC of his absolute outrage at the thought of wealthy outsiders using their surplus affluence to grab off the area. It is, he said, the last good swimming beach on Maui not overshadowed by condominiums and it should be kept free of development as a recreational resource for the public. This tended to be typical of much public thinking.

At a previous KCA meeting, its president, William E. Maschal, had strongly supported the development. He told that meeting of 150 persons that "The Kihei Development Plan, in existence for eight years or so, calls for this particular area to be developed for apartments. The revised plan has the same designation. The general plan is our bible. That's the true situation for almost ten years now. It calls for development for apartment use. It looks to me as if it is absolutely useless for agriculture."[12] As an aside I must say that many members of the KCA own property gold mines resulting from the zoning of the Kihei plan, that undoubtedly a number of its members see themselves in the future in the same position as Mr. Fuhrman and, as many of them have a variety of commercial stakes in the area's growth, continued development may be more in the interests of many KCA members than for the district as a whole.

At the LUC meeting in August almost three months later, KCA testimony strongly favored the project because it conformed to the Kihei General Plan. Speakers noted that it would beautify the area, and bring people here who would spend money without competing for local jobs. Fuhrman's own testimony drew attention to what he saw as disregard for his rights. He reminded listeners that he bought the land and owned it while the County plan designated it for urban use. Ultimately, in December 1978 the

LUC approved the requested reclassification from agriculture to urban use and for the first time the parcel was legally urban.

It is sad to see a plan, believed by planners to be one of the worst possible, used by both the county and the developer and his supporters to pressure the state to make even more urban land available. It is also sad that the following statement, curiously from the plan too, was not considered seriously in the way it might have been. "Adjoining Wailea is the Makena area, a thriving Hawaiian community. The plan would place strict development controls in Makena with special emphasis on the conservation of Makena's historic sites. The planners believe Makena can become one of the most valued assets of the entire planning area if emphasis on its development is placed on conservation, the prevention of unwanted development, so that when maximum urbanization is reached in the rest of the planning area, Makena will remain as now, a quiet place of natural beauty and historic interest."[13] Strangely one of the plan's authors, now in another capacity, presented the case for the developer.

The controversy was taking place in an exceptional area, the Maalaea-Makena resort region, the largest in the state with almost 5,000 units completed and 37,000 units officially the present ceiling. Outside Waikiki no other region comes close to it.

The hearings occurred when the governor of the state was deploring unnecessary in-migration, and the mayor of the county was insisting such high-priced developments as the Poolenalena proposal drastically affected local values and did nothing to alleviate the local housing shortage. The mayor had also recently said that Maui had enough development on the books already without any new projects. It was a time too when the state plan and the draft county plan both deplored unnecessary crowding and the beyond-capacity reliance on Hawaii resources. The Hawaii State Plan priority directions already in effect stressed that economic activity "should provide needed jobs for Hawaii's people without stimulating unnecessary in-migration." No evidence of need appears to have been given. As at least one-half to two-thirds of the labor force would likely be new in-migrants, the provision of jobs for local people was not a strong argument. The provision of future investment opportunites was a strong motivating factor acceptable if the great social and environmental costs were forgotten along with the fact that similar investment opportunities on land already zoned urban abounded elsewhere on Maui and on every island. Neither the state nor the county had a legal obligation to Mr. Fuhrman, and every policy document seemed to say no. The specific zoning became legal only after—and not before—the state made its decision to designate the land urban. Substantial public opinion said no, an unbiased Warnecke report gave an emphatic no, even the Kihei plan narrative said "control strictly, emphasize conservation," yet approval was given. Even after approval, the opposing community members did not give up. A group, The People to Save Makena, was formed to take the matter further.[14] This they did in the form of several challenges to the Seibu Maui Makena project, a discussion about which follows soon.

In the Chang's Beach case, powerful local interests, old values of individualism and an antipathy toward government interference came into conflict with community interests and new values embraced by state and projected county plans. In this instance, however, newer attitudes did not prevail. The concerns of environmental groups such as deteriorating life-styles, crowding, environmental and cultural preservation, and a general growing awareness of public versus individual rights were turned aside. Furthermore, there was the confusing example of two public interest groups, the KCA and the Sierra Club, apparently pulling in different directions, reflecting individual and public rights respectively. For the LUC which had already processed land use changes from agriculture to urban for the Wailea and Seibu projects, there were sufficient precedents to grant approval on this occasion. Why should Rolph Fuhrman be singled out for discriminatory treatment? He received the approval and subsequent approvals from the Planning Commission but not without court challenges concerning procedural errors, inadequate notice before holding a contested case hearing, and conflict of interest.

The Makena Maui Project

To the south of Poolenalena and of much greater significance is the Seibu Corporation's Makena project, 1,000 acres of former Ulupalakua ranch land. At the time of purchase the land was designated agricultural by the state, but the Kihei 701 Plan showed its probable availability for hotel, apartment, and related resort development if the state were willing to change the designation. The state did so, but for half the area only.

In late 1974 the Maui Planning Commission and the State Land

Use Commission reviewed plans and heard submissions about the project. Twenty-seven persons testified. Nineteen spoke in opposition to the project and eight in favor. Objections centered around the fact that no need for the project had been demonstrated, that land values and taxes would skyrocket, that the quality of life would be endangered, and that plans would conflict with a proposed state park for the area. At least three of the four contentions have proven to be true. Despite public opposition and the fact that there was already more than enough urban classified land—one witness asserted that north, along the same coast, there was enough land zoned for residential use to maintain 250,000 people —the state with county went ahead and approved the project.[15] In 1980 it possibly would not have been approved.

One spokesman asked that the LUC enact a moratorium on all reclassification for resort development so that planners on Maui and at the state level could at least assess the long-range effects of those resorts already completed or under construction on Maui. A Hawaiian spokesman, Charles Maxwell, referring to the fact that the Japanese family owning the Seibu group wanted Makena to be its "jewel in the Pacific" countered by saying "Makena is already a jewel" belonging to and enjoyed by local people.

Certainly some Makena residents supported Seibu's application. Apart from increasing land value they envisioned both improved water supply and new roads, deficiencies the settlement had always suffered. Others saw a resort as the best use for poor agricultural land, and what has become something of a conventional viewpoint was expressed by Domingo Amano who said his four thousand ILWU members had been convinced by the preliminary presentation of Seibu that the planned resort would generate direct and indirect employment for thousands of people on this island. But today I understand that any new employment will serve as many, if not more, newcomers as well-established residents.

The Maui Planning Commission endorsed Seibu's application despite the fact that the Kihei Community Association, several hundred members strong and the only group then representing district residents, came out against reclassification. The commission said it had listened to all arguments pro and con and felt the project should proceed because it conformed to Maui's quality growth objectives. In reply to criticism of overdevelopment, planning director Ishikawa attempted to allay obvious fears by saying that the Makena project was not geared to massive construction. Only one hotel was planned, he said, but announcements made by Seibu officials and published materials at the time quoted 1,200 hotel rooms—not modest by any means—and almost 5,000 residential units, together capable of accommodating 6,000 to 8,000 persons. Hardly a miniscule operation.

Often the public is treated in a cavalier manner. In this case, probably fewer than twenty persons decided the issue. Who knows what the people of Maui or the district really thought? A referendum in which everybody voted may have come out in favor of the project but this can be only a guess. All the state or the county had was the evidence presented. The public hearing responses were decidedly negative yet approval was given.

Confrontation at Makena Landing

From 1978 to 1980, as the result of dissatisfaction at Poolenalena, the construction of the first golf course at Makena, and growing public awareness of plans for the first hotel, resentment mounted. This was not aimed at the company, not against development per se, but against development at Makena. For many Maui people, Makena is like Hana. It is theirs and is not for outsiders. When so much of an island seems to be given over to visitors I can well appreciate the sentiment. I also suspect that the fact that the developer was a powerful foreign company unconsciously tipped the balance for some protesters.

Public protest came to a head in the spring and summer of 1979 with the formation of a group called The People to Save Makena. Concern about the impact of the development was voiced at a May 1979 County Planning Commission meeting during a hearing in which Seibu requested under the Coastal Zone Management Act a Special Management Area Permit. The *Maui News* in one of its rare editorials addressing tourism and development noted that the concern voiced by the new group had merit "but came nearly ten years too late to stop the granting of a Special Management Area Permit requested by Seibu Hawaii Inc." Too late it went on to say "because the development is permitted under two county ordinances adopted in 1969." Both ordinances concerned the Kihei 701 Plan and its associated zoning.

I agree entirely with the editorial concerning the protest coming too late, but what the editorial did not mention were the deficiencies of the plan, changing public and county administration views over a decade, that in 1969 there was no development south of Kihei (Wailea was deserted) to enable the community to visualize impact, and that besides public hearings and possibly a county plan still in draft form there was no effective way community organizations could be heard with the same potency as developers. The editorial seemed to give good advice to the group: "Those who oppose Seibu's request have a 'better-late-than-never' alternative for stopping future developments. The county council is now drafting a new General Plan for the County of Maui. Anti-development forces need to band together now and let the council's planning and economic development committee speed action on the plan—which has been stalled in committee for sixteen months."[16] The editorial, like most media statements, did not differentiate between anti-development and opposition to specific development which was the case here.[17] No one protests development at Kaanapali or Wailea; but they do at Makena.

The group found itself somewhat alone in conditions quite unlike Kauai where considerable local support was forthcoming or on Oahu where neighborhood boards appear to be listened to. Its approach to the council, encouraged by the *Maui News*, got them nowhere, but a lawsuit was filed in the Second Circuit Court challenging the Maui Planning Commission's decision to grant Seibu a permit to build its hotel. Plaintiffs were individuals including the president of the Maui chapter of the Sierra Club and People to Save Makena. The allegations were that the hearing was not in compliance with the objectives, policies, and guidelines of the Coastal Zone Management Act and that a later closed-door meeting violated the State Sunshine Law.[18] The charges were not sustained.

One cannot help feeling a degree of sympathy for the community group, Seibu Hawaii which was somewhat of a bystander yet vulnerable to the proceedings, and an overworked planning department. Seibu seemed to be doing everything expected of it but was not able to dodge the issue. The weak link seemed to be between the county and some of the people it represented.

What happened in this instance is typical of what has happened in every county. Some if not all the participants might do well to get their acts together in the interests of a first-rate tourism industry and a satisfied community. A county plan setting out development guidelines and public objectives was still being considered more than two years after its first draft had been distributed, yet one of the pressing questions of today's Hawaii is still unanswered: How can county planners, developers, and a responsible representative community coalition be brought together from the start of deliberations so that at every step of the development/planning process they work in cooperation and not in confrontation? Invoking legislation in this case provided a short-term temporary remedy but it was difficult to see what was realistically accomplished. The long-term remedy is within grasp but still remains to be taken.

Behind the Scenes Connections

By late 1980, hitherto unknown facts about Makena, felt by many to be of a fundamental nature, began to emerge. The Makena Surf property (Chang's Beach) was originally bought in 1970 by an eighty-seven member hui, Waipao Joint Venture, for $1.6 million. In 1977 the parcel was sold to the present developer for $6 million. The hui's membership included a judge of the Second Circuit Court, who had formerly been an officer of Valley Isle Realty, two members of the Maui Planning Commission, the deputy director of the Maui Planning Department, several state and county officials, local businessmen, and other persons of note, none of whom one could assume would want the property back once it were sold.[19]

Despite the fact that the deputy planning director, a hui member, shepherded Makena Surf approvals through the Planning Commission, which he had chaired before his present appointment, and that two other members of the hui were planning commissioners, Second Circuit Court Judge Richard Komo ruled that such occurrences did not constitute conflict of interest.[20]

A *Maui News* report noted that the hui was managed by Masaru "Pundy" Yokouchi, president of Valley Isle Realty, former aide to Governor John Burns, and now a strong supporter of Governor George Ariyoshi.[21] It also recorded the fact that during 1979 the deputy planning director had resigned in order to work for Valley Isle Realty.

I have referred to the Nukolii, Kauai, controversy. Here it provides a further dimension to the two studies at Makena and interest group activity on Kauai. The construction of the Nukolii project of Graham Beach Partners, Pacific Standard Life Insurance Co. of California, and Hasegawa Komuten which was overwhelmingly voted down by public referendum in November 1980 was, nevertheless, given the official green light by Circuit Court Judge Kei Hirano who based his decision on what he viewed as vested rights acquired by the developers before the vote.[22]

The 60-acre property just north of Lihue, in an area much loved by the public, had been bought in 1973–1974 from Amfac for $1.2 million by a hui managed by Yokouchi. In a matter of months it was sold to Pacific Life Insurance Company of California for $5.25 million.[23] In the following year the Amfac official who handled the sale left the company and joined the Maui hui. Later he became project manager for Makena Surf.

One might ask what other connections there are between the Nukolii and the two Makena projects? Makena Maui was sold to the Japanese Seibu Corporation by Valley Isle Realty broker Yokouchi on behalf of Ulupalakua ranch owner, Pardee Erdman, himself a representative of the Waipao Joint Venture hui.[24] There are other threads connecting the projects. All projects have recently been controversial and have engendered much community interest, a number of the same actors are common to all projects, each parcel occupied now by resort construction was sold to the current developer by Valley Isle Realty for a considerable sum, and the specific figures reflected high expectations for early resort zoning from the agriculture classification each parcel was in.

There has been some discussion of all projects in the news media but on fundamental points concerning values, ethics, and philosophy it has been unaccountably silent. A partial explanation of the hui's actions with reference to Makena Surf was given by its attorney, Walter T. Shimoda. "Those who had a faith in Maui," he said, "lived through the difficult period (prior to the 1960s) and invested in real estate [there]. Now they are entitled to and deserving of their profits . . . Without huis most of the ordinary people in Maui would have been unable to invest and participate in the growth of Maui to which they contributed . . . Our antagonists forget the hard times suffered by the ordinary citizens of Maui prior to the 1960s. . . . This is not to say," he added, "that profit justifies the ravishing of our environment. We are just as concerned as the next citizen in [its] preservation."[25]

The statement is revealing. In the cases noted investments were made not in the sixties but in the mid-seventies after Maui had proved herself. Faith in Maui was not involved, especially, as was pointed out to me by a perceptive Kauaian observer, when the group seemed equally prepared to invest in the Garden Island's future. Hui membership was not representative of "ordinary citizens" and that fact alone made news throughout Hawaii.

Makena and Nukolii deserve more thorough study than I can give them here. Stories about the projects are still breaking. I have pointed out what I believe to be some of the relevant facts. Thoughtful and thorough interpretations and conclusions need to be drawn as more information becomes known. I believe they may become classic cases concerning public interest, the exercise of power, the long-term effect of community hostility to development, and the apparent unjustifiable extension of urban areas into rural districts when adequate areas of urban zoned land already exist. Of equal importance should be discussions concerning the desirability of permitting private development on exquisite coastlands vitally needed in their primitive state not only for community recreation but also for the maintenance of high quality tourism.

An End for Some, a Beginning for Others

In May 1979, *Hawaii Business* ran a story on Makena in its annual Maui issue. It highlighted problems of a general nature concerning human impacts at Makena. At the time the article was written, the Seibu project looked as though it was about to get off the ground, but long before this the few dozen families living in the idyllic surroundings of the Makena–La Perouse Bay area were already being plagued by swarms of U-drives coming in on the new roads in the area. If the occupants of these U-drives were not getting stuck on the treacherous lava near La Perouse Bay, they were asking directions or inquiring about the availability of land to buy. "There's none available," says Sam Garcia who lives on his five acres. He continues with a smile, "Unless you want to offer $8–$9 a square foot." Well might he smile, but his price was not particularly outrageous. When the hotel goes in next to Sam's house, values will skyrocket and with sales already at $11 a square foot and listings at $15 at Wailea, $8–$9 must now be on the conservative side.[26] The pressure on all residents to sell is great but unfortunate. Climbing land taxes will not help the situation at all. Pressure now is nothing to what it will be within five or more years.

Actual residents—as opposed to sympathizers and People to Save Makena who are not Makena residents—are also disquieted at what is happening. Helen Peters has mixed feelings about what is about to take place and she, like others, is determined to retain the property in the hands of her extended family, an unlikely prospect if the example of West Maui is anything to go by. "Already," Mrs. Peters says, "we have to go way out in the water to get *akule* [a kind of fish]. They used to come in right in front of the house. Also maybe in the future we'll have to ask permission to go to the beach not like before when everybody could use the beach and let their animals go onto everybody else's property. Also we're going to miss the quiet. [But] if it provides new jobs, the development will be all right. Before, there was only the cowboy life, and work on the road. Life was pretty good then but it was also very hard."

Life is likely to be very hard for some in the future. A few persons will find themselves nearly millionaires, but land will be sold ultimately to settle estates, a few original buildings may remain to provide housing for tourist-related enterprises and activities, and the Makena that Maui residents have known, identified with, and for some fought for, will disappear. If there are any remaining relatives of old-time residents left in fifteen to twenty years, I will be surprised. There will be houses of course and other residential units of exceptional value owned or occupied by successful business or entertainment people from the mainland and Japan.

The sun is setting on old Makena. A new, beautiful, manicured, and contrived Makena will emerge, the product of alien drawing boards, foreign design concepts, mainland and Japanese visitors' tastes, and American and Asian private capital seeking luxury and rapid economic growth. The cost-benefit analysis for this and other Hawaii projects must ultimately be done by residents now, not "ten years too late," as the *Maui News* editorial admonished, otherwise the public will always lose by default.

An Overview

This and the three preceding chapters have been concerned with tourism's and related investment's impact on landscape, man, and society. It is obvious that tourism has been a godsend to the state's economy in a number of ways. It is, however, related to high inmigration, and does contribute to coastal zone pollution and deterioration, a high cost of living, a high crime rate, and to high land values which prevent low and moderate income local people from owning homes or living in the areas of their choice—in some cases the districts where they spent their childhood.

Some impacts may be measured then analyzed in a straight-forward way. There are gifted members of the public and some influential leaders who intuitively discern change in a reliable manner. In public forums these people can make useful input depending on their stature and the quality of presentation, but such a contribution is usually looked upon with a degree of suspicion by many people. Nonmeasured or nonmeasurable impacts must be evaluated carefully by wise and trusted observers. How otherwise can decisions be made about the maintenance of the tranquility of the Na Pali coast or about the aesthetics of construction? In certain topical areas, impacts can be measured especially for some economic elements, but there are still benefits and many costs which defy quantification. There may be ways of objectively analyzing data but no way of objectively interpreting them or making wise decisions based on them. What we must understand clearly is that both quantitative and qualitative methods of evaluation are essential. No matter how scientific enquiries might be, it is a fact of life that decisions are frequently made using criteria which may have only limited bearing on the data arising from supporting studies. If the studies have been done and the decision makers are aware, the tendency will be to take greater cognizance of the studies and to make better decisions.

Policy studies, problem-solving studies, and baseline studies still need to be done and to be completed quickly. Scientific contributions are essential using whatever data are available. Comprehensive and systematic basic studies are needed desperately. Only then can change be monitored with confidence. Monitoring of as many elements as possible by simple field mapping, Landsat imagery, or whatever other methods seem appropriate is essential. Just as important is the necessity for well-selected groups to establish critical limits, if only arbitrarily, above which concentrations, or densities, should not transgress.[27] The Pacific Urban Studies and Planning Program at the University of Hawaii is providing a data base including maps for forty different elements. The Hawaii legislature has instructed the State Transportation Council to monitor the growth of transportation and suggest limits. Other agencies have already had discussions about carrying capacity. Tourism is so important that government agencies, private consultants, and the university should all be involved in a program of study. The time seems appropriate to fill in the blanks and to bring all studies, monitoring, and limit setting into some degree of systematic coherence. When that is underway and the information readily available, then another major step will have been taken toward measuring identifiable changes and impacts. University departments and the School of Travel Industry Management should be seen as a source of relatively low cost short-term and long-term studies. With the aid of advanced undergraduate and graduate students a continuous program of both basic and practical studies could be pursued. In this way the university could make an appropriate contribution to the state which supports it.

I have talked frequently about differing individual and group perceptions of resources or of environmental change. At times perceptions of honorable observers vary widely. They do not, because of this, constitute aberrations of reality. They are the true situations—together they contribute to reality. We must therefore be prepared to meet all types of views ranging from precise to the confused and nebulous, similar to those heard at a town meeting. Each may be as close as one can ever get to a true situation especially where community groups are concerned. This may be the only data on which a decision can be made. This is why I would prefer that a community cross section—businessmen, professionals, interest groups, public leaders, trade unionists, and scientists —be involved in setting guidelines and limits, especially where evaluation must be done in subjective terms. Environmental guidelines, for instance, devised only by scientists are likely to be as biased as tourist industry guidelines set only by tourism operators. No one group has that infallible, unquestionable, certain knowledge. It is not that separate groups are untrustworthy and need watching. It is that they are incapable of making decisions which have a chance of acceptance and of working reasonably well within the total community. I see this as a useful way to proceed acknowledging that in times of emergency, the community may have to defer in the interim to a group with greater knowledge than any other group.

There are four major interrelated and overlapping concerns: crowding, environmental stress, the diminution of the distinctive Hawaii way of life, and the resolution of conflicting values. Crowding in separate concentrations in some of the state's most attractive areas or threatening good agricultural land is a lead element. It is partly or largely a manifestation of the total activity of tourism and the direct culprit for the deterioration of environment and culture.

It seems clear that the time has arrived for a new decisive approach. Hit and miss methods do not work. The depression of quality in the total environment means a direct effect on the industry. If tourism managers want at least the same quality they have now, they will have to work much harder for it, not on their own but in cooperation with a more aware and educated total community. Although we know there are some who say all is lost, I prefer to agree with the late Dr. Thomas Hamilton who said that the economic and social future of Hawaii is precarious. But the chance is there. So, let's not miss it.

In any consideration of impact, scale is tremendously important. Smaller scale and slower development ensure less trauma in the population. They allow more time for changing strategies, general planning, and ascertaining the reactions of visitors and local people alike. "Slower" does not necessarily mean slow. Pace must be decided on an ad hoc basis reflecting changing attitudes, the region, and the time. Although I have implied that preferred growth, quality growth, controllable growth, and similar terms are imprecise and frustrating symbols to those who charge inaction and bureaucratic lip service, they have their value. They are being used more and except for "quality growth," few of them were used a decade ago. Inherent in each is a plea for a reasoned approach, and they prepare the community for a coming period when individual gain in many areas could start yielding to the common good. In hastening the arrival of this day, community groups have a vital part to play.

Sociologist Dean MacCannell in the introduction to his book *The Tourist: A New Theory of the Leisure Class* addresses what he sees as the "two poles of modern consciousness. Tourism is willing," he says, "to accept, even venerate, things as they are" while revolution represents "a desire to transform things."[28] In Hawaii we might argue that the two poles have come together and appear to replace each other. In making provision for the first "polar" function of appreciating what is there, tourism as an organized activity has inadvertently cast itself in the role of revolutionary— transforming landscape and society to accommodate newcomers. Fresh tourists then arrive to experience what is actually a transformed scene and the industry then extends itself again to provide for the extra visitors. The process in theory goes on and on.

CHAPTER 13

Plans, Trends, and the Future

Feelings toward the Industry

THE past two-and-a-half decades before the economic downturn of the early eighties constituted a period of rapid economic growth. It is generally agreed by most residents, notwithstanding the views of some citizen groups, that during this time as a result of tourism more people were employed, more economic opportunities were made available, the neighbor islands moved toward the mainstream of development, fewer people were poor, housing was of a higher quality, schools were improved, and more extensive health facilities existed than before development. Benefits have been in the areas of material improvement. In social and educational matters and in the understanding of one group by another, there is still a long way to go if development is conceived as a balanced process.

There are people who are not wholeheartedly impressed with tourism and some who are downright hostile such as the radical wing of the Hawaiian Movement which sees tourism as a symbol of oppression and a vulnerable area of future attack. "There always have been residents who react negatively to cultural fatigue: that is, they have unfavorable reactions when people from foreign lands come to their country in excessively large numbers. While the majority of the residents of an area may not react, a minority becomes very vocal . . . These noisy minorities," said a local official to a group of Japanese hotel executives, "frequently have sufficient influence on their local governments to cause the passing of laws to restrict the growth rate of the visitor industry."[1] Almost a decade after these remarks were made attitudes were changing. The response now is increasingly "Why the noise? Are there real grounds for disquiet?" A misinterpreted "vocal minority" may grow into a community furor, the case with Nukolii, and come back to haunt developers, the industry, and the community for years.

Although to some there may seem to be a consensus concerning feelings toward tourists and tourism, government planners and decision makers concerned with the industry need to be sure of their ground. In 1972 a survey conducted for the Hawaii Visitors Bureau reported that 69 percent of residents felt that tourism was good for the state while 8 percent saw it as bad.[2] A later survey prepared for the Department of Planning and Economic Development, mentioned elsewhere in this study, showed a very solid statewide majority, 74 percent, who believed tourism good for Hawaii while a diminished proportion, 5 percent, felt it bad. On the surface this seemed to indicate an increase in tourism's supporters, but it could be accounted for by the characteristics of a different sample or different community feelings at the time of the poll. I cannot see the likelihood of support increasing in the future with increased growth. I imagine the approval of the industry by three-quarters of the population is as high as anyone might expect it to be. The second survey did not by any means imply unconditional support. Support was given in the context of a faltering plantation agriculture and other limited resources. It was also given by people who wished to see a degree of control or its equivalent in the form of a room tax (52 percent) and the limitation of out-of-state investment. It must also be understood that the generation of opposition is partially a function of group dynamics and that it is cumulative. Without much increase in development, opposition could increase dramatically given the appropriate circumstances and time. Opposition over time reinforces sensitivity to all irritants which multiply and possibly create overt hostility. It could be described as cumulative, agglomerative, and self-reinforcing. But with decline, or unaccustomed slow growth, support for the industry may appear in unlikely places. Community reactions are not simple and are probably impossible to forecast statistically.

Neighborhood boards, considered at the end of the seventies to be reliable indicators of public feeling, indicated a stiffening of attitude in rural Oahu. On the North Shore and along the windward side except for the village of Kahuku, residents were determinedly against further development, a similar situation developed along the Waianae coast, although in this latter case, some argue, hostility to outsiders no matter what the cause might be lessened if residents had the opportunity to share more in the rewards of tourism.

Positive Effects of Tourism

In previous chapters I have examined change, much of which was either not acceptable to a significant group of people or not desirable for Hawaii. Here I want to summarize those aspects of the industry which are attractive to the public.

The overwhelming benefit of tourism is that it provides a major indigenous source of income at a time when the only other major source, agriculture, is everywhere struggling or temporarily on a heady upswing. Where agriculture has failed there is no doubt the slack has been taken up or the blow softened by tourism. However, tourism is by no means a complete substitute for agriculture as I have pointed out.

In a 1978 poll by the *Honolulu Advertiser*, 64 percent of respondents favored growth of the visitor industry to create jobs, yet in the same poll there was marked anti-population growth sentiment. Respondents did not connect the expanded tourism with what was perceived as overpopulation. The discussion of the poll noted that "employment . . . [and] the pocketbook issue outweighs environmentalism in the minds of most islanders." The 2 to 1 in favor of tourism growth was reported in all areas of the state. Stronger support was shown by Caucasians and those of Japanese ancestry. Hawaiians and part-Hawaiians, with a 3 to 2 vote produced a smaller margin than the average. In the eighteen to thirty-four age group those in favor were again 3 to 2, but this increased markedly to a 4 to 1 for persons over 50 years of age.[3] Another poll conducted for the Housing Constituency in 1980 added another component related to resident attitudes to development in general. Nearly 90 percent of respondents favored the imposition of strong controls on developers, 74 percent did not believe what developers told them, and 60 percent believed "developers did not care about the community."[4]

Another element commonly perceived as exceptionally important but about which much has yet to be learned, both in Hawaii and elsewhere, is the ripple-like multiplier effect of tourist spending.[5] Conventional wisdom says that in the tourist business a dollar is not just a dollar because it is in fact spent over and over again. It could be the equivalent to three dollars. Not so, is the answer given by many studies done around the world. It may range from 0.2 to 1.5 which is very high. At least one study says that a multiplier that exceeds 2 should be subjected to critical review before acceptance or use in future analysis.[6]

The process is based on the theory that for every dollar spent in tourist business some is used for local interindustry purchases, some for wages (direct household income), some for the payment of taxes to local and nonlocal governments, and the remainder, lost to the system, is transferred outside the region as dividends, cash flow to head office, or for the payment of imports. Whatever is lost to the system is leakage. Household income is further allocated to local purchases, savings, taxes, or import spending outside the system.

In the next round, and any subsequent rounds of spending, each business involved has the opportunity to convert receipts into the same pattern as tourist businesses did. In this round direct household income becomes indirect income and this too can be allocated in the same pattern as previously.[7] In every round something leaves the system. In an actual situation on a small remote island in which most food, drink, clothing, and industrial materials are imported, in which local wages are low, and where tourism is in the control of a few large overseas establishments, the substantial leakage which ensues would result in a very low multiplier characterizing the operation.

In a comprehensive study, Juanita Liu, now with the School of Travel Industry Management, University of Hawaii, pointed out several deficiencies associated with the conventional ways of calculating multipliers especially those measuring income. The work built on that of Brian Archer who has done much for the understanding of the concept.

Liu points out that multiplier impacts represent only part of the total picture and that they ignore costs while assuming the existence of infinite resources.[8] The multiplier, too, is an entirely economic notion and does not assess social costs or benefits. Liu's studies confirmed the hypothesis that the conventional method of determining income multipliers tends to overestimate the value. She calculated multipliers by considering establishments of the same type separately. "Even smaller values," she says, "might be achieved if all other industrial sectors were disaggregated."[9]

The studies show that high performance and high multipliers are not necessarily related. Different types of establishment have different levels and modes of performance. Central, large, affiliated, externally owned establishments have small multipliers because of the limited linkages they have in the local economy and because of economies of scale.[10]

A study of multipliers can be misleading. Liu's study supported a conclusion that within the context of income multipliers locally owned establishments provided the maximum multiplier values but smaller enterprises maximized employment. High multipliers did not necessarily indicate what was best for a region. In the studies cited, large externally owned establishments captured the bulk of tourist receipts, provided the bulk of direct income, and operated at a high level of performance, none of which was indicated through multipliers.[11]

One might postulate for Hawaii that during the first decades of tourism many establishments were local and smaller than they are now. This would have created higher income multipliers and a maximization of employment per establishment. Today local ownership is down, sizes of establishments are much greater, and the overall level of performance is probably as high as it has ever been. Critics of tourism in a particular place might point to the fact that rather than being high, multipliers are ominously low. Liu's study showed that neither high nor low multipliers meant much unless one knew how they were calculated and to what use they were to be put. Even then they could be of more academic than practical importance. What is invalid is to imbue the industry with a rather magical quality derived from operations which invariably produced high multiplier effect. In Hawaii, federal spending is the most important component of state income. Because so much of it goes toward providing direct income its multiplier effect, which is virtually never mentioned, is probably greater than that of tourism.

Associated with the benefits of tourism is the fact that it provides over one hundred thousand jobs directly and indirectly—one quarter of the state workforce. Populations on the neighbor islands ceased declining as a result of tourism and family members were able to remain at home rather than migrate to Oahu or to the mainland to find work.

From the business point of view, the industry makes very good use of available resources and contributes to a relatively stable economic climate in which most satisfactory returns are available to entrepreneurs and investors in a number of activities. It pro vides a magnificent vacation destination for millions of mainlanders who work in an economic and social milieu which makes the possibility of leisure travel a reality.

The industry and its ramifications provide the traveling public and the local community alike with superb restaurants, good entertainment, fine shopping centers with a much wider variety of goods than they otherwise would have had, and relatively cheap, efficient, reliable air transportation to other islands and to the mainland.

The tax base is such that both medical facilities and higher education units are at a level above that found in other Pacific island countries and territories. Part of this of course is that Hawaii is a state of the United States, part stems from the high volume of economic activity associated with tourism.

Local people have access to the facilities provided for travelers. They can enjoy the tasteful landscaping of great resort areas, the stores, hotel amenities, art and cultural centers, tennis, and golf. This is particularly true on neighbor islands where recreational facilities abound and where local people are relied upon to support operations when facilities first open. I must point out, however, that even where discounts are offered until a clientele is established, many facilities, except on infrequent occasions or for a limited group of participants, are beyond the financial reach or outside the interests of many local citizens. Nobody of course would dispute the fact that in the main, the facilities are for visitors.

Previous Planning and Exploration

One of the most influential and comprehensive of early plans was a 1960 publication of the Hawaii State Planning Office, *Visitor Destination Areas in Hawaii—An Action Program for Development*. The study arose, first, from a growing need for extra accommodations and, second, from the obvious need for the state to attempt to improve the economy of the neighbor islands. The plan designated visitor destination areas and made a number of recommendations concerning appropriate capital improvements, the use of state lands for resort development, visitor promotional funds, state aid for hotel construction on neighbor islands, and other roles the state might play.

Later in the decade because of some public criticism of tourism, the Hawaii Visitors Bureau, in an unusual move, assembled a large Committee on the Statewide Goals of Tourism which included "a number of more strident critics of tourism." With this action a turning point in the perception of tourism management was reached. A report followed a number of meetings but "more important," said Dr. Thomas Hamilton, "was the recognition that it would be healthy for tourism to become a topic for discussion by a broadly representative body of the citizenry."[12]

The way was now prepared for the late Governor John A. Burns to convene the Governor's Travel Industry Congress (1970) attended by four hundred widely representative delegates. Although the congress had no official status, it provided direction to decision makers in the years that followed and made the state aware of tourism in a new constructive way.

During the 1960s the School of Travel Industry Management of the University of Hawaii under its founder, Dean Edward Barnet had been making its own special contribution behind the scenes, first as a department of hotel and tourism administration from 1959 and then as a school since 1966. The concept of travel industry as a wide, inclusive activity extending to land development, transportation and hotel keeping originated within the school, part of a newly developing broad base for the study of tourism. Before professional courses were offered in Hawaii, management for the industry came from the mainland or Europe.[13] Today under the leadership of Dean Chuck Y. Gee the school is continuing to make very positive contributions.

In the early 1970s the Department of Planning and Economic Development published two very useful documents, each discussed elsewhere in this work. The first, of help in the preparation of the contemporary tourism plan, was a cost-benefit analysis prepared by Mathematica.[14] The other was the two-volume Hawaii Tourism Impact Plan,[15] a major comprehensive tourism assessment of Hawaii. The first volume evaluated the industry, gave physical guidelines, and presented a list of major state-planned projects; volume two was a study of West Hawaii.

As a result of the interest stimulated by the congress, the 1972 legislative session established a Temporary Visitor Industry Council which in the following year submitted a detailed report as complete as anything up to that time.[16] Its recommendations carried policy several steps forward. Recommendations fell within three headings: growth regulation keyed to needed jobs, an office of tourism coordination, and Waikiki growth limitation. Unfortunately the legislature took no action concerning the report. Nevertheless, it set the stage for the work of the Tourism Planning Advisory Committee and the Interim Tourism Advisory Council which along with the DPED staff carried the burden of preparing the ten-year tourism master plan. All committees from the Temporary Visitor Industry Council through to the Interim Tourism Advisory Council were under the level-headed chairmanship of Dr. Hamilton, former president of the University of Hawaii and later with the Hawaii Visitors Bureau.

Governor Ariyoshi appointed the Tourism Planning Advisory Committee to start on the tough job of formulating tourism policy, assessing previous reports, and preparing materials for action.[17] These finally came in several forms: Act 133, the Interim Tourism Policy Act; the tourism section of the Hawaii State Plan; and the specifics of the State Tourism Plan of which supporting material was published in 1978 as the State Tourism Study.

In talking to a public gathering in New Zealand on the same subject, Dr. Hamilton said this: "I relate this background and I regret that it has taken this long, not to establish that we in Hawaii are terribly slow to act, for the truth of the matter is that most democratic governments do not act all that quickly and all things considered this may not be necessarily a bad thing. My purpose was rather to demonstrate how difficult the task of arriving at consensus is in an area where tourism is such a central social and economic factor as it is in Hawaii."[18]

In 1975 and 1976 groups of legislators, newsmen, and representatives of counties and government agencies traveled to the Caribbean and the Pacific Islands to observe the tourist industry in action elsewhere.[19] The indirect value to Hawaii of these two excursions was very great. Every place visited by the group had some telling message for Hawaii. Some were flashbacks to Hawaii twenty years ago, many showed pitfalls Hawaii should guard against. Virtually every problem found in Hawaii had its counterparts elsewhere. Although there was revulsion against stringent control which it was avowed was not Hawaii's way, there was nevertheless secret admiration for effective controls observed in several places. Generally group members were happy with what they had taken for granted in Hawaii, but saw only too well the competitive threat presented by other countries, all ready to step in should Hawaii falter. The trip underscored the problem of Waikiki and above all it showed the sensitivity and fragility of tourism which had soured so easily in some other places and could do the same in Hawaii if quality were not vigilantly maintained.

The Tourism Ten-Year Plan

The ten-year tourism plan or the "tourism master plan" was a massive undertaking providing basic data and charting the course of Hawaii tourism until 1985. Its background information is summarized in five volumes as the 1978 *State Tourism Study.*[20] Never before has tourism in Hawaii been subjected to such exhaustive scrutiny. The work involved hundreds of thousands of words sifted, organized, and written in final form. Despite the study's sheer length, comprehensiveness, and questioned recommendations which brought forth a flood of criticism, it nevertheless provided in one set of publications something the public has never had before—useful basic facts and interpretations in one place.

It did not appear out of thin air. A number of essential technical reports were called for, a cost-beneift analysis was updated, former tourism plans were studied, and the governor appointed the Tourism Planning Advisory Committee to assist the Department of Planning and Economic Development with its formulations. In January 1976 the committee submitted recommendations for a State Interim Tourism Policy, later approved as Act 133, a set of major guidelines to help direct the intensive planning already underway. These remained in effect until the Hawaii State Plan was approved in 1978 at which time the tourism plan was legally required to conform to the tenets of the more comprehensive Hawaii State Plan.

Act 133 also established the thirteen-person Interim Tourism Advisory Council which superseded the comittee. The council, chaired by Dr. Hamilton, had an even representation from industry, the public, and the counties. As each portion of the plan advanced, the council systematically discussed it, suggested modifications, and ultimately made recommendations to the director of the Department of Planning and Economic Development.

The plan was required to reflect the thinking lying behind Act 133 concerning the provision of high-quality tourism service, protection of scenic beauty, the enhancement and appreciation of Hawaiian and other ethnic heritages, and the sustenance of tourism's health in a way which would not impair those critical elements of Hawaii life. In short it was seen as a plan to develop policies that would maximize employment while minimizing negative social, environmental, and economic impacts.

The State Tourism Plan underwent two phases seeking approval: the first in 1978–1979 and the second—reoriented, rewritten, and revised—in 1980–1981. A brief study of its uncertain progress reflects changing times, varying attitudes, dissatisfaction with past impacts, a disquiet with accelerated growth, fear of recession-induced decelerated growth, a growing awareness of social impacts, legislative appreciation of intensifying public reaction to tourism, and increasing community input during the second phase after rejection in 1979 and 1980 and nonapproval in 1981.

State Tourism Plan: First Phase

Although all students of Hawaii tourism understand the varied and profound ramifications of tourism, the plan focused on largely economic matters to the exclusion of many social matters of a pressing nature. Tremendous concern was shown with creating sufficient jobs to accommodate future needs. As tourism appeared obviously to be the major employment generator, the regulation of growth upward or downward was an integral component of planning. Too much growth would not only look after needs but also would be a positive force toward in-migration. Zero growth would result in high unemployment but it was estimated that at 7 percent it would curb in-migration and maintain unemployment at a manageable 6 percent. The 7 percent growth rate was adopted, but in order to take the heat off more heavily developed Oahu a greater than 7 percent growth became the obligation of neighbor island counties. To meet the estimated visitor increase until 1985, 36,200 additional hotel and accommodation units were needed, and of these, destination areas outside Oahu were expected to provide almost 60 percent. This approach did not sit well with many neighbor island communities nor with county spokespersons.

Tourism growth would have to provide the jobs because no alternative part of the economy was in a position to make more than a minor contribution. It was believed that there would have to be tourism jobs or none at all. The jobs would provide opportunities for both local people and recent arrivals. But only 50 percent of the industry's work force now is Hawaii-born, and about 16 percent is arrivals of the past two years.

The new arrivals, in-migrants, and immigrants (aliens) represent a special burden. They must be housed, educated, and provided with other extra facilities. Although in the past this has been a growing component of the population, it was argued that it is difficult to determine to what extent tourism is responsible for it. Researchers calculated that in a static economic situation, close to 8,000 newcomers would arrive annually in the islands regardless of the local economic situation.

Although a hotel tax would help offset some of the wear and tear of tourism and in theory make a direct visitor contribution to infrastructural maintenance, no recommended actions were made for such a tax in the plan. It was reported that the governor was neither for nor against such a tax.

A tourist tax had been discussed over a long period of time. Citizens' groups and some legislators were for it, and usually industry speakers were fervently against it. It was not strange then that it became an important item for discussion by the Tourism Planning Advisory Committee. The state commissioned a full study of the question so that it could be used as supporting data for the plan and for whatever recommendations might be made.[21] This technical report was developed by James Mak and Edward Nishimura of the University of Hawaii.[22] Mak and Nishimura found that a hotel tax would have two effects: first, it would discourage some marginal tourists from coming to Hawaii; and secondly, those who did come would reduce their stay by 0.1 days. A tax would in effect raise the price of a Hawaiian vacation.

The state interpretation of the findings was that any tax up to 5 percent would have about the same effect. It would bring "substantial tax revenue to the State government but a loss to private industry. A tax of 1 percent would bring $2.5 million to the State and cause a loss of $1 million to the industry."[23] The loss was interpreted by some as the result of a tax purporting to be levied against tourists penalizing residents as well.

Public response to the plan took several forms. Counties felt they were losing their control of tourism despite the Interim Tourism Advisory Council's pains not to appear to take decision-making powers away from counties.

The fact that neighbor islands were designated to make an unusual contribution in the future exacerbated the situation. There was reason for planning to take the direction it did. On Oahu the lid had already been placed on Waikiki, Makaha had not had an encouraging past record, Kahuku had felt the sting of public reaction, and other areas had yet to be approved. A look toward the neighbor islands showed almost a dozen major developments under way and several others given the right conditions might be off and away during the next few years.

The industry's reaction initially seemed resigned. It appeared happy that signs pointed to Waikiki smartening up. A room tax did not seem to be a threat. No ominous controls appeared to be in the wind, and the general feeling seemed to be that physical accommodation of a 7 percent increase in overnight visitors was an optimistic assessment on the part of the planners. No one then anticipated the shocks that were to come in 1979–1980. It was not felt then to be a question of visitor demand, just doubt that the industry could meet the allocations. Lower growth rates might worsen the not particularly bright financing situation. Lending institutions already saw tourism as being unpredictable. No one could foresee which way airline fares would ultimately go or the effect of increased gas prices, possibly restricted fuel allocations, protracted airline strikes, and competition from other countries. Inflated costs would make costs per room in the future $75,000 to $100,000 compared with the much lower costs of building in the boom period of 1965–1975. To get a reasonable return, room tariffs would have to increase to $60–80 a day (a greater impact than any room tax would have). "It looks real nice on paper but it's not realistic," said House Tourism Committee Chairman Gerald Machida, with reference to the industry's susceptibility to factors outside its control.

Hawaii Business had a greater degree of reservation. "The plan gives the reader a gnawing sense of unease . . . Tourism is . . . the most important growth industry in the forseeable future and should be nurtured to insure the State's economic health . . . But the authors have also swiss-cheesed the documents with caveats that could, if worse comes to worst, carry with them the seeds of heavier unemployment and economic dislocations for the State in the not-too-distant future . . . It has now codified [tourism] as the cornerstone ingredient in governmental approaches to Hawaii's economic future [and it has made the assumption] that without the proper tourism growth, the State is in for some difficult times . . . The State has decided to make one of the world's most fragile and tenuous industries the mainstay of Hawaii's economic well-being. Other potential growth industries such as agriculture,

aquaculture, manufacturing, and manganese nodule processing
have been shunted aside as long range and of only minor consequence . . . Nowhere do the documents tell how the goals might be
achieved." The article quoted an observer claiming "that the plan
is based on mostly outdated data and is dotted with guesstimates
which raise doubts about whether the final analysis is on
course."[24]

Counties felt that indeed rather narrow state and industry views
were being forced on them. No neighbor island county, nor for
that matter the City and County of Honolulu, was happy about
what was being considered. Each county had its own views how it
could best contribute; Kauai was developing very firm views on
growth, and nowhere did the plan seem to reflect the essence of
county aspirations for the future.

The plan was not clear and straightforward; it did not, as some
interest groups pointed out, present alternatives, and it did not
question its own assumption that full employment in the state
using tourism to achieve it should take precedence over all else.

The public—for the most part—tended to ignore meetings to
which they could contribute their views; nevertheless, some public
reaction was observable.

In order to relieve a social problem on Oahu, the plan suggested
interisland immigration into rural areas where moderate or low-
priced housing is usually not available. Visitor income derived
from hotel rooms is likely to be spent at larger urban areas, in
Honolulu, or the mainland where the resort or hotel corporate
headquarters may be located. As the developments would be
staffed with a large component from other states or Oahu, any argument that development solves local employment problems
needs considerable critical questioning. Neighbor islands and
more especially rural districts in which resorts are located would
receive some income/compensation along with an influx of outsiders, increased crowding, a possible lowering of development
quality, and a certain change, possibly a deterioration, of existing
life-style.

There are reasons as well to ask what the impact would be in
other regions of neighbor islands especially those with declining
agriculture away from resort districts. Tim Chow, in two interesting articles, stresses the importance of not only solving state problems but planning regionally to try to eradicate area disparities as
they occur.[25] Each island is different and each suffers different

impacts—facts ultimately taken into greater consideration in 1979.

A valid argument could be put forward that the areas identified in the plan were due for development in any case. I have no argument with development per se, but there is a big difference between normal development—which may well be responsive to both quality and local wishes—and pressured development responsive to what might be interpreted as a state emergency. It seemed the plan could be manipulated just as we have seen with some county plans. If growth rates set by the state, whatever they are when plan approval is received, are not met, some of the originally predicted widespread impacts mentioned will not eventuate and the state may not have solved its predicted unemployment problem. Following plan arguments, higher unemployment would result in an outflow of population to the mainland. This could be a situation which we might become used to in time. It might be predicted that the ultimate trauma of temporarily high unemployment must come sometime in the future if a high degree of quality in the industry and the environment is to be maintained for future generations.

Virtually full employment unfortunately may mean tourism growing more quickly toward that future point where the resources of tourism are strained or overloaded to a level we would perceive now as beyond recall. The hub of Hawaii's tourism, Waikiki, if not already at that point is as close as one would dare have it. This has already caused visitors to be less impressed with Oahu than with any other part of the state.

Resource overload is achieved two ways simultaneously: by too many visitors, and by too many local residents, a great percentage of whom were attracted in the first place by those things including promotion which bring tourists. Using the first plan's thinking as a model and projecting indefinitely into the future, always balancing growth and jobs, would eventually bring Hawaii to a resource breaking point. How soon this would be is not known. All experts agree tourism is fragile; consequently, the breakdown which must ultimately come, if the model assuming unwavering steady growth were followed, may come sooner than later. At that time there would be no growing employment in tourism and if tourists turned away from Hawaii, which is likely, there would be massive unemployment. If it is inevitable that in good economic times a resource and employment breakdown must ultimately take place, we should now tackle the problem of establishing limits to prevent massive unemployment and to conserve human and physical resources.

A New Modified Version: Phase II, 1980–1981

After an early start with public hearings in 1977, the plan, in a considerably modified form, was still being reworked and aired in 1979 and 1980 in order to gather community and legislative support for its approval by the 1980 legislature. By then the original planning period 1975–1985 was half over and the new projections extended it to 1990. Like the 1978 and 1979 legislatures, the 1980 session was not satisfied and sent the tourism plan off with other functional plans to be integrated with each other and with the State Plan as a whole. All going well, approval can be expected in 1982.

Conditions since 1977 had changed markedly. When the original plan was being prepared the economy was improving; in 1979 the tide had turned and the nation was preparing for some further belt tightening. By the summer of 1980, economic conditions had deteriorated even further—the worst for tourism in thirty years. DPED had new consultants to pull the loose ends together, and three years had provided time to reconsider the validity and emphases placed on former parameters, to introduce new methodologies, and to devise what was considered more appropriate strategies. I have already spoken about the value of work already completed. This the new authors used as a substantial foundation. In addition, they benefited from the "kite flying" done previously and were as aware as they ever would be of the reactions likely to be generated by certain types of recommendations. Although looking back the whole procedure seemed to a degree messy and inefficient, in the absence of adequate public information, the intervening years allowed time for a better evaluation of community wants and a better appreciation of possible legislative responses as the result of suggestions raised during hearings or received from the public, the legislature, and the advisory committee. By the end of 1980 all sectors of Hawaii's people were very much more aware than they were three years before.

The old advisory council had become the State Tourism Plan Advisory Committee and its chairmanship had been assumed by Aaron Levine, president of the Oahu Development Conference.

In mid-1979 the possible specific recommendations of what was now being called more cautiously the State Tourism Plan (rather than the grander "ten year tourism plan" or the "tourism master plan"), one of twelve functional plans, underwent refinement. Local newspapers noted with inadequate understanding of the situation that the former projections [the old plan] for tourism growth and development were based on questionable data and were far too high and did not fully take into account the tourism plans of the four individual counties. Although marked changes were implied, this, advisory committee members said, was not in fact the case. In reality old assumptions had been tested and modified, the time frame extended to ensure currency and some of the more general predictions refined and made more specific.

The State Tourism Plan has much about it which is creditable.[26] It is to the point, and easily grasped. More than anything else I have read, it draws attention to the human impacts of Hawaii tourism and emphasizes a number of the same questions to which I have drawn attention in this book. The plan is constantly updated. An earlier version notes, on the first page, that its goal is "to ensure the continued health of the industry and the State, planning needs to take into consideration such additional important factors as the social effects of tourism, the social and cultural health of its people, the protection of our Aloha Spirit and the protection of our precious environment." The most recent update says the same thing in different words.

The persuasive emphasis now given community concerns is further elaborated by a prominent listing of possible critical changes brought about by tourism in the areas of life-style, aloha spirit, impaired resident access, increased use of public facilities and resources, loss of open space and agricultural lands, increased cost of living and property values, crime, and population increase. As a reflection of this understanding the 1979 legislature appropriated funds to define the scope of work necessary to evaluate the important impacts that can and should be measured, to discuss the relationships of these impacts to the tourism planning process, and to develop policies for future tourism development. At the time of this writing, a proposal to do the work had been received but needed substantial modifications to be approved. Legislative support for a full study then went into abeyance.

Residents' needs, interests, and attitudes were tied to three major concerns—the provision of jobs, visitor satisfaction, and the activities of the visitor industry in general. Both developers and county government were urged to consult and be guided by state functional plans, the State Tourism Study's Physical Resources Inventory, and "by whatever means possible, protect Hawaii's environment and communities." In the section The Development Approval Process, the roles of the state and the counties were discussed. The plan noted that the Land Use Commission could seek assurance from a developer that he would comply with submitted plans, once districting took place he and the appropriate county should come to an agreement concerning the adequate provision of worker housing.[27] Earlier in this work I noted that this had become policy in Maui under two administrations.

Although, the plan states, a well-documented agreement binding the developer to his intentions could be drawn up, considerable difficulties were anticipated as most parameters of development change over time. Further, government plans and regulations at present are inadequate to protect residents.

As mandated by the Hawaii State Plan, the tourism plan filled its role in making recommendations which would maintain a strong viable industry, preserve an attractive environment, develop a high quality of life, improve the quality of existing destinations, assist with tourism promotion, and above all provide jobs for Hawaii's people. In addition, the plan addressed such matters as the provision of adequate training within the industry, means of conveying to the public the contributions of the industry, and the need to perpetuate the aloha spirit.

To provide jobs, a steady increase of visitors was considered essential but the increase was seen in terms of declining rates of increase. That is to say, the original forecast of 7 percent from 1975 to 1980 seemed to be on target, but then for greater specificity than previously, the rate for 1980–1985 was computed at 5 percent, for 1985–1990 4 percent, 1990–1995 3 percent, and 1995–2000 1 percent. The published draft plan took the increases only up to 1990. If maintained, the increases would be sufficient to meet employment needs with no more than 6 percent unemployment, the critical value on which the plan is predicated. It might be pointed out that with a growing work force and a declining visitor count—not the 5 percent increase considered essential by planners—unemployment, under these extreme conditions, averaged only 5 percent. The plan implied a higher rate should be expected. Some of this can be explained by employees taking shorter hours, transient employees leaving for the mainland and the previously understaffed nature of some establishments.

To meet perceived needs, county increases for 1980–1990 were placed at 6 percent for Maui, 6.8 percent for the Big Island, 5.5 percent for Kauai, and 3.3 percent for Oahu—a closer approximation to county wishes than previously. By the end of the same period the approximate number of additional hotel rooms needed in each county would be 7,500 for Maui, 7,400 for the Big Island, 3,100 for Kauai, and 8,100 for Honolulu. A particular concern of planners was the provision of tourism and related jobs for the neighbor islands where unemployment was higher, the sugar industry vulnerable, and the economy less diversified than on Oahu.

As with the original projections, the state economic model was used with modifications. Some previous assumptions were changed to reflect more closely what was actually occurring and the 163,200 extra jobs needed by the state between 1980 and 1990 were redistributed throughout various sectors of the economy, leaving 87,000 or over 53 percent to be supported by tourism. More jobs would be needed in the early rather than later part of the period to reduce unemployment and to provide for the larger number of recent entrants into the labor force. The greater job creating contributions expected of the nontourism economic sectors appeared most encouraging, well worth past state efforts.

Greatest projected contributions were from diversified agriculture and food processing, the movie industry, the precious coral industry, commercial fishing, and textiles and apparel in that order. An analysis of these contributions in the light of today's conditions, without changes in public attitudes and behavior and primary production demand and marketing, underlines the present dependence on tourism.

Attempts were made to solicit as wide a variety of suggestions and recommendations as possible before the final plan was drafted. Counties probably felt that new approaches, including a closer recognition of their wishes, represented a move toward retrieving greater autonomy, something they felt they had previously lost. Nor were interest groups overlooked. Members of Life of the Land, the Sierra Club, the Council of Presidents, and other groups made worthwhile submissions.

Several strategies were used to achieve the recommended goals. These included a judicious allocation of state or county capital im-

provement programs to encourage development where it is needed
and wanted, especially on the neighbor islands, or the rehabilitation of existing amenities such as the twelve-point plan for the improvement of Waikiki. Counties were also encouraged to give preference or streamlined approval to projects which in terms of the
plan seemed desirable. This would include giving preference to
full-service hotels over any other type of accommodations in the
long-term interests of both the residents and the industry.

A considerable number of activities interestingly were designed
to develop a much greater awareness of all facets of the industry
and included teaching, learning, advising, training, monitoring,
making inventories, recording, surveying, and researching. Never
before in similar Hawaii studies had such emphasis been placed on
the gathering, analysis, dissemination, and updating of relevant
information. Although most of this had no budget estimate, this
new activity of tourism management would place an inordinate financial burden on county and state agencies, the university, community colleges, and the Hawaii Visitors Bureau. Lasting quality
in the industry must be paid for.

In a systematic way the plan addressed itself to nine tourism-
oriented policies of the parent Hawaii State Plan. For each, appropriate implementing activities were suggested. The plan named
one or more organizations to supervise, monitor, or assist the proposed actions, suggest a time frame, identify a priority, and indicate a source of financial aid. Unlike so many plans which leave
final implementation up in the air, this one was specific. The recommended implementing actions are too numerous to detail here,
but anyone interested in the state's first industry and its ramifications should have a copy of the plan and study it well.

By mid-1980 it seemed that all possible useful input to the plan
had been made. One well-known city planner told me he believed
that the plan first discussed in 1977 had already lost its momentum and was in a state of decay. Perhaps this was correct in one
way, but in another, considerable benefit had been gained by reassessment and soliciting further input.

Although a conflict appeared to develop between House and
Senate concerning the plan, the topic of tourism was considered
critical enough for some legislators to speak out publicly. This on
its own constituted a new approach. In a *Honolulu Advertiser* article Representative Anthony Takitani (West Maui-Molokai-Lanai)
strongly opposed the plan's revised growth figures which he said

would "give our state over six million visitors by the year 1990 representing a growth of approximately 53 percent" in a decade.[28] Representative Ken Kiyabu, chairman of the Committee on Tourism and State General Planning, replied by saying that he fully understood his colleague's disquiet and felt that the "Hawaii we know and love" would be far better served by growth management through a functional plan than by a situation in which "the expansion of tourism was unplanned and unmanaged."[29]

Newspaper comment was not restricted only to House members. Senator Joseph T. Kuroda, chairman of the Senate Tourism Committee, in giving notice of his intention to introduce a bill to fund a $100,000 study of the social impact of tourism, said he had attended tourism plan workshops on all five islands. "These," he said, "produced grass roots feedback that the social costs of an expanded tourism industry appear to outweigh the corresponding economic benefits. Although opinions heard do not constitute a representative sample, they do raise a 'red flag' and suggest an element of caution in considering the proposed State tourism functional plan."[30]

In early 1980 some senior county officials forecasted that legislative approval would be virtually impossible until some of the plan's rough edges were smoothed off. This proved to be accurate. A criticism, not inappropriate, was that the plan did not suggest how a stable long-term climate could be created to facilitate required development. "This is par for the course," said one county officer. "The State's record of working closely with the private sector has still a long way to go." Related to this and to the function of counties, it was pointed out that there was little sign of real coordination between the state and the people—individuals, groups, or institutions—who would be expected to implement the plan. "Without a satisfactory investment climate and specific strategies for coordination, a plan can be just hollow wishful thinking," so continued the criticism.

One group which unanimously supported the plan was the State Tourism Plan Advisory Committee, a sixteen-person group representing public, counties, labor, and the visitor industry. The committee felt that "the Plan would officially establish a direction for tourism growth throughout the State and would furnish a basis for determining the levels of both public expenditures and private investment. And perhaps most important it would make available to the community relevant information about the future of each island." After noting that every facet of the economy showing promise should be pursued rather than placing great emphasis on the visitor industry, for the decade 1980 to 1990 the committee saw "no comparable economic activity to replace the visitor industry in terms of payroll and number of jobs."[31] The committee was concerned with criticism that the state and counties differed concerning both designated resort sites and tourism growth rates. In neither area was there important divergence, so it learned from its own well-placed county representatives. Without the plan, the committee believed, "decisions may be made on an individual basis with little relationship to the remainder of the County or [to] the future of the State."

Dean Chuck Y. Gee of the School of Travel Industry Management, University of Hawaii, after serving on the committee in Honolulu, made the following observations to a Pacific Area Travel Association workshop in Manila: "The State through prudent, reasonable and appropriate regulations should assure that the tourism product is created, distributed and consumed in a manner which benefits the community best."[32] Although highly dependent on the private sector, tourism, it was argued, relies heavily on common or public resources. As it passes certain critical levels it rapidly erodes the resources upon which it is based. Tourism, then, cannot be viewed as just an economic activity and the sole responsibility of the private sector. The resident and the tourist must be considered. The state through a plan attempts to balance competing and sometimes conflicting claims for the same limited resources taking into account both the broad and long-term interests of society. Tourism's part in economic development is the natural province of the private sector; the government's proper role is the protection of the rights of two publics—the resident and the visitor. "A joint responsibility of the private sector and government which may determine the ultimate survival of the industry," the dean said, "is making an appropriate response to resident attitudes towards tourism."[33]

Dean Gee's conclusions were very close to those of another member of the advisory committee, David Raney, who had been closely associated with the Hawaii Chapter of the Sierra Club and the Council of Presidents. He concluded a submission to the State Tourism Plan Advisory Committee as follows:

It seems to me that citizens of Hawaii are being asked to accept a continuing loss of some of the State's prime coastal areas to hotel/

condominium projects in exchange for promises of economic opportunities for some residents. The challenge for the Tourism Plan is to
honestly address the trade-offs for Hawaii's residents, to forge a
plan which will help to assure that the trade-offs are acceptable to
the public and that the potential benefits of tourism are actually realized in a manner which assures the continued health of the industry. In my opinion this requires that the industry must operate in
an environmentally sound manner and with the support of neighboring communities.[34]

Although technical studies were available to the writers of the
Hawaii State Plan, public contributions were exceedingly thin.
Yet it was the nine Hawaii State Plan policies and their implementation which formed the basis for three years of discussions and extensive input from diverse groups, all after the original policies
had been formulated. I hope it strikes others too that this mode of
operation seems highly illogical. The essential policies might well
have been arrived at after considerable debate rather than before
it. Perhaps as a result of the implementation of some of the
community-oriented recommendations of the State Tourism Plan,
the procedure might be reversed in the preparation of the next
plan. The formation of community councils which I suggest later
in this chapter would help immeasurably in this matter.

Planning and forecasting tourism has its pitfalls. Information
must come from a variety of sources and few interests speak with
one voice. The industry had many spokespersons, each representing only a facet of the total activity. No government department
oversees the affairs of tourism, and public interest groups are more
factious than the industry.

This is a reflection of what Henry Fairlie sees as one of the
country's present-day ailments—"single issue or single interest"
narrow-minded policies and politics substituted for the wider sov-
ereignty groups which the country once had and wielded.[35]

No one can accurately forecast crippling airline strikes, the
price and supply of jet fuel, the strategies of competing areas, the
effects of new airline technologies on Hawaii and competing
areas, the state of the money market, the behavior of foreign markets, the tastes of Americans, the mood of a resident population or
changed attitudes in Hawaii. The disparity between goals and reality is in the hands of so many forces, close accommodation may
result from luck as from good planning or effective methodologies.
Nevertheless many groups will imbue the plan with a special aura

of authority and use it for their own agendas. David Raney aptly calls this syndrome "the Trojan Horse."[36] This does not diminish a great need for planning. The entire exercise of several years was, from start to finish, long and difficult and something of a milestone in Hawaii tourism planning.

This brings me to an obvious question. Why not make future plans equally resource and carrying-capacity oriented? When the facts are known this orientation, I believe, would appeal to the industry and the public alike. By not predicating the future well-being of an industry and that of island peoples and life-styles largely on jobs and employment but on quality, as Colin Cameron suggests (the plan is moving more in this direction), the industry will end up in better shape. The results will ultimately be more humane for both the environment and its people.

Finally, until some better organization is devised I agree wholeheartedly with the suggestion that an advisory committee or a similar body remain to update the plan and to help provide accommodation to changing times. To disband this body upon the approval of the plan would be a retrogressive step.

Jobs and Income

The question is frequently asked in Hawaii: "But does tourism really provide jobs and does it raise incomes?" This has to be answered on an ad hoc basis. In Hawaii there seems to be no doubt about it. On a very simple basis it would be possible to use a neighbor island such as Maui as an example. Its earlier post-World War II economic character of declining population has already been discussed. Today, opportunities have multiplied dramatically despite a decreased overall importance of agriculture now characterized by great economic instability. By the end of the seventies, Maui County had a reputation for having the most buoyant economy in the state. The standard of living was high, recreational facilities abounded, and far more employment openings existed than could be met by Maui or Hawaii-born applicants.

In the last few years several studies focusing on tourism have been completed by economists from the University of Hawaii. In a statistical analysis, Moheb Ghali attempted to assess the relative contributions of exports—including tourism receipts—and investment to the growth of Hawaii. Put another way, an answer was attempted to the question, "What would have happened if . . . [tourism] had not grown?" The years 1953–1970 were compared using two situations: first, the active growth path of personal income between 1953 and 1970; second, the path as it would have been with the contribution of tourism frozen at 1952. The comparison showed that without tourism, personal income in Hawaii would have grown because of the growth of federal government expenditures, nonhotel construction investment, and state and local government expenditures. It was found that by 1970 personal income would have increased to a figure 17 percent lower than it actually was at that date with tourism. The average rate of growth of income in the absence of tourism was 6.87 percent compared with 7.99 percent with tourism. The growth rates would remain unchanged if similar calculations were made for per capita income. The analysis addressed the question: "How well did tourism contribute?" It finished by noting that it did not ask the more interesting and critical question so difficult to answer: "Was it worth it?"[37]

We have seen that most people in Hawaii accept tourism. Many do so with caution, while others with reluctance feel that although there are other contributors to the economy, tourism is the only one which can satisfy the state's needs in the immediate years to come, international economic conditions being equal. The State Tourism Study made this assumption and took note of several forecasts included in an article, "U.S. Tourism Seen as a Major Industry by 2000," published in *Commerce America*.[38] Here Herman Kahn was cited as predicting that tourism would continue a growth rate of 10 to 20 percent a year up to the year 2000. The same article cited the United States Travel Service's (USTS) prediction that the tourism sector of the economy would, during the next twenty-five years, grow more rapidly than the United States economy as a whole. Tourism, thus, would become of increasing importance in the international sector of the United States economy.

A second assumption made by the tourism study was that Hawaii would be part of this international growth of tourism and that this growth would be associated with increased accommodations and employment. In 1960 the total direct hotel employment in Hawaii was 4,300. In 1970 it was 13,400, by 1980 26,000. Hotel employment is just one category of a number of tourist-oriented occupations. There are other direct jobs in transport, retailing, and in service industries. The study sees tourism-related jobs—

direct, indirect, and induced employment—as 1.44 times the total for direct jobs. For 1980 the State Tourism Plan estimated the total tourist-related jobs at 124,100, of which approximately one-third were associated with hotel services and over one-quarter in a category called "eating and drinking."[39] The Department of Labor's estimate for 1980 was 114,000.

The State Tourism Plan forecasts the growth rate required to generate the industry's contribution to employment needs in the planning period 1980–1990. From a 2.83 million visitor total in 1975, a 7 percent per annum increase grading down to 1 percent at the end of the century would bring 3.97 million by 1980, 5.25 million by 1985, 6.43 million in 1990, and 7.46 million in 1995 (7.83 million in the year 2000). These growth rates would provide 87,000 new jobs between 1980 when 345,000 total jobs would be required in Hawaii and 1990 when the figure would be 508,200.

The State Tourism Plan treads very lightly around the admittedly complex subject of in-migration. This has been discussed in another context previously (chapter 11). The plan stresses the need for growth and from the vantage of 1980–1981, this seems essential. What is not at all certain is what rate of growth best satisfies the needs of all sections of the Hawaii community with the least cost to society and environment, the aim of the plan. An increase in tourism well beyond the 1979 level seems likely to be associated with an increase of in-migrants which in the decade of the seventies averaged 8,000 persons a year.[40] To provide employment for a newly augmented local population further tourism becomes essential and the stimulated industry then attracts more in-migrants. The progression from one to the other appears endless and the results poorly understood. Much more needs to be known about the dynamics of these interrelated processes. This is especially so when simultaneously the Hawaii State Plan seeks ways to curb a major problem, crowding; the industry seeks healthy, quality tourism; and the State Tourism Plan is concerned with promoting sufficient tourism to provide the number of jobs considered necessary.

The State Tourism Study profiles industry employees for 1977 and although we can expect minor changes every few years, we can assume overall characteristics will remain largely the same. The industry is dominated by female workers (58 percent) whereas in the state only about two-fifths of the workers overall are women.[41] Half the industry's employees are married and half are less than thirty years old, making it a young group in comparison with state workers as a whole. The fact that many are young in-migrants influences the profile and helps determine a number of characteristics. There are two recognizable groups in the industry: local career people and a young Caucasian group, many of whom are in Hawaii for the experience for a limited period of time. This latter group which is drawn to the state primarily by the special appeal of Hawaii rather than career opportunities has a relatively high educational level.

Thirty-six percent of employees have been in the industry for less than two years reflecting youth and recent arrivals. One exceedingly important characteristic is that 51 percent were born outside Hawaii and a third of these have been in the state for less than two years. In other words, a new hotel will not contribute as it might to local job generation. When hiring has finished it is possible that from one-third to three-quarters of the new employees are outsiders with only limited residential claims. At the recently opened Kapalua Bay Hotel a very large percentage of employees are outsiders. Local people from the other side of the island feel the commute to West Maui too far and it is asserted that because of high rents and the apparent unattractiveness of hotel positions, local employees are difficult to find. Some employers are meeting this problem with increased hourly rates.

Because of the nature of tourism, a greater number of part-time workers are employed in the industry compared with the state as a whole. Only 27 percent are union members. Unlike other places in the Pacific, about half have some post-secondary or college education or better compared with 29 percent for the state. The largest ethnic groups represented are Caucasian and Japanese.

In comparison with the average, it is interesting to see the profile for industry management. Fifty-eight percent of managers are male compared with the female domination of the industry, and 47 percent are Caucasian as opposed to 31 percent among non-management employees. This is the highest percentage of Caucasians of any occupational group in the visitor industry. Nineteen percent of managers have a Japanese background and 12 percent are Hawaiian.

Immediately prior to the State Tourism Study, William Dickie Merrill, a well-known Honolulu architect, completed an especially useful doctoral study at the University of Edinburgh.[42] His thesis, Hotel Employment and the Community in Hawaii, analyzed the impact the hotel industry had on employment and surrounding communities especially on neighbor islands. Up to this time the industry had used what they considered a reliable rule of thumb to estimate the job impact of new hotel rooms. When the thesis was read it caused some consternation among industry officials and planners. "The basic thing that was important was that the assumption always has been that each hotel room produced 1.77 jobs per room," said the late Dr. Thomas Hamilton, then chairman of the Governor's Tourism Planning Advisory Committee. "You could do a lot of projecting on that basis. This begins to screw up the projects—but good."[43]

What Merrill showed was that using neighbor islands as a model, 100 hotel rooms created about 76 hotel jobs of which 34 were primary jobs sought by heads of households and the remainder secondary jobs employing spouses of household heads working elsewhere, dependent children, and other household members. Merrill's classifications of jobholders, not jobs, used primary to mean the primary source of support for a household; secondary meant that the income from the job in that family was supplementary. It could be the principal income for the individual but not the main source for the family.[44] Based on 1973 examples of seven neighbor island hotels, the 34 heads of families with primary jobs supported 84 persons altogether and the 42 secondary jobs benefited 156. In summary then, 100 rooms did not provide the pattern of hotel jobs previously imagined, only 76 distributed in a quite unexpected manner but nevertheless benefiting, in all, 240 persons.

The findings probably helped account for the overestimate of predicted Kona population in the hotel construction years 1960–1970. It also has a very useful application: "If the local labor supply is inadequate and the importation of labor is necessary, only those who could—and would—support themselves as householders by this employment will be attracted to the area as new residents. Secondary beneficiaries would retain their present place of residence: they would be either prior residents of the community or commuters living in households of another person elsewhere. In any event these secondary beneficiaries would not increase the community populations or the demand for services although as an indirect effect, the increased community income might produce a demand for improved services.[45] With changing population distribution, high rentals, and constraints placed on new hotels to provide employee housing or to employ only those with accommodations in the area the situation could have changed from the time the study was done. An update would be valuable.

What Merrill provided were new insights into the dynamics of employee-community relations. And in the light of the tourism plan he underscored the complexities and logistics of matching up job-generating room growth with the people who are supposed to fill those jobs and for whom hotel growth, especially on neighbor islands, is being encouraged. There is of course the essential relationship between primary jobs and the provision of on-site employee housing—sometimes not popular because even when produced close to cost, it is still too high for most purchasers—and the added road congestion contributed to by holders of secondary employment who choose to live elsewhere and commute. Today, with the high price of gasoline, if jobs are available in town, hotel jobs remain vacant in some resort areas.

Education and Learning

The activity of tourism as I perceive it is comprehensive. It affects every major facet of Hawaii life. It is so complex and little known that the small amount of space I can devote to knowing about tourism is in no way commensurate with its importance. If there is one aspect that represents a glaring deficiency in the overall activity I would point to public lack of knowledge. I would say that every group in every area should learn more about it. I would extend the message to industry managers, visitors, agents, and wholesalers on the mainland and in foreign countries. If we could achieve just part of what I consider the ideal, the people of Hawaii and the industry would have done each other a very great service.

When I refer to tourism education my concern includes everything relevant: research, professional education, general education through the schools, public enlightenment, and the flow of tourist or tourism-related information in any form.

Much has been written about tourism and tourists by the university, banks, Hawaii Visitors Bureau, and government researchers. Most contributions are mentioned in the notes and the bibliography of this book. Some long overdue work has now been done on research priorities. Although a good start has been made, many problems of a specific nature need still to be studied. I would like to see joint projects conducted by academic researchers and industry officers who could bring to the study practical insights often not within the grasp of an institutional researcher.

Professional training concerning the visitor industry is of course necessary and this is given at the University of Hawaii School of Travel Industry Management, community colleges, and, in certain areas, by the Hawaii Visitors Bureau and the City and County of Honolulu. It is understood that facilities are adequate for the future planned needs. Further information on the topic can be gained by referring to the Hawaii Tourism Study and the State Tourism Plan.

One of the most important contributions which could be made would be to design an integrated course which would extend from the elementary school level to university. This could be achieved under the rubric of established programs and disciplines but better still would be a total approach, an interdisciplinary view of development, tourism, and a host of related activities and their impacts.

This course of studies would constitute a regular part of the curriculum, not presented for a special occasion, not financially supported by the industry, not a contentious issue such as faced parents on Maui in 1976,[46] not prepared to aid a special interest but an honest critical approach to a topic basic to the state. Despite its initial reception in Maui, the Hawaii Visitor Industry Council's program is making a modest contribution but not in the manner or with the emphasis I believe is essential.

Public Information

Although it may be impossible to teach many of the four million visitors much about Hawaii, its lands, manners, and customs (the plan with admirable determination says it must be attempted), it is essential that the 1980s move toward greater dissemination of public information. Much information about tourism is already collected. A worthwhile project would be to turn some of the state material into readable book form for the public, colleges, and high schools. Basic data have already been collected; only more extensive interpretations and the identification of problems would be needed.

Radio and television might be encouraged to present thoughtful public affairs programs on tourism, and all newspapers, especially those on neighbor islands, could contribute through series of worthwhile, well-balanced articles. Hawaii residents live among a plethora of industry newspapers and promotional materials, so much so that it must be difficult to distinguish between fantasy and reality.

Informational workshops to engender debate among the public would be invaluable. There have been valuable workshops and others with great potential which seemed to end disappointingly. Often early public meetings about the State Tourism Plan were failures in terms of attendance. Not all were like this nor do they have to be. In 1977 Maui County ran a day-long forum on the visitor industry entitled "Maui's Future: Choice or Chance."[47] Held in the ballroom of the Hotel Intercontinental Maui, it attracted 350 persons. Although there was minimal controversy and almost nothing concerning some of tourism's less attractive impacts, it was nevertheless a model which could readily be followed in the future. The Maui forum provoked superlatives like "terrific," "superb," "outstanding" describing talks by a number of government, university, and industry leaders. Despite the careful course it appeared to plot, more than anything else it acknowledged that the public had a right to know in detail—even if they were not told—about what had taken place in Maui's tourism and what might be in store for the community.

Another most important aspect of public education is the training of leaders to act as community spokespersons who would help train others all of whom could present a community side to industry and government. Both the state and the counties, I feel, have a deep responsibility to assist public groups to participate more fully in the planning and management of tourism. The days should be over when haphazard and disorganized statements are made by local organizations which have been thrown together for the occasion or assembled with the minimum of preparation for a particular crisis situation. Elsewhere I have discussed the strengths and inadequacies of community groups. Each county with state or federal assistance should be prepared to set up a participating community council or consortium of public interest groups each with a small full-time supporting staff with access to the mayor, councillors, committee chairmen, the planning commission, legal advice, and, especially, relevant information. Where expertise is lacking, the staff could obtain experience through internship programs with the industry and with private county or state planning organizations. In each county the staff would work with a specially appointed community planner. What is suggested takes the

Oahu neighborhood boards several steps further and applies this concept of representation to all counties and to the state.

The new organization 1,000 Friends of Kauai already discussed fills some obvious gaps. It takes as its model the 1,000 Friends of Oregon which has assumed the role of watchdog of state and local government activities. This in many ways is commendable as is the development of a high degree of professionalism which is characteristic of the Oregon organization; but, nevertheless, the principle of confrontation is still central to activities. In the past a community group may have achieved something through confrontation but not as much as they may have achieved if other strategies were possible.

A community council would provide the third side of a triangle, the other sides of which would be represented by the county and the industry. There is no reason why a community council should not be equipped to make as polished and professional a presentation as a developer or his consultant planning firm at a public hearing. The confrontation this might suggest should not be necessary as a common practice. I have already said that I feel developer and council should work in close cooperation with minimum friction. I believe the community council should be part of this working group presenting community views to both the county and the developer early so that problems can be ironed out before public hearings are begun, ideally during the initial planning stages. The county would represent the people in a more formal manner, supervise the process, and attend to the law. Developer and community would then be more on an equal footing than ever before in an atmosphere of cooperation.

A state community council would be available for appropriate tasks including the supplying of membership to governor's committees or to a tourism advisory council. This would be completely in keeping with state views as they have developed through the 1970s.

Existing groups, radical or conservative, would not be superseded but would be expected to make an input to community councils which would then research topics, gather information, and take grass roots views further to a forum where they would be, as a matter of course, discussed seriously. The thrust of this suggestion is to provide a representative group made up of persons of worth and substance reflecting the community and recognized by both the counties and the state. The industry is adequately represented on major committees and at two levels of government by its own organizations. Other than through normal channels of elected officials who may be out of touch with specific public re-action to immediate tourism issues and through public appointees, the community has no viable voice which both government and the industry can respect. It should have.

The cooperation I am suggesting between various groups will be difficult. Channels of communication may not be easy to devel-op while marked disparities in perception exist between various influential groups. With effort these can be overcome. Miracles are not accomplished by education alone or by allowing every group to have its finger in the pie. Sensible compromises will have to be worked out at every stage.

A recent survey of the views of decision makers (from govern-ment and industry), influentials (from the news media and non-tourism business leaders), and observers (from community service groups and the university) showed that vast perceptual differences existed between these groups even when the mission was merely to ascertain research priorities for Hawaii tourism.[48]

All groups felt that the major question for research was an anal-ysis of the tourist dollar as it flows through the economy in terms of how much remains in the economy and who is affected. Other important questions on which there was agreement concerned the feasibility of alternative futures for tourism in Hawaii, the necessi-ty for greater knowledge of the costs and benefits of tourism to the government and to the economy, tourism's need for land and its effects on nearby land use, the necessity of knowing more about resident attitudes to the industry, and the importance of finding out how residents' attitudes affect visitors.

The items in which decision makers had much greater interest tended to be items specifically oriented to the tourist industry: Hawaii's image in attracting visitors and its effect on visitor satis-faction; needs and deficiencies of employee training programs; in-formation capable of being used to predict visitor arrivals; threats to the aloha spirit; and an analysis of government revenue and spending at various stages of tourism growth.[49]

Less important items to decision makers were changes in urban-ization and population patterns resulting from tourism, tourism's effect on the price of real estate and the cost of living, the impacts of tourism on the distribution of income, the effects of tourism on in-migration patterns, and an analysis of which types of residents get which types of jobs.

It is obvious that the accommodation of disparate views as

hinted at in the survey would be a barrier which would have to be overcome in developing easy communication between groups. This is important as the state appears to wish to move toward wider community involvement in tourism. Decision makers who responded surprisingly took a short-term view of some of the state's major problems, some of which—urbanization, in-migration, crowding, and high costs of living—if they get out of hand can have a substantial long-term impact on the industry.

Programs such as those outlined would at least go some of the way to insure an aware public, an understanding government, and an enlightened industry in years to come. This is how I believe cooperation and preservation of the aloha spirit are achieved. Every individual and every group is then prepared to make a worthwhile contribution to the state's major activity. They are then prepared to promote, to regulate, to encourage, to create, to participate, or to slow—whatever is appropriate for the times.

Some see the present situation in terms of the interaction between a fairly knowledgeable and deeply interested group and the rest who must be taught to smile, to appreciate, and to understand what is being done for them. As one industry spokesman described it to me, "This is the industry of Hawaii and the sooner they know what puts the bread on their tables the better." This reflects frustration but it can be a dangerous, nonproductive attitude which may be all too prevalent.

The Foreign (Out-of-State) Component in Hawaii Tourism

Japan and Canada are two foreign countries that contribute to Hawaii tourism. Japan far surpasses Canada and has significant hotel or development investments in every county. Canada comes in a much less important second with investments in several hotels and condominiums mostly on the island of Maui. Individual Canadian investment in condominium units is unknown and could be high.

"Foreign" in this section's title means different things to different people. Here I take a cue from Governor Ariyoshi when in 1973 he testified to a congressional committee as follows: "When we at the State level speak of foreign investment, we're talking about all kinds of capital wherever it may come from whether it be the mainland or foreign countries."[50]

This being so let's look at the ownership of hotels in Hawaii. For most of the 1960s and 1970s, as the result of energetic foreign activity, it was assumed by many members of the public that most hotels were owned by interests outside Hawaii. Names like Sheraton, Hilton, Holiday Inn, Westin (formerly Western International), and Hyatt seemed to dominate the scene. With close to 6,000 rooms, Sheraton does manage the most rooms; but management and ownership have to be clearly defined. The above corporations tend to be contract managers for separate owners and of the ten which Sheraton manages, seven belong to Kenji Osano of Japan. In a 1972 series of articles concerning ownership of Hawaii's tourism plant, Bob Krauss said that the orders for Sheraton came out of Boston just as those for Holiday Inn originated from Memphis; but within a few years of the statement, one could have said with equal validity that Sheraton in Hawaii also receives instructions from Kokusai Kogyo Co. (the personal conglomerate of Kenji Osano) and Ohbayashi-Gumi Ltd. of Japan as well.[51]

It was perfectly true that rapid changes had taken place. Not only were Japanese-owned hotels found on all islands but also large tracts of land bought for resorts existed on Maui and the Big Island. Investment did not end here. Japanese also owned golf courses, real estate and development companies, travel organizations, and restaurants. A 1974 listing of foreign investments in Hawaii names thirty-seven Japanese corporations operating in the area of development, hotels, real estate, and golf course operations. There were fourteen restaurant companies and seventeen in the travel business.[52] A later survey shows fifteen investors in hotels with assets of $249 million and sixty-one in real estate with a total of $176 million. A 1981 *Hawaii Business* listing shows fifteen hotels, some of the best known in Hawaii, now under Japanese ownership in Waikiki.[53] All tourism-related investments make up something more than a third of Japan's $1.8 billion invested in Hawaii.[54] Total foreign investment in Hawaii is estimated at $3 billion.[55]

But how to ferret out ownership is difficult indeed. In his article, Bob Krauss tried to answer the question why "from 50 to 80 percent of Hawaii's tourist industry is owned and controlled by interests outside the state, why is so much of the largest industry under absentee ownership?" "Jaca" Simpson of the Hawaii Visitors Bureau noted that "when you talk in terms of major components of our tourist industry, I'd say 70 to 80 percent is a reasonable estimate for outside ownership."[56]

Dr. Thomas K. Hitch of the First Hawaiian Bank remarked that it was extremely difficult to determine ownership. "The picture is always changing. You read in the paper that Sheraton has bought the Matson hotels. Then you read that ITT bought Sheraton. In the meantime Kenji Osano has bought three Sheraton hotels. But Sheraton not Osano is running them. How can you tell who is doing what to whom?"[57]

At the end of 1978 an analysis of the ownership of hotels showed the out-of-state ownership situation had not worsened over six years if indeed the earlier estimations had any foundation.[58] Of the total number of hotel rooms in Hawaii, it was determined that 55 percent were owned by Hawaii interests (table 12); about one-fourth of the rooms were owned by mainland owners; the remainder, about 8,200, were owned mainly by Japanese, but the situation is not quite as clear-cut as it seems. Some of the Hawaii hotel firms had out-of-state stockholders as did some hotel-owning Hawaii huis. The analysis also pointed out that "large mainland insurance companies held mortgages in a number of Hawaii's hotels both locally and foreign-owned."[59] Having completed something of a circle we are now back to Dr. Hitch's "who is doing what to whom."

A condominium market specialist quoted in the same analysis estimated that out-of-state ownership of Waikiki condominiums is 60 percent, on the neighbor islands probably closer to 80 percent.[60]

Ten years after the first wave of foreign buyers of hotels started in 1963, Robert and Emily Heller were commissioned to investigate foreign investments.[61] The Heller Report, using 413 respon-

TABLE 12. *Ownership of Hawaii*
Hotels, 1978

Location of Owners	Percent
Hawaii	55.0
Mainland U.S.A.	23.9
Japan	17.0
Canada	1.2
Hong Kong	1.1
Korea	.8
Taiwan	.5
Unknown	.5
TOTAL	100.0

SOURCE: First Hawaiian Bank, 1978.

dents, indicated that most people in Hawaii did not welcome
future Japanese investment (48 percent against, 38 percent for)
though previously it had been acceptable (45 percent approved,
39 percent disapproved) to a point.

Two years after the report an attempt was made to verify what
appeared to be the feelings of Hawaii's residents. The new research used a sample five times the size of the original.[62] It did indeed show that a plurality of respondents felt past investment had
done the state "good," only 25 percent felt past performance
"bad." The bulk of respondents (71 percent) felt future investment
should be attracted from the mainland. Almost a majority felt that
it was still important to attract some investment from truly foreign
sources.[63]

Almost a quarter of respondents did not want to encourage foreign investment. Another group of similar size would have investment only in areas like scientific research and aquaculture which
are largely unattractive to foreign investors. Together these two
groups accounted for half the respondents. Only 10 percent suggested hotels as an appropriate place for investment. Respondents
seemed to be saying in a roundabout way that although they felt as
a result of their backgrounds they might be expected to welcome
investment, deep down they did not really want it.

A most interesting issue relevant to this study was control although in most questions it was never clear whether "foreign"
used with control meant "mainland" as well. For this reason the
published survey's effectiveness was diminished. Nevertheless, an
overwhelming proportion of respondents, close to 90 percent, required some control of foreign investment. A third would forbid
investment in land and as many would prohibit investment in critical industrial activities. Other groups, not going as far as prohibition, insisted that in both land and business investments local people have more than a 50 percent voice.

I found this a fascinating study not so much for what it told me
about foreign investment, but for what it told me about residents'
attitudes to outsiders and their willingness to institute controls
when their resources were at stake. Obviously people do not feel
secure with outside intrusion and in this I do not exclude the mainland. They meet it with certain acceptance, yes, but by no means
with complete satisfaction.

About the same time, the Japanese government and numerous
Japanese business organizations were concerned about the invest-

ment exuberance of their nationals. Because of this they instituted a set of guidelines—preferred behavior for overseas entrepreneurs.[64] The Ministry of Foreign Affairs also let the Japanese business world know about the "delicate change in the way Hawaii's public sector perceives the Japanese influence . . . increased Japanese capital . . . and an influx of Japanese tourists."[65]

But as soul searching was taking place in two dissimilar parts of the Pacific, Japan was hit by an OPEC-induced energy crisis in which the country's surplus balance of payments could be wiped out overnight by the cost of imported oil. "To conserve foreign exchange [Japan] decreed that overseas investments in the real estate, tourist, and leisure fields would have to be approved on a case-by-case basis. Membership in Hawaii golf clubs was banned and exportable holiday money for tourists was reduced from $3,000 to $1,500 (ample for a vacation at tour rates). [Hawaii] legislators, who were spending a lot of their time in gas lines, were content to believe that the Arabs had dammed the [investment] *tsunami* and that the issue was dead."[66]

Suddenly the Japanese incursion into Hawaii was slowed and, with relief, legislators felt it would now be unnecessary to pursue the matter further. The threat seemed to be over. Scale and rate of development, two important psychological elements in tourism, diminished, but the Japanese still remained. By 1980 the Japanese government amended its foreign exchange regulations making it easier for individuals to own property abroad but by then exceptionally high interest rates and a sluggish economy seemed to signal to all but huge corporate investors to "wait and see."[67]

Since the initial flurry of concern, further research has been conducted which suggests that there is insufficient evidence to indicate "that Japanese investors control the passage of their countrymen through Hawaii." In addition, of the five thousand jobs available in foreign-owned hotels virtually all are held by permanent residents of Hawaii.[68]

By 1981 a consensus of influential people whose views I read or to whom I listened seemed to be that foreign investment was good for Hawaii and even if it were not, nothing could be done to change it. In a somewhat defeatist manner it indicated that ultimately land would be owned by the very rich and those not rich and wanting some would have to migrate to the mainland. Virtually all informants ignored the unbelievable social consequences of such a proposition. Canada's predicament today in its desire to control its resources and consequently its destiny, should be an object lesson to Hawaii and a hint of how the state could be thinking tomorrow. Real concern for the future would see the entire question analysed and evaluated now, not only in economic terms but also in a social and political context.

The Japanese Tourist

Just as the beginning of Japanese investment constituted a trend in Hawaii tourism still continuing so too did the increasing flow of Japanese tourists. Today, with a sluggish economy at home, approximately half a million (570,000 in 1980) Japanese tourists arrive annually in Hawaii. This represents almost 15 percent of the state's total. Over a ten-year period, 1968–1978, Japanese visitors registered an average 26 percent annual increase. This is the highest rate of growth for any group, just ahead of Canada. This strong eastbound flow—together with Canadians—provided a valuable buffer against the declining volume of westbound tourists experienced in late 1979 onward. But by May 1980 Japanese tourists too were feeling the economic pinch and ended the year with a decline of 1.6 percent over the previous year.[69]

The Japanese tourist has a specific unique character: 99 percent stay in hotels, a very large number are in their twenties with the bulk between twenty and forty, males outnumber females and over 88 percent of them are part of tour groups.[70] Unlike mainlanders they have a relatively short vacation in Hawaii, four nights and five days mainly on Oahu. Two-thirds of them visit neighbor islands for a very short period of one or two days, and of all the islands Kauai, which 72 percent visit, is far and away the favorite.[71]

An exceptional characteristic of Japanese tourists is their capacity to spend—$213 per day in comparison with $77 for mainlanders.[72] They enjoy traveling in groups, the conventional mode at home, probably because for almost 80 percent of them this is their first trip to Hawaii, and for many of them to a foreign country where both culture and language are different. They are avid picture takers and when they are not traveling for a quick look at a neighbor island, they are single-mindedly shopping, mainly in Waikiki. They outspend mainland visitors on clothes, gifts, and souvenirs almost six to one on a daily basis and their total expenditure exceeds longer staying mainlanders by almost three times. It is estimated that their contribution to the $2.2 billion (1978) spent by visitors in the state could well be in excess of $400 million.[73]

An important contribution to high spending is the homeland custom of *omiyage*, an obligation to bring back gifts to friends, relatives, and neighbors. Japanese travel mainly as couples, are particularly quality conscious, and purchase expensive items for their own use. For some these tend to be items from European designers—Cardin, Gucci, Dior, and Givenchy. For the neighbors and relatives they bring back lower-priced articles: macadamia nuts, Hawaii perfume, candy, papaya, and pineapples. The high-priced items cost perhaps $400 or $500 but may be half the price of similar goods at home. The high value of the yen and the custom of paying semiannual bonuses mean that the traveler arrives in Hawaii with the will and most certainly the cash with which to buy.[74]

Considerable sums of money are spent at Honolulu's number one retailer to Japanese tourists, the Netherlands Antilles-owned Duty Free Shoppers Ltd. This is one of a number of places to which it is said every Japanese visitor is subtly directed by tour guides who it is alleged are rewarded for their work. They patronize a number of retailers attuned to their tastes and pattern of buying and would-be competitors complain that it is an extremely tough market to crack. Selling to Japanese is an art so far mastered by a few who doggedly retain their individual positions of strength. Just what exactly a Japanese tourist is worth to Hawaii is hard to evaluate. High-priced gifts bought in Waikiki are nearly always imported, other purchases may be duty free and purchased from a foreign-owned retailer. The leakage factors in these cases must be particularly high. However, heavy spending is likely to offset this possible disadvantage.

Local people and industry representatives are now beginning to understand the complexities of Japanese travel behavior. Each group is by no means identical but there are common threads, knowledge of which makes it easier to accommodate such visitors. Japanese demand quality, are suspicious of discounts, patronize good hotels, book at the upper room rates, but do not complain when complaint is justifiable.[75]

For the older visitor especially, travel is purposeful, not just fun, and this extends even to a game of golf. Market and consequently behavior is many faceted. Japanese travel officials are able to identify special markets with particular interests. These may include bridal couples, senior citizens, office ladies, modern youth, and one labeled "sun and sea plus".[76] Each require different attractions and different treatment by tour officials and local hosts.

Immediate improvements which could be made now in Hawaii would be the inclusion of Japanese explanations at entertainment shows, more Japanese signs and greater numbers of Japanese speakers on hotel front desks. Extensive instruction as well might be given in the use of safety deposit boxes, the danger of carrying too much cash, locking hotel doors and being aware of security in general.[77] Until now the domestic mainland market has dominated Hawaii. A future market with exceptional potential lies with Europe and Asia. To handle this successfully Hawaii must learn to cope with a variety of cultures with considerable skill. The Japanese market is a start. How this is managed will help determine the future.

Tomorrow's Tourism

I believe that in the future, if not all visitors and all residents, then a greater proportion will have an educated awareness and sensitivity toward the interchange of hosts and guests and about the industry which makes this possible. In accommodating these changes together with greater numbers of Japanese, other Asians, and possibly West German visitors, it will be necessary for planners to look beyond the standard resort and its conventional offerings toward a system which can offer culturally and creatively oriented leisure. Orthodox facilities will no longer be sufficient to accommodate the educational, intellectual, and creative needs of cultures very different from those found residing within Hawaii. Changes will have to be made to accommodate new breeds of Americans—the new look we see now will be prominent into the 1980s and there will inevitably be new life-styles emerging. Already the industry has noted the changed patterns associated with Japanese tourists who come despite limited provisions being made for their special needs. It will be up to Hawaii to decide just how far it will change established patterns, but there is no doubt that resorts of the 1960s and 1970s will not be appropriate to the needs of travelers at the beginning of the next century.

Traditional visitors and seasoned travelers will come more often than previously as FITs; however, visitors from new markets in Southeast Asia, the Middle East, China, and perhaps Brazil might well arrive in groups as Japanese do today and will probably continue to do so in the future. Old mainland markets cannot be relied on indefinitely. The industry will have to promote foreign markets, especially Europe, innovatively if Hawaii is still to prosper.

Various forces will be at work. Adam Krivatsy and Peter Sanborn both see a more noticeable concern for environment and resources than ever previously. Sanborn emphasizes too a move toward a greater emphasis on the quality of life.[78] Both people, keen observers, are intimately connected with tourism in Hawaii —Krivatsy with resort design and Sanborn previously with resort management, now with marketing. Krivatsy postulates a two-tier system developing for a time because of inflation, rising costs, and crowding. He feels old-time gracious living, privacy, and elegance will become a thing of the past, remaining only for the declining percentage who can afford the luxury. Persons who are not very affluent demanding a Pacific holiday will get it in an atmosphere of greater austerity than before with prices kept within limits by markedly diminished personal attention. Occupancy rates will be at 90 to 95 percent or higher. The run-of-the-mill holiday will be experienced with a considerable loss of privacy and decreased standards of luxury.

This if it comes about will be a trend which will run counter to the expressed aim of quality made by many tourism managers together with state and county governments. It may in fact run parallel. While Kapalua has seen its future if not immediately as one in which densities can be lowered by constructing fewer buildings of higher value—cottages possibly offered at $1 million each to consumers who can pay and will buy—Waikiki may very well become more automated, more efficient, and less human as suggested—super institutionalized tourism. Once imposed limits have been reached at Waikiki, and improvements made upgrading the area, occupancy rates may quickly be in the range suggested. Neighbor islands will cater to a dominantly well-heeled clientele.

Trends toward more control by state and county, concern for coastal lands and for residents' ways of life have already been mentioned but some of these will certainly yield to increased crowding and other pressures already strong on the mainland. Without a doubt the gaps in the neighbor island resort regions will fill up. This is taking place now and will continue into the future as a response to corporate plans and some county direction. The state tourism plan may contribute urgency and an illusion of order but the trend would continue nevertheless.

Already air charters have all but disappeared only to be replaced by scheduled airlines using every possible device to compete with one another. There will be long competitive battles as companies attempt to meet inflation, fare schedules, and high-priced fuels. To combat inflation, the most fuel-efficient design of aircraft will prevail. Whether these will be the largest is yet to be seen. Applications for higher fares will characterize the industry.

In 1978 Raymond Dasmann, talking about the Pacific, saw the fares just about as low as they would go. Then as a result of scarce high-priced fuel, he expected only fare increases in the future. This he felt would screen out lower income tourists and allow tourism to become "a luxury reserved for the 'leisured classes' or those with access to government or business expense accounts."[79]

What Dasmann says for the Pacific could well be heeded in Hawaii knowing full well that in relation to such places as Tahiti or Samoa, Hawaii has outstanding advantages. The more restrictive energy resources become on the mainland and the less dependable private road transport becomes, the greater may be the demand for Hawaii travel. While as the result of continuing gasoline crises minor air routes would perish, Hawaii remains on the major east-west air artery of the Pacific. But as Dasmann sees it, chronic gas shortages and soaring air fares could place a considerable brake on mass tourism as it is now known. This would of course result in marked economic dislocation.

L. W. "Bill" Lane, Jr., chairman of the Pacific Area Travel Association, on the same theme, sees today's energy problem "as the Achilles' heel" of tourism's continued growth.[80] "Energy," he said, "will take a higher percentage of our income" and this without doubt will affect tourism. Other PATA representatives were saying escalating fuel prices could rule out long distance air travel for all but the well-to-do.

What has been said is not idle speculation. Hawaii is already having a taste of what might be in store. In an effort to revitalize the present soft visitor market, Governor George Ariyoshi has proposed a one-time program, "Hawaii 82." This is a $4 million promotion effort toward which the state will provide $200,000 and the remainder will come from the private sector. At the same time it is hoped that a long-term strategy will be devised.

The forces likely to be operating in the future underline the good sense of emphasizing tourism quality over everything else. Those who can pay high air fares can also afford to pay for something first-rate in Hawaii. If we assume a rather extreme scenario of an exceptionally tight fuel situation, private transport would be hit first while available supplies would likely be allocated more readily to essential services and public transport including airlines. Under these conditions, Hawaii would, at least in the short-term benefit from a huge market with few moderately-priced places to go and a well-served trunk route.

There are other forces too needing attention—most notably a markedly changed pattern of United States discretionary spending. Marketing analysts have become particularly attentive to the 35–44 age group frequently with two wage earners, few children, and a passionate interest in leisure pursuits. In 1979 there were 12.2 million families in this bracket with an average family income of $25,000. In 1990 there will be over 18.2 million with a family income approaching $30,000 (1979 dollars).[81] These are the post-World War II baby-boom children. A recent article sees these people as "children of inflation, born with credit cards in their mouths, and oriented to spending rather than saving. They are part of the instant gratification, self-indulgent, 'me' generation which has a taste for high-priced gadgets and little interest in self-denial." The group outspends the average consumer by 50 percent for furniture, 30 percent for appliances, and buys 25 percent of all vans and pick-ups. Tennis, racquetball, and exercise salons are something of an obsession for a group that Louis W. Stern, professor of marketing at Northwestern University, says "wants the outward visible things that say 'I have made it and I want to live comfortably'."[82]

Given reasonable interest rates and accessibility, massive demands for mortgages will be made by the group who will be a major sophisticated affluent group of the 1980s and a potent economic force. Double salaries, high discretionary income, and willingness to spend will make the group ideal visitors to the state. They will continue to come even when air fares are drastically hiked, will spend well, and will likely become a major market for mid-range and more highly priced neighbor island and Waikiki condominiums. Even when volume falls and the cautious say they are staying at home this year, this group will help bolster Hawaii's occupancy rates.

The affluent American public, a product of their times and their culture, many feeling annihilated by an overwhelming boredom and having done everything they feel they can do at home, will keep visiting Hawaii while there is a means of getting there and quality is as good or better than in competitive destinations.

CHAPTER 14

Where Now?

HAWAII has a remarkable array of resources for tourism: climate, beaches, clear water, magnificent coastal scenery, fascinating mountain vistas, open spaces, attractive rural industries, tourism facilities of high quality, a high level of industry expertise, and a friendly, hospitable, interesting multi-ethnic population. Like all resources, these may be preserved, conserved, damaged, and perceived differently by different groups.

Some Human and Political Components of Tourism

The resources listed have at least four kinds of users: the visitors, the tourism managers and investors, the in-migrants, and the old-time well-established resident population. Each has a different ethos and mode of behavior toward resources and a special function in relation to the industry. All contribute to its operation.

The visitors come to Hawaii to enjoy and use the resources and above all—in the eyes of the state and the industry—to spend money. Their relationships are transient in the extreme. The tourism managers run the industry with expertise, marshall the resources necessary for its operation, pay wages, and buy varying amounts of goods and services from local people. Their responsibilities are primarily to local and overseas corporate shareholders (or to themselves as the investors) and to the visitors. The industry-oriented "new public" and the established residential "old public" provide services and derive a significant part of their income from these activities. The old established residents, a vital resource themselves, supply what the industry considers the most vital component of tourism, "aloha spirit." Except for public resource use, no group provides largess to any other. Together the four groups (with financial institutions) make the industry. They are the industry, a fact usually not understood and, by the industry, largely overlooked. It is commonly considered that those with managerial skills or capital to invest are providers of opportunities from which the entire community benefits. There is no doubt about the value of the skills provided or the essential needs for capital for which the investor is rewarded. But in reality all provide portions of a very good tourism operation and all contribute to its strengths and weaknesses. In terms by which tourism is usually judged, Hawaii has something it can be proud of. If the nature of the joint enterprise becomes better understood, tourism in Hawaii can be in an even stronger position.

As a destination area, Hawaii has characteristics which make it quite different from other Pacific island groups. Its political and historical connections create a tropical, exotic, removed, and distant extension of the United States. This is important. It does not have to depend exclusively on world prices for agriculture like other Pacific islands. If the cost of sugar production gets too high, its price is supported by the mainland taxpayer, or regulated by international agreement. Should tourism disappear tomorrow, the island group would still be better off than others in the Pacific. It would still have something no Pacific country has—massive federal spending, not aid, and a higher level of investment. Physically Hawaii has much of what other Pacific islands have—obviously in very attractive proportions—but both agriculture and tourism exist at the present scale and quality only by virtue of their political and social linkages. These vital connections prop up what in the immediate past was a decidedly shaky agriculture and give the state direct access to about the one best tourist market it could have. Its potential, however, is by no means unlimited.

Hawaii then is very different from other places in the Pacific. But a cost is paid for these advantages. In Fiji, for example, with a population of 500,000 people and an area comparable to Hawaii, fewer than one-half its residents has rights to the land. In Hawaii, on the other hand, with a population of around a million, over 220 million people have potential rights to land—rights of unlimited access. Within the span of a lifetime, a large number of those people have the opportunity of visiting the state and with them they bring mainland culture, high technology, and prevailing attitudes to environment and life. As an insular piece of tropical exotica alone in the central Pacific, Hawaii more than pays its dues. If the situation did stop at this point, it might be workable, but it does not. The millions with rights to land similarly have the right to migrate to Hawaii, and there is yet no known appropriate way of stopping them. Left to their own devices and without regulation, they will arrive until such time as the state no longer attracts them. If this were to be the case then the tourist industry would for all intents and purposes, no longer attract tourists, and, possibly any shred of local cultural integrity would have by then disappeared. The possibilities of an unattractive, crowded urban tropical outlier of the United States in the mid-Pacific constitutes a real problem which all in the state must come to grips with now or suffer with later. The islands will remain, the coastal and mountain vistas will remain, but the present jewel as we know it today will have virtually disappeared.

Interrelatedness and Balance

This study attempts to emphasize the comprehensive interrelatedness of virtually all aspects of Hawaii land and life and to draw attention to the fact that a weak or unreliable agriculture is a problem of tourism; that a dissatisfied, resentful public results in poor quality tourism and few sources of finance; that climate, landscape, and soil are as much tourism components as they are essential to aquaculture or macadamia nut farming; that mainland values and local cultures are confusingly intertwined parts of tourism; and that a good visitor industry and its future direction is as much a responsibility of the public as it is of the industry.

Attitudes have wide and important ramifications. The reaction of residents to visitors at Hanalei could affect the income of a tour wholesaler in Long Beach, an article in a magazine such as *Sunset* or *National Geographic* could bring unexpected hundreds to the Waipio Valley, while disrespectful tourists from Chicago could bring discomfort to a family in Lahaina. Each element —landscape, industry, agriculture, open land, clear air and water, local ethnic groups, single individuals, visitors, government, and developers—is a part of the whole. The objective and obligation of the human components are to hold this dynamic ensemble in a precise and rewarding balance so that each part is in a reciprocally sympathetic interrelationship with every other part, allowing each to develop its potential but not to the extent that it impairs the reasonable operation of any other part. This does not come about by osmosis or by propinquity. It is arrived at by good management and full participation; but what is considered reasonable today may not be considered so in a decade.

Balance is an important concept. It suggests an acceptable and healthy proportion which must be maintained. It is important to maintain a satisfactory balance between urban land and rural areas, open land and forest, resort areas and residential districts, used areas and wild lands. Agriculture must always be balanced with tourism to widen the economic base, to help maintain ethnic variety, to preserve the Hawaii way of life, and to maintain open space. A reasonable balance between visitors and residents is essential as is that between local people and recent in-migrants. This is particularly important on islands like Kauai and Molokai where new arrivals could easily overwhelm old residential patterns and destroy the way of life.

Too much development, inappropriate development, development where it is not wanted or where the population is reluctant to increase momentum—the case on Kauai, for example—may very well upset essential balances with undesirable repercussions. The motivation to develop must be balanced against the forces to constrain.

A prevalent belief stemming from a fundamental mainland religious tradition is that man must inevitably transgress, that he is essentially evil, and that he will eventually destroy any aspect of nature or mankind he comes in contact with. Because of this, selfless groups are prepared to act as watchdogs in the interests of good over evil. The actions of persons motivated by this belief, of those having self-serving objectives, and others completely sincere and motivated by a sense of public good need careful analysis.

Developers have frequently been the target for attack, not unjustifiably because of their frightening power to change land and society. By exercising their prerogatives, they are no less and no more virtuous than the environmentalists or others who oppose them. This fact is discussed by Bernard Frieden in his book, *The Environmental Protection Hustle*. In this context one must question the validity of those who would prevent development at all costs (often "gangplankism") as much as one should question those who, without being guided by local residents, approve major development projects in sparsely populated rural areas.[1] And by doing so, as an exercise in power or for personal gain and against the wishes of the people, create the potential for great urban enclaves which could degrade both landscape and society. This is not an argument against development per se but an argument for the very careful study of any development creating major in-migration and leisure-oriented urbanization in an area where the people have not been thoroughly consulted or have not given their approval. Long and thorough consultation is essential. The ceremonial public hearing as mandated by law is not enough.

Conflicting Values and the Regulation of Tourism

This leads naturally to another balance which is yet to be worked through in Hawaii—that between individual freedom and public good. Both are encouraged within the context of American values but one is frequently incompatible with the other. Hawaii is too precious a collection of resources to allow the state to become a battleground for conflicting forces. The stakes for each force are high. Yet without the moderating influence of a more neutral regulation, a few interests will be served while the majority may be ignored.

A number of individual developers operate in a dualistic framework combining with consummate skill the ability to create and the ability to conserve.

Former Maui Mayor Elmer Cravalho understood probably better than many politicians the potency of conflicting elements and the delicate balance that must be maintained between the maintenance of life and quality on one hand and innovative entrepreneurship on the other. One man alone can be a tempering force as he was, but it would be folly to put all one's faith in a political leader just as it would be folly to rely on the good sense of disparate groups. In this regard, judiciously providing direction and facilitating a participatory management is a proper function of government.

Within American society there is an abhorrence of control equated with unnecessary government interference, yet there is reverence for government-enacted law. In crises, people expect control. In adversity, government interference is accepted, sometimes demanded, as Lockheed, Chrysler, and the railroads know. The pursuit of activities with minimum hindrance but with government protection when appropriate relates closely to two sets of American values—freedom and individualism on the one hand and democracy and equality on the other. When individualism gets out of hand, government and law may intervene to prevent damaging impacts to members of society, or to contain one group in the interests of another and thus establish, to a degree, equality of treatment. Individualism usually means inequality, especially economic inequality. It is this conflict between equality and inequality, this inherent incompatibility between democracy and individualism which is at the heart of the situation in Hawaii today. Henry Steele Commager puts it this way:

> Americans do not want economic equality . . . and present a fascinating paradox . . . They have a passion for political and social equality plus a passion for individualism. And individualism, as Americans see it, is not compatible with democracy. For democracy means equality, individualism inequality. The average American, I think we can say, is in favor of equality for everyone but himself . . . he doesn't want equality for his children, he wants to send them to Harvard . . . he doesn't want equality in income for himself, he wants to make more money. Individualism is leaving the door as wide open as possible to each individual to go as far as he can.[2]

Herein lies a great dilemma. In Hawaii the door has been left wide open. In going as far as he can, the venturesome individual finds his path impinging on the lives of others and impacting on the land about him. More and more persons, some in high places, are clammering to have the door closed at least a little—not to inhibit the individual but to circumvent those cases where he may inhibit others. Almost everyone concerned with any aspect of development would say that leaving the door wide open endangers scarce and precious resources and impairs quality. The question then is not open versus closed, as some persons may interpret this statement, but "how far closed?"

There are other forces also in conflict across the United States. Two of these are discussed by Walter Karp and described as "republican virtues" and "the cult of the nation" (sometimes confusingly referred to as "neo-conservatism" although this term seems to have a variety of meanings depending on the perceptions of the user).[3] They are paradigms whose shared values lead to two distinct Americas, two contrary codes which conflict at many points. "The republic," says Karp, "is the great central fact of American life." It is the constitution of liberty and self-government—Jefferson's energizing principle, a constantly alert antagonist of oligarchy, special privilege, and arbitrary power. It preserves and perfects self-government, secures for each citizen an equal voice in government, and provides for honest political utterances. It was the protective umbrella under which men and women of diverse cultures, without having to assume patriotic symbols of the country of adoption, could be proud of their backgrounds while simultaneously being true to the spirit of the American republic. One's loyalty was not judged by the extent of one's cultural assimilation. There was in fact no need to be molded to the will of a nation.

Against this, during a half century from the 1890s to the 1940s, a hollow devotion to the "nation symbol" developed. Other symbols, a flag for example, assumed as much importance as the maintenance of a founding creed. The "cult of the nation," Karp says, "exalts the repressive virtues of wartime." It cloaks with patriotic ardor its hostility toward the virtues of a republic at peace. The true "nationist," he indicates, in the interest of "complete internal peace" forgoes the exercise of liberty to speak, to act, and to voice independent judgment. The absence of internal turbulence and ferment, its followers believe, strengthens the nation in the performance of its international duties which are often more important than those at home. To question authority weakens the nation. It is well to heed the mode and not rock the boat. Mutual respect is replaced by polarization. To the "nationist" preservation of the "republic" is seditious, un-American. It is more admirable to submit to the rule of the few than to maintain an endless struggle for self-rule. The search for the republic is a search for fundamentals; the cult of the nation is the religion of patriotism, the pursuit of symbols, images, and the consecration of the state above everything else.[4]

Karp's views, somewhat oversimplified and summarized in two paragraphs, offer two models—many realities exist somewhere in between. The point here, however, is that the two forces provided the components of a context in which Hawaii became a state and in which development occurred. During the period of greatest change, as Hawaii the state was finding its feet and through the 1970s, "nationism" became for many an easy substitute for the difficult-to-maintain "republicanism." Whereas under "republicanism" alone a greater respect might have been paid the needs of local people, their way of life, their different cultural backgrounds, and their rights to participate, this did not come about in the way it might have. The struggle for survival in the face of cultural and economic submergence from outside was made more difficult.

"Nationism" in its various grades and guises and admixtures represents shared assumptions. People are not necessarily black or white, neo-conservative or republican. Some may be, but most draw attitudes from both poles. The forces or models are there, however. Other than the elements discussed above, nationism includes a greater-than-normal emphasis on individualism, a strong defense, the rights of property holders, free enterprise with no government control or interference, and the unassailable superiority of the mainland way of life. As a corollary, fuzzy questions such as social welfare, ethnic or indigenous rights, programs for those on lower incomes, women's rights, and affirmative action tend to receive low priorities and sometimes little more than passing attention. Unfortunately, within this general paradigm, respect for the environment, conservation of the Hawaii way of life, and the maintenance of cultural values are classified similarly: not quite the lowest priority but certainly not the highest.

In the previous chapter I drew attention to a new market made up of young-to-middle-aged, two-wage earner, no-children families to whom attaining material desires is the primary goal. Christopher Lasch in his *The Culture of Narcissism* discussed this group in a fascinating way.[5] The group saw its greatest development in the 1970s. Personal fixation on awareness, self-absorption, and various degrees of narcissism, Lasch argues, stems from "the dangers and uncertainties around us and a loss of confidence in the future. The poor have always had to live for the present, but now a desperate concern for personal survival, sometimes disguised as hedonism, engulfs the middle class as well."[6] This is a new cultish overlay not as significant as the more fundamental modes already discussed but nevertheless a contemporary phenomenon portrayed in Hawaii by residents and visitors alike. Their attitude to life insulates them against the social problems which propelled them toward this frame of mind in the first place—poverty, racism, injustice, and so on—all of which are neatly dodged in their centripetal world. These are not people from whom thoughtful action can be expected; they are significant only as a growing group unlikely

to work toward an improved situation in Hawaii. Although a resigned and growing self-indulgent group on the mainland makes
an extremely useful tourism market, in Hawaii as residents "a society that fears it has no future is not likely to give much attention
to the needs of the next generation."[7]

Taking this further, Henry Fairlie sees this not in its trivial "me
decade" form, but as a fundamental long-building change reflecting the absence of any concerted public stance against the current
absorption with self, a manifestation of uncurbed individualism.[8]
Associations of family, church, and union which historically
checked excesses to provide the self-restraint of self-government
have not done so. Nothing was done to encourage wider obligations to offset the superficially attractive pursuit of personal interest; individual indulgence promoted by the media did not help.
The present national preoccupation with individualism Fairlie
sees as cyclic, but also a situation which at present reduces "political and national authority . . . to making unrelated compromises
with narrow, shifting, trivial, self-absorbed claims of relatively
well-to-do people who have little care for the past or the future and
not much more for the present."[9] The implications here are that
although all conditions described may not be applicable to
Hawaii, several most certainly are. In addition, taking special care
that the state and the counties focus on the fundamental picture
rather than on trivial or self-serving activities would be wise indeed.

I have discussed forces which tend to restrict or defuse advocacy. The popular advocate who often comes from a peripheral
tradition persists while being frequently treated as a person of limited consequence. Because people operate in paradigms—if you
don't share my assumptions wholeheartedly you must belong to
the other group—and because legislators, other decision makers,
and the industry managers are largely from the same tradition, an
unfortunate pattern is set: how can one group bring pressing problems to another group to take action upon when each group wears
blinders? It is also a courageous person who would appear to criticize the system into which he or she has been systematically social-
ized. This is speaking out, not revolution. The combination of attitudes all but stifles the development of a viable and respected
voice raised on behalf of all people and the environment in relation to tourism activity.[10] Those who speak out on behalf of all
people, in an area where decision makers are certainly not rad-

icals, run the risk of being classified as such. The speaker and the reactors become enmeshed in a situation where symbol and reality are inextricably confused. Advocacy of conservation or, retention of a way of life may end in the speaker being branded anti-development or radical. The concept of radical is then immediately associated with a mode of dress, a way of life, a system of morals, and a weakening of security and the American way to the extent that no matter how worthy the topic, its impact is nullified by the patterned thinking on the part of those who could do much to help if they could only see beyond the paradigm. Breaking down the paradigms in the interests of a better quality of life for all including quality within the visitor industry is a major priority for Hawaii today. Again this is a function of attitudes and education or education and attitudes—hardly resolvable when one always affects the other. The pressing overarching problem is to raise priorities concerning tourism and its impacts in and on all groups. As time goes by, this becomes increasingly difficult to do.

Elsewhere I have talked about the values and aspirations of local people. Not that I believe that these are the antitheses of mainland values or that they are homogeneous or uniform within Hawaii, but they can be seen as having enough common threads to be able to speak of a local way of looking at things, coping with life, and viewing the world. The industry readily recognizes a part of this distinctiveness which it identifies as being the very special aloha spirit. But it is very obvious too that local well-established residents (other than those whose roots are on the mainland) live in two worlds—one a creation of the founding ethnic groups, the other cultivated and imposed, associated with the mainland connection. Under such circumstances is it little wonder that at times local people exhibit a high degree of ambivalence revering Hawaii custom on the one hand, while enthusiastically seeking patterns of behavior and mainland symbols of affluence which are believed will give them a truly American stamp. A local person may operate in the two modes simultaneously, may espouse each alternately when the occasion demands, or may cast his lot entirely with one or the other. Whatever is chosen is never comfortable and a greater or lesser degree of discomfort is aroused with the realization that the essence of local integrity and authenticity—which alone is his—appears to become less each decade.

My purpose here is not to say this should not be. It is as it is. Choices have been made. But mainland values are extremely potent and the people of Hawaii, who in a number of ways are becoming a minority in their own state, should be given a chance to practice social self-determination while there is something left of their own to revere. I am pointing out the danger of the tyranny of a dominant society, not necessarily an inevitable outcome of tourism but nevertheless a possibility in the presence of thoughtless and relentless tourism.

Direction and Limits

The value dilemma is a tough one. Society, at least the mainland American component in Hawaii, rewards the builders of buildings and the developers of resorts lavishly. While admiring one facet of society, we find ourselves bewailing crowding, pollution, and other ills, all of which result from a number of the activities we rate so highly. Years of imbibing values and reinforcing those already held have told us that such behavior is admirable, it is the American free-enterprise way, it realizes the best in the individual and society, it begets freedom, it provides jobs. In a number of contexts, the above is true. At an earlier period of Hawaii's growth I would have agreed, but there comes a time when development, no matter how economically desirable, comes up against hard physical limitations. This is especially so in a situation where growth is pitted against finite resources, physical and social. It is nowhere truer than in Hawaii. The state is so small one can know every mile of coastline, every beach. One can count them. Where else can Honolulu grow but around the base of every mountain, engulfing good agricultural land in the process? How much more can be built at Waikiki? Oahu, Maui, and the Big Island are hard pressed for water. Every year greater difficulties appear. If problem follows problem with alarming rapidity on Oahu, it will happen too on every other island.

The leading edge of development is in the hands of the entrepreneur who pays lip service to conservation and protection (most people do). But in an attempt to derive the greatest possible profit, the rather thin and shadowy conservation-development ethic may be pushed aside. Limits, the entrepreneur contends, inhibit individuality, impair freedom, infringe rights, encourage bureaucracy, invite corruption. The programmed list can go on interminably. Without doubt it applies to some situations but certainly not to all. Setting limits, like the law, provides a thread of security which everyone inherently feels the need for in a threatening situation. Without them, the life and livelihood of a million residents and the pleasure of four million visitors would be at stake.

Control in one form or another is talked about by every citizens group, every county mayor, the governor, and thoughtful citizens. It has little to do with government interference. There is no guarantee government would not interfere—no reason why it should. This is if interference means unnecessary limitation or the placement of an unnecessary impediment in the pursuit of a legitimate enterprise. It has a lot to do with responsible government activity which, when done properly, will bring a mature response. It is not selling out, not anti-tourism, not radical activism. It is merely invoking, for the benefit of the many who make up Hawaii society, that other very estimable value, democracy, or as previously discussed republicanism, which in this case through law and government will emphasize equality—and equally, quality. It will ensure the right of every resident to share reasonably in the benefits of all resources and will also, if applied correctly, preserve what is considered good and valuable for future generations to enjoy.

The suggestion here is that real regulation wisely using legislation, probably all of which is available, is urgently needed for a healthy sustained total environment and an equally healthy industry. Legislation in Hawaii has come as far as reflecting the good intentions of community leaders and legislators, but good intentions alone without action are never enough. In the past, it seems agencies which might have been able to implement measures decisively were themselves caught up in conflicting forces and pressure brought about by incompatible values. From time to time, the ambivalence of lawmakers allowed blind eyes to be turned to inaction. Yet solid virtues stand as tokens enshrined in various plans and legislation. In the state and counties, it appears that the attitude sometimes has been: "Now that intentions have got as far as legislation, we've done all we need to do and it's business as usual." If tourism in Hawaii is to be at all sustained, such barriers must be overcome. Legislation is there, and it must be applied swiftly and effectively for the long-term economic and social good of the state until changed attitudes make legislative props unnecessary. Within the prevailing economic system, all should be asked to give more attention than has been the case to the public good and, consequently, to the long-term survival of the state. It is time now for thoughtful appraisals and worthwhile decisions.

Awareness, Participation, and Reevaluation

Education and general awareness can do much but they are not a panacea for all ills. If effective, they would allow those who read or listen to the views of well-known conservatives to do the same for equally well-known radicals. It may also go some of the way toward ensuring that future articles in national magazines such as Michael Demarest's frothy Maui feature in the 26 March 1979 issue of *Time* catch just some of the burning issues, treat local people differently from the 1950s stereotypes, give people as much space as "things for visitors to do," and stop regaling readers with ersatz pidgin.[11] His was a good travel article and a marvelous tourism plug for Maui ("the last paradise with panache") but is this as far as we have come? Doesn't Maui have an identity beyond condos and interesting restaurants?

Education will also encourage the media not to brand everything critical as "anti-development." I am fascinated by Hawaii's development. Some things I am enthusiastic about—some things I am against. I have no category for myself for or against. It does not apply. To be polarized to the extent that one can justify applying a label of pro-development or anti-tourism to oneself does not help. Development has been and will be essential to the state's well-being in certain places under certain conditions. In different places and different conditions it could be disastrous. To classify as black or white all such behavior does no good. In fact, it may deter positive action by thoughtful persons. The industry requires useful, critically constructive input from every possible source.

Greater awareness on all sides would go a long way toward removing the emotional cloud surrounding tourism. Many academics, middle-class intellectuals, environmentalists, and liberals are biased against the industry. Industry spokesmen are equally narrow. A middle view may be seen as wishy-washy, yet is an absolute necessity for balance and stability. Greater awareness may also eliminate the industry dictum that criticism projects a bad image. Constructive criticism is the first step toward improving quality.

Much time has already been spent indicating a need for research, public information, teaching, and above all preparing the public for greater managerial participation in an activity in which it is already a major component.

There is a need for a reassessment of all planning goals, for wording plans in a straightforward way, and for going beyond the motherhood statements which seem the penchant of writers for both the state and the counties. There are good reasons for starting from scratch again in counties, but the understanding must be that planning is not merely zoning and a series of ordinances but management in the interest of the citizenry, asking their full participation, not just listening to community suggestions. Ways of achieving this have been discussed earlier and to my mind are of critical importance. It also means establishing critical limits, monitoring changes, evaluating public opinion, assaying social impacts, implementing law, dedicating land to appropriate uses, surveying the impact of taxation, placing hotel or apartment zoned land not in use in a long-term reserve status, considering devices to prevent speculation, and evaluating large-scale and small-scale developments in terms of their overall effects. The list could go on and on.

The County of Maui has so far been highly successful in its tourism endeavors despite limited public participation. In the state with any question which develops into a contest—developers and operators versus the people—the outcome has been traditionally stacked against the people for reasons already discussed. In Maui, a strong and astute mayor took up the cudgels on behalf of the people. An expert manipulator of developers and people, he tipped the balance in such a way that the public felt it benefited from tourism activity. As a result of a greater degree of public confidence in the industry through the mayor, the economy boomed. However, without that specific mayor who resigned in 1979, development could have been in disarray and the results disastrous —or more disastrous than some feel they have been.

The public cannot gamble on similar situations. It must have safeguards and strategies to ensure its views are heard. So that residents as a group can stand on their own feet, I believe the active and full participation of community councils is absolutely essential. With an ever-increasing hotel-condominium capacity and the resources of some areas stressed to the limit, no person or group with limited representation can be allowed to assume alone the huge responsibility involved.

Aloha Spirit

For centuries European and American travelers have admired the Polynesians and, brought up in a tradition of personal restraint, have never concealed their envy of the open, generous, hospitable, less inhibited culture of Pacific islanders. Hawaii is not unique. Here that special character of the Pacific was developed and enhanced by succeeding cultures. The aloha spirit, as it has been called since World War II, before which it was referred to more as aloha, has developed an almost magical mystique especially in the eyes of the industry. To it, aloha spirit is the essence of the best of Hawaii tourism. Eileen McCann O'Brien in a 1946 *Paradise of the Pacific* editorial wrote eloquently as follows: "[The chief fascination of Hawaii] is this blend of races and cultures which has taken place both literally and figuratively within the Hawaiian's Spirit of Aloha as the prompting urge . . . the indefinable aloha of the Hawaiians . . . a gentle, kindly friendliness towards others . . . is a living reality in the islands of Hawaii."

Gavan Daws feels it has been made a commodity of incalculable value to the industry and the HVB and there is no doubt that it has been contrivedly cultivated.[12] Nevertheless it remains acknowledged by all as a component essential to island life and tourism. In insensitive hands it becomes debased. "Our busy season approaches," said one industry spokesman. "Visitors expect the aloha spirit to be dead in Waikiki but it's certainly alive here. It's up to you. Those folks we've invited deserve our aloha."[13] So turn it on and tune it up.

Aloha is nevertheless a factor to contend with. It has its roots in Polynesia but today represents the best of the collective consciousness of the state. Each statement made above has a germ or more of truth to it. It can be exploited and people can be exploited for it. It has two important self-reinforcing aspects—actual displayed characteristics and belief that it is there and exists. If there is one thing above all others that is untrue, then it is the belief aloha can be turned on at will. It cannot. It develops. It is part of a group's integrity and it can disappear. It most certainly will if human dignity and cultural integrity disappear.

It stems from Polynesia, a unique Hawaiian tradition, and the rural areas where numbers of Hawaiians and other ethnic groups lived together; it is helped by new groups identifying with the old simple friendly ways; and it is strengthened by an attractive environment. For the tourist industry, it is an adaptable quality which can be used with respect but never exploited. By many of the thousands of industry employees imbued with high economic expectations of the American dream, it might very well be sustained for personal reasons where otherwise it might have become strained.

The antithesis of aloha spirit is crime and violence perpetrated on tourists and local residents alike. Crime and a lowered aloha spirit go hand in hand. Apologists say that crime is no greater in Hawaii than in other parts of the nation, but such an attitude in a tourist state is decidedly dangerous. Conditions are not the same in Hawaii as elsewhere and no one knows what incidence must be reached before crime competes with a recession or transport strikes in the destruction of a tourist industry and its dependent community. Not a month passes without a major mainland newspaper featuring a documented horror story of crime and tourism in Hawaii. The industry for obvious reasons prefers low profile reporting, and the apologists say it is not really that bad. That is not true. It is bad when beach parks are closed by excessive violence, when local people and visitors fearfully keep clear of a growing number of areas, and when rape, robbery, and murder become commonplace. It is then that a crisis of inestimable proportions, which should have been solved long before, has descended on the industry and the state. Comprehensive remedies, not just police or legislative action then become necessary. The crime problem may be solved but the visitor industry by then may have sustained irreparable damage.

Used wisely, aloha is a resource of exceptional value. It is sensitive, vulnerable, and could readily disintegrate at the hands of industry leaders who do not see its connections with other facets of Hawaii society and economy. For the industry to select preservation of the aloha spirit as a question of the utmost concern while playing down such problems as the cost of living, affordable housing, crowding, psychological stress of tourism, income distribution, and cultural authenticity is folly indeed.[14] It is in fact the outward reflection of the social foundations of tourism, an expression of community well-being. A minimally exploited, respected host group which feels its way of life remains largely intact virtually guarantees preservation of the aloha spirit.

State self-sufficiency, which under the circumstances outlined can never be complete but can be improved, is a worthy and necessary goal for making the tourist dollar go further in the interests of the local community as well as making the state less vulnerable to world and mainland economic conditions. It means the encouragement of local capital to invest in Hawaii, attractive wages so that local labor will stay in the state and will work in the industry; the creation of high value Hawaii-made artifacts which may be able to supplant exotic imports purchased as visitor gifts; the development of every conceivable indigenous source of energy; and the encouragement of diversified agriculture and industry to use resources more fully, to maintain openness, to improve the balance of trade, to decrease the importation of food stuffs, and to broaden the economic base. It could mean for the state the equivalent of greatly increased tourist spending and also more jobs without an associated increase in tourist arrivals, of making the tourism multiplier really multiply. It would also provide a buffer against tourism's vulnerability demonstrated so forcefully in 1979 with United Airlines' strike followed by a grounding of DC-10s, a police strike where tourists were asked to keep off the streets at night, and the manifold implications in Hawaii and throughout the world of skyrocketing petroleum prices.[15] High oil prices not only appreciably increase the cost of travel but also contribute to inflation and tend to lower standards of living within tourism market areas and potential areas. Should there ever be the need for federal allocation of jet fuel with tourism given a low priority, Hawaii's economy could suffer immeasurably.[16]

Along with self-sufficiency there is a need for greater self-appreciation. The industry could be encouraged not only to do more for Hawaiian art and culture through its direct use in entertainment but also through the concrete encouragement of the resurgence of Hawaiian culture which is starting to take place. This is separate from conventional hotel entertainment and embraces the provision of facilities for Hawaiians and all other ethnic groups to participate in cultural growth through industry help. Protection and reconstruction of historical sites and buildings can also enhance local living, increase the authenticity of the visitor's experience, and most importantly impart a greater sense of self-worth to local people.

I cannot separate environmental respect from ethnic respect which is part and parcel of self-appreciation and ecodevelopment. Respect represents an appropriate approach to each area by both hosts and guests. Respect, though, seems too mild; awe might be more apposite. The Hawaii environment has been emphasized in every chapter. It belongs to the people in the same way as culture. It is a Western habit to speak of the two separately. A deterioration of one is as significant as the deterioration of the other; both are inextricably interrelated and both provide much of the essential foundations for tourism. Both deserve more attention by the industry than aloha spirit.

Scenarios and Suggestions

One cannot follow an interest for the time I have without scenarios of the future continually coming to mind.[17] Nobody can say what will be. Here I indicate with reluctance what could be, what some groups would like to see, and realistically what might be.

Scenario 1 follows the model "The system has done well elsewhere so don't interfere with it. Leave it alone. The market works." Left entirely alone, little that was originally Hawaii other than the physical outline and appearance of the land would persist. Remaining spaces in urban classified areas would be filled with haphazard small-scale tourism and construction primarily for investment. There would be great pressure for spot-zoning outside today's resort areas and variances of all types would be commonplace. Mainland values would prevail. Land values would be so high that only the wealthy could afford to buy. Some would see a simplistic division between the privileged and the proletariat. The residue of an Asian-Pacific people would remain in hostile pockets under the shadow of an indifferent majority. There would be corresponding cells of people who would raise voices about environmental and cultural erosion to little avail. At the slightest threat of government interference those who derived most from the economy would vehemently protest that controls only stultify. A part of the work force would be potentially unstable and volatile, and in the interests of security, state or national, provision would be made to stabilize the situation should it show signs of getting out of hand. Others of the public, rather confused and misled, would feel that this was the acceptable free enterprise way leading to high expectations and ultimate fulfillment. Their turn would come eventually. The economy would likely be run in the interest of the few who deserved the remainders' admiration because of their achievements. Many decision makers could end up in the hip pockets of those they should be directing.

The visitor industry would increasingly be promoted at the fastest rate outside constraints would allow. In-migrants would not be discouraged despite the excessive strain they placed on the land. This would, through crowding, lead to dramatic deterioration of the coastal zone especially in the availability of water, the quality of air, and the state of beaches and coastal waters. Resource limitations would be largely forgotten as new people still arrived to compete for jobs still available. Some industry spokesmen would bravely maintain quality was as good as anywhere else in the world. Crime would be exceptionally high and extensive areas of local hostility on all islands would virtually be out of bounds for tourists. As the result of crowding, violence, and an overall decline in quality, tourism would sour. The bad, lacking control, would overwhelm the good and islands of excellence could no longer be maintained by escaping to hideouts away from the rapidly advancing condominium front. Agriculture, strong or weak, would be in a very secondary position. And in the face of high population and a huge growing group of unemployed dependent on the state, Hawaii could ultimately become a cross between Puerto Rico and Florida—with subsidies and large numbers of retirees.

The deficit would be bridged by massive federal grants and in an attempt to encourage further investment and to save corporations left with run-down resorts, further tracts would be opened up for half-acre lots and retirement villages. At best there would always remain pleasant spots in depressed rural areas if one could obliterate from mind what was rapidly becoming an extensive Caucasian-occupied tropical slum in high density urban areas. Great income disparities would exist between the haves and have-nots. Population pressure would be relieved by a migration reversal back to the mainland. Remittance checks from relatives on the mainland, pensions, annuities, federal grants, and greatly lowered visitor spending would be the sources of income. Tourism's vulnerability and its resource base would be such that it could never return to its past high level.

For those living in Hawaii, it may not be as bad as it sounds now. After a long period of socialization to the inevitable, conscious rationalization, and habituation, some people would be prepared to say with a shrug of the shoulders, "Well you can't have progress without some cost and at least we're better off than they are in the Caribbean. Surely beach crowding is no worse than in Southern California."

Scenario 2 would be associated with ambitious education programs at all levels—focusing both on the top and the bottom. Education would stress the fact that healthy tourism needed regulation and wide public participation. Residents would learn that if control means the maintenance of life-style, a good environment, and a quality industry, then in Hawaii it should no longer be a dirty word. While a steady rehabilitation of Hawaii rather than a complete acceptance of mainland values took place, well-supported active lobbying would take place in Washington, exploring then eventually finding ways to amend the constitution in order to regulate in-migration and immigration. Investment for investment's sake, on prime agricultural land or along fine coastal lands would be kept well in bounds. Both state and counties through existing legislation and cooperation would keep a firm check on the environment, water allocation, housing for residents, speculation, inappropriate investment, a desirable level of foreign investment and so on. Diversification in agriculture and industry would be an increasingly important component of the economy. Through the allocation of state and federal lands a compromise would be reached with the Hawaiian community. Educational thrusts would result in extensive changes of attitude in all groups. For many people the state would be a pleasant place in which to live. Development would be desirably slow always allowing time for reevaluation and a change in direction. Higher unemployment may well accompany slower development.

Realistic? Scenario 1 is too horrifying to contemplate but we should. Scenario 2 is possible but under the circumstances and, considering the backgrounds of the players, not particularly realistic in its entirety.

In scenario 1, possibly 20 percent of the people may gain immeasurably while 80 percent would be manipulated, exploited, or oppressed in some way or other. In scenario 2, the 20 percent would feel their initiative stifled and put upon. They would feel hamstrung by unnecessary controls and would threaten to take their money elsewhere for investment. A large number of persons in the middle might feel reasonably satisfied. But, and this is important, the 20 percent who would be decidedly unhappy would be those who have the greatest economic and political clout now, and consequently, would be unlikely to let the scenario come to pass.

Is there then a scenario both realistic and reasonable? Scenario 3? At the present time among the diverse threads making up the total tourism fabric there are bright spots, tarnished areas, and some real black spots. The bright spots—some concrete, some abstract —represent advances in enlightenment like an imaginative first-rate development, a genuine move to have greater public participation, the neat balancing of creative development with a measure of community-oriented regulation, or the thoughtful parts of a plan. Black spots, the polar opposites in the concrete sense, represent the disasters or mistakes. They are those areas, activities, or buildings which I have already identified, and nothing would be gained by belaboring the point here. It is possible that with the

wise application of parts of the Hawaii State Plan and with the re-
building and rehabilitation of existing areas (newly designated urban areas are not needed and would delay rehabilitation of existing ones), bright spots would counterbalance black spots but not
without occasional retrogression (excursions into scenario no. 1)
and not infrequent court battles. Compromise would be the name
of the game. Black spots are already with us and with changing social conditions and attitudes, their replacement may or may not be
always with tourism-oriented facilities. Growth rates and recommendations of the tourism plan would be closely reevaluated with
a much greater emphasis placed on the impact of imposed arbitrary rates on conditions in specific areas. Compromise may result
in the general acceptance of slower but steady growth. As with
scenario 2, great attention in scenario 3 would be paid to diversification and self-sufficiency in an even more determined way than
at present. All would compromise more. To a degree all would become aware of resource limitations. All would be prepared to accept wider participation and reluctantly a greater degree of regulation. This course would be erratically charted between the first
and the second scenarios. Increasingly it would veer to the second
scenario. But often the more careful observers of the community
would feel the course dangerously close to the first.

Scenario 3 is achievable. It would be unsystematic, unspectacu-
lar, but could proceed in a positive manner. Its characteristics
would reflect the ascendancy of the more thoughtful aspects of the
conflicting forces I have discussed. The stage is set already for this
course. In all chapters suggestions have been made. In the pages
immediately preceding I have tried to summarize some main
points set within their rather complex contexts. Some views no
doubt will seem unpalatable now but I suspect will ultimately become acceptable in the sense of compromise essential to this model
of steady if not spectacular improvement. The slowdown of the
present allows for contemplation of the mistakes of the past and a
very cautious but highly innovative approach to the future.

No one can forecast changes in attitudes which will inevitably
take place in the next half century. Changes in direction—as opposed to pure economic change—have taken place in the past decade; they are small, one must look for them, but they are nevertheless there and are encouraging. The direction must be positive.
The cost of taking a wrong course does not bear consideration.

There is possibly nothing in this chapter which is original although some of the interpretation and emphasis might be. Every state and county plan includes, explicitly or implicitly, some of the ideas and notions mentioned here. Wording is often so loose and structure so amorphous that a number of the documents could be used to justify any of the three scenarios presented. I have included discussion, analysis, and interpretation unusual in plan narratives. In response to what I have written, some readers will conclude that unmerited attention has been given to industry managers (developers and operators) rather than to other groups. This attention I feel justified because they have created so much, have assumed such monumental responsibilities, and are at present the prime movers in Hawaii's number one industry. Both they and the community should be fully aware of the roles groups play. If not directly, by implication I have rebuked the public in allowing situations to occur, for being apathetic, and for approaching problems in a half-hearted, dispirited, and haphazard way. What has been said is in the belief that some of the forces against reasonable order and the conservation of those elements which are so worthwhile in Hawaii are becoming stronger each decade and because of this the people of Hawaii, now in a better position than ever before to speak and act, must do so. Better now in thoughtfulness than later in absolute desperation.

In one not too rosy future, we can see the United States assuming a lesser place in the world order, energy crises becoming increasingly critical, economic conditions becoming markedly worse, and the population looking inward as personal survival becomes preeminent. At that time Hawaii priorities would be rearranged and the time for speaking, acting, and reevaluating in the contexts I have discussed could be over. It is not difficult to believe: one sees some of these signs already.

It is important then that the people of Hawaii think about this carefully. The future direction can largely be in their hands. Researchers and analysts can expend immense energy in placing materials at their disposal but only the residents of the state can decide what they want and how it should be in the future.

It would be ridiculous to blame tourism for all Hawaii's ills while overlooking frenzied investment by both local people and outsiders, in-migration not attributable to tourism, and the influence of the mass media both at home and from the mainland.[18] Tourism and associated development have done much for Hawaii. They have provided the means by which some of the worthwhile things of the mainland United States may be combined with the good things of Hawaii in a unique setting and a unique way of life. Often results have not reflected this.

Today Hawaii development has reached a critical point and people are looking for direction. This is especially so on Oahu, Maui, and Kauai. The future of Maui is largely unknown, but many already think things have gone too far. On Kauai forces for development and those for conservation (for want of a better word) have reached the crossroads. On all islands, one direction leads to overcrowding, cultural smothering, condominium lotteries, confrontations, and a lack of local integrity. Another way leads to respect for people and the land, to a pride in culture and surroundings, and to overall quality. Tourism plays an essential part in both. In one it can be destructive, in the other a proud partner.

To achieve what I believe to be the preferred route implied by existing plans, the system has to be worked on. Contrary to conventional wisdom, the system does not work on its own. In this chapter and elsewhere, I have talked about steps to what is believed to be a more satisfying future in which tourism plays an important part. These included the raising of essential priorities to the point where action is taken, increasing public participation, maintaining critical balances, understanding conflicting values, developing imaginative planning, and slowing mainland cultural encroachment. I also stressed regulating with wisdom, allowing for business creativity, facilitating cooperation rather than confrontation, creating a tourism and development ethic, maintaining local cultural integrity, improving tourism quality, and working in the interests of future generations where land and people are treated with gentleness and respect. That attractive image—the legend—is still there, but it can so easily tarnish and disappear. Certainly it sells—but is it for sale?

Notes

Introduction

1. Valene L. Smith, ed., *Hosts and Guests: The Anthropology of Tourism*, (Philadelphia: University of Pennsylvania Press, 1977), p. 2.

2. Nelson H. H. Graburn, "Tourism: The Sacred Journey," in *Hosts and Guests*, ed. Smith, p. 18.

3. Dean MacCannell, *The Tourist: A New Theory of the Leisure Class*, (New York: Schocken Books, 1976), p. 1.

Chapter 1

1. Harold T. Stearns, *Geology of the State of Hawaii* (Palo Alto: Pacific Books, 1966), p. 76.

2. Raymond Fosberg, "Guide to Excursion III: Tenth Pacific Science Congress," mimeographed (Honolulu: Tenth Pacific Science Congress & University of Hawaii, 1961), p. 17.

3. Ibid., pp. 17–18.

4. Where indigenous peoples and indigenous flora or fauna are referred to, I use the word *Hawaiian*. For the contemporary life-style, economy, or legislators of various ethnic groups, I use *Hawaii* as an adjective (e.g., Hawaiian legends and Hawaii legislators).

5. Richard and Mary Elizabeth Shutler, *Oceanic Prehistory* (Menlo Park: Cummings Publishing Co., 1975), p. 85.

6. S. B. Dole, "Evolution of Hawaiian Land Tenure," *Papers of the Hawaiian Historical Society*, no. 3 (1892), p. 44.

7. Marion Kelly, "Some Aspects of Land Alienation in Hawaii," *Hawaii Pono Journal* (November 1970).

8. Norman Meller and Robert Horwitz, "Hawaii: Theories in Land Monopoly," in *Land Tenure in the Pacific*, ed. R. G. Crocombe (Melbourne: Oxford University Press, 1971), p. 25.

9. Marion Kelly, "Changes in Land Tenure in Hawaii, 1778–1850" (M.A. thesis, University of Hawaii, 1956), p. 25.

10. Evidence from Samoa, Fiji, and New Zealand suggests that postcontact

knowledge of precontact traditional land tenure systems was characteristically confused and at best very vague.

11. Jean Hobbs, *Hawaii, A Pageant of the Soil* (Stanford: Stanford University Press, 1935), p. 27.

12. The later undistinguished record of Ladd & Co., who planned to dispose of all unoccupied Hawaiian land to overseas entrepreneurs is documented in Gavan Daws, *Shoal of Time* (Macmillan: New York, 1968), pp. 120–124.

13. Kelly, "Aspects of Land Alienation," p. 5.

14. Jon J. Chinen, *The Great Mahele* (Honolulu: University of Hawaii Press, 1958), p. 31. *Konohiki* (chiefs) and *kuleana* land had to be claimed properly by an individual before the Land Commission would make an award. Payment of survey charges and a commutation tax to the government were also necessary. The division of 1848 was one in name only. Necessary individual procedures, surveying, and the issuing of a Royal Patent and Award took considerable time assuming an individual was aware of his rights, knew the procedures, actually claimed land, and could financially pay the charges.

15. An act of 10 July 1850 authorized the sale of land in fee simple to resident aliens. Jon J. Chinen, "Original Land Titles in Hawaii," privately published, Honolulu: 1961, p. 4; and R. S. Kuykendall, *The Hawaiian Kingdom* (Honolulu: University of Hawaii Press, 1938), p. 287.

16. Kelly, "Aspects of Land Alienation," p. 7.

17. Lawrence H. Fuchs, *Hawaii Pono: A Social History* (New York: Harcourt, Brace and World, 1961), p. 16.

18. W. P. Alexander, *History of the Later Years of the Hawaiian Monarchy* (Honolulu: Hawaiian Gazette, 1896), p. 3.

19. Daws, *Shoal of Time*, p. 313.

20. Gerritt P. Judd, IV, *Hawaii: An Informal History* (New York: Collier Books, 1961), pp. 143–146.

21. William V. Frame and Robert H. Horwitz, *Public Land Policy in Hawaii: The Multiple Use Approach*, report no. 1, Legislative Reference Bureau (Honolulu: University of Hawaii, 1965), p. 4.

22. Herman S. Doi and Robert H. Horwitz, *Public Land Policy in Hawaii: Land Reserved for Public Use*, report no. 2, Legislative Reference Bureau (Honolulu: University of Hawaii, 1966), pp. 9–10.

23. E. B. Scott, *The Saga of the Sandwich Islands* (Crystal Bay, CA.: Sierra-Tahoe Publishing Co., 1968), p. 125.

24. My thanks are offered here to Dr. Edward Barnet who read an early draft and drew my attention to the omission of any reference to the Haleiwa Hotel which stood until 1952.

25. Judd, *Hawaii*, p. 150. For a detailed description of the evolution of Waikiki see J. L. Taylor, "Waikiki: A Study in the Development of a Tourist Community" (Ph.D. dissertation, Clark University, Worcester, MA, 1953). For the most thorough exposition of the history of the tourist industry, see L. J. Crampon, "Hawaii's Visitor Industry, Its Growth and Development," mimeographed (Honolulu: University of Hawaii, School of Travel Industry Management, 1976).

26. Thomas Hitch, "A Brief Political, Social, and Economic History of Hawaii" (Honolulu: First Hawaiian Bank, 1971), p. 1.

27. Ibid.

28. *Hawaii '78* (Honolulu: Bank of Hawaii, 1978), p. 32.

29. Mathematica, "The Visitor Industry and Hawaii's Economy: A Cost-Benefit Analysis," mimeographed (Also known as the Baumol Report). Prepared for the Department of Planning and Economic Development, Honolulu, 1970, p. 1.

30. State of Hawaii, *State Tourism Study: Executive Summary* (Honolulu: Department of Planning and Economic Development, 1978), p. 109.

31. Ibid., p. 111.

Chapter 2

1. Eleanor C. Nordyke, "Slowdown Recommended," *Honolulu Advertiser*, 11 August 1976. For a comprehensive treatment of Hawaii's population, see Eleanor C. Nordyke, *The Peopling of Hawaii* (Honolulu: University Press of Hawaii, 1977).

2. Nordyke, *Peopling of Hawaii*, Table 13, p. 182.

3. *Economic Indicators*, March 1979.

4. W. Armstrong, "Our Ecology in the Pacific" (paper presented to the conference Ecology, Law and Public Policy, Honolulu, May 1971). The term *conceptual resources* as used by Armstrong implies a dominance of the mind over the perceived stimuli which can themselves change independently of the perceptions based upon them. The term *ambient resource* used in this work attempts to embrace the interaction between the mind, thoughts, and behavior of the perceiver and those things about him—people, air, water, rocks, life-styles, activities, perfumes, color, lighting, warmth, sounds, sky, clouds, landscapes, seascapes, moonlight, underwater gardens, buildings, and a host of other elements which create the ambience on which a Hawaii tourist experience is built.

5. Bryan H. Farrell, "The Tourist Ghettos of Hawaii," in *Themes on Pacific Lands*, eds. M. C. R. Edgell and B. H. Farrell (Victoria: University of Victoria, 1974), p. 1.

6. M. Clawson, *Land and Water from Recreation* (Chicago: Rand McNally, 1963), p. 15.

7. A. S. Svendsen, "Det Moderne Reiseliv og det private masse konsum av reiser og recreajon," *Ad Novas* 8 (1969): 124. See also J. J. Parsons, "Southward to the Sun: The Impact of Mass Tourism on the Coast of Spain," *Yearbook of the Association of Pacific Coast Geographers*, 1973, pp. 129–146.

8. Statistical data for this section are from *1979 Annual Research Report* and the *1977 Visitor Expenditure Survey*, Hawaii Visitors Bureau; State of Hawaii, *Data Book* 1980 (Honolulu: Department of Planning and Economic Development, 1980); *Hawaii '80* (Honolulu: Bank of Hawaii, 1980); and most recent estimates of the Hawaii Visitors Bureau, the Bank of Hawaii, and the Department of Planning and Economic Development.

9. *Hawaii Business*, February 1979, p. 52.

10. Ibid., p. 14.

11. *1977 Visitor Expenditure Survey* (Honolulu: Hawaii Visitors Bureau, 1978).

12. City and County of Honolulu, *The Economy of Oahu* (Honolulu: Department of General Planning, 1977), p. 8.

13. State of Hawaii, *State Tourism Study: Physical Resources* (Honolulu: Department of Planning and Economic Development, 1978), pp. 328–340.

14. Ibid., p. 328, as quoted from the original document.

15. Ibid., p. 331, from a report prepared by the State Tourism Study's Waikiki Subcommittee.

16. Ibid., p. 332.

17. "Improvements Planned for Historic Waikiki," *Hawaii Economic Review*, November–December 1971, p. 1.

18. State of Hawaii, *State Tourism Study: Physical Resources*, p. 336.

19. City and County of Honolulu, "Summary of an Assessment of Potential Off-Waikiki Resorts on Oahu," mimeographed (Honolulu: Department of General Planning, September 1978), p. 3.

20. City and County of Honolulu, "The Future of Resort Development on Oahu," mimeographed (Honolulu: Department of General Planning, May 1979), p. 11.

21. Ibid., pp. 12, 16, 17.

22. Ibid., p. 37.

23. See State of Hawaii, *Tourism in Hawaii: Hawaii Tourism Impact Plan 1* (Statewide) (Honolulu: Department of Planning and Economic Development, 1972). At the time of its publication, this was the only complete document listing a large number of proposals. By the end of the decade when the *State Tourism Study* was published, there were only half the number of original proposals still current and most of these had been reduced in size.

24. City and County of Honolulu, "The Future of Resort Development on Oahu," p. 11. See also City and County of Honolulu, "An Assessment of Potential Off-Waikiki Resorts on Oahu," mimeographed (Honolulu: Department of General Planning, August 1978).

25. James Mak and Karen Ah Mai, "Employment and Population Impacts on Resort Development at Five Oahu Sites," mimeographed (Honolulu: Department of General Planning, March 1978), p. 61.

26. *Hawaii Coastal Zone News*, February 1979, pp. 11–12.

27. Mak and Ah Mai, "Employment and Population Impacts," pp. 55 and 61.

28. Much information for this and other descriptions of resort areas that follow may be found in "Workshop on Resort Economics," mimeographed (Honolulu: Hawaii Resort Developers Conference, 1976).

29. *Honolulu Advertiser*, 18 July 1975.

30. Scott C. S. Stone, "Hawaii '69: Beauty and the Bulldozer," *Saturday Review*, 13 September 1969, p. 54.

31. *Hawaii Business*, July 1967, p. 52.

32. Ibid., p. 56.

Chapter 3

1. H. L. Baker, *Maui's Land Situation* (Honolulu: University of Hawaii, Land Study Bureau, 1960), p. 3.

2. Estimates of units vary. Sometimes only rental units are listed; at other times all units may be estimated. Sometimes numbers change with the agency listing them.

3. Esme Chu, *An Economic Study of the County of Maui*, vol. 2: *Past Development and Future Growth of Tourism* (Honolulu: University of Hawaii, Economic Research Center, 1965), pp. xvi and 49.

4. "Ten Year Trend Analysis of Hawaii's Visitor Industry, 1966–76," mimeographed (Honolulu: Hawaii Visitors Bureau, 1977), p. 23.

5. *State of Hawaii Land Use Districts and Regulations Review* (Honolulu: Eckbo, Dean, Austin & Williams, 1970).

6. "Urban" here is purely technical. There are "urban" areas in Maui which would be described now as rural. The expectation is that in the foreseeable future these will become urban in the usual sense of the word.

7. County of Maui, *A General Plan for the Lahaina District County of Maui* (Kahului: Hiroshi Kasamoto, and Muroda and Tanaka Inc., 1968); and County of Maui, *Kihei, Civic Development Plan* (Kahului: Noboru Kobayashi, Howard K. Nakamura, and Robert O. Ohata, 1970).

8. *A General Plan for the Lahaina District*, p. 6.

9. See County of Maui, Ordinance No. 371, Bill No. 13, 1964, *Napili Bay Civic Improvement District*.

10. Jack Millar, Napili Kai Beach Club: personal communication.

11. Industrial Relations Manager, Pioneer Mill: personal communication.

12. State of Hawaii, *1975 Census Update Survey*, Maui County (Honolulu: Community Services Administration, 1976).

13. See *Hawaii Business*, May 1980.

14. *Maui: Community Profile*, State Planning Systems—Community Action Program, Honolulu, 1970, p. 48.

15. Norman Meller and Robert Horwitz, "Hawaii: Theories in Land Monopoly," in *Land Tenure in the Pacific*, ed. R. G. Crocombe (Melbourne: Oxford University Press, 1971), p. 33; State of Hawaii, *Land in Hawaii* (Honolulu: Department of Planning and Economic Development, 1970), p. 17.

16. Peter Sanborn, "The Developer and His Role in Pacific Tourism," in *The Social and Economic Impact of Tourism on Pacific Communities*, ed. Bryan H. Farrell (Santa Cruz: Center for South Pacific Studies, 1977), p. 24.

17. Walter C. Witte, Kihei 1973: personal communication. See also "The Condominiums Come to Kihei" (cover story on Walter Witte), *Hawaii Business*, August 1973, pp. 37–48.

18. Ewell G. Pope, "The Developer's Point of View," *Tourism Investment and Finance* (San Francisco: Pacific Area Travel Association, 1976), p. 4.

19. Donald Tong, "Planning for Tourism on the Island of Hawaii," in *A New Kind of Sugar*, eds. Ben R. Finney and Karen Ann Watson (Santa Cruz: East-West Center and the Center for South Pacific Studies, 1977), p. 158.

20. *Hawaii Business*, August 1973, p. 86.

21. Pope, "The Developer's Point of View," p. 4.

22. Adam Krivatsy, "Planners and Planning for Tourism," PEACESAT Conference, The Impact of Tourism Development in the Pacific, mimeographed (Suva: University of the South Pacific, 1978).

23. Adam Krivatsy, "The Role of the Tourism Development Planner," in *The Social and Economic Impact of Tourism on Pacific Communities*, p. 21.

24. Donald Wolbrink and Associates, *Physical Standards for Tourism Development* (Honolulu: Pacific Island Development Commission, 1973).

25. Ibid., p. 11.

26. Ibid., p. 20.

27. State of Hawaii, *State Tourism Study*, Executive Summary (Honolulu: Department of Planning and Economic Development, 1978), p. 257.

28. Brian Nicol, "Maui '80: A Community Struggling with Success," *Honolulu*, March 1980, pp. 56–89.

29. Ibid., p. 57.

30. *Hawaii Business*, May 1980, p. 22.

31. Ibid., p. 45.

Chapter 4

1. Earl Stoner, former president, Amfac Communities-Hawaii, 1971: personal communication.

2. Peter Sanborn, "The Developer and his Role in Pacific Tourism," in *The Social and Economic Impact of Tourism on Pacific Communities*, ed. Bryan H. Farrell (Santa Cruz: Center for South Pacific Studies, 1977), p. 25.

3. Belt, Collins and Associates Ltd., *Kaanapali Beach, Land Use Study* (Honolulu, 1953), p. 5.

4. Louis G. Van Der Linden. 1971: personal communication.

5. Harland Bartholemew and Associates, *A Study of Pioneer Mill Company Lands at Kaanapali, Maui, Territory of Hawaii* (Honolulu, 1957).

6. Earl Stoner, recorded in transcript of a public hearing by the Maui Planning Commission, Re Amfac Application for Zoning Changes, 12 November 1968.

7. *Hawaii Business*, May 1979, p. 57.

8. Ivan Tilgenkamp, planner, Honolulu, 1973: personal communication.

9. *Maui News*, 31 January 1979.

10. *Maui News*, 2 April 1979.

11. *Maui News*, 8 December 1978.

12. *Workshop on Resort Economics* (Honolulu: Hawaii Resort Developers Conference, 1976).

13. *Hawaii Business*, May 1979, p. 39.

14. *Proposed Kapalua Master Plan, Maui, Hawaii* (Kahului: Belt, Collins and Associates Ltd. and Charles Luckman Associates, 1973), p. 1.

15. Frederick Simpich, Jr., *Anatomy of Hawaii* (New York: Coward, McCann and Geoghegan, Inc., 1971), p. 122.

16. *Honolulu Project, Economic Evaluation* (Kahului: Western Management Consultants, Inc., 1970), p. 1. It is interesting and a reflection of the time needed to implement large-scale projects to note that of three major projects on Maui, not one was implemented by the original sponsor. Planning was started by Pioneer Mill (now Amfac) for Kaanapali; by the Matson Navigation Co. for Wailea (now A&B); and by A&B (now ML&P) for Kapalua.

17. Work was summarized in a brief paper, "Honolua Design Workshop" prepared by Ernest J. Kump Associates, Palo Alto, California, 1971.

18. *Honolulu Advertiser*, 15 June 1973.

19. *Maui News*, 16 June 1973.

20. Colin Cameron 1971: personal communication.

21. *Hawaii Business*, May 1977, p. 52.

22. Ibid.

23. Ibid.

24. *Hawaii Business*, May 1979, p. 17.

Chapter 5

1. Shelley M. Mark, in a speech given June 1973 to the "Conference on Organizing and Managing the Coastal Zone," Annapolis, Maryland, 1973.

2. See George Chaplin and Glenn Paige, eds., *Hawaii 2000* (Honolulu: University Press of Hawaii, 1973).

3. State of Hawaii, *Growth Policies Plan, 1974–1984* (Honolulu: Department of Planning and Economic Development, 1974).

4. Remarks to the Hawaii State Association of Counties, Wailea, 9 December 1976, mimeographed.

5. The Seibu-Makena project on Maui had land reclassified from agricultural to urban in 1974, a time when there was no convincing need for that particular project on Maui.

6. State of Hawaii, *The Economy of Hawaii in 1976* (Honolulu: Department of Planning and Economic Development, 1976), p. 21.

7. See State of Hawaii *Annual Report 1974* (Honolulu: Department of Planning and Economic Development, 1975).

8. State of Hawaii, *Report to the People: Second Five-Year District Boundaries and Regulations Review* (Honolulu: Land Use Commission, 1975), p. 14.

9. Shelley M. Mark, "State Planning in Hawaii," *Hawaii Economic Review*, September–October 1970, p. 7.

10. State of Hawaii, *Report to the People*.

11. Gordon Kemmery Lowry, Jr., "Control and Consequence: The Implementation of Hawaii's Land Use Law" (Ph.D. diss., University of Hawaii, 1976), pp. 216–217.

12. Ibid., p. v.

13. *Honolulu Star-Bulletin*, 13 February 1980.

14. State of Hawaii, *State Comprehensive Outdoor Recreation Plan* (SCORP) (Honolulu: Department of Planning and Economic Development, 1973).

15. State of Hawaii, *1975 Annual Report* (Honolulu: Department of Planning and Economic Development, 1976), p. 8.

16. Deborah N. Lee, "CZM Program Supported at Hearing," *Hawaii Coastal Zone News*, May 1978, pp. 1–2.

17. *Hawaii Coastal Zone News*, September 1977, p. 7.

18. State of Hawaii, *State Tourism Study: Executive Summary* (Honolulu: Department of Planning and Economic Development, 1978), pp. 245–249.

19. State of Hawaii, *Report: Governor's Tourism Planning Advisory Committee* (Honolulu: Department of Planning and Economic Development, 1976).

20. State of Hawaii, *Tourism in Hawaii: Hawaii Tourism Impact Plan* 1 (Honolulu: Department of Planning and Economic Development, 1972).

21. Allan Sommarstrom, "Stress and Competition for Space," *Proceedings of International Geographical Union*, 1975, Palmerston North, pp. 165–166.

22. The Tourism Impact Plan was valuable as far as it went. It provided good

design information and references to a socioeconomic study of North Kohala. It made recommendations for more open space, further beach access, against speculation, for design review, adequate employee housing, and against overbuilding. Both volumes are light on social aspects.

23. Overview Corporation, *Shaping the Future of Hawaii's Environment: A Special Report on the Comprehensive Open Space Plan,* Honolulu, 1972.

24. *Legislative Accomplishments—State of Hawaii, 1976 Session: Economic Development,* p. 2.

25. State of Hawaii, *Draft Document: The Hawaii State Plan* (Honolulu: Department of Planning and Economic Development, 1977).

26. State of Hawaii, *Act 100 A Bill for an Act Relating to Planning,* Sec. 8, 1978.

27. *Maui News,* 19 April 1978, editorial.

28. *Maui News,* 24 April 1978.

29. State of Hawaii, *State Tourism Study* (Honolulu: Department of Planning and Economic Development, 1978), five volumes.

Chapter 6

1. *Hawaii 78* (Honolulu: Bank of Hawaii, 1978), p. 13.

2. State of Hawaii, *Annual Overall Economic Development Program* (Honolulu Department of Planning and Economic Development and Economic Development District Committee, 1977), p. 104.

3. Wesley H. Hillendahl, Bank of Hawaii, address to a group of West Maui businessmen, *Maui News,* 18 August 1978.

4. Virginia Goldstein, "Planning for Tourism on the Island of Hawaii: The Effects of Tourism on Historical Sites and Culture" in *A New Kind of Sugar,* eds. Ben R. Finney and Karen Ann Watson (Santa Cruz: Center for South Pacific Studies and the East West Center, 1977), p. 161.

5. *Bank of Hawaii Monthly Review,* October 1978, p. 2.

6. Details of the statement were included in *Hawaii County in 1978* (Honolulu: First Hawaiian Bank, September 1978).

7. Lynette A'alaonaona Roy, "Planning for Tourism on the Island of Hawaii: The Effects of Tourism on Natural Resources, Natural Beauty and Recreation," in *Sugar,* eds. Finney and Watson, p. 165.

8. *Hawaii Business,* July 1976, pp. 26–37.

9. *Honolulu Advertiser,* 3 August 1977.

10. *Hawaii Business,* July 1977, p. 8.

11. *Hawaii Business,* July 1978, p. 6.

12. *Kauai County in 1976,* (Honolulu: First Hawaiian Bank, October 1976), p. 1.

13. *Maui News,* 28 August 1978.

14. *Honolulu Advertiser,* 6 August 1977.

15. *Maui News,* 19 September 1977.

16. *Maui News,* 25 September 1977.

17. County of Maui, *Proposed Goals and Objectives for a Long-Range Comprehensive Plan of Maui County* (Wailuku: Office of the Mayor, 1977).

18. *Hawaii Business*, May 1976, p. 46.

19. County of Maui, *Open Space and Outdoor Recreation Policies Plan* (Honolulu: Marshall Kaplan, Gans, Kahn and Yamamoto, 1974), two volumes: general and technical reports.

20. *Hawaii Business*, May 1976, p. 26.

21. County of Maui, *Proposed Goals*, p. 62.

22. *Maui News*, 27 September 1978.

23. *Maui News*, 2 October 1978.

24. *Maui News*, 8 February 1980.

25. *Maui News*, 25 September 1978.

26. Elmer Cravalho, 19 August 1975: personal communication.

27. *Hawaii Business*, January 1978, p. 32.

28. *Honolulu Star-Bulletin*, 3 January 1973.

Chapter 7

1. Agricultural statistics are from *Hawaii '79*, Twenty-eighth Annual Economic Review (Honolulu: Bank of Hawaii, 1979); State of Hawaii, *Data Book 1979* (Honolulu: Department of Planning and Economic Development, 1978); Bank of Hawaii, *Monthly Review*, January 1980; and State of Hawaii, *Statistics of Hawaiian Agriculture, 1978* (Honolulu: State Department of Agriculture; United States Department of Agriculture, 1979).

2. *Sunday Star-Bulletin and Advertiser*, 22 August 1976.

3. J. A. Mallet, *Hawaii Future Agriculture*, Agricultural Economic Report, no. 59, 1962; and *Statistics of Hawaiian Agriculture*, 1978.

4. Yields in 1908, 1939, and 1968 were respectively 39, 65, and 98 short tons of unprocessed cane per acre, *Sugar Manual* (Honolulu: Hawaiian Sugar Planters' Association, 1968), p. 21.

5. Thomas Hitch, "The Future of Agriculture in Hawaii," in *Economic Indicators*, September 1972.

6. State of Hawaii, *1979 Annual Overall Economic Development Program* (Honolulu: Department of Planning and Economic Development; Hawaii Economic Development District Committee, 1979), pp. 111-3 and 111-4.

7. A. Gerakas and R. H. Suefuji, *Preservation of Agriculture and Agricultural Lands in Hawaii* (Honolulu: Department of Planning and Economic Development, 1971).

8. *San Francisco Chronicle*, 18 February 1977.

9. *San Francisco Chronicle*, 23 February 1977.

10. *Honolulu Advertiser*, 12 July 1977.

11. *Ampersand*, 11 (1977): 25–32.

12. Elmer Cravalho, "Submission to the United States International Trade Commission on its Section 201. Investigation of Sugar Imports . . . San Francisco, 30 November 1976," mimeographed, (Wailuku: County of Maui, 1976).

13. *Hawaii Business*, May 1979, p. 4.

14. Smaller areas are found on Molokai. A new experimental area for fresh pineapple was started on Kauai in 1979. On Molokai the situation is confused. While phase out was in progress, some discussion had taken place concerning

new areas being planted under different management (United Brands) for the fresh pineapple market.

15. State of Hawaii, *Economy 1978*, p. 38.

16. *Hawaii Business*, July 1979, pp. 60–62.

17. *Maui News*, 7 April 1978.

18. *Hawaii Business*, July 1977, p. 23.

19. Chuck Gee in *Research Priorities in Pacific Tourism*, ed. B. H. Farrell (Santa Cruz: Center for South Pacific Studies, 1977), pp. 22–24.

20. *Maui News*, 3 December 1975.

21. *Honolulu Star-Bulletin*, 13 February 1980.

22. State of Hawaii, *State Agricultural Plan* (Honolulu: Department of Agriculture, 1980).

23. *Hawaii Business*, October 1979, p. 31.

24. *Honolulu Advertiser*, 21 August 1977.

25. *Hawaii Business*, May 1977, p. 52.

26. *Honolulu Advertiser*, 5 August 1977.

27. State of Hawaii, *Statistics of Hawaiian Agriculture*, p. 1.

Chapter 8

1. *Maui News*, 26 April 1978. Report of Annual Neighbor Island Meeting of the Hawaii Visitor Bureau.

2. Allan Sommarstrom, "Stress and the Competition for Space: The Case of Tourism in Hawaii," in *Proceedings of the International Geographical Union Regional Conference and Eighth New Zealand Geography Conference* (Palmerston North: New Zealand Geographical Society, 1974), p. 163.

3. State of Hawaii, *What Hawaii's People Think of the Visitor Industry* (Honolulu: Department of Planning and Economic Development, 1976), p. 3.

4. City and County of Honolulu, "The Future of Resort Development on Oahu," mimeographed (Honolulu: Department of General Planning, May 1979).

5. *Maui News*, 17 June 1975.

6. Thomas H. Creighton, *The Lands of Hawaii: Their Use and Misuse* (Honolulu: University Press of Hawaii, 1978), p. 341.

7. Ibid.

8. State of Hawaii, *The Hawaii State Plan* (Honolulu: Department of Planning and Economic Development, 1978), p. 9. This is the published interpretation of the plan and its associated procedures followed by a copy of the actual plan.

9. R. F. Dasmann, "Reconciling Conservation and Development in the Coastal Zone," in *Nature Conservation in the Pacific*, eds. A. B. Costin and R. H. Groves (Canberra: Australian National University Press, 1973), p. 285.

10. See G. B. K. Baines, "The Environmental Demands of Tourism in Coastal Fiji," in *The Melanesian Environment*, ed. J. H. Winslow (Canberra: Australian National University Press, 1977), pp. 448–457; Freda Rajotte, *A Method for Evaluation of Tourism Impact in the Pacific*, Data Paper no. 9 (Santa Cruz: Center for South Pacific Studies, 1978); Freda Rajotte, "Evaluating the Cultural and Environmental Impact of Tourism," in *Pacific Perspective* 6 (1977): 41–48; R. F. Dasmann and F. Doumenge, "Conservation Problems in the Pacific," *South Pacific Bulletin* 24 (1974): 37–45; and R. F. Dasmann, J. P. Milton, and

P. H. Freeman, *Ecological Principals for Economic Development* (New York: John Wiley and Sons, 1973).

11. Lewis Thomas, *The Lives of a Cell: Notes of a Biology Watcher* (New York: Viking Press, 1974).

12. For a description of these processes and others leading to final formation of coral reefs, see M. S. Doty, "Interrelationships between Marine and Terrestrial Ecosystems in Polynesia," in *Nature Conservation*, eds. Costin and Groves, pp. 241–251.

13. State of Hawaii, *State Tourism Study: Executive Summary* (Honolulu: Department of Planning and Economic Development, 1978), p. 262.

14. Dasmann and Doumenge, "Conservation Problems," p. 41.

15. Dave Raney, "Kealakekua Bay—One Cesspool Too Many," *Hawaii Coastal Zone News*, May 1976, p. 93.

16. *Hawaii Coastal Zone News*, November 1977, p. 3.

17. C. H. Lamoureux, "Conservation Problems in Hawaii," in *Nature Conservation*, eds. Costin and Groves, p. 317.

18. Burl Burlingame, "What's in Store for He'eia?" *Hawaii Coastal Zone News*, August 1978, pp. 4–5.

19. *Hawaii Coastal Zone News*, March 1978, p. 8.

20. Robert Hill, "Bay Recovery Slow Process," *Hawaii Coastal Zone News*, April 1978, p. 6. Also see A. V. Banner and J. H. Bailey, "The Effects of Urban Pollution upon a Coral Reef System," Hawaii Institute of Marine Biology, *Technical Report* no. 25, 1971.

21. Hill, "Bay Recovery," p. 2.

22. Paul E. Shulz, "The Public Use of Underwater Resources," in *Towards a New Relationship of Man and Nature in Temperate Lands*, IUCN Publication no. 7, Morges, 1967, p. 159.

23. Application of Ashford no. 4516, 440 *Pacific Reporter* 2nd Series, (1968).

24. State of Hawaii, *State Comprehensive Outdoor Recreation Plan: Executive Summary* (Honolulu: Department of Planning and Economic Development, 1972), pp. 4–5.

25. Steve A. McKeon, "Public Access to Beaches," *Stanford Law Review* 22 (1970): 579.

26. For a broad summary of conditions in Hawaii, see Michael Anthony Town and William Wai Lim Yuen, "Public Access to Beaches in Hawaii: 'A Social Necessity'," *Hawaii Bar Journal* 10 (1973): 3–29.

27. *Honolulu Advertiser*, 18 July 1975.

28. *Maui News*, 24 May 1978.

29. Ibid.

30. *Maui News*, 15 July 1975.

31. *Maui News*, 23 October 1978.

32. "Mariner's Notebook," *Maui News*, 25 October 1978.

33. Michael Seiler, "Keeping a Hawaii Paradise That Way," *San Francisco Examiner and Chronicle*, 26 November 1978.

34. "Public Opinion Survey for the Development Plan Program," mimeographed (Honolulu: Survey & Marketing Services, December 1978).

35. *Honolulu Star-Bulletin*, 17 February 1980.

36. The Hawaii Sugar Planters' Association is investigating the by-products of

ethanol production which include yeast and another byproduct which might be converted into fertilizer. An HSPA demonstration plant will work on gasohol as well.

37. "Public Opinion Survey," p. 12.

38. State of Hawaii, *State Tourism Study: Physical Resources* (Honolulu: Department of Planning and Economic Development, 1978).

39. Ibid., p. 323.

Chapter 9

1. Lawrence H. Fuchs, *Hawaii Pono: A Social History* (New York: Harcourt Brace and World, 1961), p. 24. See chapter 1 of this work.

2. Frances Cottington, "Socio-Psychiatric Effects of Luxury Hotel Growth and Development on a Rural Population," mimeographed (Honolulu: University of Hawaii Medical School, 1970), p. 2.

3. Andrew W. Lind, *Hawaii's People* (Honolulu: University Press of Hawaii, 1967), p. 73.

4. Terence A. Rogers and Satoru Izutsu, "The Japanese" in *People and Cultures of Hawaii: A Psychocultural Profile*, eds. John F. McDermott, Jr., Wen-Shing Tseng, and Thomas W. Maretzki (Honolulu: University Press of Hawaii, 1980), p. 98.

5. Danilo E. Ponce, "The Filipinos: Introduction," in *People and Cultures of Hawaii*, p. 155.

6. Ibid, p. 162.

7. Ibid.

8. Sheila Forman, "The Filipinos: Hawaii's Immigrants from the Philippines," in *People and Cultures of Hawaii*, p. 177.

9. State of Hawaii, *The Economy of Hawaii 1977* (Honolulu: Department of Planning and Economic Development, 1977), p. 62.

10. Benjamin B. C. Young, "The Hawaiians" in *People and Cultures of Hawaii*, p. 14.

11. Nancy B. Graves and Theodore D. Graves, "The Impact of Modernization on the Personality of a Polynesian People or How to Make an Up-tight, Rivalrous Westerner out of an Easygoing, Generous, Pacific Islander," mimeographed (Auckland: South Pacific Research Institute, August 1975), Research Report no. 7.

12. Peter Rosegg, "AJAs are Real Minority on Mainland," *Sunday Star-Bulletin and Advertiser*, 26 August 1977.

13. Karen Horton, "Conflicts Not Always Racial," *Honolulu Advertiser*, 27 June 1975, (one of a series of six articles).

14. JoAnn Yukimura, Lihue, 13 July 1977: personal communication.

15. *Maui News*, 10 January 1979.

16. Alan Howard, *Ain't No Big Thing* (Honolulu: University Press of Hawaii, 1974), pp. 240–245.

17. Leilehua Omphroy, "The Effects of Acculturation on Self-Identification in Hawaiian Children," in *New Neighbors: Islanders in Adaptation*, eds. Bradd Shore, Cluny Macpherson, and Robert W. Franco (Santa Cruz: Center for South Pacific Studies, 1978), pp. 181–184.

18. Howard, *Ain't No Big Thing*, p. 245.

19. County of Kauai, *A General Plan for the Island of Kauai* (Lihue: prepared by Eckbo, Dean, Austin, et al., 1970), p. 15.

Chapter 10

1. For further references to the complicated area of human impact, see the following works: DiAnne Reid Ross and Bryan H. Farrell, eds., *Source Materials for Pacific Tourism* (Santa Cruz: Center for South Pacific Studies, 1975); Valene L. Smith, ed., *Hosts and Guests: The Anthropology of Tourism* (Philadelphia: University of Pennsylvania Press, 1977); Ben R. Finney and Karen Ann Watson, eds., *A New Kind of Sugar: Tourism in the Pacific*, 2d ed., (Santa Cruz: East-West Center and the Center for South Pacific Studies, 1977); Bryan Farrell, ed., *Research Priorities in Pacific Tourism: A Satellite Discussion on the PEACESAT Network* (Santa Cruz: Center for South Pacific Studies, University of California, and School of Travel Industry Management, Social Science and Linguistic Institute, and the PEACESAT Project, University of Hawaii, 1977); Bryan Farrell, ed., *The Social and Economic Impact of Tourism on Pacific Communities* (Santa Cruz: Center for South Pacific Studies, 1977); Bryan Farrell, "The Golden Hordes and the People of the Pacific," An Inaugural Lecture (Santa Cruz: University of California, 1978); John M. Knox, "Resident Visitor Interaction," paper presented at PEACESAT Conference, *The Impact of Tourism Development in the Pacific*, April 1978, (Suva: University of the South Pacific, in press); Raymond Noronha, *Social and Cultural Dimensions of Tourism: A Review of Literature in English* (Washington: Tourism Projects Department, International Bank for Reconstruction and Development, 1977); Louis Turner and John Ash, "The Golden Hordes," *New Society* 19 (1973): 126–128; Louis Turner and John Ash, *The Golden Hordes* (London: Constable, 1975); and UNESCO, "The Effects of Tourism on Socio-Cultural Values," *Annals of Tourism Research* 4 (1976): 75–100 (Translation of UNESCO document SHC/OPS/TST 100).

2. For an extended discussion of the interaction of visitors and local people, see Bryan H. Farrell, "Tourism's Human Conflicts: Cases from the Pacific," *Annals of Tourism Research* 6 (1979): 122–136.

3. Philip Frick McKean, "Tourist-Native Interaction in Paradise: Locating Partial Equivalence Structures in Bali," mimeographed (paper presented at the Seventy-First Annual Meeting of the American Anthropological Association, November 1972), p. 1.

4. Knox, "Resident Visitor Interaction," p. 8.

5. *Honolulu Star-Bulletin*, 14 June 1974.

6. Knox, "Resident Visitor Interaction," p. 11.

7. Ibid., p. 12.

8. Farrell, "Tourism's Human Conflicts," p. 126.

9. Knox, "Resident Visitor Interaction," p. 7.

10. Claude Steiner, ed., *Readings in Radical Psychiatry* (New York: Grove Press, 1975), p. 12.

11. Tamara Wong, "An Hawaiian-Chinese-English-Irish Nineteen-year-old Activist," in *The Social and Economic Impact*, ed. Farrell, pp. 70–72.

12. Irwin Altman, *The Environment and Social Behavior* (Monterey: Brooks/Cole Publishing Company, 1975), pp. 112–123.

13. Farrell, "The Golden Hordes and the Pacific People," p. 19.

14. Eric Berne, *Transactional Analysis in Psychotherapy* (New York: Grove Press, 1961).

Chapter 11

1. John M. Knox, "Classification of Hawaii Residents' Attitudes toward Tourists and Tourism," *Tourism Research Project*, Occasional Paper no. 1 (Honolulu: University of Hawaii, 1978).

2. Ibid., p. 1.

3. Ibid., p. 12.

4. Ibid., p. 6.

5. State of Hawaii, *Data Book 1978* (Honolulu: Department of Planning and Economic Development, 1978).

6. Noel Kent, "Escape Mecca of the World," *Hawaii Pono Journal*, October 1971, p. 42.

7. "Report on the Compensation Structure for Hourly Employees of the Hawaii Hotel Industry for the Year 1968," mimeographed (Honolulu: Touche, Ross, Bailey and Smart, 1969).

8. Thomas Hale Hamilton, "Tourism in Hawaii." (Written for the Encyclopedia of Hawaii, 1976. Manuscript in Hawaii State Archives), p. 17.

9. Willard Tim Chow, "Tourism and Regional Planning: The Legend of Hawaii," mimeographed (paper presented at the Fifth Pacific Regional Science Conference, Vancouver, B.C., August 16–19, 1977), p. 12.

10. *Hawaii Business*, April 1978, p. 62.

11. Ibid., p. 64.

12. Ibid.

13. "Why Hawaii's Per Capita Income Rank has Fallen," *Economic Indicators*, September 1979.

14. State of Hawaii *Long-Range Population and Economic Simulation Model for the State of Hawaii* (Honolulu: Department of Planning and Economic Development, 1978); and Eleanor C. Nordyke, "Relationship Between Tourism and Population Growth" (Paper presented at a workshop of the Commission on Population and the Hawaiian Future, Honolulu, 1979).

15. Darwin Labarthe, Dwayne Reed, J. Brody, and Reuel Stallones, *American Journal of Epidemiology* 98, 3 (1973): 161–174.

16. Frances Cottington, "Sociopsychiatric Effects of Luxury Hotel Growth and Development on a Rural Population," mimeographed (Honolulu: The Queen's Medical Center, 1970). See also Lawrence Fukunaga, "A New Sun in North Kohala: The Socio-Economic Impact of Tourism and Resort Development on a Rural Community in Hawaii," in *A New Kind of Sugar: Tourism in the Pacific*, eds. Ben R. Finney and Karen Ann Watson (Santa Cruz: East-West Center and Center for South Pacific Studies, 1977), pp. 199–228.

17. Ibid.

18. Fukunaga, "A New Sun," p. 216.

19. Cottington, "Sociopsychiatric Effects of Luxury Hotel Growth," p. 6.

20. Fukunaga, "A New Sun," p. 211.

21. John Ventura, Kihei, 1974: personal communication.

22. David Y. S. Kong, Kihei, 1977: personal communication.

23. *The Hawaiian Realtor*, May 1977, p. 29.

24. *Forbes*, 18 September 1978.

25. *Honolulu Star-Bulletin*, 14 December 1978.

26. *Forbes*, 18 September 1978.

27. *Barron's*, 4 December 1978.

28. *Pacific Business News*, 9 February 1981.

29. *Maui News*, 12 August 1977.

30. R. F. Dasmann, "Reconciling Conservation and Development in the Coastal Zone," in *Nature Conservation in the Pacific*, eds. A. B. Costin and R. H. Groves (Canberra: Australian National University Press, 1973), p. 294.

31. *Hawaii '78* (Honolulu: Bank of Hawaii, 1978), p. 12.

32. Noel Kent, "Tourism and the Rising Political Awareness in the Hawaiian Working Class," in *The Social and Economic Impact of Tourism on Pacific Communities*, ed. Bryan H. Farrell (Santa Cruz: Center for South Pacific Studies, 1977), p. 75.

33. Thomas Creighton, *The Lands of Hawaii: Their Use and Misuse* (Honolulu: University Press of Hawaii, 1978), pp. 359–363.

34. Bob Krauss, "A New Mahele?" *Honolulu Advertiser*, 26 December 1977.

35. *Honolulu Advertiser*, 16 July 1975.

36. Edwin T. Fujii, James Mak, and Edward Nishimura, "Tourism and Crime," mimeographed, Tourism Research Project, Occasional Paper no. 2 (Honolulu: University of Hawaii, 1978).

37. The study does not use a component which includes the ethnic mix of the population. Care would have to be taken before transferring results applicable in Hawaii to New Zealand or Fiji where different ethnic groups within the total population would have associated with them different values and, consequently, different patterns of crime.

38. Fujii, Mak, and Nishimura, "Tourism and Crime," p. 10.

39. *Honolulu Star-Bulletin*, 8 August 1970.

40. James Dooley, "Japanese Tourist Special—Hotel with Love for Sale," *Honolulu Advertiser*, 21 March 1978.

41. Noel Kent, "A New Kind of Sugar," in *A New Kind of Sugar*, eds. Finney and Watson, p. 171.

42. *Hawaii Business*, February 1979, p. 34.

43. "Tourism, Crime Explored," *Maui News*, 16 September 1971. The study referred to was conducted by Dick Meyer, Maui Community College.

44. Fukunaga, "A New Sun," p. 212.

45. *Honolulu Advertiser*, 18 March 1980.

46. County of Hawaii, *The Kona Community Development Plan* (Hilo: Donald Wolbrink and Associates, 1975), p. 1.

47. This is coined by analogy to the notion in the South Pacific of the "Pacific Way," an easygoing, nonviolent, hospitable, gentle manner of living.

48. Thomas Creighton, "Honolulu's Opportunities," *Sunday Star-Bulletin and Advertiser*, 27 January 1980.

49. John Carl Warnecke and Associates, *Environmental and Urban Design Study of the Makena-La Perouse, Wailuku, and Lahaina Areas* (Honolulu: State Foundation on Culture and the Arts, 1970).

50. Krauss, "A New Mahele?"

51. *Sunday Star-Bulletin and Advertiser*, 17 July 1977.

52. "Condominium Construction in Hawaii," *Economic Indicators*, January 1979, p. 1. Also "Condominium Inventory," *Monthly Review*, June–July 1979.

53. Michael Hopkins and Marjorie Penseyres "A Study of Resort Condominium Visitor Expenditures," mimeographed (Honolulu: University of Hawaii, School of Travel Industry Management, 1979). Prepared for the Hawaii Resort Developers Conference, 21 June 1979.

54. Bryan Farrell, "The Tourist Ghettos of Hawaii," in *Themes on Pacific Lands*, eds. M. C. R. Edgell and B. H. Farrell, Western Geographic Series vol. 10 (Victoria: University of Victoria, 1974), pp. 181–222.

55. W. Edgar Vinacke, "Stereotyping Among National Racial Groups in Hawaii: A Study of Ethnocentricity," *The Journal of Social Psychology* 30 (1949): 265–291.

56. See Max E. Stanton, "The Polynesian Cultural Center: A Multi-Ethnic Model of Seven Pacific Cultures," in *Hosts and Guests: An Anthropology of Tourism*, ed. Valene L. Smith (Philadelphia: University of Pennsylvania Press, 1977).

57. Midori Matsuyama and Theodore Brameld, "The Polynesian Cultural Center," mimeographed (Paper presented at the 73d Annual Meeting of the American Anthropological Association, Mexico City, 1974), p. 23.

58. John M. Knox, "Police Escorts Back-up Public Relations Approach," *Honolulu Advertiser*, 6 July 1972; Allan Sommarstrom, "Stress and Competition for Space: The Case of Tourism in Hawaii," in *Proceedings of the International Geographical Union Regional Conference and Eighth New Zealand Geography Conference* (Palmerston North: New Zealand Geographical Society, 1975), pp. 163–165; Noel Kent, "A New Kind of Sugar," p. 196.

59. *Honolulu Star-Bulletin*, 17 March 1980.

60. Farrell, "The Tourist Ghettos of Hawaii," p. 203.

61. *Honolulu Advertiser*, 28 March 1980.

Chapter 12

1. Ernest J. Donehower, former Deputy Director of Research, HVB, 1976: personal communication.

2. *Maui News*, 27 October 1978.

3. Considerable information about Kauai groups came from conversations with JoAnn Yukimura, Tamara Wong, and David Chang.

4. Alan Cline, "SHOK," *San Francisco Sunday Examiner and Chronicle*, 15 January 1978.

5. Neighborhood board information was derived from discussions with Ned Wiederholt, Department of General Planning, Honolulu; "An Evaluation of the Effectiveness of the Neighborhood Boards and Neighborhood Plan," mimeographed (Honolulu: Pac West Community Associates, Inc., 1979); and Gail Suzuki, "Planning for the Visitor Industry of Oahu" (senior thesis, Environmental Studies Board, University of California, Santa Cruz, 1980).

6. Bryan H. Farrell, "Breaking Down the Paradigms: The Realities of Tourism," in *The Social and Economic Impact of Tourism*, ed. Bryan Farrell (Santa Cruz: Center for South Pacific Studies, 1977), p. 2.

7. Ibid., pp. 2–3.

8. John B. Connell, "Proliferation or Planning," *Hawaii Coastal Zone News* (June 1976): 3–4.

9. Ibid., p. 4.

10. "Kihei, Civic Development Plan" (brochure, undated).

11. John Carl Warnecke and Associates, *Environmental and Urban Design Study of the Makena-La Perouse, Wailuku, and Lahaina Areas* (Honolulu: State Foundation on Culture and the Arts, 1970), p. 5.

12. *Maui News*, 24 May 1978.

13. "Kihei, Civic Development Plan." In the discussion the plan is referred to as the Kihei 701 Plan, the Kihei Development Plan, and the General Plan.

14. David Hoff, "Makena Fight is Probable," *Maui News*, 6 April 1979.

15. *Maui News*, 5 October 1975.

16. *Maui News*, 11 May 1979.

17. A good example of specific rather than blanket opposition was shown by Poipu Beach condominium owners opposed to the proposed highrise Waiohai Hotel yet supporting Kiahuna Golf Village nearby. The first spoiled the view, the second provided welcome recreational facilities and increased the value of nearby condominiums.

18. *Maui News*, 6 July 1979.

19. *Maui News*, 24 December 1980.

20. *Maui News*, 25 February 1981.

21. *Maui News*, 24 December 1980.

22. *Honolulu Advertiser*, 10 February 1981.

23. Ibid.

24. *Maui News*, 25 February 1981.

25. *Maui News*, 24 December 1980.

26. *Hawaii Business*, May 1979, p. 32.

27. See Alan J. Wagar, *The Carrying Capacity of Wild Lands for Recreation* (Washington: Society of American Foresters, 1964), p. 2. Also see G. H. Stankey and D. N. Lime, "Recreation Carrying Capacity: An Annotated Bibliography," USDA Forest Service, General Technical Report INT-3, 1973.

28. Dean MacCannell, *The Tourist: A New Theory of the Leisure Class* (New York: Schocken Books, 1976), p. 3.

Chapter 13

1. Wesley H. Hillendahl, "Development of the Visitor Industry in Hawaii —Past and Future," mimeographed. (Address presented to a group of Japanese hotel executives, Honolulu, 7 November 1974), p. 12.

2. Thomas Hale Hamilton, "Tourism in Hawaii." (Written for The Encyclopedia of Hawaii, 1976. Manuscript in Hawaii State Archives), p. 18.

3. *Honolulu Advertiser*, 22 January 1978.

4. *Honolulu Advertiser*, 22 April 1980.

5. See Brian Archer, "The Uses and Abuses of Multiplier," in *Planning for Tourism Development: Quantitative Approaches*, eds. Charles E. Gearing, William W. Swart, and Turgut Var (New York: Praeger, 1976). A multiplier is a ratio of primary or direct spending and indirect or spending secondary to the direct spending, e.g., $100 direct and $50 indirect would give a multiplier of 1.5.

6. Robert O. Coppedge and Russell C. Youmans, "Income Multipliers in Eco-

nomic Impact Analysis," _Special Report_ 294 (Corvallis: Oregon State University, Cooperative Extension Service, 1970), p. 3.

7. Juanita C. Liu, "Differential Multipliers for the Accommodation Sector," Working Paper no. 80–07, mimeographed (Honolulu: University of Hawaii, School of Travel Industry Management, 1980), p. 16.

8. Juanita C. Liu, "Tourism Income Multipliers at the Establishment Level," Working Paper no. 80–08, mimeographed (Honolulu: University of Hawaii, School of Travel Industry Management, 1980), p. 17.

9. Ibid., p. 14.

10. Liu, "Differential Multipliers," p. 28.

11. Ibid., p. 28.

12. Thomas Hale Hamilton, "Hawaii's Tourism and Controlled Growth," mimeographed (Address to the New Zealand Institute of Travel, Auckland, 26 October 1976), p. 4.

13. Chuck Y. Gee, Testimony presented before House Committee on Tourism, 2 February 1981.

14. State of Hawaii, _The Visitor Industry and Hawaii's Economy: A Cost-Benefit Analysis_ (Honolulu: Department of Planning and Economic Development, 1970).

15. State of Hawaii, _Hawaii Tourism Impact Plan_, Vol. 1, _Tourism in Hawaii_; Vol. 2, _Regional West Hawaii_ (Honolulu: Department of Planning and Economic Development, 1972).

16. State of Hawaii, "The Report of the Temporary Visitor Industry Council," mimeographed (Honolulu, November 1973).

17. Hamilton, "Hawaii's Tourism and Controlled Growth," p. 6.

18. Ibid., p. 7.

19. Activities and observations were covered in two reports each starting with an introduction by Thomas Hamilton and containing duplicated copies of newspaper articles and a concluding statement. The reports were "Legislators Seaside Resort Study Mission May 25–June 14, 1975," and "A Report of a Tourist Study Mission to the South Pacific made by Representatives of the Public and Private Sectors of Hawaii, November 20 to December 9, 1976."

20. State of Hawaii, _State Tourism Study_, 5 vols. (Honolulu: Department of Planning and Economic Development, 1978). Volumes are as follows: _Economic Projections, Public Revenue/Cost Analysis, Manpower, Physical Resources, and Executive Summary_.

21. State of Hawaii, _Report: Governor's Tourism Planning Advisory Committee_ (Honolulu: Department of Planning and Economic Development, 1976), p. 39.

22. James Mak and Edward Nishimura, "The Economics of a Hotel Room Tax," _Philippine Review of Business and Economics_ 14 (1977): 65–80.

23. State of Hawaii, "Summary of a Study on the Economics of Hotel Room Tax," mimeographed (Honolulu: Department of Planning and Economic Development, 1977), p. 2.

24. _Hawaii Business_, April 1978, p. 52.

25. See Willard Tim Chow, "Tourism and Regional Planning: The Legend of Hawaii," mimeographed (Paper presented at the Fifth Pacific Regional Science Conference, Vancouver, B.C., August 16–19, 1977); and "Tourism Policy and

Regional Development in Hawaii," mimeographed (Paper presented at the 40th Annual Meeting of the association of Pacific Coast Geographers, Hilo, Hawaii, June 21–24, 1977).

26. I have revised portions of this book again and again as new material comes to light. This particular section was written without the benefit of the final document but with the draft—*State Tourism Plan* (Honolulu: Department of Planning and Economic Development, 1980). In addition, I had invaluable conversations with Chuck Y. Gee, Elizabeth Johnson, John Kelsh, Gay Larned, and the chairman of the Tourism Plan Advisory Committee Aaron Levine, all concerned with the plan either in its earlier or later forms or both.

27. Ibid., pp. 11–80.

28. Anthony Takitani, "Growth of Hawaii Tourism Opposed," *Honolulu Advertiser*, 12 March 1980.

29. Ken Kiyabu, "Planned Tourism Growth Supported," *Honolulu Advertiser*, 14 March 1980.

30. *Honolulu Star-Bulletin*, 7 February 1980.

31. "The State Tourism Plan and the Visitor Industry," *ODC Planning Issues*, Winter 1980, p. 2.

32. Chuck Y. Gee, "Establishing Better Communications Between Public and Private Sectors in Tourism—The Hawaiian Experience," mimeographed (Paper presented to the Pacific Area Travel Association Workshop, Manila, 3 January 1980).

33. Ibid.

34. J. David Raney, "Community Concerns Regarding Tourism," mimeographed (Submission to the Hawaii State Tourism Plan Advisory Committee, Honolulu: 27 August 1979).

35. Henry Fairlie, "Constitutional Complaints," *Harper's*, June 1980, p. 28.

36. J. David Raney, "Community Concerns Regarding Tourism," p. 5.

37. Moheb Ghali, *Tourism and Regional Growth* (Leiden: Martinus Nijhoff, 1977); and Moheb Ghali, "Tourism and Economic Growth: An Empirical Study," *Economic Development and Culture Change* 24 (1976): 527–538.

38. "U.S. Tourism Seen as a Major Industry by 2000," *Commerce America*, 19 June 1977, cited in *State Tourism Study: Executive Summary*, p. 49.

39. State of Hawaii, *State Tourism Plan*, p. 38.

40. State of Hawaii, "The Population of Hawaii, 1980: Preliminary Census Results," Statistical Report 141 (Honolulu: Department of Planning and Economic Development, 1980), p. 1.

41. State of Hawaii, *State Tourism Study: Manpower*, pp. 20–49.

42. William Dickie Merrill, "Hotel Employment and the Community in Hawaii" (Ph.D. dissertation, University of Edinburgh, 1974). For newspaper evaluation of the thesis, see A. A. Smyser, "Jobs in Tourist Industry," *Honolulu Star-Bulletin*, 30 March 1976.

43. *Honolulu Advertiser*, 30 March 1976.

44. Merrill, "Hotel Employment and the Community in Hawaii," p. 258.

45. Ibid., pp. 258–259.

46. In 1976 a curriculum package for grades 4, 5, and 6, "Getting to Know Hawaii's Visitor Industry," was prepared by two social studies teachers for the Hawaii Visitor Industry Education Council to be used first as a pilot study on

Maui. Parent and group opposition was predictable and energetic. To allow an industry to finance part of an overall curriculum and to paint any picture of the industry was considered a dangerous precedent. See *Maui News*, 14 April, 27 September, and 15 November 1976.

47. *Maui News*, "Maui's Future: Choice or Chance," 4 February 1977, special supplement.

48. John Knox, "Research Priorities in Hawaii and the Pacific: An Overview," *Tourism Research Project*, Occasional Paper no. 3 (Honolulu: University of Hawaii, 1979).

49. Ibid., p. 12.

50. Richard D. Johnston, "The Japanese Have Hit the Beaches in Hawaii," *Fortune*, September 1975, p. 133.

51. *Honolulu Advertiser*, 21 July 1977; also Bob Krauss, "Tourist Industry Owners in a Calabash": first of three articles, *Honolulu Advertiser*, May 1972.

52. *Hawaii Overseas* (Honolulu: Department of Planning and Economic Development, 1974), pp. 4–11.

53. *Hawaii Business*, February 1981, p. 48.

54. State of Hawaii, Hawaii International Services Agency, *Foreign Investment in Hawaii* (Honolulu: Department of Planning and Economic Development and U.S. Department of Commerce, 1979), pp. 161–163.

55. *Hawaii Business*, February 1981, p. 45.

56. Krauss, "Tourist Industry Owners."

57. "Hotel Ownership in Hawaii," *Economic Indicators*, September 1978.

58. Ibid.

59. Ibid.

60. Ibid.

61. The original study was published by the Economic Research Center, University of Hawaii, December 1973. Information here is from H. Robert and Emily E. Heller, *The Economic and Social Impact of Foreign Investment in Hawaii: A Special Summary* (Honolulu: Hawaii International Services Agency, Department of Planning and Economic Development, 1974).

62. *What Hawaii's People Think of Foreign and Mainland Investment in the Islands* (Honolulu: Hawaii International Services Agency, Department of Planning and Economic Development, 1975).

63. Ibid., p. 7.

64. *Guidelines for Investment Activities in Developing Countries*, reprinted from the Japanese (Honolulu: Hawaii International Services Agency, Department of Planning and Economic Development, 1973).

65. *Hawaii's Reaction to Japanese Investment in the Islands* (Tokyo: Ministry of Foreign Affairs, 1973), reprinted by Department of Planning and Economic Development, Honolulu, 1973.

66. Johnston, "Japanese Have Hit the Beaches in Hawaii," pp. 135–136.

67. *Hawaii Business*, February 1981, p. 48.

68. State of Hawaii, *Foreign Investment in Hawaii*, p. 121.

69. State of Hawaii, "Statistical Data on Japanese Tourism," *International Business Series* (Honolulu: Department of Planning and Economic Development, 1981), p. 16.

70. Figures where appropriate are from *1978 Annual Research Report* (Hono-

lulu: Hawaii Visitors Bureau, 1979) or a Hawaii Visitor Bureau Japanese Visitor Opinion Survey, 1979.

71. State of Hawaii, "Statistical Data on Japanese Tourism," p. 13.

72. Hawaii Visitor Bureau preliminary estimate for 1980. The 1979 figure was $175.

73. "Looking for More than Sunshine," *Hawaii Business*, February 1979, p. 29.

74. For a good summary of the behavior of Japanese tourists see Juanita C. Liu, "The Japanese Tourist in Hawaii," mimeographed (Paper presented to the Fifth Annual Pacific Islands Studies Conference, Honolulu, April 1980).

75. Barbara Mills, personal communication; and remarks made by Kiyomi Sugahara, World Tour Operators, and Thomas C. Hoadley, Amfac Resorts, at a seminar, "Japanese Tourism through the 1980s" Honolulu, February 1981 (Hawaii International Services Agency).

76. Remarks made by Joseph E. Hale, Pan American World Airways, at a seminar, "Japanese Tourism Through the 1980s."

77. Remarks made by Thomas C. Hoadley, Amfac Resorts, at a seminar, "Japanese Tourism Through the 1980s."

78. Adam Krivatsy, "Tomorrow's Tourism—As We See It Today," in *The Social and Economic Impact of Tourism on Pacific Communities*, ed. Bryan H. Farrell (Santa Cruz: University of California, 1977), pp. 99–101; Peter Sanborn, "The Future of Tourism in Hawaii," in *The Social and Economic Impact of Tourism on Pacific Communities*, pp. 106–107.

79. Raymond Dasmann, "The Future of Tourism in Relation to Energy Costs," mimeographed (Paper delivered at a PEACESAT Tourism Conference, "The Impact of Tourism in the Pacific," Suva: University of the South Pacific, 1978).

80. *Honolulu Advertiser*, 14 February 1980.

81. "The Over-the-Thrill Crowd," *Time*, 28 May 1979.

82. Ibid.

Chapter 14

1. Bernard J. Frieden, *The Environmental Protection Hustle* (Cambridge: MIT Press, 1979).

2. "Democracy in America: A Conversation with Henry Steele Commager," *Bill Moyer's Journal*, PBS, 16 April 1979, mimeographed transcript (New York: Educational Broadcasting Corporation, 1979), p. 6.

3. Walter Karp, "Republican Virtues," *Harper's*, July 1979, pp. 27–34.

4. Ibid.

5. Christopher Lasch, *The Culture of Narcissism: American Life in an Age of Diminishing Expectations* (New York: W. W. Norton & Co., Inc., 1978).

6. Ibid., p. 27.

7. Ibid.

8. Henry Fairlie, "Constitutional Complaints," *Harper's*, June 1980, p. 32.

9. Ibid.

10. See Robert Lekachman, "Looking for the Left," *Harper's*, April 1979, pp. 21–23. For a discussion on the question of shared assumptions, see Bryan H. Far-

rell, "Breaking Down the Paradigms: The Realities of Tourism" in *The Social and Economic Impact of Tourism on Pacific Communities*, ed. Bryan H. Farrell (Santa Cruz: Center for South Pacific Studies, 1977), pp. 1–6.

11. Michael Demarest, "Maui: America's Magic Isle," *Time*, 26 March 1979, pp. 74–80.

12. Gavan Daws, *Shoal of Time: A History of the Hawaiian Islands* (New York: Macmillan Co., 1968), p. 394.

13. *Maui News*, 14 December 1974.

14. John Knox, *Research Priorities in Hawaii and the Pacific: An Overview*, Occasional Paper no. 3 (University of Hawaii Tourism Research Project, 1979).

15. See also *Hawaii, The Most Vulnerable State in the Nation* (Honolulu: First Hawaiian Bank, 1973).

16. Jet fuel represents approximately 36 percent of Hawaii's total petroleum consumption, compared with 5 percent for mainland consumption. The direct and indirect effects of high energy costs cannot be overemphasized as a deterrent to travel.

17. After a decade of study, these are the possibilities I see. They should not be confused with thorough studies based on alternative futures theory. Such studies seem essential.

18. UNESCO "The Effects of Tourism on Socio-Cultural Values," *Annals of Tourism Research* 4 (1976), p. 93.

Selected Bibliography

Bank of Hawaii. *Hawaii '69–Hawaii '80.* Annual.

———. *Monthly Review,* 1969–1981.

Banner, A. V., and Bailey, J. H. "The Effects of Urban Pollution Upon a Coral Reef System." Hawaii Institute of Marine Biology, Technical Report no. 25, 1971.

Chaplin, George, and Paige, Glenn, eds. *Hawaii 2000.* Honolulu: University Press of Hawaii, 1973.

Chow, Willard Tim. "Tourism and Regional Planning: The Legend of Hawaii." Paper presented at the Fifth Pacific Regional Science Conference, Vancouver, British Columbia, 16–19 August 1977. Mimeographed.

———. "Tourism Policy and Regional Development in Hawaii." Paper presented at the 40th Annual Meeting of the Association of Pacific Coast Geographers, Hilo, Hawaii, 20–24, June 1977. Mimeographed.

Cottington, Frances. "Socio-Psychiatric Effects of Luxury Hotel Growth and Development on a Rural Population." Mimeographed. Honolulu: University of Hawaii Medical School, 1970.

Crampon, L. J. "Hawaii's Visitor Industry: Its Growth and Development." Mimeographed. Honolulu: University of Hawaii, School of Travel Industry Management, 1976.

Creighton, Thomas H. *The Lands of Hawaii: Their Use and Misuse.* Honolulu: University Press of Hawaii, 1978.

Dasmann, Raymond; Milton, J. P.; and Freeman, P. H. *Ecological Principles for Economic Development.* New York: John Wiley and Sons, 1973.

Daws, Gavan. *Shoal of Time: A History of the Hawaiian Islands.* 1968. Reprint. Honolulu: University Press of Hawaii, 1974.

Demarest, Michael. "Maui: America's Magic Isle." *Time,* 26 March 1979.

Eckbo, Dean, Austin & Williams. "Hawaii Land Use Districts and Regulations Review." Prepared for State of Hawaii Land Use Commission. Honolulu, 1969.

Farrell, Bryan H. "The Golden Hordes and the People of the Pacific." An inaugural lecture. Santa Cruz: University of California, 1978.

———. "Tourism's Human Conflicts: Cases from the Pacific." *Annals of Tourism Research* 6 (1979): 122–136.

_____. "The Tourist Ghettos of Hawaii." In *Themes on Pacific Lands*, edited by
    M. C. R. Edgell and B. H. Farrell. Victoria: University of Victoria, 1974.

_____, ed. *The Social and Economic Impact of Tourism on Pacific Communi-
    ties*. Santa Cruz: Center for South Pacific Studies, 1977.

Finney, Ben R., and Watson, Karen Ann, eds. *A New Kind of Sugar: Tourism in
    the Pacific*. Santa Cruz: Center for South Pacific Studies, 1977.

First Hawaiian Bank. *Economic Indicators*. 1969–1981. Monthly.

Fuchs, Lawrence H. *Hawaii Pono: A Social History*. New York: Harcourt, Brace
    and World, 1961.

Fujii, Edwin T., and Mak, James. "The Impact of Alternative Regional Develop-
    ment Strategies on Crime Rates: Tourism Versus Agriculture in Hawaii.
    Mimeographed. Honolulu: University of Hawaii, 1979.

Fujii, Edwin T.; Mak, James; and Nishimura, Edward. "Tourism and Crime."
    Tourism Research Project. Occasional Paper no. 2. Honolulu: University
    of Hawaii, 1978.

Gee, Chuck Y. "Employment Opportunities Created by Tourism Development."
    Mimeographed. Honolulu: University of Hawaii, School of Travel In-
    dustry Management, n.d.

_____. "Establishing Better Communications between Public and Private Sec-
    tors in Tourism—The Hawaiian Experience." Paper presented to the
    Pacific Area Travel Association Workshop, Manila, 3 January 1980.
    Mimeographed.

Ghali, Moheb. *Tourism and Regional Growth*. Leiden: Martinus Nijhoff, 1977.

Gray, Francine du Plessix. *Hawaii: The Sugar-Coated Fortress*. New York: Ran-
    dom House, 1972.

Hamilton, Thomas Hale. "Hawaii's Tourism and Controlled Growth." Address
    to the New Zealand Institute of Travel, Auckland, 26 October 1976. Mim-
    eographed.

_____. "Tourism in Hawaii." Written for The Encyclopedia of Hawaii, 1976.
    Manuscript in Hawaii State Archives.

Hawaii Business. 1969–1981. Monthly.

Hawaii, County of. "The Kona Community Development Plan." Hilo: Donald
    Wolbrink and Associates, 1975.

Hawaii Economic Review. 1969–1981. Quarterly.

Hawaii, State of. *Data Book*. 1969–1981. Annual.

_____. *The Economy of Hawaii*. Honolulu. Department of Planning and Eco-
    nomic Development. Annual.

_____. *Growth Policies Plan, 1974–1984*. Honolulu: Department of Planning
    and Economic Development, 1974.

_____. *The Hawaii State Plan*. Honolulu: Department of Planning and Econom-
    ic Development, 1978.

_____. *Hawaii Tourism Impact Plan*, vol. 1 *Tourism in Hawaii*, vol. 2 *Regional
    West Hawaii*. Honolulu: Department of Planning and Economic Develop-
    ment, 1972.

_____. *Long Range Population and Economic Simulation Model for the State of
    Hawaii*. Honolulu: Department of Planning and Economic Development,
    1978.

_____. *Report: Governor's Tourism Planning Advisory Committee*. Honolulu:
    Department of Planning and Economic Development, 1976.

————. *Report to the People: Second Five-Year District Boundaries and Regulations Review*. Honolulu: Land Use Commission, 1975.

————. *State Comprehensive Outdoor Recreation Plan* (SCORP). Honolulu: Department of Planning and Economic Development, 1973.

————. *State Tourism Plan*. Honolulu: Department of Planning and Economic Development, 1980.

————. *State Tourism Study*. Honolulu: Department of Planning and Economic Development, 1978. Five volumes.

————. *What Hawaii's People Think of the Visitor Industry*. Honolulu: Department of Planning and Economic Development, 1976.

Hawaii Visitors Bureau. *Annual Research Report*, 1969–1981.

————. *Research Report* 1969–1981. Monthly.

————. *Visitor Expenditure Survey*, 1979.

Heller, H. Robert, and Heller, Emily E. *The Economic and Social Impact of Foreign Investment in Hawaii: A Special Summary*. Honolulu: Hawaii International Services Agency, Department of Planning and Economic Development, 1974.

Hillendahl, Wesley H. "Development of the Visitor Industry in Hawaii—Past and Future." Address presented to a group of Japanese hotel executives, Honolulu, 7 November 1974. Mimeographed.

Honolulu Advertiser. 1969–1981. Daily.

Honolulu, City and County of. "An Assessment of Potential Off-Waikiki Resorts on Oahu." Mimeographed. Honolulu: Department of General Planning, August 1978.

————. *The Economy of Oahu*. Honolulu: Department of General Planning, 1977.

————. "Evaluation of Off-Waikiki Resort Sites: Fiscal Impacts, Transportation System, and Beach Use Analysis." Technical Report no. 4. Honolulu: Department of General Planning, 1978.

————. "The Future of Resort Development on Oahu." Mimeographed. Honolulu: Department of General Planning, May 1979.

————. "Progress Report on the Evaluation of Off-Waikiki Resort Sites." Mimeographed. Honolulu: Department of General Planning, 1978.

————. "Public Opinion Survey for the Development Plan Program: Oahu Report." Mimeographed. Honolulu: SMS Research, 1978.

————. "Summary of an Assessment of Potential Off-Waikiki Resorts on Oahu." Mimeographed. Honolulu: Department of General Planning, 1978.

Honolulu Star-Bulletin. 1969–1981. Daily.

Kauai, County of. *A General Plan for the Island of Kauai*. Lihue: Eckbo, Dean, Austin, et al., 1970.

Kelley, John. "Tourism, Land Alienation and Foreign Control in Hawaii." In *The Melanesian Environment*, edited by John H. Winslow. Canberra: Australian National University Press, 1977.

Kelsh, John. "Government Planning for Tourism." Paper presented at PEACESAT Conference, the Impact of Tourism Development in the Pacific, Suva: University of the South Pacific, 1978. Mimeographed.

Knox, John M. "Classification of Hawaii Residents' Attitudes toward Tourists and Tourism." Tourism Research Project: Occasional Paper no. 1. Mimeographed. Honolulu: University of Hawaii, 1978.

_____. "Research Priorities in Hawaii and the Pacific: An Overview." Tourism Research Project: Occasional Paper no. 3. Mimeographed. Honolulu: University of Hawaii, 1979.

_____. "Resident-Visitor Interaction." Paper presented at PEACESAT Conference, The Impact of Tourism Development in the Pacific, Suva: University of the South Pacific, 1978. Mimeographed.

Krivatsy, Adam. "Planners and Planning for Tourism." Paper presented at PEACESAT Conference, the Impact of Tourism Development in the Pacific, Suva: University of the South Pacific, 1978. Mimeographed.

Lamoureux, C. H. "Conservation Problems in Hawaii." In *Nature Conservation in the Pacific*, edited by A. B. Costin and R. H. Groves. Canberra: Australian National University Press, 1973.

Lind, Andrew W. *Hawaii's People*. Honolulu: University of Hawaii Press, 1967.

Liu, Juanita, "Differential Multipliers for the Accommodation Sector." Working Paper no. 80–07. Honolulu: University of Hawaii, School of Travel Industry Management, 1980.

_____. "Tourist Income Multipliers at the Establishment Level." Working Paper no. 80–08. Honolulu: University of Hawaii, School of Travel Industry Management, 1980.

_____. "The Japanese Tourist in Hawaii." Paper presented at The Fifth Annual Pacific Islands Studies Conference, University of Hawaii, 1980.

Lowry, Gordon Kemmery, Jr. "Control and Consequence: The Implementation of Hawaii's Land Use Law." Ph.D. dissertation, University of Hawaii, 1976.

MacCannell, Dean. *The Tourist: A New Theory of the Leisure Class*. New York: Schocken Books, 1976.

Mak, James E., and Ah Mai, Karen. "Employment and Population Impacts of Resort Development at Five Oahu Sites." Technical Report no. 1. Honolulu: Department of General Planning, 1978.

Mak, James E. and Nishimura, Edward. "The Economics of a Hotel Room Tax." *Philippine Review of Business and Economics* 14 (1977): 65–80.

Mathematica. "The Visitor Industry and Hawaii's Economy: A Cost-Benefit Analysis." Mimeographed. Honolulu: Department of Planning and Economic Development, 1970. (Also known as the Baumol Report)

_____. *The General Plan for the County of Maui*. Wailuku, 1980.

Maui, County of. *A General Plan for the Lahaina District County of Maui*. Kahului: Hiroshi Kasamoto, and Muroda and Tanaka Inc., 1968.

_____. *Kihei, Civic Development Plan*. Kahului: Noboru Kobayashi, Howard K. Nakamura, and Robert O. Ohata, 1970.

Maui News. 1969–1981.

Maui Sun (formerly *Lahaina Sun*). 1969–1981.

McDermott, John F. Jr.; Tseng, Wen-Shing; and Maretzki, Thomas W. *People and Cultures of Hawaii. A Psychocultural Profile*. Honolulu: University Press of Hawaii, 1980.

McKean, Philip Frick. "Tourist-Native Interaction in Paradise: Locating Partial Equivalence Structures in Bali." Paper presented at Seventy-First Annual Meeting, American Anthropological Association, November 1972. Mimeographed.

Meller, Norman, and Horwitz, Robert. "Hawaii: Theories in Land Monopoly." In *Land Tenure in the Pacific*, edited by R. G. Crocombe. Melbourne: Oxford University Press, 1971.

Merrill, William Dickie. "Hotel Employment and the Community in Hawaii." Ph.D. dissertation, University of Edinburgh, 1974.

Nordyke, Eleanor C. *The Peopling of Hawaii.* Honolulu: University Press of Hawaii, 1977.

————. "Relationship Between Tourism and Population Growth." Paper presented at a workshop of the Commission on Population and the Hawaiian Future, Honolulu, 1979. Mimeographed.

Pope, Ewell G. "The Developer's Point of View." *Tourism Investment and Finance.* San Francisco: Pacific Area Travel Association, 1976.

Project Wailea: City of Flowers. Honolulu: Alexander & Baldwin, 1970.

Proposed Kapalua Master Plan, Maui, Hawaii. Kahului: Belt, Collins & Associates, Ltd. and Charles Luckman Associates, 1973.

Rajotte, Freda. "*A Method for Evaluation of Tourism Impact in the Pacific.*" University of California, Data Paper no. 9. Santa Cruz: Center for South Pacific Studies, 1978.

Smith, Valene L. ed. *Hosts and Guests: The Anthropology of Tourism.* Philadelphia: University of Pennsylvania Press, 1977.

Sommarstrom, Allan. "Stress and the Competition for Space: The Case of Tourism in Hawaii." In *Proceedings of the International Geographical Union Regional Conference and Eighth New Zealand Geography Conference.* Palmerston North: New Zealand Geographical Society, 1974.

Taylor, J. L. "Waikiki: A Study in the Development of a Tourist Community." Ph.D. dissertation, Clark University, Worcester, MA, 1953.

"Ten Year Trend Analysis of Hawaii's Visitor Industry, 1966–76." Mimeographed. Honolulu: Hawaii Visitors Bureau, 1977.

Turner, Louis, and Ash, John. *The Golden Hordes.* London, Constable, 1975.

UNESCO. "The Effects of Tourism on Socio-Cultural Values," *Annals of Tourism Research* 4 (1976) 74–105.

Wagar, Alan J. *The Carrying Capacity of Wild Lands for Recreation.* Washington: Society of American Foresters, 1964.

Warnecke, John Carl & Associates. *Environmental and Urban Design Study of the Makena-La Perouse, Wailuku, and Lahaina Areas.* Honolulu: State Foundation on Culture and the Arts, 1970.

What Hawaii's People Think of Foreign and Mainland Investment in the Islands. Honolulu: Hawaii International Services Agency, Department of Planning and Economic Development, 1975.

Wolbrink, Donald and Associates. *Physical Standards for Tourism Development.* Honolulu: Pacific Island Development Commission, 1973.

Index

Production Notes

This book was designed by Roger Eggers and typeset on the Unified Composing System by The University Press of Hawaii.

The text and display typeface is Compugraphic Caledonia.

Offset presswork and binding were done by Halliday lithograph. Text paper is Glatfelter Offset, basis 55.